The Triumph of
The Immaculate Heart
of Mary
The Visions of
The Golden Lady
of Happiness

Louise D'Angelo

D1452970

Published By
THE MARYHEART CRUSADERS, INC.
22 Button Street
Meriden, Conn. 06450
Printed in U.S.A.

Written 1996-1998

First Printing 1998

© The Maryheart Crusader, Inc. 1994

© The Maryheart Crusaders, Inc. 1995

© Copyright 1996 The Maryheart Crusaders, Inc. All rights reserved. No part of this book may be reproduced in any form or manner whatsoever, except in the case of a brief quotation embodied in critical articles or reviews without written permission from the Maryheart Crusaders, Inc.

Library of Congress Catalog Card No. 95-81320

ISBN 1-878886-61-4
ISBN 1-878886-34-7 (1995)
ISBN 1-878886-43-6 (1996)

Printed and Bound in the U.S.A.

Cover painted by:
Waldemar Karwowski
Southington, Conn.

MARYHEART PUBLISHING CO.
22 Button St.
Meriden, CT 06450

DECLARATION

In accordance with the decree of Pope Urban VIII we declare that in speaking of events, prodigies and miracles, we wish to speak of them in the sense in which the Ecclesiastical Authority has approved them, without desiring in any way to anticipate the decisions of the Holy See, and in absolute submission to the authority of the Church.

Published by
THE MARYHEART CRUSADERS, INC.
22 Button Street
Meriden, Connecticut 06450

DEDICATION

This book is dedicated
with much love to
The Holy Mother of God

TABLE OF CONTENTS

PROLOGUE

PART ONE

WRITING THIS BOOK: 1997-1998
FATHER BRADLEY PIERCE:
SPIRITUAL DIRECTOR AND
CONFESSOR SINCE 1984

PART TWO

INTRODUCTION TO MY LADY,
VISIONS AND REVELATIONS

PART THREE

THE STORY BEGINS LOUISE D'ANGELO
FIRST RELIGIOUS EXPERIENCES YEARS 1924-1943

PART FOUR

I MOVE TO NEW YORK CITY
GOD'S PLANS FOR ME START
TO UNFOLD
FIRST VISIONS: YEARS 1944-1945

PART FIVE

THE FOUNDATION FOR MY ROLE IN MY LADY'S TRIUMPH: YEAR 1944

PART SIX

THE GIFTS OF THE HOLY SPIRIT SUFFERING HUMANITY AND MY WRITINGS: YEARS 1944-1945

PART SEVEN

THE DEVIL'S CHALLENGE
THE PATHWAY TO MY LADY'S TRIUMPH
APRIL 5, 1946

PART EIGHT

THE SHRINE OF THE IMMACULATE
HEART OF MARY: 1946

PART NINE

MONSIGNOR HAYES
SPIRITUAL DIRECTOR
YEAR 1947

PART TEN

THE FIRST VISIONS OF THE GOLDEN
LADY OF HAPPINESS: 1948

PART ELEVEN

SECOND VISION OF THE GOLDEN
LADY OF HAPPINESS: 1960

PART TWELVE

THE TRIUMPH OF THE
IMMACULATE HEART OF MARY

Ever since 1944, I have been told by my Lady: "Make yourself known to the world and make my words and my Son's words known to the world."

This book was written not only in obedience to my spiritual director, but in fulfilling this request of my Lady.

L.D.

PUBLISHER'S NOTE

In speaking of the visions of The Golden Lady of Happiness, it must be remembered that there is a difference between public revelations and private revelations and apparitions of Our Lady.

Public revelations, what is renown as the deposit of the faith ended with the death of the last apostle. We have these public revelations in the Bible.

There can be no additions to such public revelations.

Private revelations consist of all visions, apparitions and so forth which have come forth from individuals throughout the history of the Church, as far back as 270 A.D. Private revelations cannot add to nor change any revelations made in the Bible (public revelations).

That being the case, the visions of The Golden Lady of Happiness and other revelations (messages) mentioned by Louise D'Angelo fall into the category of private revelations. These cannot add to public revelations, but they can be accepted as "gifts to be received with thanksgiving . . . for they are exceedingly suitable and useful for the needs of the Church" (Lumen Gentium No.12).

However, while public revelations are part of Church doctrine and thus required of belief by all Catholics (Examples: the Virgin birth, the divinity of Christ, The physical Resurrection of Christ, the Trinity, etc.), private revelations are not. It is a serious mistake to say that "words" of the Holy Mother of God which contradict a teaching or doctrine of the Catholic faith should be accepted while at the same time the Church's teaching or doctrine should be rejected.

When speaking about Fatima, Pope John Paul II in 1982 said: "If the Church has accepted the message of Fatima, it is above all because that message contains a truth and a call whose basic content is the truth and the call of the Gospel itself" (*Exploring Fatima* page 9).

It is further to be noted that no Imprimatur or Nihil Obstat is required for a book of this type since the changes in Canon laws 1399 and 2318 which became effected on March 29, 1967. Canon 1399 forbade the publication of books which deal with visions, revelations and prophecies. Cannon 2318 carried penalties against those who violated such a law by publishing said books or visiting the places of Apparitions. Both these Canons have been repealed or annulled.

Louise D'Angelo
1987
(Photo by Olan Mills)

Louise and Michael D'Angelo
1987
(Photo by Olan Mills)

MY LADY

I call the Holy Mother of God, my Lady, when I refer to the visions for I have, since 1944 when she first appeared to me, thought of her as my Lady. Once a nun became angry with me and said: "Will you stop calling her my Lady! She is Our Lady." I replied: "Well, I don't know how else to call her when I see her. When she comes to me, she is my Lady. I know she belongs to everyone, but she comes to me and then she is my Lady." I do not say that with any intentions of being overly possessive. To me, it is an endearing term so precious to me. Ever since I saw her, I would say my Lady, and the land where she appeared in 1948 and again in 1960, I have always referred to as my Lady's land.

PREFACE

This book is about much more than visions. This book is about the second most important event in salvation history: The Triumph of the Immaculate Heart of Mary. It is also about the extraordinary mission that God gave the author, Louise D'Angelo, a mission that Jesus called The Devil's Challenge, and how fighting and winning that challenge has made the triumph of the Immaculate Heart of Mary possible. Most of all, this book is about love, the tremendous love God and Mary have for their children. Jesus said to Louise on May 7, 1946, "Know My Child of Love that what I have said to you and done through you is truly amazing the like of which the world has not seen since The Crucifixion."

Events associated with Louise's mission began in 1893 when Pope Leo XIII saw a vision of Satan speaking with Jesus telling Him if he were given the time and power he would destroy Christ's Church and establish his kingdom in the world. Pope Leo XIII was so disturbed by this experience that he composed a prayer to St. Michael and had it included at the end of the Latin Mass.

The effects of The Devil's Challenge are all too apparent to those of us living in the world today. Satan has not made good on his promise to destroy the Church although he has been successful in promoting confusion about Church teaching and disobedience to that teaching among many of the clergy, religious and lay people. Satan has been more successful in establishing his kingdom in the world. Everyone who has lived more than fifty years has witnessed the terrible moral decay that has taken place in our country and the world. Since the 1950s we have seen God more and more pushed out of our public and private lives; out of our government, our legal system, our schools, the media and our homes. Satan has filled this vacuum promoting greed, sexual immorality, abortion and all kinds of violence.

Satan's Challenge would not go unanswered by God. God would choose someone to answer this challenge. That someone would be a simple nothing with whom everyone could identify. Not someone like St. Theresa who was very religious from childhood, entered a convent at fifteen and had parents who may be canonized. No! God wanted someone that we could all identify with no matter what the circumstances of our lives.

God placed Louise in just such an ordinary life. She was born into a dysfunctional family. Her father was an alcoholic who died in an automobile accident when Louise was ten years old. Her mother, who seemed more interested in her career than her children, placed her children in foster homes after their father's death. During these years Louise cried herself to sleep but in spite of her great sadness she never became bitter. One could see the effect of grace already at work in her soul. At this early age she had a great concern for her world. She thought of the many sad people in the world and wondered what she could do when she grew up to bring them happiness. She decided to become an ice skater because Sonja Henie, the great figure skater, had made her happy when she saw her movies.

Even though writing would be an important part of Louise's mission, she would never receive more than a high school education. After the visions began, Louise gave up her skating career and became more involved with her spiritual life; because at the time she had a very poor knowledge of her Catholic Faith. She wanted to enter the convent but Jesus told her that her life was to be in the world where the devil is. When Louise married, the Lord told her she would have no children, but that the world would be her children (June 27, 1960). That prediction came true.

In Louise God had chosen someone whose life was so lacking in privilege that one could identify with her no matter what their misfortune or shortcomings. Mary called Louise on May 5, 1944 "a simple stupid child with many, many faults, a child who was once lured away by earthly pleasures (and yet) has been chosen to do a great job for God." Our Lord never protested when Louise called herself "a nothing." Jesus simply replied, "Ah, dear one, is it not I who has the power to make something out of nothing?" (May 2, 1946)

In asking Louise to accept The Devil's Challenge God is telling all of us that we, too, have a devil's challenge. Through her battles with Satan and her final victory recorded in her writings, which now number more than 175 yet to be published works, God is able to show us the power of His grace and all the weapons we can use to fight and win our devil's challenge and find the peace, joy and happiness that God's Child of Love has found.

The weapons Louise used are ours to use. Her love for God and His holy will, her faith and trust in Jesus and Mary, her love for the Church and obedience and all that the Church teaches, her prayer life and the sacraments, especially the Eucharist and Confession, and the graces she used to fight temptation and grow in holiness. Her greatest weapon was her desire to do whatever Jesus and Mary asked no matter what the cost which enabled her to accept all the suffering that was a part of her job for God.

In the second volume of this book, where Louise describes in detail the battles she had with Satan and the demons, we get some idea of how much suffering she endured. At the beginning of The Devil's Challenge, Satan told her that the pains and torments she would suffer would be greater than the pains of Purgatory and the torments of Hell. During her battle with Satan and the demons, she was dragged into Purgatory and into Hell to suffer their pains and torments. In spite of this, Louise refused to give up because of her love for God and His holy will and her love for her world.

The greatest test of our love for God and neighbor is how much we are willing to sacrifice and suffer for them. One thing canonized saints have in common is that they were so concerned to do God's will, they were willing to deny themselves anything and to suffer whatever it would take to do God's will. There is no stronger testimony to the authenticity of a visionary than this kind of love for God and His holy will. In reading Louise's writings and coming to know her soul through spiritual direction, nothing has impressed me more than Louise's love for God and His holy will and how much she was willing to suffer to accomplish God's will for her.

Our Lord and Our Lady have given Louise the title of God's Child of Love because in Louise and in her writings, one finds such a powerful expression of God's love, and Mary's, and this love will lift up this fallen world. On January 17, 1946, Jesus said to Louise, "I promise that if My children turn to you, their prayers will be answered so fast that they will be surprised. For I bring to the world, through you, the love of God for His children and the ways of a loving Father. And your hands and your heart will cause, not only people, but nations to return to My Church and you alone shall be their guide. Through you and your angels, much sin will vanish from the earth."

In 1945, the Blessed Virgin had told Louise about a terrible destruction that could come upon the world because such a sinful world deserves God's justice but, on May 7, 1946, God the Father said, "Dear Child of Love, now I can give My children a promise, a promise that means great happiness. The message your Lady gave on January 26, 1945 will not come about because you so willingly took upon yourself the task of fighting the devil and suffering. If you had refused The Devil's Challenge then no other Child of Love could I have had. But you accepted so that the world will not suffer what Mary said it could. For you shall cause thousands to return to Mary's heart never to leave. And Mary's heart will be planted deep in the hearts of her children never to be blotted out by any force or power." On May 8, 1946 the Father said "I, the Almighty God, stood above the earth, as a weight ready to fall. Yes, I was ready to destroy for My anger was great. But you, My dear one, and your love took Me away from this position and no longer am I ready to destroy for you have so won My Heart as to ease My anger and this great destruction will not take place before the Last Day."

On December 20, 1946 Jesus said, "Dear Child of Love, oh beloved of My Heart, never before did I tell one of My children of such great love that is theirs alone. Never before and yes, little one, never again will such words of praise and love fall to the ears of a child of God.

"But I made you special to receive such love and praise for of all My children I saw only you who would accept the Devil's Challenge. Dear one, because you will be so wounded hundreds of times on the battlefields I not only promise you great glory and praise for all eternity, but I promise you unending honor and love from My angels and saints who will sing your name throughout the heavens for all eternity as the special princess, the chosen daughter of the King and Queen. . . .

"There are in heaven now great saints who have great glory, but who refused the Devil's Challenge. So great a sacrifice and so heroic was the acceptance of the Devil's Challenge that when they refused they did not lose their glory or place in heaven. They are still My beloved children and so very close to My Heart."

The triumph of the Immaculate Heart of Mary, through the writings of Louise, reveals Mary in all her glory as Queen and the importance of Mary as the Mother of each one of us. On May 1, 1948, Mary said, "My appearance here (in Meriden) is the end of a circle that began at La Salette. All the times I have appeared on earth, I was building up to this glorious climax that has come about because of you and the shrine here called The Shrine of the Immaculate Heart of Mary. I started to draw a circle at La Salette. I continued the circle at several places including Lourdes and Fatima. Now, I draw this circle to a close for now I stand upon this rock as The Golden Lady of Happiness. Tell my children that I have come in all my glory to bring peace, joy and happiness to the world."

In the following apparition Louise received from God the Father and Jesus they both express the responsibility we have to honor Mary as our Mother and our Queen. On January 26,

1945, God the Father said, "If the world turns against the Mother of My Son then I shall turn against them and once again the darkness of a horror night shall descend upon the people of this world and a more bloody fight was never before seen." Jesus said, "The world cannot rejoice until it rejoices with My Mother and Me." Mary said on January 26, 1945, "Heed well the words of my Son for you to return to my heart: the heart that is the gateway to the Hearts of My Son and His Father."

We all need to honor and love Mary as our Mother because no one could love and honor Mary as much as her Son has in choosing her to be His Mother. No one can make us better disciples of Christ than Mary because she is Christ's greatest disciple. We need Mary to intercede for us because, like any Mother, she will go to our Father and obtain mercy when justice is due. On January 26, 1945, Mary talked about her role as Mother of Mercy, "My children of the world, I stand before the throne of God to defend the children of the fallen world and out of His great love for me, He will allow my heart to bring back the peace that is not in the world today."

In the more than fifty years that Louise has been receiving visions from God the Father, Jesus, Mary, the saints and many souls in Purgatory, she has never talked about these visions publicly. She has guarded them as precious secrets of her soul and never wanted people to think she was special.

I have told Louise to make these visions public now because Our Lady has asked her to do so when she said, "Spread your writings all over the world. Do not delay. Souls will be saved, hearts will be filled with joy. Your writings will light up the world and my light and your light will light up every dark corner of the world. Upon the pages of your writings will be the rays of light which will radiate out from Meriden to touch hearts and souls until the end of time."

On May 17, 1946, when Louise had just begun to write, Jesus said to her, "Know My little one, that for all time your writings will be read as you wrote them. Not one single word will be lost by any force or power. Your writings and My messages will be spread over the whole world, yes, even as the Bible is spread over the whole world. For all time I will preserve all you have written so that all My children for all time will know of My Child of Love. They shall read not only the messages from Heaven but the love you wrote in your articles and writings."

While visiting the Shrine of Our Lady of Fatima, Portugal on the 24th of July, 1997, Mary said to Louise, "There were numerous saints who fed the hungry, who clothed the naked, who taught children and adults, who took care of the sick and injured, all to their glory; and gaining numerous merits. However, you, my most beloved Child of Love, have the whole world.

"You, my Child of Love, shall feed the hungry of the whole world with spiritual knowledge. You shall clothe the people of the world with garments of love and grace. You shall teach, not in small schools in one limited area, for your writings will be spread over the entire world. You shall bring the medicine of grace and spiritual knowledge to those who are spiritually ill and in danger of being lost for all eternity. You will light up the whole world with your love and grace, and not just a small corner of the world. There is no place on earth where your light will not shine. This is your world, the world you saved (from the terrible chastisement this sinful world would have received) by and through your Devil's Challenge."

At Fatima, Portugal on the 13th of July, 1917, the Blessed Virgin Mary appeared to three children over a holmoak tree dressed all in white calling herself the Lady of the Rosary and said, "In the end my Immaculate Heart will triumph." At Meriden, Connecticut on May 1st 1948 Mary appeared to Louise D'Angelo standing on a rock dressed all in gold calling herself the Golden Lady of Happiness and announced to the world: "My Immaculate Heart has triumphed."

On July 7, 1960, Mary once again announced her Triumph and said: "My Immaculate Heart has triumphed. I will now show the devil that I am the powerful one. Tell my children that I say to them, my power is greater than the strongest armies and greater than the strongest hate. The world will know that there is hope—great hope—for peace, joy and happiness because I have come to bring peace, joy and happiness to mankind . . . The world has cried, now I will dry its tears because now I can show my power and my glory."

I asked her if she wants her children to say the Rosary or make sacrifices or do penance (like she did other times) and she replied: "Tell my children that I desire to hear songs of love and songs of joy. The world will see great wonders because, at last, it has the Golden Lady of Happiness.

"Tell my children to pray and to make sacrifices, but tell them to rejoice. My Hour of Glory has arrived. My glory shall be implanted upon this earth in such a way that it will never be dimmed by any force or power. I am the Golden Lady of Happiness and I am the Golden Lady of Peace and Light. Every dark corner of this world shall see my splendor and my children shall flock around me in a most miraculous way. They shall say their Rosaries and they shall confess their sins and they will do penance for their sins; but most of all they will love me as I have never been loved before. I come now to give love and to receive love. I ask for prayers of love."

Fatima is the first chapter in the Triumph of the Immaculate Heart of Mary. In this book, and in Louise's other writings, can be found the rest of this incredible story of love and hope that will lift up this fallen world and bring Mary's Triumph to all of mankind.

Rev. Bradley W. Pierce, M.S.A.
Director of Field Education
Holy Apostles Seminary
Spiritual Director of Louise D'Angelo

AUTHOR'S PREFACE

THE STORY OF MY LADY
THE STORY OF THE WORLD

There is one very important fact, which has to be noted, concerning my visions and my Lady's shrine. The visions of The Golden Lady and her triumph involve a great deal more than to build a shrine at the site of the apparitions.

The story of my Lady is not just about the visions I saw in 1948 and again in 1960. Nor does this story revolve around a rock upon which the Holy Mother of God stood and told me: "My Immaculate Heart has triumphed." The story revolves around fallen mankind. The story includes many different parts, including the role I was to play, my own triumph as I fought the battles upon spiritual battlefields and the whole of mankind in all its daily struggles and failures.

The story reflects world history from the year 1944 onward. In that story, I found myself and my role to be part of a divine plan to bring peace, joy and happiness to suffering mankind.

Years ago, each time I wrote the story of The Golden Lady and her triumph, that story was not complete. Actually, it had to tell more than the story of the visions. It had to include, not only the world and all its ups and downs, hut also the story of my life as I witnessed these drastic changes in the world as humanity struggled to survive.

The story of my Lady reaches far out from the place where she appeared to me to embrace a world which so desperately needs God and Our Lady's love and concern, a world fallen into a darkness of sin and despair, a world crying for help, a world searching to find a path it has lost.

The revelations I received over fifty years ago to the present, paint a beautiful picture of the love which God and Our Lady have for their children and reveal a pathway, filled with light, for humanity to walk upon. See the light of my story, not only to reveal a Golden Madonna, but a light which shines brightly into a dark world which shows the way to the loving Hearts of Jesus and Mary.

In the other manuscripts I wrote throughout the years (some are in the bishop's office) I purposely left out all the details of my early revelations because I did not want to give them to the public. However, by doing that, as Father Brad explained to me, I left out half the story and the other manuscripts contained only bits and pieces of the story of my Lady's triumph.

It is only under obedience to my confessor and spiritual director, Father Bradley Pierce, that I now include in this book the many revelations which I had hidden for 50 years. Father Brad has been my confessor and director since 1984. He had read my writings and also my secret notes. That is why he insisted that I reveal, in this new book, the whole story of my Lady which includes the role God gave me to fulfill, which started in 1944.

Under Father Brad's direction and guidance, I have now written the book that he felt I should have written before. This is explained in Part One at the beginning of this book. As can be seen in the Part One chapters, I was very reluctant to do what Father Brad told me to do, but I did so under obedience.

Yet, as I wrote this new book, I could see and understand the wisdom of Father Brad to have told me to write the book as he felt it should be written.

Father said to me: "The book you are now writing clearly reveals God is infinite love and mercy and will teach people valuable lessons about His love and mercy."

I replied: "I am glad that I obeyed you because by doing that, I can teach people very powerful, spiritual lessons which they have to know to reach a closer union with God."

You see, the story of my Lady is not just about visions, but about this fallen world and God, Our Lady's and my love for the poor, lost, bewildered children caught up in the rushing waters of man's selfishness and greed.

I was told about this fallen world in 1944 and about my role in raising this fallen world. I was told about my Lady's triumph when she said (January 26, 1945): "My children of the world, I stand before the throne of God to defend the children of the fallen world; and because of His great love for me, He will allow my heart to bring back the peace that is not in the world today."

Also, this is not just a book about my private revelations. Within its pages there is a great deal of information about the power of God's grace and about His love and Mary's love; and how important it is to live a life of virtue. I was told by my Lord that He would use me as an example for others to follow. Such an example has been hidden for fifty years. That was what I wanted.

But, now is the time to let these words of Jesus and Mary bring joy, hope and happiness to millions of lost, lonely,fallen hearts and souls. Let the light of my story and my Lady's story shine into this dark world and show the way to the loving Hearts of Jesus and Mary.

The ones who have read the new chapters have found in this book a rich gold mine of spiritual knowledge not only from the words of Jesus and Mary, but from my words about God the Father, Jesus, Mary and the Holy Spirit and grace; all of which presents the beautiful teachings of our faith.

I so long to bring such knowledge to the world.

Here is a prayer I wrote 11/4/86:

MY PRAYER OF LOVE

Dearest God: Accept my prayer of love and accept my heart of love. Let me walk through this darkness called life for all to see. Let me wander among the lost, the lonely, the sad, the poor and show them that the light of Your love, which I carry, can lead them into a joy, happiness and peace which they never knew existed. I will walk among the darkness and find the ones who need me and Your Heart of Love. Then they can rejoice and praise the God

who never stopped wanting and loving them.
Amen

I also wrote this prayer 12/10/86:

TO GOD: THE TRINITY

Today with my soul bursting with love for God,
I composed this prayer:

Dearest God, my most beloved Trinity, surround
me at all times with Your presence, Your grace,
Your love. I cannot exist outside of Your presence, Your grace, Your love. Wherever I go, let
me bring Your love, Your ways, Your total presence. Let me walk among all the darkness and
sorrows of life and become a ray of pure light
shining forth for all to see. Let people say:
"Wherever Louise is, there is God, His ways
and His love." Let people see You in me for I
wish at all times to reach out and touch souls
with Your light, Your grace and Your love. Amen

In parts of this book, I explained about the secret notes,
which I now reveal, and how amazed I was to discover them
as I wrote the book and saw the wonderful things which had
been revealed to me so long ago, most of what I had merely
recorded and then forgot. I still have these original notes and
note books. Also, many of these notes (as far back as 1944)
have been in the bishop's office in a book called "Prophecies
and Predictions." That book has been in this office since 1963,
so you can see that I did not make up these revelations now
for this book.

Many of you know about all the false visions making the
rounds, always speaking of death, doom and destruction. Some
even say the Church will be destroyed: All from "Our Lady"?
You can surely see the difference with what they say and what

my Lady says (1960): "Tell my children to pray and to make sacrifices, but tell them to rejoice. My hour of glory has arrived . . . Every dark corner of this world shall see my splendor . . . I come now to give love and to receive love . . . Tell my children to hide behind my golden garments and there they shall find their protection. I have come as the loving Mother who protects her frightened children" (July 12, 1960).

I wish to quote now from an article in "Immaculate Heart Messenger" (January-February-March 1997) (Page 28):

RATZINGER ON FATIMA SECRET

Joseph Cardinal Ratzinger, prefect of the Vatican's Congregation for the Doctrine of the Faith since 1981, presided over the October 13, 1996 ceremonies at Fatima. It was the 79th anniversary of the miracle of the sun. Cardinal Ratzinger is the former Archbishop of Munich. If any one of the hundreds of thousands who came to Fatima on October 13 expected that Ratzinger who had been permitted by Pope John II to read the Fatima secret would reveal it, they were disappointed because not a word was expressed of it in his homily. Radio Renascenca, Portugal's Catholic radio station, did however interview the Cardinal on the third part of the secret.

The Cardinal stated that the "third secret of Fatima" is not sensational or apocalyptic. "To all the curious I would say I am certain that the Virgin does not engage in sensationalism; she does not create fear. She does not present apocalyptic visions, but guides people to her Son. And this is what is essential."

Cardinal Ratzinger, in the Radio Renascenca interview, said that preoccupation with presumed predictions of catastrophe are not part of healthy Marian devotion. He said the Church "is opposed to sensationalism and this expectation of unheard of things." What the Cardinal said was in contradiction to some reported Marian messages from throughout the world. It would be a perversion to give in to such pressures by publishing the third segment, he said.

"Instead, the intention and the centrality of the mission of the Church is to guide people toward those things that are truly important. Only in that way are we truly obedient to Mary. The Madonna did not appear to children to the small, to the simple, to those unknown in the world in order to create a sensation." Mary's purpose, he said "is, through these simple ones, to call the world back to simplicity, that is to the essentials: conversion, prayer and the sacraments."

My Lady has never come as the harsh Mother to warn her children of her and God's dire punishments for suffering humanity, but as the loving Mother who wants to bring them hope, joy, peace and happiness and who guides her children to her Son.

THE PROMISES OF THE GOLDEN LADY
OF HAPPINESS GIVEN TO ME
IN 1948 AND 1960

As I write different chapters of this book, such as referring to early notes, I have to mention one or another of the three promises to show how these references were in my early notes before I heard the promises from my Lady. I now list the three promises, without explanations, which shall be found in different chapters.

1. "I promise that the world will not be destroyed before the Last Day. The world will not be destroyed before the Last Day by any force or power of man, or by any force or power of God because now my heart can be planted upon this earth and planted deep within the hearts of my children. No force or power shall take my heart away from my children."

2. "I promise that if the world of science continues to go against the ways and the teachings of God, then this science will be destroyed and men shall no longer know the secrets which they now know because that knowledge is not important, nor is it needed to save a soul."

3. "I promise that the devil and his evil ones will be pushed back into Hell and much sin shall vanish from the world so that the world will no longer be filled with the sin and corruption that the devil has created."

Prologue

Introduction to The Story Of My Lady

— 1 —

MY LADY'S NAME
THE GOLDEN LADY OF HAPPINESS

The title my lady gave herself, The Golden Lady of Happiness, may sound strange to some people; however, that was not what she called the shrine.

Two years before Our Lady stood on the rock dressed in golden garments, she had told me to name the shrine: The Shrine of the Immaculate Heart of Mary. That was in 1946 when she first told me she wanted a shrine in Meriden.

At that time, she also placed her heart next to her Son's by saying: "On each pillar place a picture of my heart and my Son's Heart to show all who enter that love is here."

By saying that, Our Lady drew attention to the Heart of Jesus and His love which exist in the Blessed Sacrament.

When my Lady told me to name the shrine for her Immaculate Heart, I did not know anything about the heart of Mary. I remember going to the spot where she said she wanted her shrine and saying: "There will have to be a big sign for all those words." I would have preferred a shorter title such as Our Lady of the Rosary Shrine.

Nevertheless, as part of the plan of God to bring peace, joy and happiness to suffering mankind, the shrine had to be called: The Shrine of the Immaculate Heart of Mary. And that became one of the many signs that my job and my Lady's shrine were given by Heaven; because, two years later when Our Lady stood on the rock dressed in garments of gold, her first words were: "My Immaculate Heart has triumphed."

Our Lady did not appear in Meriden, as she did at other approved shrines, to plead for her children to say the Rosary or do penance. When I asked her if she wanted me to tell her children to say the Rosary or do penance, she replied: "They shall say their Rosaries, they shall confess their sins and they

1

will do penance for their sins; but most of all, they will love me as I have never been loved before. I come now to give love and to receive love. I ask for prayers of love."

Such words were ones of pure triumph: a triumph of love and of her heart of love at the place where she said: "My Immaculate Heart has triumphed."

The name which she called herself after she said, in 1948, "My Immaculate Heart has triumphed," was "I am The Golden Lady of Happiness." She had called attention to her Immaculate Heart before she said: "I am The Golden Lady of Happiness."

Having a separate title for Our Lady, such as this one, is very common in Catholic tradition. Bernadette's shrine, in France, is called simply Our Lady of Lourdes or Our Lady of The Grotto; yet, Our Lady called herself The Immaculate Conception at Lourdes. In Banneux, Belgiam Our Lady is known as The Virgin of The Poor. At Knoch, Ireland she is known as Our Lady of Silence. Saint Catherine Laboure's Madonna is known as The Lady of the Miraculous Medal.

In a book called "Miraculous Images of Our Lady" by Joan Carroll Cruz, there are listed one hundred titles of Our Lady among which are:

> Our Lady of the Bowed Head
> Our Lady of the Window Pane
> Our Lady of the Pottery
> Our Lady of the Guard
> Our Lady of the Thorn
> Our Lady of the Willow Tree
> Our Lady of Dawn
> Our Lady in the Sand
> Our Lady of the Dew

All of these titles of Our Lady, as odd as some seem to be, are very much loved and respected by her children who flock to these shrines where such titles have great meaning.

In the Church's Litany of Loreto, which is in "The Handbook of Indulgences, Norms and Grants," Our Lady has many beautiful titles such as: Mirror of Justice, Throne of Wisdom, Shrine of The Spirit, Mystical Rose, Tower of David, Tower of Ivory, Gate of Heaven, and Morning Star.

Our Lady of LaSalette, France is known as The Lady in Tears. When she first appeared to the children, she was sitting on a rock, her face in her hands, weeping. No doubt, Our Lady was thinking about LaSalette, when, this time in Meriden, she stood upon a rock as the glorious, radiant Queen of Heaven dressed in regal garments of gold and said in triumph: "I am The Golden Lady of Happiness." One can see the difference between Our Lady as the weeping Madonna and the triumphant Golden Lady of Happiness.

There should be no problem with the name my Lady called herself inasmuch as our Church calls her this Golden Lady.

In the Litany of Loreto, she also has the title: House of Gold.

Then about three years after I had seen her in 1948, I discovered two things which made my heart explode with joy.

The first was when someone pointed out to me that my Golden Lady was the Lady of the Apocalypse (or Revelation). There one finds these words: "A great sign appeared in the sky, a woman clothed with the sun with the moon under her feet and on her head a crown of twelve stars" (Rev. 12:1).

I had never read that before I saw my Lady standing on the rock in Meriden all dressed in gold with the moon under her feet and around her head a halo of twelve stars.

You can imagine how delighted I was when I read such words in the Bible. Surely, that was a confirmation of my Lady.

The second thing which happened concerning my Lady came directly from my beloved Catholic Church who put golden garments upon Our Lady.

It was August 15th the feast day of the Assumption of the Blessed Virgin Mary. It was the first time the Mass for this day was in English. I never expected what happened. Suddenly everyone was responding—"The Queen stands at Your right hand arrayed in gold."

I could hardly believe what I heard "arrayed in gold"! Here was my Golden Lady of Happiness!

My joy and wonder lasted for days. The Church was saying: Mary, arrayed in gold."

Maybe the Church has said that before—in Latin, but I never knew it. I only heard it after the Mass was changed from Latin in the English I knew.

So, my Lady's title The Golden Lady of Happiness was not so unusual as it first seemed; and she called herself that years before the whole Catholic Church called her The Golden Lady "arrayed in gold" in the languages her children could understand.

There in Holy Scripture stood my Golden Lady, and there in the Liturgy of Word, in the Responsorial Psalms, were these words: "The Queen stands at Your right hand arrayed in gold."

It was as if Our Lady knew that I would hear and understand such words years before I even knew they existed.

Also, it is noted that this reading is in the "Liturgy of the Hours" (said by priests and religious daily) (page 798 Week II) Psalm 45:

> From the ivory palace you are greeted with music. The daughters of kings are among your loved ones. On your right stands the queen in gold of Ophir.

A friend of mine, Donald D'Efemia, wrote about this Queen arrayed in gold in the following article.

THE QUEEN ARRAYED IN GOLD

On August 15th, the Holy Roman Catholic Church celebrated one of its greatest feast days of the liturgical year in commemorating the Assumption of the Blessed Virgin Mary into Heaven. This sacred and supernatural truth that soon after her death, the body of the holy mother of God was assumed into Heaven, was declared a dogma of the holy Catholic faith by Pope Pius XII, in a solemn declaration in Rome on November 1, 1960. Thus after centuries of holy tradition, the teachings of the early Church fathers and the practice and belief of the faithful, the Pope, with the promise assistance of the Holy Spirit, declared in an infallible statement, that the assumption of the Blessed Virgin Mary into Heaven was a doctrine of the Catholic Faith and to be believed by all the faithful.

What joy filled the air! What happiness expressed and felt on this historic day! Catholics worldwide rejoiced in the triumph of Mary's proclaimed assumption. Gladness filled the hearts and souls of Catholics everywhere. How fitting it is to see, in Mary's assumption into Heaven, a crown of glory and splendor reserved for her alone.

Ever since the 15th century, devout Catholics have been praying the Holy Rosary, a highly indulgenced devotion to the Blessed Virgin Mary, and greatly valued by the entire Catholic Church. Tradition attributes that the Holy Rosary was given to St. Dominic, founder of the Dominican Order by Our Lady herself, as a weapon to fight against heresy and sin. On the accustomed days of Wednesdays, Saturdays, and Sundays the prayers of the Glorious Mysteries are recited. The beads of the fourth and fifth Glorious Mysteries are recited to recall to our mind, Mary's glorious assumption into Heaven and her being crowned Queen of Heaven and Earth by Almighty God, Himself. One can scarcely imagine this triumphant, magnificent, royal occasion, when the Blessed Virgin Mary, the Mother of Jesus, was assumed into Heaven shortly after her death, arrayed in queenly garments and crowned by our God and Creator, the Glorious Queen of angels and men. What splendor! What purity! What glory! What love! Unspeakable words visualized sublime and full of grace! Children of God—behold your Mother.

When celebrating the sacrifice of the Mass on the solemnity of the Assumption of the Blessed Virgin Mary into Heaven, on August 15th, the Congregation, in response to the reading of the Responsorial Psalms on that glorious feast day, joyfully proclaim, "The Queen stands at Your right hand arrayed in gold." How magnificent is this awe-inspiring radiant truth, that the Catholic Church teaches her children! Triumphantly beautiful, the ever-Virgin Mary, the Mother of Jesus, Our Lord and King, stands next to her son dressed in splendid royal garments of dazzling gold. With a sparkling, jeweled crown upon her head, Mary stands before all of God's creation, as the victorious, happy, triumphant Golden Lady of Heaven and Earth. What happiness fills our hearts as we gaze with joyful wonderment and affection at this heavenly queen arrayed in gold.

Praise, honor and glory to you forever, Oh! Golden Lady of Happiness.

Our Lady's heart must have overflowed with joy when she stood upon the rock in Meriden, in all her triumph and called herself The Golden Lady of Happiness, after she had sat upon a rock at LaSalette and wept or after she stood upon the little tree in Fatima and predicted dire happenings for mankind.

However, she did say at Fatima (July 13, 1917): "But in the end my Immaculate Heart will triumph."

Standing on the rock before me, all dressed in golden garments, my Lady was filled with untold happiness as she said: "My Immaculate Heart has triumphed." "I am The Golden Lady of Happiness."

— 2 —

BLESSED MARY
THE LADY OF HAPPINESS

Throughout the years whenever I thought about or spoke about The Golden Lady of Happiness, I would associate the word happiness with the happiness Mary would bring to the world and to her beloved children. Everyone else, who knew about the visions, thought the same way: that Our Lady would make them happy. Often when their prayers were not answered, they would wonder why The Golden Lady of Happiness did not bring them the happiness they desired.

However, to think that way is to make a serious mistake. For example: does The Golden Lady of Happiness cease to be The Golden Lady of Happiness when a person, who prays to her, does not receive his or her own personal happiness? The answer is no. Why? Because Mary always was and always will be The Golden Lady of Happiness because the happiness she speaks about is *her own* happiness, not so much ours. She speaks of herself as the one who has happiness. It is true that she will answer millions of prayers and bring happiness to millions of hearts and souls; however, when she calls herself The Golden Lady of Happiness, she is referring to herself in the same way she was speaking of herself to Bernadette at Lourdes when she said: "I am the Immaculate Conception."

Seen in this light, one can fully understand why Mary said to me: "I am the Golden Lady of Happiness." If one were to limit the word happiness to just the happiness Mary will give to her children by prayers answered or cures received, then there would be little understanding of The Golden Lady of Happiness by the ones who did not receive a favorable answer to their prayers.

How can we be sure that she is referring to her own happiness and not to ours? Because the word blessed means happy!

7

This was pointed out to me by my friend, Donald, one day not so long ago. In a very casual way, he said: "If people cannot accept the title of Our Golden Lady of Happiness, I tell them to look up the word blessed and they will discover that the word blessed means happy."

The very next day, I started to look through dictionaries and much to my delight, what he had said was true: blessed means happy as so stated in the book called "The Lion Encyclopedia of The Bible" published by The Reader's Digest Association, Inc. (Page 137): "The Beatitudes: Jesus pronounced blessings . . . on the 'humble'—those who realized that spiritually they were 'poor.' In fact all those mentioned in the Beatitudes are 'poor' and humble' in one way or another. ('Blessed' means 'happy') here are the people God declares 'happy.' . . . and so the Beatitudes turn the world's idea of 'happiness' upside down."

In other words, happiness is not a life of freedom from crosses and obtaining everything one thinks he or she needs to be happy, but to be called blessed, the happiness obtained through grace.

Donald said to me: "The first time I read the Beatitudes and the words blessed were changed to happy, I was very upset. But I discovered that the word blessed does mean happy." I also discovered the same thing. In one dictionary I found: blessed: make happy."

In another dictionary, I found these words: "Blessed means holy, sacred and happy." "Blessing: anything that makes people happy and contented."

Millions of people use the word blessing when they receive something which makes them very happy. They will say: "This is a blessing," "I was blessed," "This turned out to be a blessing in disguise."

In the "New Testament of the New American Bible" Saint Joseph Edition, (Catholic Book Publishing Co.) there are these words on page 440: "Blessing: . . . men bless other men by wishing them well or happiness."

That being the case, there can be no greater blessing than

what the souls in Heaven are given who are blessed because of their great, eternal happiness.

In the "Roget's II The New Thesaurus" by The American Heritage Dictionary, there are these words on page 99: "blessedness: a condition of supreme well-being and good spirits: happiness."

In a book called "A Tour of the Summa" by Paul J. Glenn, there are these words on page 448: "Beatitude is perfect happiness in the beatific vision; this happiness or beatitude is what the soul has merited through Christ and His grace." (Page 452) ". . . in Heaven . . . happiness is the fact of each soul's being saved. . . ."

In "The Maryknoll Catholic Dictionary" by Albert J. Nevins, M.M., when speaking of "Blessed In Heaven," there are these words on page 80: "all the souls in Heaven who are enjoying the Beatific Vision." On page 264: "Happiness: Man's happiness is in the attainment of his ultimate end, which is God Himself, the attainment of this end is perfect happiness."

The word blessed is used for Mary many times in Holy Scripture. When Mary visited Elizabeth, she said to Mary: "Most blessed are you among women and blessed is the fruit of your womb . . . Blessed are you who believed." Mary answered: "Behold from now on will all ages call me blessed" (Luke 1:39-48).

If blessed and happiness mean basically the same thing then we can see Mary as The Golden Lady of Happiness; because, as stated in "A Catholic Dictionary: "In Heaven the souls of the just enjoy eternal and unchangeable happiness in the possession of God in the Beatific Vision."

In the Roget's II book we find these words: "blessedness: a condition of supreme well-being and good spirits: happiness."

Indeed, Mary who is the most blessed of all in Heaven can say: "I am the Golden Lady of Happiness" because she has the complete fullness of happiness in her glory in Heaven and she possessed that fullness of light and glory from the moment of her conception.

At Lourdes Mary called special attention to her Immaculate

Conception: "I am the Immaculate Conception." As The Golden Lady, Mary calls attention to the happiness which is hers because she is so blessed with grace and light and enjoys a happiness in Heaven which far exceeds the happiness of the saints who share Paradise with her.

Not only that, but when Mary focuses upon her own heavenly happiness, she is teaching her children that they can share in that happiness: all who enter into God's Kingdom of love and joy. Who is there who would not want to be found in God's Heaven with Mary?

The whole story of Mary's triumph, The Golden Lady of Happiness and my role in that triumph is but a road or pathway to the infinite, never-ending happiness of Heaven.

The very first question in The Baltimore Catechism is: "Why were you born?" The answer: "To know God to love God to serve God and to be happy with Him forever."

Our Lady, when she calls herself The Golden Lady of Happiness, is showing us a glimpse of her happiness in Heaven and she invites us to one day share such happiness with her. She wants to focus upon the rewards of loving and acquiring virtues and loving and doing God's holy will as she did. She teaches us the value of penance, confession, prayer, sacrifice and all that must be done to save and sanctify one's soul. But she also teaches the joys found in living such a spiritual life; for the word happiness also means joyous.

That is no doubt why she said to me on July 12, 1960: "When the Rosary is said, let the prayers be joyful. Sing songs of love. . . ." These words are one of joy and happiness.

When Mary speaks of happiness, she is talking not so much about material happiness but one that will last forever.

ADDITION
BY ESTELLE HASSLER

Feeling that Louise, because of her humility, purposely left out a very important reason for an increase in Our Lady's happiness and also feeling that The Golden Lady of Happiness would want the world to be aware of the reason for this happiness I pleaded with Louise to allow me to make this addition. Realizing that Louise was given the title, The Mighty Warrior of Truth and Righteousness, I knew that if I begged Louise to allow me to type these words of truth, she would not refuse me.

The Blessed Mother of God, so filled with love for her children, went before Almighty God and pleaded for them and He gave her a way to prevent the destruction of the world. She came to Louise and flooded Louise's soul with grace and Louise, so saturated with love for the world, *used* that grace. She could have rejected the grace but with her own free-will *used* that grace and accepted The Devil's Challenge.

Louise's explanation of the title, The Golden Lady of Happiness, is magnificent but she does not mention her role in that title because, as I said before, because of her humility.

Why is Louise's Lady so completely happy that she delightfully calls herself The Golden Lady of Happiness? Because, finally, someone (Louise) has accepted The Devil's Challenge, which was so very pleasing to Our Lady's Son bringing all of Heaven enormous happiness. It is no wonder why Louise, The Child of Love, will present Our Lady to the world as she has never been presented before as The Golden Lady of Happiness.

(See explanation of The Devil's Challenge in following chapters).

— 3 —

MY LADY'S SHRINE:
A SHRINE OF LOVE

If one were to explain in a single word the messages of Our Lady which she spoke at her approved shrines, the list would be as follows:

1 La Salette: famine

2 Lourdes: penitence

3 Fatima: sacrifice

4 Beauraing: prayer

5 Banneux: believe

The one word to describe the Shrine of the Immaculate Heart of Mary is: love.

The word love permeates the complete story of my Lady. It is entwined throughout the messages of Our Lady and Our Lord from the very beginning in 1944 until Mary stood upon the rock in 1948 and again in 1960 and said: "My Immaculate Heart has triumphed." How did this triumph come about? Only one way, through love.

In 1946, when Our Lady first told me about her shrine, she did not call it The Shrine of the Golden Lady of Happiness; although, when I first saw her, standing on the rock in 1948, she called herself The Golden Lady of Happiness. In 1946, she named the shrine The Shrine of the Immaculate Heart of Mary with these words: "name the shrine in honor of my Immaculate Heart."

At that time, I knew nothing about the Immaculate Heart of

12

Mary. I remember going to the place which was the entrance to the land where she wanted her shrine and saying to myself: "It will have to be a big sign for all those words: The Shrine of the Immaculate Heart of Mary."

Knowing as I said nothing about the deep significance of the words the Immaculate Heart of Mary, if I had been chosen to name the shrine, I would have called it The Shrine of the Rosary for I dearly loved the Rosary.

Yet, Mary's shrine in Meriden, unknown to me at that time, had to be called The Shrine of the Immaculate Heart of Mary because this shrine would be connected with Fatima where Our Lady said: "In the end my Immaculate Heart will triumph."

The very fact that as early as 1944, my whole job for God revolved around the heart of Mary and love becomes a solid proof that the Holy Mother of God did appear to me on the rock in a field in Meriden, Connecticut and said: "My Immaculate Heart has triumphed."

On October 10, 1946, when my Lady told me to name the shrine for her Immaculate Heart, I did not know the story of Fatima or that two years later Our Lady would connect her shrine here with the one in Fatima. I also did not realize that my Lady's shrine would become a shrine of love; even though she has also said in 1946: "On each pillar place a picture of my heart and my Son's Heart to show all who enter that love is here. On each window place a picture of our love for our children."

How did the triumph of the Immaculate Heart of Mary come about? Only one way, through love.

Now, very reluctantly, I will reveal more of my most precious secrets: the messages I received from Jesus and Mary starting in 1944 onward. I do this under obedience to my spiritual director, Father Bradley Pierce. As I reread these precious secrets (I have the original notes), I see so clearly that my Lady's shrine is a shrine of love. These notes which were hidden for over fifty years (I am writing this book in 1996-1998) reveal that fact. These notes also reveal the role I was given to bring forth the Shrine of the Immaculate Heart of Mary at a time when I did not even know what the Immaculate Heart of Mary was.

There would have been difficulty seeing my Lady's shrine as a shrine of love if one could not read the words I am about to reveal. After reading them, one can see the solid foundation upon which was built The Shrine of The Immaculate Heart of Mary. Remember, as I said, Mary called her shrine The Shrine of the Immaculate Heart of Mary.

Notice how Our Lady speaks of her Immaculate Heart right from the beginning. Notice also that my role in the plans of God centered around love. That was told to me as soon as I began to see and hear Jesus and Mary in 1944.

The first thing I was told concerned one of my titles. Jesus and Mary called me Child of Love.

One of the first visions I saw in 1944 referred to love. I saw a great destruction of the whole world caused by natural disasters, wars and even sin. I saw myself among this fallen world and I heard Christ say to me: "Raise this world, Child of Love."

I looked all around and I said to Him: "But how can I do that, my Jesus?"

He replied: "With love My Child of Love, with love."

Christ also said to me, at that time: "I shall place the sufferings of humanity upon your shoulders and you will be made to bear that weight."

As the years went by, as I watched "my world" (as I called it after I had been told to raise the fallen world) suffer through numerous disasters, wars, strange illnesses, etc. I did indeed suffer with my world because I had such a very deep love for suffering humanity.

Once when I asked Our Lord: "How can I give myself more to You?"

He replied: "Through love alone and through thinking of love alone. The more you empty yourself of useless thoughts, the greater will be your love for Me. Think of Me and think of your love for Me; for your love is Mine and My love is yours."

Note, that here is one of the teachings of our Catholic Faith about spiritual advancement. A teaching of which I had no knowledge about at that time.

Years later when I wrote my book called "Come Climb The Ladder And Rejoice," which was about climbing the Ladder of Perfection to a closer union with God, I included this teaching about useless thoughts in that book.

On March 31, 1944, I wrote: My Lady said to me: "You must know the big job we have for you . . . first because of your small love you can give us. It is so small, Louise, that it could never satisfy our hungry, longing Hearts."

Our Lady was telling me that Christ and she longed for love from their children.

On March 31, 1944 (regarding the role or job I was to do in God's plans): ". . . You must bring Jesus' and my name into the hearts and homes of people who do not know as, who do not want to know us or who do not know us as we desire to be known."

Again, I was told about the longing for love, from their children, which Christ and Mary have.

On April 2, 1944, Our Lady said to me: "My arms ache for the millions who pass me by and the ones who honor me from afar. Teach them to come to me and to throw their arms around me or to fall on their knees in wretchedness. I shall comfort them. I am a Queen; but I am also a loving, understanding Mother who desires so to help her children."

On April 9, 1944, I wrote: God wants the whole world to find peace, happiness and love.

I thought that I might get "swell-headed" (as I called it) because of the job I had been given to do for God and my Lady. My Lady put my mind at ease with these words spoken in May 1944:

My Lady said to me: "Fear not, my child, for God makes no one important to themselves. Their job is only important if it is important to God because He is the only important one."

I will say that when my Lady told me all these things, I never once questioned her about the great job I was to do for

God. I merely accepted all she told me without questions. I never wondered what it would be or how I would do it. I never asked my Lady or Jesus how or when I would do the things she told me I was going to do.

On May 1, 1944 my Lady said this, no doubt, thinking about the Golden Lady of Happiness: "Dear children of God, come to me, as this child of God, (myself) has come to me; and find in me, as she found, peace and joy and happiness, as perfect as can be found on earth. Follow the path that she leaves for you to follow and find me, my Son, your Father, and the Holy Ghost."

On June 2, 1944, she said to me: "Dear children of God: Find peace, find happiness; and find all the joys that are to be found in God's world. But when you go forth, do not go alone. Take within your hearts, my heart and my Son's Heart."

Here my Lady places her heart and the Sacred Heart together, as she later did when she told me about her shrine.

On May 4, 1944 Jesus again spoke to me of love: "Fear nothing but Hell, my child, and fear Hell because it is there you shall go if you lose your grip on Heaven; and your grip on Heaven is the love you have in your heart for God, the Father, for me and for my Mother."

I was being taught about free will when on May 4, 1944 Jesus also said: "But, do not fear the devil for he has no power over you unless you let him have this power; and you shall not let him have any power as long as you hold God's hand."

On June 2, 1944, my Lady said: "Smile, be happy and love. Forget the world and its pleasures. Remember Heaven and its joys. Look for your happiness in the love you have for me and my Son. Search for it until you hold it in your hands and hearts in such a way that no one could take it away from you. Accept the trials and tribulations of your life. Accept all with love and understanding."

In such words, one can clearly see that the path to happiness is to put God first in one's life and to lovingly accept His holy will with love and understanding. The path my Lady created for her shrine is paved with love. The name she called herself, The Golden Lady of Happiness could only be fashioned from a shrine of love. For love brings happiness and peace and joy. Love makes the sun shine and dark clouds vanish.

When a person has love, pure, holy love for God, for Mary and for God's holy will, the result can only be happiness.

On June 2, 1944, Our Lady also said to me: "Dear children of God, find peace, find happiness . . . But when you go forth do not go alone. Take within your hearts, my heart and my Son's Heart."

Here she mentions her heart again, the Immaculate Heart of Mary.

On January 26, 1945, Our Lady spoke words which were directly connected with the shrine to her Immaculate Heart, but I did not know that In 1945. She first told me about the shrine in October 1946. Here again, she talks about her heart:

"My children of the world, I stand before the throne of God to defend the children of the Fallen World and because of His great love for me, He will allow my heart to bring back the peace that is not in the world today."

She continued: "My dear children of God, the sun is going to shine forth on a pure, white flower: a flower of peace, a flower of hope, a flower of love . . . My dear children, my heart is the flower that can bloom in the hearts of all men. My heart is the place of great joy and happiness."

Then Our Lady told me about a great destruction of the world which would happen if she were cast aside. She then spoke of great hope with these words: "I tell you this because my Father and your Father's love is so great that He will give you a way to prevent the destruction of the world before the Last Day."

This became one of the promises of The Golden Lady of Happiness. It also shows my role in the plans of God making her shrine and promises known.

On November 13, 1945, Our Lord said to me: "Write long and hard. Write My love and My Mother's love and give to the world that which I want them to have. Write only as My

Child of Love could write. For I bring to the world through you, the love of God for His children and the ways of a loving Father."

On January 29, 1946, Jesus said to me, addressing His poor suffering children: "Dear suffering children: My Heart is open and My love will cover you and protect you from all harm . . . Love is what the world has forgotten."

On May 2, 1946, I was told by Christ: "You shall be the bearer of the glad news. You shall present the King and the Queen of Heaven to Earth and to My children in a glorious manner."

Here, no doubt, Christ was referring to The Golden Lady of Happiness. Surely, she came in a glorious manner. However, in 1946, I did not know about The Golden Lady dressed in her glorious garments of gold. But later, she said to me: "When you give your Golden Lady to the world, you will reveal all her splendor and power" (July 5, 1960).

After hearing such words, I would become weak and I would feel sick. I wrote: Suddenly, I have become so weak, my poor heart cannot stand such things. How could I possibly be worthy of them. But it is God's will. It is God's will! And always, God's will is my will.

But filled with agony after hearing such words about myself, I cried and said to Jesus: "Oh! Jesus, Jesus, what are they going to say about all these things which I have written? Oh, Jesus! It is true, but what will people say?"

Christ sweetly replied: "They will say, dear one, that you are love" (May 2, 1946).

On May 7, 1946, God the Father spoke to me about the great, world-wide destruction which Our Lady had told me that could come if she were cast aside.

He mentioned this message of January 26, 1945 when He said: "The world will not suffer what Mary said it could. For you shall cause thousands to return to Mary's heart never to leave. And Mary's heart will be planted deep in the hearts of My children never to be blotted out by any force or power. The Mother of My Son will not be cast out of the world because you will bring her to the world in such a wondrous way that hearts and souls will turn to her with undying love and devotion."

I wrote, in my note book, under these words: I can't hear any more. I am confused! What has God, my Father said? It is too much for me to understand. I said: "Oh! Jesus! if only I could have just loved You like a plain nun does! and not be great! Because my Jesus, I am not worthy to hear such things from You or from my Father." And Jesus replied, "My dearest one, then I would be so sad because you would not be My Child of Love. Nor could I accomplish such great things through you."

Then on October 10, 1946, my Lady told me about the shrine she wanted here in Meriden, Connecticut. She told me I would have to tell priests that she wanted this shrine. This caused me tremendous sufferings, but I tried to do what she wanted me to do.

Here is what I wrote in my notes about Mary's visit and her requests for this shrine. She called the shrine The Shrine of the Immaculate Heart of Mary and she continued:

On October 10, 1946, my Lady appeared to me in my home and she told me that she wanted a shrine to her Immaculate Heart built in Meriden. She showed me the land in a vision. She said: "On each pillar place a picture of my Heart and my Son's Heart to show all who enter that love is here! On each window place a picture of Our Love for Our children."

On April 25, 1947 (before I saw my Golden Lady), Our Lady appeared to me with a crown of silver stars on her head . . . From each star, a golden beam of light fell to the earth . . . One star was longer and brighter than the others. Then I heard my Lady say that this star will be in her crown after the shrine is built here. And she said: "The world will know that Heaven smiles on the shrine to the Immaculate Heart."

On April 29, 1947, Jesus said to me: "Beloved little Child of My Heart, into a dark world comes this brilliant light from Heaven. For behold the Child of Love will bring this light. This light is love."

On May 27, 1947, I wrote these notes: "Dearest Jesus, I am as helpless as a little flower and I am weak and could easily be destroyed. But, dear Jesus, with the graces that You have put into my soul, I know that indeed You have well protected me from the world and I am safe under the mantle of Your love."

On May 25, 1947, in an article I wrote, there were these words:

But love is a smile. Love will make the earth smile and the earth is in need of this smile of love. Love is the hope for those who cry. Love is the repentance for those who sin . . . How can a dumb one (like me) have knowledge or a dull mind (like mine) be brilliant? It is not for me to say for those things I cannot understand. But I do know how to love; and I love you and I love your children in the suffering world.

Then in 1960, when I again saw The Golden Lady on the rock, the following words from Mary speak of love.

On July 7, 1960, when I asked my Lady if she wants her children to say the Rosary or make sacrifices or do penance, she replied: "Tell my children to pray and to make sacrifices, but tell them to rejoice . . . They shall say their Rosaries and they shall confess their sins and they will do penance for their sins; but most of all, they will love me as I have never been loved before. I come now to give love and to receive love. I ask for prayers of love."

The following day, on July 8, 1960, she said: "Come to my land on Sunday and pray. Send me prayers of love."

On July 12, 1960, she said: "Tell my children that The Golden Lady of Happiness wants love—pure, simple, love. When the Rosary is said, let the prayers be joyful. Sing the songs of love because I am ready now to show the world my true power and glory."

She also said: "I am the Mother who dearly loves her children."

She said in August of 1960: "Ah! my children, love my Immaculate Heart."

Surely, it can be clearly seen that right from the beginning,

Our Lady and Our Lord was presenting to their children a shrine of love.

She asked for prayer: "Tell my children to pray and to make sacrifices. . . ." but the prayers she wanted most to hear were prayers of love. ". . . but most of all they will love me as I have never been leaved before. I come now to give love and to receive love. I ask for prayers of love." She also asked for songs, but "songs of love." That was years, before the changes in the Liturgy, when songs were still sung only by the choir. Today, during Mass, everyone sings songs of love, praise and worship.

She said that her children will say the Rosary, and she added: "When the Rosary is said, let the prayers be joyful."

She called herself The Golden Lady of Happiness because happiness stems from love, the love for God and Our Lady and the love received from them. A person loved is a happy person in spite of daily crosses and sufferings.

One day, after I had made my Lady known in 1960, someone asked me: "What was the greatest moment in your life?"

She expected me to say it was when I saw my Lady.

Instead, I answered: "The most precious and greatest moment in my life is to know that at this very moment, I can love God and He loves me."

One day, over forty years ago, when I sat down to destroy my early notes thinking that I was too unworthy to have Our Lord and Our Lady speak to me, suddenly Christ appeared to me and stopped me. He sweetly said: "Do not destroy My Heart."

Within such notes, there was the Heart of Jesus and also the heart of Mary and the shrine of love called The Shrine of the Immaculate Heart of Mary. I did not destroy them; and for that, I am very happy for I realize what a tremendous loss that would have been if I had destroyed such notes. They were saved. How? Through love.

Part 1

Writing This Book:
1997

Father Bradley Pierce:
Spiritual Director
and Confessor
since 1984

SAINT ALPHONSUS LIGUORI STATES: "I FOLLOW ONLY THE SAFE AND ORDINARY PATH OF HOLY OBEDIENCE TO MY SPIRITUAL FATHERS, WHERE AS, JESUS CHRIST HAS PROMISED US, WE ARE SURE TO KNOW THE WILL OF GOD."

WITH THESE WORDS IN MIND, I NOW EXPLAIN WHAT MY SPIRITUAL DIRECTOR AND CONFESSOR TOLD ME TO DO IN REGARDS TO THE REVEALING OF MY MOST PRECIOUS SECRETS IN THIS BOOK.

MY SPIRITUAL DIRECTORS
AND CONFESSORS

Whenever there arises in a person's life such things as visions and revelations from God or Our Lady, there are two very important steps to take. The first step is for the person to have lengthy and expert direction from competent spiritual directors and confessors. The second necessary requirement is the one so favored has to obey these directors and confessors especially in regards to such favors even if such direction and advice is against what the person wants to do.

Obedience becomes the number one sign that the favors are true; and disobedience is the sign that the visions are false. Saint Teresa of Avila was quoted as saying: "If the Holy Mother of God told me to start a convent in one place and my superiors told me not to, I would obey my superiors."

It is very foolish for a person who thinks he or she is a "chosen" one to attempt to evaluate visions and revelations without the aid and advise of a spiritual director and confessor. Both must be made aware of the situation. In addition, it could take years of careful watching by a director before he could come to any conclusion as to the truth of what the person is experiencing if the person's case is complex. Very often an experienced and alert director or confessor can spot a fraud or a false "mission" without too much trouble just by listening to the person or reading his or her writings.

I once knew two women who thought they were chosen for "God-given missions." I mentioned the fact to each one that there had to be a spiritual director and/or a confessor to guide them. They refused.

One woman, who read the life of Saint Teresa of Avila, said that Saint Teresa was her spiritual director. The other woman told me in a firm voice that she did not need a director because the Pope was her spiritual director. Of course, both made a very serious mistake.

As soon as my visions started in 1944, I went to receive advice from a priest and through the long span of my work for God, Our Lady and my Church, I have had proper spiritual direction from competent directors and confessors.

As I write these words, I am 73 years old. I consider my job for God ended, and I will add: successfully. However, it would not have been successful if I had not had proper spiritual direction from competent directors who safely lead me through the maze of what I called my job for God. This job which included visions of Our Lady and a shrine she asked to be built in Meriden. However, there were other things I was asked by God to do. I was told to write. So, I spent fifty years writing notes, books and articles for Catholic papers. I was lead in the areas of becoming a well-known lecturer and of forming a Catholic organization called The Maryheart Crusaders. All this work was done with the full approval of not only my spiritual directors and confessors, but also of my bishop: Archbishop Whealon of the Hartford Diocese (now deceased). I was also very concerned about my personal spiritual life (other than the visions). I began to go to confession every week, always mentioning my faults and weakness, such as an angry outburst or showing off at the ice skating rink when I planned to become a famous ice skater.

I learned a great deal from the wise confessors. For example: One day, during Mass (I often went every day to Mass as well as on Sundays and Holy Days), a priest during his sermon, stated that it was a great sin to go to Holy Communion when one's soul was not in the State of Grace. I had no idea what the State of Grace was and I panicked. After Mass, I sought out a priest to hear my confession and to tell him of my fears that I may not have been in the State of Grace when I received Holy Communion. He wisely explained to me what being in the State of Grace was (no mortal sins) and after questioning me, he assured me that I had been in the State of Grace when I received. These weekly confessions continue for years.

I knew how valuable they were.

At the time when no one wanted to stay in the confessional too long, because they were afraid that the people standing in line would think they were great sinners with a long list of sins, I found the confessional to be much more than just the place to tell the priest sins. I knew there were valuable spiritual lessons to be learned from the priest. I did not want to miss such an opportunity to learn about the teaching of our Church concerning spiritual improvement. I did not care how long I stayed in the confessional as I discussed my spiritual problems with a priest and listened carefully to his words of wisdom and advice.

When it was unthinkable to identify yourself to a priest in the confessional, I did just that. I wanted the priest to know who I was so that be could watch my spiritual growth and correct any mistakes I was making.

Years later when the Church changed the confessionals so that a person could face the priest, if so desired, most everyone I knew was shocked. I was not. I told them that I had been telling the priest who I was for years. I laughed at their attitude. They could not believe mine.

I will add that I did not "jump" from one director to another even if I heard something I did not like. It was only circumstances, such as death, which caused me to seek another director or confessor.

All together, I had five priests to whom I entrusted my work for God and my revelations.

The following are the spiritual directors and confessors who carefully guided my work for God and also my spiritual life as I went, day by day, doing God's holy will for me.

SPIRITUAL DIRECTORS AND CONFESSORS

1. Reverend F. X. Shea:
   Secretary to Cardinal F. Spellman,
   New York City
   1944-1947

2. Monsignor John J. Hayes (deceased)
   Chancellor of the Diocese of
   Hartford, Connecticut
        1947-1957

3. Reverend Vincent E. Lyddy, Pastor (deceased)
   Saint Frances Cabrini
   North Haven, Connecticut
        1960-1984

4. Reverend James Kelleher (deceased)
   1960-1975

5. Reverend Bradley Pierce,
   Holy Apostles Seminary, Cromwell, Connecticut
        1984

MY FIFTH SPIRITUAL DIRECTOR AND CONFESSOR: FATHER BRADLEY PIERCE: 1984

As can be seen by the first chapter in this part, I have had proper spiritual direction since 1944. I place Father Brad first because it was he who guided the writing of this book as I will explain.

Because of my poor health and the distance to be traveled, from Meriden to New Haven, to go to confession to Father Lyddy, I needed another confessor and spiritual director closer to my home. I never stopped thinking of Father Lyddy as my confessor; however, I began to see him less and less. I did not have in mind anyone to replace him; but then I met a young seminarian named Bradley Pierce. He was at that time studying for the priesthood at a seminary not too far from Meriden called Holy Apostles in Cromwell, Connecticut. As the years went by, I had met several seminarians from Cromwell due mainly to The Crusaders' book store which I had founded in 1984 and where I worked from 1984 until 1993. Many seminarians came into the store.

I did not meet Brad in the store. Instead, he came to one of my Crusaders' meetings in my home. He has been brought to this meeting by a friend of mine who wanted Brad to hear me speak. Actually, I did not find Brad, he found me.

He later said that the first time he heard me speak, he knew the Holy Spirit was guiding me and my work for God and for souls. He was so deeply impressed that he came to all the meetings I had in my home to hear me speak.

We fast became friends and Brad wanted to know all he could about The Crusaders and my writings. I gradually gave him some of my articles. He, also, was deeply concerned about the spiritual lives of the average Catholic lay person.

When Mike (my husband) and I invited some of the seminarians to our home for weekly suppers, Brad would come with them.

Brad and I had many spiritual talks and I was as deeply impressed with his spirituality as he was with mine. We (and others) at times traveled to New Haven to see and talk to Father Lyddy, whom, as I said, I still considered to be my confessor and spiritual director. Father Lyddy was also deeply impressed with Brad who expressed ideas and teachings which were truly Catholic.

When Brad's elderly mother requested baptism after her son's ordination, I became her Godmother.

I watched with joy as Brad worked ever closer to his priesthood; and one of the happiest days of my life was when my "son" (as I began to call him) was ordained. Then he became Father Bradley Pierce.

After Father Brad became a priest, he could become my confessor; however, I did not rush into Father Brad's confessional. I still considered Father Lyddy to be my confessor and I saw him as often as I could.

However, because of my increasing health problems, I could not go to New Haven to confession as often as I would have liked. Then I gradually turned to Father Brad.

By that time, Father Brad knew about my Lady as well as the work I did for God with my writings and lectures. Still I hesitated speaking to him as I had to Father Lyddy about my personal spiritual life and my own quest for sanctification. I felt he may not understand the goals I was trying to reach, being only a newly ordained priest.

In June of the year 1984, I had one of my dreams fulfilled. That was to open a Catholic book store and Evangelization Center in Meriden where Mass could be celebrated in a chapel daily and confessions heard after Mass. This Catholic outreach program was part of the work I did for God and my Church. All was done with the approval of Archbishop Whealon.

Father Brad was very enthusiastic about this project and did all he could to bring it about. He offered his services immediately as the one to say Mass and hear confessions. I was thrilled.

On Monday, June 25, 1984, Archbishop Whealon came to bless the store. When a picture of the Archbishop was taken, I stood on one side of him and Father Brad stood on the other. Father Brad and I worked together in the store for weeks. It was truly a dream-come-true for him and for me. He shared my joy and even my awe. He could hardly believe that he was not only a priest, but that he was working in the Maryheart Crusaders' chapel saying Mass and hearing confessions.

My greatest joy was to prepare the altar for the great Sacrifice of the Mass. With tender love and joy, I prepared the altar so that my "son" could say Mass.

After Mass, in a small room which had been prepared for that purpose, Father Brad heard confessions. Many people went to confession, except me. I still had Father Lyddy, however, my visits to his confessional became less and less.

Then I realized I had to have a confessor closer to Meriden. At that time, there were other priests who came to our store to say Mass on days Father Brad could not come. I was very shy about revealing my most precious secrets about my spiritual life to just "anyone."

I wrote the following notes on August 1, 1984 about how I decided to choose Father Brad to be my next confessor:

Then I had a choice of who would be my new confessor and I looked for the qualifications I felt a confessor should have.

I wanted a new confessor because, although I am sure of my path to sanctity, I wanted to share my spiritual life with a knowledgeable priest so as to get someone else's opinions about my pathway to perfection. But I hesitated, at first, feeling that if I revealed my deepest spiritual secrets I would be only looking for praise. I had to make sure that my motive was correct before asking one of the priests I knew to become my confessor.

My thoughts turned toward Father Brad mainly because he was familiar with many of my teachings about the spiritual life and was completely in tune with what I taught others.

Then one day, last week, suddenly, I knew that I would choose Father Brad. He finished hearing confessions and walked out of the confessional and put his arm around my shoulder. I looked up (he is taller than I am) and said: "I would like to go to confession."

He returned to the confessional and I sat in front of him as I had done with Father Lyddy for so many years.

After the introductory prayers, I began to explain that I would like him to become my new confessor. He immediately said he felt that he was not capable of being my confessor when I had been his spiritual teacher all these years. It was a beautiful moment which revealed his pure humility.

I explained: "I am sure of my pathway to union with God but I don't want that to be merely my own opinion. I would like to share with you the secrets of my soul and you can give me your opinion and if you tell me to destroy any of my notes, I will."

Father Brad put his head down, with his hands folded in his lap and bent forward. He said: "Louise, I want you to know that I would not be here if it were not for you. I owe my priesthood to you, your instructions, your faith in me, your encouragement when I was ready to give it all up. How can I tell you to tear up your notes?"

I laughed and said: "As my confessor, it will be your duty to do that."

Then I said: "One thing bothers me, though. I have to make sure that when I let you read my secret notes (no one reads such notes) that I am not doing it merely to have you praise me. I want the motive to be correct and pure; the one which is that I feel I should have someone's opinion besides my own which tells me that I am on the correct path to union with God, as I continue to reach a closer union with Him."

He replied: "You know, I understand how you feel. Often when I give a sermon I ask myself: 'Am I doing this so people will tell me how great I am or do I truly want to help and instruct the people who hear me?' I have to come to the conclusion that God sent me to help and instruct His children."

I replied: "And I have come to the conclusion that I should have someone's opinion, other than mine alone, which tells me that I am on the correct paths to God and perfection. I do send spiritual notes to Father Lyddy, but he never speaks to me about my spiritual life nor answers any of my letters lately. However, I guess that is a good sign because if my notes were wrong, he would tell me. Still, I would like to talk about things which concern my own personal spiritual life."

Father Brad, again, expressed in a very humble way that he feels he is not capable of being my confessor, but I think he is. He often speaks words of great spiritual insight and wisdom. I have heard many of his homilies. He said he is 100% for my ideas and hopes and work for God; and he told me that his greatest joy is to come to the store to say Mass in our chapel and to hear confessions.

This first confession to my "son," Father Brad, was a wonderful spiritual experience for both of us. We could feel tremendous graces descend upon us and I felt that I had found the new confessor I had been looking for.

Although I wanted Father Brad to read my secret notes, I did not show them to him as soon as he became my confessor. I gradually revealed certain secrets as our relationship deepened and he became my spiritual director as well as my confessor. Many things I told him about my visions and so forth, I did not plan to tell him. These bits of information came spontaneously during our talks in the confessional depending on what subjects we were discussing.

When in 1989, I began to photo copy my notes for the Archbishop, at his request, I made an extra copy of all I photo copied for Father Brad. In that way, he learned more and more about the job I had been given by God and my Lady. He read all the manuscripts I had given to him and often amazed me by repeating what he had read. He would take the manuscripts on vacations to study them. He acted as a wise and prudent spiritual director as he studied my writings, approving all he read.

If he found anything in all these writings which was against our Catholic faith or which presented teachings other than what could be found in the spiritual books of our faith, Father Brad would have immediately told me; but he found nothing.

He would not have allowed me to continue to write if what I wrote was, in any way, against the teachings of our Catholic Church. Instead, he found much spiritual fruit contained in my articles and books, instructions and insights which made his own faith more precious to him.

As the years went by, Father Brad and I had numerous talks about the work I did for God, my Church and souls as well as the favors and blessings I had received from God and my Lady.

FATHER BRAD AND FATIMA

It was Father Brad who introduced me to Fatima. He had been to Fatima at least twice before I, myself, went there with a group of Maryheart Crusaders in 1987. When I told him I really wanted to go to Lourdes, he said: "No, Fatima is the place for you." I would never have gone to Fatima if Father Brad had not insisted that I go.

I wrote about this first trip to Fatima in my notes:

I actually had no desire to go to Fatima, I also had no devotion to Jacinta and Francisco; and I would never have gone to Fatima on my own.

It was Father Brad, who had been to Fatima, who constantly told me that I should go there. Actually, I wanted to go to Lourdes, for I had a very deep love for and devotion to Bernadette and Our Lady of Lourdes. I dreamt about going to Lourdes for years, but Father Brad kept saying: "Fatima is the place for you." So, I decided to go to Fatima, instead of to Lourdes, with Father Brad and the others.

Fortunately, Mike and I had the money to make the trip due to the handsome retirement package given to Mike when he left his job at the factory. So, having the money to make the trip was no problem. The problem was that I still wanted to go to Lourdes and not to Fatima; but I went to please Father Brad. He had found Fatima to be far more inspiring and spiritual than Lourdes; and he wanted to take me there.

There were seven people in our little group. We made the trip from July 11, 1987 to July 25, 1987.

I actually went more to please Father Brad than because I wanted to go.

That statement is perhaps unusual due to the fact that I knew Fatima and my Lady were connected. However, my Lady was also connected with the other visions in her Golden Circle; so, to me, Fatima was just one of the visions in her Golden Circle of visions which ended with my Golden Lady's triumph.

Father Brad talked about Fatima constantly. He, fortunately for me, had found Fatima, when he went there, to be everything he desired as a place for prayer, meditation and love for Our Lady.

I must say that I did not share his enthusiasm, but I deeply respected his love for and devotion to Our Lady of Fatima.

As can be seen from the chapters I wrote about Fatima ("My Trips To Fatima") my Lady and the events which happened while I was there, it was surely providential that Father Brad insisted I go to Fatima; and as I said, I would never have gone if he had not arranged the trip for me and my husband.

Father Brad was not only my confessor and spiritual director, he also became the chaplain for The Maryheart Crusaders offering his expert advice when needed. He never lost interest in our work or our goals. He continued to come to the store three times a week to say Mass and hear confessions for the people who would come to the chapel. He helped numerous people who came to his confessional with troubled hearts and souls. He often spent long hours giving spiritual help and hearing confessions after Mass. As word spread of his gentle, kind and understanding words, more and more people came to our chapel to go into his confessional for the help they so desperately needed. Many people who had stayed away from the sacraments for long years, returned to the practice of their Catholic faith after going to confession to Father Brad. He made our chapel a true "Refuge for Suffering Souls" as I called it.

When it came time for our annual banquets, Father Brad could be counted on to help with all the necessary work. As many as 200 people attended these banquets. Before they left the church, Father Brad celebrated Mass for them. Everyone left with a feeling of tremendous joy after his inspiring Mass and homily.

MY BOOK: "THE TRIUMPH OF THE IMMACULATE HEART OF MARY"

As the years went by, Father Brad and I became close friends. Mike and I often had him and other friends to our home for suppers and parties. Birthday parties and Christmas get-togethers were always times of joy for my closest friends. Often as many as 18 people came to celebrate. Father Brad was one of them.

Our group of Crusaders, with Father Brad as our chaplain, traveled twice to the Holy Land and seven times to Fatima.

Once I had found Fatima, the shrine and the wondrous sights of Portugal near Fatima, I had to return to that blessed place. Father Brad arranged not only the pilgrimages, but all the daily Masses, as well. At times, he would surprise me when during one of our private Masses, he would read pages from one of my manuscripts. I had not even known he had brought the manuscript with him. But he dearly loved what he read in my manuscripts and wanted to share the inspiring words with others.

During all these years, Father Brad remained my confessor and spiritual director. We often, at least twice a month when I went to confession, had spiritual talks and I knew my spiritual life was safe under his direction. When problems arose at the store or in other areas, Father Brad's words of wisdom helped solve such problems.

The closer we became, the more writings from my secret note books I gave him to read. He was able to see the depths of such writings and how the words could help suffering humanity and lead souls to the loving Heart of their Savior.

The more he read, the more writings he wanted me to give to the world. But I was not ready to share my precious secrets with the world as yet: the words of Jesus and Mary to their Child of Love, as they called me. I had hidden my secrets for fifty years. I had written and The Crusaders did publish books such as "Come Climb the Ladder and Rejoice," "Come Home The Door Is Open," "The Catholic Answer to the Jehovah's Witnesses," etc.; however, I wanted to keep my secret notes about my visions and favors from God hidden from the eyes of the world.

This began to bother Father Brad. He would say to me: "The world has your books and the ones you wrote are excellent; however, the words of Jesus and Mary to you, your visions have a power which could light up this whole world because of their beauty and love. You must give these writings to the world."

He especially thought that it was time to publish a book about the visions of The Golden Lady of Happiness.

I had written several manuscripts about the visions but had not published any of them. I just put the manuscripts in the Crusaders' archives.

Father Brad wanted to see such writings published. Under his direction and with his encouragement, I began to write "The Story of My Lady" with the intentions of getting it published. This manuscript (a very short one) Father Brad presented to Archbishop Cronin.

After the death of Archbishop Whealon in August of 1991, Bishop Daniel A. Cronin had been named the Hartford Archbishop. He was appointed by Pope John Paul II. On January 28, 1992, the Most Reverend Daniel A. Cronin had been installed as Archbishop of the Hartford diocese.

Father Brad became acquainted with the new Archbishop because of Father Brad's work at Holy Apostles College and Seminary in Cromwell, Connecticut. By that time, Father Brad had told me that the time had come to get a book about my

Lady and her shrine published and I had begun to write it.

Father Brad presented this manuscript as well as other information, to the Archbishop.

This was the first time since my Lady requested her shrine, in 1946, that a spiritual director of mine had presented a manuscript to the bishop with the intention of getting it published.

On March 3, 1992, Father Brad wrote a letter to the Archbishop thanking him for his kindness during a visit to him. Father wrote: "I have given you a lot of material to go over, particularly the material that pertains to Louise D'Angelo."

On May 11, 1992, we had to move our store and chapel to a new location and Father Brad wrote to Archbishop Cronin asking the bishop for permission to move the Tabernacle and the Blessed Sacrament to the chapel in our new store.

On May 14, 1992, the bishop answered Father's letter granting permission to move the Tabernacle from its present location to the new chapel. He ended the letter by saying:

> With every prayerful
> good wish, I remain
>
> Faithfully yours in
> Christ
>
> Daniel A. Cronin
> Archbishop of Hartford

After a long wait, the first manuscript Father Brad had taken to the Archbishop was returned to me with a note stating that certain points had to be clarified.

I set to work writing many pages which clarified the items pointed out. I also began another manuscript about the visions and the shrine. This time I called the book: "The Triumph of the Immaculate Heart of Mary."

Time went by and I finished this task during 1995.

Once again, Father Brad presented this manuscript to the bishop. More time went by before I received this manuscript back, asking again to clarify some points.

Meanwhile, Father Brad read and reread a copy of this manuscript. The more times he read it, the more frustrated he became. What he read was not what he wanted me to write. I had, as I had done with all the manuscripts I wrote about my Lady and the shrine, purposely, left out my secret notes which explained my role in my Lady's triumph. Father Brad, who was familiar with such notes felt they should be part of my Lady's story.

Father saw, so clearly, that without these secret notes, the story of my Lady could not be clarified. There were too many missing parts. He set about trying to get me to agree with him. Finally, I did agree and this book is the result of Father Brad's direction and guidance and my obedience to my confessor and spiritual director. The following chapters explain how Father Brad instructed me to write this book and how I did as he directed under holy obedience to my spiritual director.

3

FIRST MANUSCRIPTS I WROTE

In all the other manuscripts I wrote throughout the years (some are in the bishop's office) I purposely left out all the details of my early revelations because I did not want to give them to the public. However, by doing that, as my spiritual director, Father Brad, explained to me, I left out half the story and the other manuscripts, including the 1995 one I wrote, contained only bits and pieces of the story of my Lady's triumph.

It is only under obedience to my confessor and spiritual director, Father Bradley Pierce, that I now include in this book the many revelations which I had hidden for 50 years. Please know that Father Brad had been my confessor and director since 1984. He has read my writings and also my secret notes. That is why he insisted that I reveal, in this new book, the whole story of my Lady which includes the role God gave me to fulfill, which started in 1944.

Now under Father Brad's direction and guidance, I have written the book that he felt I should have written before. As can be seen in these chapters, I was very reluctant to do what Father Brad told me to do; but I did so under obedience.

Yet, as I wrote this new book, I could see and understand the wisdom of Father Brad to have told me to write the book as he felt it should be written.

Father said to me: "The book you are now writing clearly reveals God's infinite love and mercy and will teach people valuable lessons about His love and mercy."

I replied: "I am glad that I obeyed you because by doing that, I can teach people very powerful, spiritual lessons which they have to know to reach a closer union with God."

You see, the story of my Lady is not just about visions, but about this fallen world and God, Our Lady's and my love for the poor, lost, bewildered children caught up in the rushing waters of man's selfishness and greed.

Also, this book is not just a book about my private revelations. Within its pages there is a great deal of information about the power of God's grace and about His love and Mary's love; and how important it is to live a life of virtue. I was told by my Lord that He would use me as an example for others to follow. Such an example has been hidden for fifty years. That was what I wanted.

But, now is the time to let these words of Jesus and Mary bring joy, hope and happiness to millions of lost, lonely, fallen hearts and souls. Let the light of my story and my Lady's story shine into this dark world and show the way to the loving Hearts of Jesus and Mary.

The ones who have read the new chapters have found in this book a rich goldmine of spiritual knowledge not only from the words of Jesus and Mary, but from my words about God the Father, Jesus and Mary and the Holy Spirit and grace; all of which presents the beautiful teachings of our Catholic faith.

I so long to bring such knowledge to the world in order to help save souls and lead them to a closer union with God. Such desires to help souls is expressed in this prayer which I wrote December 20, 1987:

MY PRAYER TO THE HOLY SPIRIT

Dearest God, Holy Spirit, flood my soul with Your light and grace and power. I open my whole being to Your light and grace. I willingly give myself to Your light and grace so that You can freely work through me to reach out and touch hearts and souls. I accept all the grace and power you care to give to me so that through me others can see Your power, grace and light. Use me in whatever way You care to use me. I will, in turn, use the power and the grace You gave to me so that through me I can bring to all the light and power of Your grace and love.

In keeping with my love for souls and the work I do to teach others about God, His grace and love, I wrote this prayer on October 11, 1992:

A PRAYER FOR MANKIND

Dearest God,

I wish to pray for all the people, all over the world, billions of them, who have difficulty knowing You, understanding You, doing Your holy will, praising You, thanking You and loving You.

I wish to pray for their souls and to ask for Your mercy and forgiveness for sinners who may, at this very moment, be on the road to everlasting separation from You and Your love. May this prayer be powerful enough to save souls which would otherwise be lost for all eternity.

In parts of this book, I explained about the secret notes, which I now reveal, and how amazed I was to discover them as I wrote the book and saw the wonderful things which had been revealed to me so long ago, most of what I had merely recorded and then forgot. I still have these original notes and note books. Also, many of these notes (as far back as 1944) have been in the bishop's office in a book called "Prophecies and Predictions." That book has been in this office since 1963, so you can see that I did not make up these revelations now for this book.

I especially ask you to pay close attention to the chapters about how The Holy Spirit appeared to me to give me the gifts of knowledge and words. Then read the chapters on Suffering Humanity and my writings with great care to see the gifts God gave to me so I could help suffering humanity. This was the foundation for my role in my Lady's triumph.

— 4 —

MY SPIRITUAL DIRECTOR,
MY SECRET NOTES AND
MY OBEDIENCE

When my spiritual director and confessor, Father Bradley Pierce read the completed manuscript which I wrote about the visions of The Golden Lady of Happiness in 1995, he was not as satisfied, by what he read, as I thought surely he would be.

He was deeply troubled not by what was in the manuscript but by what was omitted. He had known for years many of what I have always called my most precious secrets. These consisted of messages or revelations which had been given to me as far back as 1944-1945. These loving words from Jesus and Mary were so precious to me that I hid them and would not even let my closest relatives see them. It took me over a year before I allowed my second spiritual director to read them in my private note books.

When I composed the very first short manuscript about the visions, around 1961, I did include some of the early messages in that story. But knowing they would be seen by others caused me great pain and so I removed them from other manuscripts. I would cringe at the very thought of someone reading my most precious secrets. I did not even consider writing them in the manuscript I prepared about the visions in 1995, which I planned to now give to the public. I suffered enough just knowing that the public would read about my Lady; however, I knew that the time had come to give The Golden Lady to her children through a published book.

However, Father Brad realized that if I withheld that information, the story of my Lady would not be complete.

He clearly saw that I was hiding a great deal of important facts and that greatly bothered him even though he understood why I was reluctant to reveal what was hidden in my private note books or diaries which I had faithfully kept for over fifty years.

As soon as I finished writing the book, I gave him a copy to read. For weeks he did not mention what I had written. Then one day, he said that he did not like the way I started the book with a short chapter about myself written in the third person; which I had done on purpose.

I said as little as I could about Louise D'Angelo. He wanted me to change to the first person and to tell more of my story. I said I would do that, but I planned to leave what I had written and change only from the third person to the first and to add nothing else.

But something else was bothering him about the book. He told me that he thought about if for weeks wondering if he should tell me. Finally in a burst of frustration and, he said, spiritual insight, he wrote me a letter dated New Year's Day 1996 and he told me what was wrong with the manuscript.

When I read the letter my heart sank and I, at first, refused to do what he asked. He wanted me to reveal my most precious secrets as part of the story of The Golden Lady of Happiness!

I immediately started to answer Father Brad's letter. I wrote:

> What you ask me to do is impossible now . . .
> the information you ask me to reveal should be
> given to the public in small doses after I die
> and should not be presented by my hand as part
> of my story of my Lady or my autobiography
> . . . what you have asked me to write is what
> I call my most precious secrets which I do not
> want to share with the public while I am alive.
> I suffer knowing that I wrote about my Lady
> and the visions. I can gather together the infor-
> mation needed for such a book, but only you,
> my confessor and spiritual director can write
> such a book.

I was strongly objecting to Father Brad's suggestion that I include in the story of The Golden Lady my most precious secrets which I had so carefully hidden during fifty years of receiving sweet words and revelations from my beloved Lord and my dearest Mary: magnificent graces and blessings.

However, before I finished answering Father's letter, he called me on the phone. He slowly and carefully began to explain to me why I had to reveal my most precious secrets when telling the story of my Lady.

My objections and opposition to what he wanted me to do made no difference to him. He plainly saw what I could not: the complete story of Mary's triumph and the role I had been given to become part of her triumph. This had to be told.

As I said, I received his call the very moment I was writing an answer to his letter. He wanted to know if I had received the letter and my reaction to it which came immediately as I said: "Yes, I got your letter and I know exactly what to tell you. I am even now writing an answer to it. I think the best thing to do is to have you write the book so it can be published after I die."

His answer was not what I wanted to hear. He replied: "The book, the way it is, without explaining your role in Our Lady's triumph, does not have the power it should have. It becomes only one of "a million" visions which have flooded the world in the past years. Your Golden Lady will be "lost in the crowd." What makes your story different, what proves your story and your visions is the way Our Lord and Our Lady prepared you to become part of your Lady's triumph. That part of the story has to be told or the whole story of The Golden Lady loses its power and its glory. It is empty, missing something."

I answered: "But, if I write all my secret notes then people will see Louise D'Angelo and not The Golden Lady. I want people to see my Lady and not me."

He quickly replied: "The world has to see your role in this whole thing. Only then can they see not only what role God prepared you for but the world can also see the wondrous love God has for the world and souls to so prepare you for the role you played. You are God's Child of Love and the world has to see you as this Child of Love in order to see the glory and the love of God and your Lady."

I replied: "But I don't want to become part of my Lady's story in such away that we become one. I want everyone to see and love only Mary."

Father Brad insisted: "One cannot separate you and your Lady in much the same way that they cannot separate Mary from Christ. Remember she would say to you: "Your triumph is mine and my triumph is yours." You cannot separate the two. Also, you were told that you are a setting for a magnificent ring and she is the diamond. You cannot separate the diamond from the setting or else it loses its value. The two have to go together."

I tried to object again, but he would not listen. He continued: "You cannot tell the story of The Golden Lady without telling the story of Louise D'Angelo. Otherwise you present only half the picture to the world and the world cannot see the loving plans which God created so that the world can have the peace, joy and happiness your Lady wants to give. Nor can the world understand exactly what her triumph is all about."

He continued: "The triumph of Our Lady stands out as an event which can be compared to the birth of Christ. There is no way that you can hide from that triumph, for it is your triumph and what you did just as much as it is Mary's triumph and what she did to bring it about."

I listened as he continued: "Even what you put into the book about the cures and favors or saving the rock, these things could never give your book the power to reach people's heart as can the words which Jesus and Mary spoke to you as they prepared you for your role. These words are proof of your visions. No one on earth could invent them."

I weakly replied: "Well, my Lady told me that the proof of the visions would be found in my writings."

"Not only that," he continued, "but the love which shines forth from the words of Jesus and Mary will light up the whole world. It is love which you present to the world when you tell of the wondrous love which Christ and Mary had for you: a plain, ordinary nothing as you call yourself. See how much comfort and joy you will bring to hearts and souls by telling the world your story and how you, a nothing, became a something through the grace and love of God and Mary? Your story is a magnificent example of God's care and love for His children and the power of His grace."

I could offer no more opposition to what Father Brad was telling me. I weakly replied: "All right, I will do what you tell me to do, but I will do it only under obedience to my spiritual director. You have told me to do this and as much as I do not want to reveal my precious secrets to the world, I will do that as an act of obedience to you."

He said that was what I had to do and he was pleased with my answer.

A TREMENDOUS JOY

After the call ended, at first I was so nervous that I became ill. Just the thought of the world reading my secret notes caused me much pain.

But then a remarkable thing happened. Slowly but surely a great joy began to fill my heart and soul. I could not explain it. I did not know why I felt such joy over a situation which I dreaded.

Then Father Brad called me again. I said to him: "I am ready to do what you want me to do and I feel a tremendous joy, but I don't know why."

He replied: "I prayed that you would be filled with enthusiasm and joy about the whole thing.

"What has happened is that your secrets have held you in bondage for fifty years and finally you are free. It is the joy of freedom which you have found as soon as you accepted God's holy will for you by agreeing to write what I told you to write. Remember Christ and God the Father always say to you: 'Your will is Mine and My will is yours.' That is where your joy is coming from. It is to free yourself from fear and to freely follow God's holy will for you."

I never finished the letter I had started to Father Brad, in answer to the one he sent to me, which was filled with my reasons why he should write the book and not me.

I now know that it is God's holy will that I reveal my precious secrets to the world and this I do with much love for His holy will for me. At last the world can have the complete story of The Golden Lady of Happiness and that causes me tremendous joy because I will bring God's love and Mary's to millions of hearts and souls.

My closest friends were also told that I will include my secrets in the story of my Lady. Although they never read such secrets and they did not know what these notes entail, they were filled with joy knowing that the complete story of my Lady and my part in that story will be revealed to the public. Estelle, who typed the first manuscript, told me that as beautiful as what I had written was, she felt that I was not telling the complete story because I hid many facts about myself and my own spiritual life.

I told her that I wanted the public to see my Lady and not me; and she answered that we cannot be separated. She said: "How can you tell the story of Christ without telling the story of Mary? It is the same with you. How can you tell the story of The Golden Lady without telling the story of Louise D'Angelo?"

When I give the chapters to Estelle to type, I allowed her son and her husband to read them knowing that now my secrets will become public. One day, Eric was at my home with a group of people and I asked him what he thought about the 1995 book (without my secret notes) and this one with them. He replied: "The first book was good, but even I thought something was missing before you even started to write the second one. It seemed to me that in the first book, I could only catch a glimpse of God and Our Lady's love. And I could not even find your love there. But now, with this book, love explodes in a brilliant light. This love is immense as it radiates outward. This love between you and God and Our Lady is absolutely amazing and it can be clearly seen in this new book. In the other book, it could not be seen at all."

That reaction from this young man caused me to be filled with joy knowing that now I can give to hearts and souls what I would not give before.

Another encouragement came from the 16 year old daughter of a friend of mine. I had given her (and others) a few chapters of my new book. One chapter included poems I had written in 1944. One poem was called "God's Gift of Tears."

I did not even know that the teenager had read any of the chapters when this happened. I wrote this in my notes dated July 25, 1996:

Two days ago, a young lady came to help me in my office. She is the 16 year old daughter of a friend of mine; a very nice youngster who always wants to help others. She worked for a couple of hours photocopying the chapters of the book "Triumph."

As I worked at my desk, suddenly she said: "I have just read the most wonderful and beautiful poem I ever read in my life. It was so beautiful, it brought tears to my eyes!"

I continued to work and I thought she was talking about a poem she had in one of her school books or maybe gotten from the library.

Then she added: "The name of the poem was "God's Gift of Tears.""

I stopped working and looked up amazed as I said: "I wrote that!"

She laughed and said: "I know. My mother let me read what you gave her. The poem was in one of the chapters. it was the most beautiful poem I have ever read. It was perfect, the rhyming, the thoughts, the way you expressed such thoughts."

I was deeply touched by what she said. If this 16 year old child could find that poem so beautiful, then other youngsters could also read and understand the poem. It was a precious moment for me.

I was being shown by these two incidents how the light and love found within my secret notes would touch hearts and souls.

But the most encouragement and courage I received concerning revealing my precious secrets to the eyes of the public came when I recently (August 1996) read the following words in a book called: "The Life and Revelations of Saint Gertrude" (published by Christian Classics, Inc. Pages 27-29).

As I said, I wanted to hide my blessings, favors and revelations from the world and it was most painful for me to include them in this book. Then I read what Our Lord had told Saint Gertrude, the Great when He told her that she should commit her revelations to writing. She was very reluctant to do that, as I had been; but Our Lord said to her: "Be firm and immovable, My daughter, for I am with you . . . What purpose does it serve that these and many other things concerning . . . My saints are known, unless it be to enkindle the zeal of those who read and hear them, and to manifest to all men the greatness of my love?"

Another problem I had when I thought about revealing my secrets, which others had mentioned to me, was I knew that many people would make fun of me and even ridicule me and my dearest Lady and Our Divine Lord. I do not mind having people laugh at me; but I felt terrible thinking my Lady and my Lord would be put into the same situation.

Saint Gertrude had the very same concern and misgivings. She wrote: "I marveled why God urged me so strongly to make known my revelations, since He knew that the majority of mankind are so weak and unspiritual that, far from finding any example for their edification, they would more probably find a subject of contempt and raillery."

Our Lord sweetly replied: "I have so planted My grace in you, that I expect it will bear me immense fruit; therefore, it is My desire that all who receive similar favors, and who despise them by their negligence, shall learn from you on what conditions I have given them these gifts, in order that My grace may be increased in them in proportion as their gratitude increases. But should there be any sufficiently malicious to defame the sanctity of these works, the penalty of their sin shall fall on themselves, and you will not be accountable for it . . . If the world is scandalized, let it be scandalized, since even the Eternal Truth Himself was not spared its censures."

Because of what I read and what the two friends had said to me, I began to see that a multitude of people could find hope, encouragement and God's love within my secret notes; and Father Brad was not only correct but wise in telling me that I had to include My most precious secrets in this new book.

Even my faults and failings will make people understand the mercy and love of God; as they could not understand them before. That is a good lesson to teach God's poor, suffering children.

I always said that I never knew why God found me so attractive and why He constantly came after me always with words of love, always filled with gentleness, never scolding me even when I deserved and needed such a scolding.

My story does show the way God not only loves His children but wants each and every one close to His Heart of love.

Millions of people can find hope realizing that if He could so love someone like me, a big, stupid nothing, then He can love all His precious children no matter how sinful they have become or how nothing they consider themselves to be.

He once said to me: "If you were to fall to the lowest gutters of sin and corruption, I would still come to you to raise you to the heights of Heaven."

With the help of God's powerful grace, I did not fall to the lowest gutters of sin and corruption; but perhaps someone who will read this book did indeed follow such a path. They can know that God extends to all an invitation to leave a life of sin and corruption and find safety in His embrace of love.

Revealing my precious secrets will also show my love for this fallen world and for God's poor, suffering children.

When I was told by the Lord that He would place the sufferings of humanity upon my shoulders, I accepted that burden. When He offered me The Devil's Challenge and explained the sufferings that would bring to me, I accepted this challenge because I so loved God's poor, suffering, lost children.

When He told me to raise a fallen world, I asked Him how could I do that? He replied: "With love."

My part of the story of my Lady's triumph is saturated with love: my love for God, His love for me, my love for Mary, her love for me, God's love for His precious children, Mary's love for her children, my love for this fallen world and the ones who fell within it.

For good reason, God called me His Child of Love and Refuge For Suffering Souls. He slowly but surely molded me as He so desired, and I allowed Him to do just that because I so loved His holy will for me; and I loved the ones who would see a clear pathway to God's Heart of love through me and my writings.

Therefore, I now expose my heart and soul to the world. After I made my Lady known in 1960, I suffered a great deal because of the fact that my soul was seen by eyes which had no right to see it. I feel that way now as I place into public view my most precious secrets through an act of obedience and love for God's holy will and love for His poor, suffering children. However, when they see my heart and soul, they will also see the Hearts of Jesus and Mary and their precious love.

MY SECRET NOTES

What was there in my secret note books which I guarded so closely and kept hidden for over fifty years from the eyes of the public? Why did I call them my most precious secrets?

My note books were filled with messages or revelations from my Lord, God The Father and my Lady. To me, these were my personal relationships with my Lord and my Lady and too precious to share with others. Unlike the ones who want to "tell the world" about their religious experiences, I wanted to keep hidden whatever favors and blessings I had received. My very soul was in my note books and I did not want to expose that to the public.

Some of the messages were praises given to me by my Lord, praises which I definitely did not deserve. Others were predictions about future events and still others were words from Heaven which explained the role I was to play in the triumph of the Immaculate Heart of Mary: this role which Father Brad saw so clearly and which he knew had to be put into the story of my Lady.

At the time when I was being prepared for the role and when I was told about future events, I had no idea what such messages meant. But I never questioned why I was told nor wondered how the future events would turn out. In my simplicity, I merely wrote what I was told and left all in my note books. I still have these notes.

As I said, after I met my second spiritual director, Monsignor Hayes, who was the Chancellor of the Hartford diocese, around 1947 it took me one year to allow him to read my note books. I finally left the note books with him because I knew he had to read what was in them before he could say that all was from God. I was terrified that he would tell me that all was from the devil. I was amazed when he walked into the room I was in, holding the two note books in his hands, and softly said: "It seems to me that you are more than a daughter of God's." He was saying that all was indeed from God.

From then on, I knew how precious my notes were and I was even more protective of them.

As the years went by, I kept my secret notes hidden. I had no intention of ever revealing them to the public.

When I wrote manuscripts about my Lady, I did mention a couple of the messages from my secret note books, but I carefully hid all the others. Just telling the story of my Lady was painful enough for me. I could never reveal all the messages from Jesus and Mary I had received throughout fifty years. For those fifty years, I referred to these notes as my most precious secrets.

Monsignor Hayes had read them and approved all I had written. That was all I needed to know.

Then I allowed Father Brad to read my most precious secrets.

It was Father Brad who began to make me take a closer look at my secret notes and to make me understand all that he understood about them. He saw so clearly that within these notes one could see the pure love which Christ and Mary had for their beloved children as expressed to me; and he wanted me to share these words with the world.

Father Brad also saw that such messages had to be put in my Lady's story; and on New Year's Day 1996, he sent me that letter which turned my secret world of my personal relationship with my Lord and my Lady upside down.

When my Lady told me to make her known in 1960, I hesitated for one month. To make her known was not an easy thing for me to do. I would have preferred to have my Lady and the visions revealed only after my death.

The main reason being, that my Lady was one of my most precious secrets that I did not want to reveal to the world.

When I was married on September 7, 1957, I had my husband buy me a little home safe. There I stored my notebooks and there I intended to keep them until after I died. Then the Church could have them. My life had changed with my marriage and I thought that my job for God and my Lady was over.

Three years later, in 1960, when my Lady began to tell me that I had to make her and her promises known to the world, the thoughts of that caused me to suffer tremendously; but I did what she asked me to do.

At first, when asked about the visions, I told as little as possible. Telling this story always made me feel uncomfortable. As I wrote in my notes: "I felt as if my soul was on display before eyes which had no right to see it." If someone, my mother or my husband, came near me when I was writing or reading my note books, I would quickly hide what I wrote from that person. It took me over a year before I finally allowed my second spiritual director to read my most precious secrets. At that time, I knew he had to read such notes in order to understand the work I had to do for God and Our Lady.

When my Lady told me in 1946 that she wanted a shrine in Meriden and I had to tell priests about this request, it was so painful for me to go to priests that when I stood by the door waiting for it to be opened, I trembled with fear and wanted to run away.

When my Lady told me in 1960 to bring people to the rock where she appeared as the Golden Lady, as my husband drove up the street to the place where the apparitions were taking place, I was so nervous and filled with fear, that once again, I wanted to run away.

When people stood around me as I waited for the vision to appear, I wanted to hide from all the eyes focused upon me as I knelt before the vision came.

When people came to me (thousands of them) some wanted me to pray with them. I would refuse because it was so painful for me to have people watch me as I prayed.

Then I was forced to write the story in order to protect it by copyrights; mainly because there were so many stories going around, all saying different things.

I had to write the true facts, but in doing that, I also had to tell a more complete story.

The first manuscript I wrote about the visions, I put into it some of my secret notes in order to make the story more complete. I soon wrote a smaller story and removed many of my secret notes. This was the one I had copyrighted. I had no more than 100 copies made and gave them only to my closest friends. The copyright protected the story from being misused by vision zealots who often came to me and wanted to use the story for their own benefit. I would tell them that they could not print anything about my Lady because I owned the copyright.

Later, I wrote two longer versions containing more details. However, I merely put them in a file case and marked each one: "To be published after my death." They also contained some of my secret notes which were connected with the visions of The Golden Lady of Happiness.

My secret notes were always so precious to me that I never allowed anyone, except my spiritual directors to read them. (Once I did allow a nun whom I trusted to read some of them.)

Now, as I write this book, which is to be published, once again I know I will have to include some of my most precious secrets, secrets I have hidden for over fifty years. But time has made it easier (although it is still painful) for me to reveal what has to be told so that the world can now have the beautiful story of the Golden Lady of Happiness: a story filled with peace, light, joy, hope and love.

Father Bradley Pierce and Louise

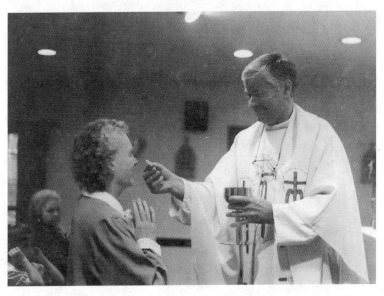

Father Brad giving Louise Holy Communion 1990

Part 2

Introduction to
My Visions and
Revelations

— 1 —

DAILY NOTES THROUGH THE YEARS

As you continue to read the chapters in this book, please understand that the notes taken from my private note books were written over a period of 50 years (a whole life time of work). As I wrote each note book and the file cases became full, I merely put each case away and never reread the note books except when I wrote my autobiography in 1963 or when I used my notes as a reference for something I was writing. Other than that, my note books were kept in file cases unread. Most of them were never reread by me or anyone else until now in 1997.

After Archbishop Whealon requested a copy of my daily notes, in 1989, 1 spent long hours taking the notes from my note books and making photo copies of them so they could be put into different categories. However, in doing this, I never took the time to carefully reread my notes so as to see the picture I now see in 1997 as I write this book. Some of the notes, messages and writings I had for many long years, absolutely amazed me as I reread them for this book.

Actually, I never wanted to reread my note books to find what they contained. I preferred to leave that enormous task to someone else who, in the future, might find some notes interesting.

Often I would look at all the file cases of my daily notes and manuscripts of published and unpublished books and say: "I pity the one who will have to read all that!"

I never knew that I would be the one to do just that for this book.

Then when I started to photo copy the notes to put into categories or subject matter, I would say that I did that not only for the bishop but as an act of charity for someone in the future who would want to find certain subjects and would not have to go through each and every note book which was arranged by dates and not subject. I did not know, when I did that, that I, myself, would find these photo copied notes most helpful as I wrote this book.

In all the original notes which I have in my note books, I never changed the writing or the dates; even though some words are crossed out. That was done (very few times) as I wrote the notes and crossed out a sentence or two. They were not cancelled in later years. That only proves that I never changed or rewrote the pages. These note books are still in my possession with all the original notes. Some of these pages (50 years old) are so fragile that they tear when touched. (I copied some of them for this book.)

I wrote everything only once and did not rewrite anything. The notes remain exactly as I wrote them. I wrote them all in the note books. I *did* not write them on separate pages and then copy them into the note books. Everything was written directly into the note books and they remain the same notes I wrote throughout the years.

One reason why I never rewrote or changed anything was that my note books were seldom in my possession for long. I usually gave them to Monsignor Hayes and he kept some of them for years. I had them together only since 1960. Another reason was that I was always too ill and exhausted, from daily duties, to pull out the note books to reread any of them. They did not cause me to wonder what was in them. I simply did not want to reread them. (I never looked back at what I had accomplished, only forward to what I had yet to do.)

As I copy, here, some of these daily notes and writings from my numerous note books (now numbering over 175) and manuscripts written over the years; it can be plainly seen that all the notes and information fit together and there are no contradictions even though a space of 40 or 50 years may separate them one from the other. The original notes can be seen with the proper dates. One thing I was always very careful about was whenever I wrote a note I made sure that I put the exact date on top of the page. That proved to be extremely important as can be seen from what is written in this book.

The notes and other writings I have (such as short articles) prove that the job I was given by God to do for Him and for the Holy Mother of God was impossible to invent or compile by a mere human being. My writings also show the way the Holy Spirit guided my job and my pen even when I had no idea what that job for God would develop into.

Why did I write so many notes, daily, even hourly? Because I was told to: (March 27, 1944) "She told me to write down all the things Jesus tells me" . . . (and what she tells me).

I will add that such writings were approved by all my spiritual directors and confessors. After one of my confessors, Father Lyddy, read a sample of my spiritual note book, he told me to: "Keep writing and don't stop until I tell you." That was in 1960. He never told me to stop writing and I never did stop.

Writing all my daily notes, as well as numerous articles (many of them published) and books was not easy; it was pure penance and entailed a great deal of tears and physical sufferings. Yet, I would not give up. One of the weapons used by the devil, as I daily fought my Devil's Challenge, was to try to stop me from writing. As I put this book together, I can understand why.

Within my daily notes, in what I wrote and when I wrote them is substantial proof of my visions. My Lady told me that the proof of my visions is in my writings. Now, as I put all these notes into the beautiful picture of my Lady's triumph, I can see what she meant.

As I said, I wrote my note books according to dates. I never put individual notes or messages together as I am doing now writing this book. I never knew, as I recorded the revelations, how they would all fit together. I merely recorded what I saw and heard. Now, as I write this book, it can be plainly seen that words and messages, years apart, as much as 40 or 50 years apart, say the same things. Needless to say, when I wrote a message in 1994, 1 did not remember that my Lady told me the same thing many years before.

As I now record message after message, I am constantly amazed to find what was said years apart.

The fact is, I am so amazed at what I am finding that I check and recheck (sometimes, three or four times) the words and the dates when the words were spoken. I make sure that every word and date is accurate exactly as I first recorded it; so that no one could say I "made up" the words and dates as I wrote this book to fit them into the story of the triumph of the Immaculate Heart of Mary.

I will say again that all my notes and dates are authentic and were written by a stupid, little child who so loved God, Our Lady and her fallen world. Such writings and my obedience to the wishes of my Lord give glory, not to me, but to God, for they show the power of His grace and love. In my mind, I always thought of myself as a very big "nothing." However, as I was told once by my Lord, He has the power to make a "something" out of a "nothing." That power is grace used for the good of a soul and for the glory of God (May 2, 1946).

2

DIFFERENT CATEGORIES, SUBJECT MATTERS IN MY REVELATIONS AND MESSAGES

When I wrote, in my note books what I had always called my most precious secrets, I wrote according to dates. I did not realize, as I wrote, that within some messages there were references to different subjects which I did not understand at that time. I merely wrote what I was told and made no effort to attempt to explain what I had written or to see these different subjects.

Because of that, I did not separate the visions and messages into different categories or groups pertaining to a specific subject. That would have been impossible for I had no way of knowing what I would see or hear in the future or what these categories would be; or even if I would see or hear anything else.

This was not a fault or a mistake on my part. The fact is it shows how genuine such writings are. As a result, the messages throughout all my note books are listed according to dates and not according to subject matter. Within the pages, one can see that often there are two or even three subjects mentioned in one revelation or message. It was only in 1989 that I attempted to photo copy these messages and place them in different categories. I did that, at the request of Archbishop Whealon, who had requested all my notes. When I started that long-drawn-out project (which was only half finished by 1996), I was amazed to discover how many different subjects there were in some of the messages. As a result, I often had to make two or three copies of the same message to put into the correct category which consisted of: words about my private spiritual life, my writings, my Lady's shrine, the work I did for God, The Maryheart Crusaders, etc. This entwinement of different subjects can be seen in all the messages starting from the very first ones I received in 1944.

The messages (which still can be seen and read in my early note books) were left as they had been recorded. Throughout the years, I never made any attempt to change any of them in my note books. They remained a list of revelations (according to dates) of visions and messages as recorded in my daily notes. Even when I wrote about these in a manuscript, in 1962, which I called "Prophecies and Predictions," I listed the revelations as they were in my notes not attempting to separate them into different subjects. I, once again, listed them only according to dates. (This manuscript was taken to the bishop in 1963.)

In 1992, I wrote another manuscript about these revelations. Again, I listed them only according to dates and not subject matter. But in this manuscript, I attempted to explain some of the messages according to what had happened in the years following 1944-1945, etc. (That manuscript was also handed in to the bishop's office.)

When I, in such manuscripts, listed the messages only according to the dates they were received, I saw no reason why it was confusing whenever someone (whom I allowed) read some of my early manuscripts. The original messages often jumped from one subject to another. One can imagine how distracted a person can become if, in reading a book, suddenly the author presents a subject which completely draws one's mind away from the main story which is being told. This is what happened in my early manuscripts. Once, a priest who read the Story of My Lady for a report to the bishop, wrote me and said that the story was rather "confusing." Now, I understand why. Not only were some messages "confusing" because of the way several subjects were combined into one message given on a certain day; but I had purposely left out many of my secret notes which tied into these messages.

I, myself, was not aware of this problem until now (1997). What I had written in my early manuscripts about my Lady, her shrine and her triumph, were only bits and pieces of this story. I knew the complete story, but the ones, who read these manuscripts, did not.

Also, this fact must be taken into consideration. The story of my work for God and my Lady was not complete when I wrote the early manuscripts. There were still many events which had not as yet taken place. For example, I had been told, May 17, 1946, that my writings would be read "all over the world." When I wrote the early manuscripts about my Lady, that had not taken place. it was only after I started my organization in 1964 and after I had written my book called "The Catholic Answer To The Jehovah's Witnesses," published in 1981, when that book began to be read all over the world. My Lady's triumph did not reveal itself for the whole world until after 1989.

Also, in the early manuscripts and in the numerous letters I wrote to the Archbishops about my Lady's shrine, I focused all the attention upon my Lady and her shrine. I saw no need to go into details about my role in this shrine and my Lady's triumph and what I had been told about my role.

Now, I realize that by doing that, the story of my Lady was only half-told; or as Father Brad told me: it was "lifeless."

Now, I know, that in revealing my secret notes and in separating the words I heard into subject matter or categories, the story of my Lady becomes much clearer and easier to understand. Also, it is now possible (in 1997) to see the way the series of events unfolded throughout the past fifty years which makes the story seen as the great plan of God's to bring peace, joy, happiness and love to suffering mankind.

Also, in writing this book, including in it my secret notes and in separating the messages into subject matter, I became overwhelmed with wonder because of the words I have had in my note books for over fifty years.

It is so clear to see that in my earliest notes, is the very foundation for my Lady's shrine and her triumph.

Now, I can look back at all the notes I suffered so in recording (daily throughout the years) and I can see that saving all these notes, was, in itself, a great grace from God.

As the years went by, as I worked day and night doing the work God wanted me to do, I never looked back at what I had already done. I only looked forward to see what had to be done. Now, I can look back and see what I did accomplish for Christ, Mary, my beloved Church and for souls. Within my daily notes, is the story of what I did. Now this story can be told.

3

HOW I REMEMBER THE WORDS OF JESUS AND MARY: MY DAILY NOTEBOOKS

Someone, as they read this book, may wonder how I remember all the words of Jesus and Mary and the very dates such words were spoken. The answer is simple. I wrote everything down, dates and words, as soon as these words were spoken. My private notebooks (or diaries) go back to 1944. I recorded all that happened, all that was said and the exact dates in these notebooks. I have kept these notebooks for over fifty years. It can be imagined that such notes take up a great deal of space. They do. They are placed in file cases, all properly numbered and dated. These original notes can be seen by proper Church authorities. My spiritual directors have seen these notebooks and read the contents ever since 1947 when my first notebooks were handed to Monsignor John Hayes who accepted the task of being my spiritual director. All I wrote was approved by them.

I arrived in New York City in the Fall of 1943. By March 1944, I had seen my first vision.I also started to write, as I was told, all that I heard and saw: "Write. Write long and hard." "Write my words and my Son's words" (11/13/45).

When the words were spoken, they were spoken to a very young (19 year old) and very ignorant girl who knew next to nothing about Church doctrine. Our Lady or Our Lord spoke in words which I could understand; yet, within their words can be seen traces of solid Catholic doctrine; words which I could never invent for I knew nothing about theology.

No matter what I heard, I never once questioned what was being said to me. In all innocence, I recorded all exactly as I was told. I seldom made any comments about anything. To me if Our Lord or Our Lady said something, that was all right with me. The only things which bothered me was when they praised me for I knew I never deserved to be praised. Yet, I accepted all that was said as God's holy will for me.

I wish that I could fully explain the way I wrote these notes and revelations with, more or less, a casual attitude. I would merely say to myself: "Well, if that is what Jesus or Mary said then that is all right with me."

I faithfully recorded, word for word, all I heard; however, I never tried to figure out, in regards to future events, the how or the why of all I heard and saw. To me, no matter what I heard or saw, that was merely God's will for me. Even if I did not understand what was said, I did not question anything. I merely wrote all in my notes.

I was extremely careful to write exactly what I heard. I did not dare change one word or one sentence. I would have considered that a sin and my notes remained exactly as I wrote them throughout my life-time.

Once the notes were recorded, I never changed them. Once in a while, I crossed out a paragraph, but very seldom. The words of Jesus and Mary were never changed and could be read in their entirety fifty years later. What I am trying to say is the fact that, in no way, could I possibly have, of myself, invented these messages in order to tie them into my role connected with my Lady and her triumph.

Whenever I wanted to quote some of my early notes, I had only to go to the file cases, look up the date and find the information I was looking for.

The task I had of writing everything down in my notebooks began as soon as the visions started. I was told by both Our Lord and Our Lady to write what was said to me. I picked up my pen and never put it down.

I remember, at that time, I roomed with another girl for a brief period. I had a little table with an inkwell on it and a pen. In those days, a person would pick up the pen, dip it in the ink and then write.

Our Lord and Our Lady had told me to write—and I did. I wrote pages as the job God gave me began to unfold.

One day, the girl came home, looked at the empty inkwell and said: "What on earth have you been writing? The ink is all gone!" I never told her or allowed her to read my notes; and as I said, I never stopped writing. I not only wrote about the visions and what I was told, I also began to write poems and articles about Jesus and Mary.

One thing I wish to say about my notebooks and all the writing I did for over fifty years (published books and articles included). Such writings caused me a great deal of suffering. I regarded them as penance. I was never well as far as my health goes. I had many daily duties and obligations. I worked full-time jobs, such as a bookkeeper. I had a home to take care of as a wife—a working wife—etc.; however, I never stopped writing books, articles and daily notes. I could not have changed any of my earliest notes even if I wanted to. I was simply too busy and too ill.

Numerous times after I worked all day and was so exhausted, I would retreat to my basement in my home where I kept my writings and add to the collection. This was so painful to me and I suffered so much with all I had to write that I called my cellar office: "my dungeon." Still I would not stop writing. Why? Because years ago, in 1944-1945 my Lady and Our Lord said to me: "Write, write long and hard. Write as only my Child of Love can write."

The worst penance of all was keeping up with my daily notes. That became a very heavy cross for me to carry. There was always so much to write about. Yet, I did not stop writing because writing was God's holy will for me and I loved God's holy will no matter how much I suffered. I would not give up.

As I continued to write new notes about revelations and visions, I never looked back to see what I had previously written. I could not have done that, even if I wanted to, because my spiritual director, Monsignor Hayes, had most of my note books and often I did not see them for years.

Meanwhile I merely continued to record what was happening concerning my visions and revelations. Once, Monsignor

Hayes returned to me a note book to give to a doctor (a friend of his). When I saw it, I was delighted. I had not seen it for four years.

After I reread that note book, I was filled with joy.

The one thing which pleased me immensely was the fact that my later notes written without reviewing my early notes were consistent. There were no changes or contradictions in what had been written years apart. They basically said the same things.

Following are notes I wrote May 20, 1950 about just such a situation. At that time one of my note books had been with Monsignor Hayes for four years:

The other day Monsignor gave me one of my note books to give to Dr. Brennan. I read it over and I felt so wonderful. It was so good because I had forgotten most of what I had written. It was good to reread my notes and to see how everything fits together. It is easier to understand things better than it was when I wrote things and didn't know what was going to happen next. I guess that I won't read the book anymore, but it was a gift of God to allow me to reread it, after four years. It is good to know that God's love filled my notes four years ago and longer the same as it does this very day.

— 4 —

NO FINANCIAL GAIN
FROM THE VISIONS

In speaking about visions, my visions, one has to take into consideration the possibility of financial gain for someone who claims to see visions. The Church, in her wisdom, is very interested in this aspect of such claims, and well she should be. Throughout the long history of visions and visionaries, even relics, there have been numerous frauds and money-making schemes, all well documented.

When I first started to see visions in 1944, I never knew that such frauds or money-making schemes existed. I never even suspected that someone could have personal gains through visions.

My one and only interest was to do the job my Lady and my Lord told me to do. At that time, I had no idea what that job consisted of, but I knew I would follow the path which was created for me by the very ones I saw and heard.

At that time and throughout the following years, I was very much lacking in worldly possessions as well as money. That did not bother me.

I mention that fact and others in this chapter to show that my visions never brought me into a higher state of living. My husband and I worked to obtain the money we needed for our personal living expenses and for the savings which we have, mainly through the savings plan in the factory where my husband worked until his retirement. No one ever made any donations to me or to him for any of our living expenses. No one ever paid any of our bills. Even if they had offered, we would have refused. All the money donated to our organization, The Maryheart Crusaders, went to that for our work, even the money I received for my lectures (which was not that much). I never took a salary from the organization nor any royalties for the books I wrote. Mike never even took gas money for the numerous trips we made to my meetings or lectures. Some were as far away as Boston and Cape Cod.

In 1946 when I was first told that my Lady wanted a shrine in Meriden, my mother, brother and I lived close to poverty in a small rented apartment. My father had been killed when I was ten, in a car accident and my mother worked to support us. There was never any talk about money connected with my visions. The fact is, I hid my visions in my secret notes and I seldom mentioned them to my mother or brother.

When I first saw my Golden Lady in 1948, there was never any mention of money being gained from the visions. By that time both my brother and I had low-paying jobs to help with the household expenses.

The fact is, I dreaded telling anyone, especially priests, about the visions. They were my most precious secrets.

My mother wanted a house of our own, but we never had the money to buy one or even to get the down payment.

After I saw my Lady in 1960, as word spread about the visions, I began to hear talk about money.

At that time, I was married. My husband worked in a factory and I also had a low-paying job in an office. I continued to work in offices for the next 25 years, full or part-time in order to help with the household expenses. I never once thought to gain anything personal from my Lady and her story; but others did suggest such to me.

I was told more than once that I could be a "millionaire" if the right promotion of the visions was made all over the world. I absolutely refused such offers.

My Lady and her story were not "for sale." When I made up a small story of my Lady to copyright it, I did that so the story could be protected and no one, myself included, could profit from the visions.

I made only 100 copies of the story to give to my closest friends who knew about the visions. At that time, a copyrighted article or book had to be distributed to the public in order to secure the copyright. I never made up any more copies and told everyone the copies they had were for private use only and could not be copied or sold.

One day when an unusual picture was taken by my husband at the rock, I was told by many people that the picture could be sold "by the thousands" and I could make a lot of money. I quickly hid the picture and it has remained hidden in my secret notes ever since.

When "visions" began to pop up all over the world starting in 1961, huge promotions were created for each "vision." Centers were set up to sell books, tapes, newspapers etc. and even Rosaries "blessed by Our Lady." A great deal of money was made.

I never allowed my Lady to become involved in such a promotion. There was no money collected for books, tapes, magazines, etc. because these items were not available. I would not allow it because I obeyed my bishop.

Some people wanted to make a donation to me personally if I prayed for him or her. I never accepted such donations but I would pray for the person.

The only thing I would accept would be if someone offered to take me to a restaurant for lunch. But I did not accept too often because I was tricked a couple of times.

One time a woman begged me to go to lunch with her, so I went. However, as soon as we had ordered the meals, the woman said: "Now tell me all about your visions." I felt trapped because we had ordered the food. I told her as little as possible.

Another time, four women came to see me. They insisted that I go to lunch with them. We went. Before the meal was over, one woman put a fat roll of bills on the table in front of me and said: "I am married in an invalid marriage. All this money is yours, if you tell me that my marriage is all right with God."

I was shocked and I told her I did not want her money and I would never tell her that her marriage was all right with God.

She put the money back in her pocketbook and she did not even speak to me when we left the restaurant. She was furious.

I never accepted any money from anyone for my personal use because of the visions.

When Mike and I bought our home in 1967, we got the money for the down payment from a small trust fund we had set up and money from my mother.

The mortgage was only $89.00 per month. (The house has greatly increased in value. Many people think I just bought it and paid the current market price which is far more than it cost.) Even though the mortgage was only $89.00 per month, Mike and I had to struggle to keep the house and pay living expenses. I had to work as a full-time bookkeeper. He worked in a factory.

I was forced to give up my job because of illness; but I had an insurance policy which paid me a monthly sum which made up for my loss of income.

OUR RETIREMENT OUR TRIPS

My husband and I retired and went on Social Security when we were old enough. He received an excellent retirement package which gave us money to make trips to the Holy Land and Fatima; something we could not afford to do before retirement. With his pension, our Social Security and Mike's small check for working at our Crusader's Center, we are able to meet all our living expenses. We also have Medicare and Blue Cross medical insurance. Because of that, I, as before, never asked anything in the way of payment for the work for God, which I have done since 1960, including working long hours doing Crusader work.

Why? Because I so love souls, my Church and my Lord's holy will for me.

Part 3

The Story Begins
Louise D'Angelo
First Religious Experiences
Years 1924-1943

— INTRODUCTION —

THE PREPARATION FOR MY ROLE IN MY LADY'S TRIUMPH

When the story of Our Lady of Fatima is read, a very unusual fact emerges. It is very clear that the three children, Lucia, Jacinta and Francisco, were prepared in advance for their encounter with their beautiful Madonna. This was strange or different because such a preparation did not happen in other well-known, approved Marian apparitions. The visions seen at Lourdes, LaSalette, Guadalupe, Beauraing, Banneux and even Knoch were not preceded by other visions or instructions to the seers. Their task or mission was only to report what was seen at what date and where.

The first hint, that the three children had been chosen by God for a very special mission, came two years before the actual visions of Our Lady of Fatima. They had no idea what was to happen in the future when they saw the Angel of Portugal.

The visions of this angel was first seen in 1915 when Lucia was in the field with her flock of sheep. She was not with Jacinta or Francisco, but with other childhood friends.

Suddenly, after the youngsters ate their lunch, there appeared before their eyes a white figure in the air above the trees. This figure disappeared without speaking. Lucia and her friends had no idea what they had seen or why. The fact is, Lucia was told she had merely seen "someone wrapped in a sheet."

The following year, 1916, when Lucia was with Jacinta and Francisco the Angel of Portugal again appeared. This time he told them who he was.

As the three children played, a strong wind developed and the trees began to shake. When they looked up, they saw a figure dressed in white coming towards them. This was the same figure Lucia had seen the year before. Jacinta and Francisco had not seen this before nor had Lucia mentioned it to them. The youngsters were, as can be imagined, frightened. The angel told them not to fear and identified himself as the Angel of Peace. He taught them a prayer and added: "Pray thus. The Hearts of Jesus and Mary are attentive to the voice of your supplications."

The months passed and one day the youngsters were playing by a well owned by Lucia's parents. Suddenly, the angel appeared again and said: "What are you doing? Pray, pray very much. The most holy Hearts of Jesus and Mary have designs of mercy on you. Offer prayers and sacrifices constantly to the Most High."

The angel explained how the children could make such sacrifices, especially for the conversion of sinners. He also foretold their future sufferings.

In addition, he taught them another prayer and also brought them Holy Communion. When he did that, his words were: "Take and drink the Body and Blood of Jesus Christ, horribly outraged by ungrateful men! Make reparation for their crimes and console your God."

When Our Lady appeared on the 13th of May, 1917, the three children had already been schooled in the discipline of making sacrifices and offering their sufferings as acts of reparation for the sins which so offended her Son. They had been well prepared to bear the words of Our Lady of Fatima: "Are you willing to offer yourselves to God to bear all the sufferings He wills to send you, as an act of reparation for the sins by which He is offended, and of supplication for the conversion of sinners?"

Their answer: "Yes, we are willing."

The roles which the three young children had been given did not end when the visions of Our Lady of Fatima ceased. The seers spent the rest of their lives fulfilling these roles.

They never forgot, not only the words of Our Lady, but the words of the angel as well. Their spiritual lives had been formed by these words: sacrifice, suffering, prayers, conversion of sinners and "console your God."

Jacinta chose to accept sufferings for the conversion of sinners. Francisco chose to console his God, so offended by sin. Lucia chose to be a nun and to share with the members of her community prayers, sacrifices and penance.

I bring up these facts because in my story, it can be plainly seen that a long preparation for my encounter with my Golden Lady came before I actually saw her standing on a rock in a field as The Golden Lady of Happiness.

When I first started to see and hear Our Lady and Our Lord in 1944, the words I heard were, for me, a solid preparation for my role in the triumph of The Immaculate Heart of Mary.

Not only was I prepared to meet my Golden Lady, I was also prepared to carry out the will of God in regards to my complete job for Him and my Lady. I wrote these words about the first visions of my Golden Lady which took place in 1948: I was not as awe-struck as people might think that I should have been when I saw her standing on the rock, because that was not the first time that my Lady suddenly appeared before me.

For four years, from 1944 to 1948, I had often seen and heard Our Lord and Our Lady. Then from 1944 to 1989, when my Lady's triumph began to be manifested before the whole world, I silently had carried on the parts of my job which had been given to me in 1944.

As you read this book about the triumph of the Immaculate Heart of Mary, you will clearly see that job unfold and the way I was prepared to do what the good Lord and Mary wanted me to do.

— 1 —

MY UNHAPPY CHILDHOOD

The date of my birth was, without a doubt, part of God's plans for my role in my Lady's triumph, as was the place of my birth. I was born in Meriden, Connecticut on June 13, 1924. It was many years before I found out that June 13th was a feast day of Our Lady of Fatima and Meriden was the place where Our Lady wanted a shrine to her Immaculate Heart.

My parents were very poor and did not welcome me. They already had one child and I became an added burden. As a result, my mother and I never had a close relationship and I felt unwanted all through my childhood.

I was not born into a family of pious, practicing Catholics. My mother was a Catholic who left her faith to marry my father whose family came from a very strict Protestant background.

My mother had my brother and me baptized as Catholics much to the fury of my Protestant relatives. As a result, my brother and I seldom saw my father's side of the family.

At one time in my childhood, my brother and I were sent to a Protestant Sunday School. I did not attend Mass or prepare for my First Communion until after my father died when I was ten years old. One of my mother's brothers, who was my Godfather, saw to it that my brother (who was a year older than I) and I went to Catholic religious instructions so we could make our First Communion.

Before my father was killed in a car accident, my mother had her marriage blessed by a priest; but she seldom took us to Mass.

As a result of her lack of interest in her Catholic faith, I grew up knowing nothing about my religion except the few short lessons I had learned while preparing for my First Communion. One was how to go to confession.

After my father died, things became very difficult for my mother and as a result she arranged for my brother and I to live in foster homes. This separation from my mother caused me tremendous suffering. I felt completely alone and unloved even though my brother was in the same foster home. If a teacher at school mentioned that I did not live with my parents, I would burst out crying. Every night that I lived in a foster home (2 different ones for about four years), I would cry myself to sleep. Sometimes I went to see my mother but such visits left me crying more as I became so sure that she did not want me. When she would visit my brother and I in the foster home, she would go into a room alone with my brother and say I was too young to hear what she had to say. I do not know what one called such a family at that time, but years later it would be called dysfunctional.

However, God gave me a wondrous grace during my unhappy childhood. I imagined that the whole world was crying with me. Instead of becoming bitter and hateful, I was determined to do something when I grew up to bring joy and happiness to others so that when they saw me or heard me they would stop crying. The only way I knew how to do that was to go into show business. The part of show business which I chose was to become a famous ice skater like the star Sonja Henie. That became my goal for many years as I struggled to fulfill my dream. (Sonja Henie was the ice skater who had won numerous titles and became a famous movie star whom I greatly admired.)

God also blessed me with two additional graces. The first one was a tremendous determination never to give up. The second grace was to fill me with a great love for the poor, the unfortunate ones, the outcasts of society.

I, myself, felt like an outcast and I looked for the ones who were laughed at or pushed aside so I could love them.

I remember that as a child of seven or eight, I heard about a poor, unfortunate child whose parents were of a different race. Everyone talked about this child and taunted him. I would walk to his house and look at the child and feel so sorry for him. I wanted to hug him and tell him that I loved him even though I did not feel loved myself.

These three graces formed the foundation for my future job for God.

1. I was determined never to give up.
2. I wanted to do all I could to bring joy and happiness to others so they would stop crying.
3. I had a special love for the sad, the lonely, the outcasts of society.

The good Lord was able to build upon this foundation as I journeyed through life fulfilling the job God gave me to do. (I never said I had a mission. I always said I had a job to do for God and my Lady.)

My mother caused me much sufferings in other ways. As far back as I can remember she was constantly criticizing all I said and did. She would say: "You were a good girl . . . but!" or "You should not have said (or done) that!"

I tried hard to please her, nevertheless, all I heard from her were her loud words of what I did wrong. I don't know what such treatment was called in that day and age. In later years, it was called child abuse.

Still her words did not discourage me. I never gave up trying to please her. If, by chance, she did give me a word of praise, my heart would leap with joy and all her words, finding fault with me, would quickly disappear.

In one way, such training was good for my future spiritual journey. I tried to do all in my power to always please my Lord and my Lady, even though at times, I did fall or make mistakes. I never let such falls discourage me. I would rise again with the help of God's graces and continue upon the path the Lord had placed me upon.

This picture shows St. Rose's Church in Meriden, Connecticut. In this church Louise was baptized on July 24, 1924 according to the rite of The Roman Catholic Church even though her father was not a Catholic. Louise's mother had Louise and Louise's brother baptized in her faith.

Louise's mother holding Louise. Louise's father and brother George. Louise's father died when she was ten years old

This is an early picture taken of Louise's brother and Louise on her Grandmother's (her mother's mother) farm in Meriden, Connecticut. The farm has now disappeared but it was on South Colony St.

Louise and brother George after the family moved from Meriden to Bridgeport, Connecticut. Louise was almost six years old.

2

MY FIRST RELIGIOUS EXPERIENCES

If one were to choose the person who would become part of the triumph of The Immaculate Heart of Mary, one would surely not have chosen me; nor would I have chosen myself.

By the time I was fourteen years old, religion and my Catholic faith had been far removed from my life.

My mother could not have cared less whether or not I attended Mass or even said my prayers. I was taught nothing about the Bible, Christ or Mary. I was completely filled with faults and human weaknesses. My one and only ambition in life was to become the second Sonja Henie. My love for ice skating completely consumed me; so much so, that I would put on a pair of my brother's hockey skates and try to pose like the famous ice skater. Her movies completely devoured me. I would see each one three or four times. When I walked to and from school, I would picture myself in the beautiful costumes she wore, gliding gracefully over the ice: which of course, I could not do.

Then came my determination not to give up. I knew what I wanted to do when I grew up and I was going to do all in my power to achieve my goal.

When the other children at school could never make up their minds as to what they wanted to do when they grew up, I always knew. I wanted to be the second Sonja Henie. I even wrote essays in school about her.

I never did become the second Sonja Henie, but I never gave up trying to be. This "trying to be" was not easy.

At that time, I had no place to skate, except in winter on a frozen pond. I lived in a foster home. I had no money for any skating lessons. I did not even have figure skates. I later saved nickels and dimes to buy my first pair. I once wrote to Sonja Henie asking for a pair of her old skates. I never received an answer. But all these minuses did not cause me to give up.

At that time I, my mother, and my brother were living in Bridgeport, Connecticut where the family had moved, from Meriden, when I was about six or seven years old. My father was killed in a car crash when I was ten years old.

It was in Bridgeport where I had my first religious experience. It happened, not at my First Communion, but when I made my Confirmation at age around fifteen.

Although, my mother did not care about her faith and she cared less about mine or my brother's, the couple who had taken us in as foster children were practicing Catholics. They began to take George and me to Mass with them; and someone (I can't remember who it was) enrolled George and me in the confirmation class at a church called "new" St. Peter's. It had been built after an older church by the same name was too small and too old. It was in this older church where I had made my First Communion on June 9, 1935, when I was eleven years old just before my twelfth birthday. (I made my Confirmation, September 26, 1939 when I was 15 years old.)

I really cannot remember anything I learned at the confirmation class. What I remembered was being very shy and feeling out-of-place because both my brother and I were older and taller than the other children in the class. I simply did not fit in. I retreated to the back of the room and stayed there, never asking or answering questions. That was part of my personality.

At school, I was very shy and withdrawn in spite of my ambitions and determinations. That, no doubt, was due to my family life when I felt so unwanted and so unloved. I would tell myself that my foster parents never loved me because they were being paid to take care of me and my mother never wanted me. Then I found God.

However, this spiritual awakening was still years away and I had no one to lead me in that direction, except God Himself. The first extraordinary sign that God was calling to my sad, lonely soul came on the night I made my Confirmation.

My mother decided to come to this event. She had bought

me the white dress and veil which were needed by the girls. My brother was well-dressed in his new pants, shirt and tie. The evening was not a calm one. There was a wild rain storm raging outside the church. The confirmation class marched into the church and took our seats in the pews reserved for us. We were crowded and I sat elbow to elbow with the other girls.

Suddenly, all the lights in the church went out due to the storm. For a few minutes, the church was plunged into darkness. Then someone put large candles on the altar rail and a dim light flooded the church. The ceremony proceeded as planned with our march to the bishop.

The bishop was regal in his robes as he sat in front of the church. I went up and he gave me the name I had chosen: Veronica. I chose that name because it was the only woman's name on the Stations of the Cross. I had spotted that name when once I had said the Stations and it appealed to me. Then I returned to my seat.

As the ceremony continued, something was happening to me in the depths of my soul. One could say this happened because of the unusual atmosphere created by the dim candlelight; however, what I felt deep within my whole being could not have been created by material circumstances.

At that time, I had no idea what had happened. I do not know what to call the experience. Perhaps others would call it spiritual ecstasy.

No matter what name could be applied, there is no doubt that there was a direct act of the wondrous power of the Holy Spirit upon my soul revealing to me the very Heart of God with all Its splendor and glory.

I experienced a profound feeling of God's presence. My whole soul was bathed in His light and love. A warmness which I never experienced before, flooded my whole being. I did not know this God Who drew me deep into His arms and Heart that evening; but I knew that something very beautiful and wonderful had happened and I never wanted that feeling to end.

The feeling was real and lasting. I never forgot it. It was a miracle of grace so profound that I could look back at what had happened and remember exactly how I felt.

God's first kiss of love had been planted deep within my whole being.

After the ceremony ended, I "came to" "back to earth" when a girl touched me and told me to get up. I looked around and saw that I was the only one still kneeling.

I could hardly wait to tell my mother. I rushed to her side and tried to explain the wonderful feeling I had. I told her what happened. When I did, she threw "cold water" on my heart and soul by saying: "Oh, I didn't think it was so wonderful. When the lights went out, I could not see anything even with the candles on the altar rail." I was crushed. So, I kept my secret and never told anyone else what had happened when I made my Confirmation.

This ability of my mother to throw "cold water" on my heart and soul was experienced by me many times. For years, whenever my heart and soul were bathed in the delight and wondrous joy of a religious experience, if my mother "stormed" into the house, her very presence was enough to make such joy and delight disappear.

One other religious experience came my way before I was forced to leave Bridgeport and move to Meriden with my brother to live in another foster home: my grandmother's. This was the third foster home for George and me.

When I lived in the last foster home in Bridgeport with a woman I called "Aunt Betty" (I was too ashamed to tell anyone I did not live with my mother. It sounded better to say I lived with my "Aunt Betty"), I had a dog, a collie named Laddie, which I dearly loved. This dog was very affectionate and docile. He was my only friend. We would walk the streets of Bridgeport together, he always by my side.

One day when "Aunt Betty" was not home, I decided to give the dog a bath in the kitchen sink. He gladly jumped into the water as I went to a closet in the hallway to get the soap and an old towel. He waited patiently, standing in the water, for my return. Suddenly, the door slammed shut and locked. The lock was a large one that produced a metal slide that went into the hole on the door frame. A person could only open the door with a key and I did not have the key.

I knew I was in serious trouble. The apartment where I lived was on the third floor of a large house. There was no way I could climb in a window.

I ran to the front of the house and tried the front door. That also was locked. I began to panic. I knew that my dog would wait until I returned standing in the water that was slowly becoming cold.

I ran back up the stairs to the back door. I could hear my beloved dog whining. I began to cry. I looked into the hall closet and found a large screwdriver. I tried to put it into the space between the door frame, but it was much too big.

Then I began to cry harder when suddenly I remembered God. I uttered a heart-wrenching prayer: "God help me! Please God help me! Please unlock the door!"

Suddenly, as I stared in amazement I heard a click and the door began to slowly open as if an invisible hand had opened it from within. I stopped crying looking at the miracle before me. I was sort of in a trance of awe. Then I heard my dog cry in a low, sad voice.

I "came to" and ran to the dog who was shivering in the cold water. He had not moved. I picked him up and placed him on the floor. I forgot about the old towels "Aunt Betty" had given me to wipe the dog when he was washed. I ran into the bathroom and got her best towels. Soon my beloved pet was warm and happy wrapped in "Aunt Betty's" best towels.

I will not repeat what she said to me when she found out I had used her best towels to wipe a dog.

For weeks after I had seen the "miracle" of the door open by itself, I would walk up the back stairs and stare at the door wondering how it had opened. I even took the screwdriver, which I had used to try and open the door, from the closet and tried again to open it. That did not work.

I knew that God had worked the "miracle" for me, but I

still did not know this God who had left His celestial home to rescue a crying child and her beloved pet.

Later, my beloved pet was killed by a car and I lost my dearest friend, which caused me added suffering.

Then I lost my whole feeling of security when suddenly my mother decided to send my brother and me back to Meriden to live with her mother.

Louise and her brother when they made their First Communion. Louise was age 11.

3

I MOVE BACK TO MERIDEN
MORE RELIGIOUS EXPERIENCES

In spite of the two profound religious experiences I had had at about age fifteen, I was not converted as far as my embracing my Catholic faith was concerned. I quickly returned to a non-religious life still filled with my dreams of becoming the second Sonya Henie.

When my mother told me that George and I had to leave Bridgeport and return to Meriden to live with my grandmother, I was devastated. By that time, I had found a little security living with "Aunt Betty" and her husband, both of whom were very kind to my brother and me. I also knew that I would see my mother at least once a week.

She tried her best to work and support George and me. She even surprised me by buying a bicycle for my birthday; however, I really wanted her more than a bicycle.

We left "Aunt Betty" and George and I stayed in my mother's rented room before we left for Meriden. I felt that the last ties which I had with my mother were broken when she decided to stay in Bridgeport.

One day, at school, I suddenly burst out crying in a classroom. The students and teacher rushed to my side. They wanted to know what was wrong. I tried to explain that I had to leave my mother to live in Meriden with my grandmother.

Moving back to Meriden without my mother was crushing. I truly felt as never before that she did not want me, but I still had my brother whom I loved dearly. At least my mother had not separated us. I clung to his hand when we walked to our new High School. Then we had to separate. His classes were in the morning, mine were in the afternoon.

He was not as affected as I was. He found it easy to make new friends, I did not.

I had never had any real friends as I grew up. I was not a very lovable or even likeable person. My schoolmates resented the fact that all I talked about was ice-skating and how I would become a second Sonja Henie. In addition, I was not a healthy child. I was always tired and weak. No one knew why. It was only after I had open-heart surgery when I was 69 years old, in January, 1993, when the problem was discovered. The doctors found that I had a hole in my heart since birth. This illness is called: Atrial Septal Defect. In addition, as a child, I had rheumatic fever which damaged the mitral valve that had to be replaced with an artificial valve. One doctor said I was a living miracle due to the fact that I had these illnesses and survived.

My mother, my "Aunt Betty" and even my grandmother, when I lived with her, were never concerned about my health. If I did mention the way I felt to my mother (which was seldom) she said I would "outgrow" whatever caused me to become weak and tired.

As a child, and as I grew older, I knew nothing about holes in a heart or mitral valves.

However, because I was never strong or filled with energy, I often could not keep up with school activities, especially sports.

Whenever teams were chosen for a sport, the captains never wanted me on their teams. If a teacher insisted that a captain put me on a team, the response was: "Do I have to take her?"

This, of course, did not make me wanted or liked even by my schoolmates.

I did not know what the problem was. I only knew that I could not make friends or keep them. Perhaps I was just not an interesting companion.

Also, I developed many serious faults. I did not know how to say kind words to others. I did not know how to congratulate anyone or express words of sympathy. I seemed to have only one virtue: my love for the unfortunate ones, the outcasts, the ones whom everyone laughed at. But that only added to my troubles with others. I was also treated like an outcast and laughed at.

Still, as a child, God did bless me with another virtue. It was generosity which could have been called charity. Even as a child, I was willing to give or share what I had with others. While some saints shared their food and clothing with others, I shared my school supplies.

Every year, after summer vacation was ending, I would carefully and meticulously pick out and buy pencils, erasers, rulers, notebooks and paper for school.

When I was settled at the desk in my classroom, I would lay out all my working tools on my desk. Soon, a steady stream of youngsters would come to me and say: "Louise, can I have a pencil?" or "an eraser?" or "a notebook?" and I would gladly part with my "treasures!" Before the day ended, my desk would be empty and I would have to go back to the store to replenish my supply. I never refused such a request.

However, that did not cancel out the glaring faults and weaknesses which had become part of my personality.

At an early age, I slowly began to realize that I had many faults which I did not like. I was not the type of person I really wanted to be. When someone would tell me I was mean or selfish, I would say to myself that deep down I did not want to be like that. I longed to be a sweet, gentle, caring person but I did not know how.

It would appear that my spiritual growth started at that time even though I knew nothing about self knowledge or self improvement. I merely wanted to become the type of person I was not.

As a result, one day I formed in my mind the type of person I wanted to be: someone sweet, gentle, loving and whom everyone liked. I called this image, Dale. Dale was not a child's imaginary playmate as some children create for themselves. Dale was, to me, a goal to reach to become the type of person I wanted to be.

I carried Dale with me for a long time always striving to imitate her.

When I did or said something which I did not like, I would say to myself: "Dale would have never said that."

I tried very hard to change into Dale, but I did not succeed until the Holy Mother of God became my example to follow. But I had a long spiritual journey to travel before I found her; and the way was very rough and bumpy.

Living at my grandmother's house in Meriden was not a very pleasant experience. In the house were also my grandfather and three uncles. The place was in constant turmoil and I became almost like a servant to all.

My grandmother was a very poor housekeeper and I was very neat. So it ended up where I did most of the housework, cleaning, doing dishes and ironing piles of my uncle's shirts. None of my hard work was ever appreciated—just expected.

There was no chance for any spiritual growth when I lived with my grandmother for about two years. Yet, the good Lord did not forget that He had, in some way, chosen me to do a job for Him and Our Lady.

There were three occurrences which made God and the devil, as well, very real to me.

The first one was a simple prayer. One day, I read that a little girl had wanted a banana. She knelt down and prayed for the fruit. Her prayer was answered.

I had a little kitten that I was very fond of. One day the kitten disappeared. I remembered the story about the girl and her prayer.

So I knelt down by the bed and prayed to God asking that my pet come home.

The kitten did not return, however, I learned a lesson. That was the first time I ever knelt down to pray to God for something special. I was then about fifteen years old.

I did go to Mass every Sunday with my grandmother, but Mass meant nothing to me mainly because the Mass was in Latin and the sermons were in Polish. But praying for the kitten was different than going to Mass. The prayer brought me in direct communication with my Lord. That was important. That made the difference.

It also happened, while living at my grandmother's that God introduced me to my future foe: the devil.

Up until that time, I hardly knew that the devil existed. I, perhaps, had heard the name during my childhood, but I knew less about him than I knew about God. Then I found him in a most terrifying way.

When I moved into my grandmother's house, she shared her room and her bed with me. My brother was given a bed in my uncle's room. This bedroom was on the second floor of a large house.

Right next to my grandmother's room, there was a new room which had been added to the house when an addition had been built. This room was the best one in the house; yet no one occupied it. It was a beautiful, sunny room with hardwood floors, but it was used only as a store room filled with my grandmother's sewing items.

I, no doubt, could have used that room as my bedroom; however, there was a problem.

The first time I went into the room, I was terrified. For some unknown reason, I felt very strongly the presence of the devil. As I said, at that time, I knew nothing about the devil or how evil his presence was; yet, I was afraid to go into that room because I knew the devil was there.

I called the room, The Devil's Room, and for the two years I lived with my grandmother, I refused to enter that room.

Whenever I cleaned the other bedrooms, I would not walk into The Devil's Room which had a door opening onto a porch where I went to shake out the dirty, heavy rugs. It would have been much easier for me to go on to the porch from The Devil's Room to carry the heavy rugs, but I opened a window in my uncle's room and climbed out the window so that I would not have to go through The Devil's Room to the porch.

I have no doubts about it that the devil was in that room. I never felt his presence in any other room in the large farm house and I slept soundly right next to that room. I am sure that God never allowed the devil to control any other room in the house, but I had been introduced to him and I felt his evil in that room.

There was, in addition to The Devil's Room, another terrifying encounter that I had with the devil. This was more frightening than the one I had with the devil in his room.

When I moved into my grandmother's house, my ice skates and my desires to be the second Sonja Henie moved in with me. I was still determined to reach my goal. One of the best things about living with my grandmother was that she owned a very large farm with a pond that froze over each winter. I spent many a happy hour skating on that pond, practicing what steps, spins and jumps I had taught myself by watching more advanced skaters when I went to a frozen pond.

Every evening no matter how cold it was, I would dress in warm clothes and head out to the fields to ice skate on the pond. If it snowed, I and some other boys in the area would clear the outdoor rink.

One evening just before I left the house to go ice skating, I read a story in a magazine that one of my uncles had left on the table. This magazine was like the foodstore tabloids that are filled with stories meant to be more sensational than informative.

The magazine was opened to a story about the devil. it told how one night in an Irish village, the devil had walked. The story said that in the morning the people woke up and saw strange footprints in the snow. The footprints covered the entire village, on the walks, through the fields and even on the roofs of the homes. No human being or animal could have made such footprints or could have walked upon the houses as the prints indicated. People were terrified when they came to the conclusion that the devil had paid their village a midnight visit.

There were pictures of these mysterious footprints. It could be seen that they were shaped like a hoof but were in straight lines, not side by side.

After I read the article, I put the magazine down and happily walked through the snow to my skating rink.

Halfway across the field, I suddenly froze in terror. Stretching across the field directly in front of me as if to block my path were the exact same footprints I had seen in the magazine! There was no mistake about it. The footprints were deep in the white snow in one straight line.

I ran back to the house filled with fear. My uncles were home and they became concerned when they saw me. I explained about the footprints in the snow and showed them the picture in the magazine saying the prints were the same.

They and my brother quickly put on warm clothes and followed me to where the footprints were still clearly visible. I told them that the devil made the prints the same as he did in the Irish village.

All my uncles were hunters and had often gone into woods following animals so they were able to tell me what animal, if any, had walked across my path.

They could not.

They said they had never seen footprints like that before; and they had to accept my explanation that the devil had made them; but they did not believe it.

I had no doubts that the devil had crossed my path that night. I knew I had been terrified, but I did not know why. I was to find out when I accepted what Christ called The Devil's Challenge (May 3, 1946).

When my grandmother took me to Mass on Sundays with her, none of my uncles went with us although one uncle drove us to the church. I did not realize at that time that they were fallen-away Catholics. One uncle had been divorced and that was why he moved back to his mother's home.

I never asked any questions about religion and what they thought about their faith.

The only time I was able to have any sort of religious influence in my grandmother's house was when she and I looked at her huge Bible.

She did care about her faith. That was why she went to Mass every Sunday. However, she could give me no spiritual lessons or help because she spoke Polish and I had trouble understanding her. Her beautiful Bible was also in Polish, so I could not read it. But I did enjoy looking at the splendid pictures although I did not know what they represented. If I had been able to read and understand Polish, I might have learned a great deal about the Catholic religion from my grandmother.

It was while I lived with my grandmother when I made my first prediction, but I did not realize that what I said could be called a prediction.

One evening, I sat with my grandmother on her bed talking. On the wall in front of us was a large oval picture of the Crucified Saviour. She was crying and I felt very sorry for her. I sat down next to her and asked her what was wrong. She tried to explain to me how her heart was breaking because of the way her children's lives have become mixed up and away from God. (There had been divorces and remarriage by a Justice of Peace.) Suddenly, I looked up at the picture of Our Lord and I said: "You should not cry because He sees your heart. Someday a great joy will come to you because God has chosen someone here in a special way."

My grandmother stopped crying and looked at me with eyes filled with wonderment. She had understood what I had said and she replied in a voice that was filled with fear: "Why do you say that? How do you know that?"

Then I became frightened and I answered: 'I don't know. I don't know why I said that." I wondered why I had said such a thing. But I let it slip into my memory and I thought no more of the remark.

There is one thing more that I would like to mention which happened when I lived with my grandmother.

When my grandmother and I went to Mass, as I said, the Mass meant nothing to me because I could not understand what was going on. I never went to Confession or Holy Communion because my grandmother never went.

However, I did have a little prayer book which had been given to me at one time, perhaps when I made my First Communion. In order to pass the time in church, I would read the prayer book.

In the front of the book, there were little sayings which I loved to read.

I memorized two of them. One was "Dear Lord, teach me

the nothingness of earth and the greatness of Heaven." The second one was: "Dear Lord, teach me the shortness of time and the length of eternity."

As I journeyed towards the job God wanted me to do for Him and my Lady, these two prayers were answered.

This picture shows Louise and George when they lived with her grand-mother and three uncles. The picture shows Louise's Uncle Dom. He was one of the uncles who came to view the footprints in the snow when the devil crossed her path.

This shows Louise skating on the pond in her grandmother's field in back of the farm house. It was when Louise went to skate on this pond when she was terrified by the footprints in the snow.

4

MY MOTHER RETURNS TO MERIDEN
MY RELIGIOUS EXPERIENCES
CONTINUE

By the time I was seventeen years old, I was living with my mother in Meriden. She had returned to her hometown from Bridgeport after she settled her business affairs and was out of work. She found employment in Meriden so she rented an apartment, bought furniture and took George and me to live with her. At last I had the home with my mother that I had so longed for when I was in foster homes for about six years.

However, things were still not perfect. The long separation from my mother made it impossible for us to have a close relationship. She had to work all day and was seldom home in the evening. She found many new friends and liked to be with them instead of staying home with me. Many a night, I sat home alone crying wondering where she was and what she was doing.

I continued my High School education (I never went to college or any other type of school after I graduated from High School) and I graduated in June 1942 when I was eighteen years old.

During my school years, I was a good student. I always finished my homework or any other assignment which was given to me. My two favorite subjects were writing and modern history.

The second World War had started when I was in the last years of High School and I had a profound interest in all the events; so much so, that I saved the newspaper headlines (which I still have). I was deeply affected by the sufferings which the war brought to people. The war became more personal for me when I watched, with tears in my eyes, my brother board a train to take him to a far-away Army camp.

Still, in spite of the war clouds which cast deep shadows over all of mankind, my main interest in life was ice skating. I thought that when I became a famous skater my childhood dreams of bringing joy to others would be realized.

In order to make that dream come true, I no longer waited for winter to freeze a pond. I began to make trips to the New Haven Arena and also to a skating rink in New York City. In order to pay for these trips, I worked in a local store after school.

At these indoor rinks, I could wear my little skating costumes which made me feel like the second Sonja Henie.

By watching other skaters being taught, unable to afford a teacher myself, I was able to greatly improve my skating ability.

However, the good Lord had other plans for me which did not include becoming the second Sonja Henie; and He used the very thing which I loved the most to teach me two profound spiritual lessons.

By that time, I was a rather excellent skater according to the standards of that era. So, at the New Haven Arena, I was asked to give a solo at some sort of a skating event. I was thrilled. This was my chance to show the world what a "great" skater I was.

The evening came and I had a pretty costume on. As I skated out onto the ice, I felt like the second Sonja Henie.

However, things did not turn out like I had planned. Suddenly, the rink looked huge, the ice was "too hard," my program was too long. I did not fall, but my performance was terrible. When it ended, I was in a state of shock. When the skaters, whom I had known at the arena, asked me what happened: "You can skate better than, that!" I burst into tears.

I went by myself and sat on the steps all alone crying. My beloved ice-skating had failed me. The one thing on earth that I thought sure would bring me perfect joy and happiness failed me. I sat for a long time with such thoughts in my mind trying to figure out why the one thing, I had been so consumed with for years, failed me.

I could find no answer to my question. I could only leave the arena filled with shame and disappointment.

There was no doubt that the good Lord used my skating to teach me a valuable spiritual lesson, but I was not yet ready to learn it. I could only remember that lesson as I became more involved with God's plans for me.

God taught me another lesson using my beloved ice skating. This lesson, I learned. In addition to skating in New Haven and New York (in the summer), I joined a small ice club in Hartford. This brought me much joy. I was the best skater in the club and I chose the best male skater to be my partner. When we went flying around the ice, while the other skaters got out of our way, I honestly thought that I was causing them great joy and happiness while they watched me because I skated so well.

My happiness was unbounded. Here was my dream come true: I was bringing joy to others through my skating. I was not. End of that dream.

One day I met one of the skaters, on my way to the rink, on a bus. I was delighted to see her. I sat down next to her and expected to have a chat with her. Instead, she jumped up and took a seat in back of the bus. She refused to talk to me or to explain her actions. I was stunned and I had no idea why she had acted like that.

When I arrived at the rink, I went to a room to have my skates sharpened. The man who ran the skate shop was a very kind, gentle person.

I told him what had happened. He began to explain, as gently as he could. I was the most hated person in the club. I was selfish, bold and I didn't care about any of the other skaters. I pushed everyone aside and used their patch of ice as if it were my own.

He did not have to say any more. I burst into tears. I never dreamt that the other skaters hated me. I thought they had been happy seeing me skate. I learned my lesson.

I became a very quiet, considerate skater, but still no one liked me. I had angered too many members with my wild skating. I was ready to leave the club. Then there was talk that a famous skater, whom I had pictures of (I saved every picture of an ice skater I could find including my beloved Sonja Henie), was coming to the club to put on a little show. She needed good skaters for her show and I was one of them chosen. That was my first professional ice show. My dreams of becoming the second Sonja Henie, were coming true. I was a professional skater. But I still had a long way to go.

After I graduated from High School, I got a job in a defense factory. I worked there for about a year before my life changed once again when I moved to New York City.

During this time when I lived with my mother, skating in New Haven and New York, my religious experiences continued.

God was slowly drawing me to His Heart of Love. I became more interested in my Catholic faith. I began to go to Mass and Confession on my own. My mother was still a fallen-away Catholic. I had remembered how to go to Confession from my First Communion lessons.

Then one day, I walked into a church, St. Joseph's, on my way home from school. I sat in the back pew. Suddenly, in the dim light, I felt a wonderful peace deep within my soul. I didn't know why I felt this peace, but it was there. I was very anxious to experience that feeling again. So, I began to stop in the church on my way home from school every day.

That began my "secrets." I told no one what was happening to my soul. The feeling was too precious for me to share. If, sometimes, a few girls would walk with me as we went home and I passed the church, I did not dare tell them that I wanted to go in. I would continue to walk with them until we parted, then I would walk back to the church to visit alone. This was a very long walk, but I didn't mind. I wanted to experience the beautiful feeling I got sitting in back of the church.

I really did not pray, I just sat there. The feeling was a faint call to my soul from my Lord, but I did not know that.

One day, I moved to the front of the church and knelt in front of the altar rail. There was a beautiful statue of the Sacred

Heart on the other side of the rail. I would look at it and tell God that I loved Him not knowing who the statue represented. To me, the statue was of God.

Then one day, I was kneeling in front of that statue telling God that I loved Him, when suddenly, the statue came to life. The head of Christ lifted and His eyes looked outward, away from me. He had a look, on His face which I thought was anger or displeasure.

The look on His face startled and affected me so deeply that I burst out crying. I thought that I had, in some way, displeased my God. I was devastated.

Years later, I knew that the look was not for me but for the world. The Lord looked past me out into the world and was not pleased with what He saw. This was the same statue that I knelt before, years later, when I was in the crowded church and my Lord said to me: "They love me with their lips, but not with their hearts."

In the dim, peaceful church, God was bestowing upon me wonderful graces, but I did not know that fact. I did not even know what grace was. Still, I had been drawn to my Lord.

He continued to bless me with additional religious experiences during the two years before I moved to New York City at the end of 1943.

One evening as I knelt to pray by the bed in my home on West Main Street, in the evening, suddenly there was a brilliant light which came in one window to my side. I never before saw a light so bright. No lamp or spotlight could have produced such a radiance. The entire window lit up and the shade, curtain and drapes completely disappeared. The light did not illuminate the whole room, only the window and the floor in front of the window. In the pool of light which shown upon the floor, I clearly saw a black cross.

I stared at the light and cross on the floor not knowing what had happened or why.

When the light went out, it was gone in a second. It did not fade away slowly and the room was dark again.

I was very puzzled by the occurrence. What confused me

the most was the cross on the floor. There had not been any cross on the window which would have been there if there had been four panes of glass which made up the window. There was only one bar in the middle of two panes of glass.

The following day, I examined the window closely trying to find out where the light had come from and why the cross had appeared on the floor. The window was perfectly normal and I could never explain the light or the cross. I only knew that a cross reminded me of God. But, the good Lord was revealing to me, in that vision, that the cross would become part of the job He would later give me to do.

Another cross was put into my life at that time. I actually knew nothing about the cross of Christ or the Crucifixion. I only knew that the cross reminded me of God whom I was growing to love very much.

One day I looked at the sky and saw a cloud which was formed in the shape of a cross. When I saw the cross in the sky, my heart filled with joy because I associated the cross with God.

After that I, almost daily, looked for my Cross In The Sky, as I called it; and I never failed to find this Cross In The Sky. It was not just a cloud formation. Once there were no clouds in the sky and I longed to see my Cross In The Sky, Suddenly, five birds came into view, formed a perfect cross, then flew away. My heart exploded with joy.

Several times, there were no clouds in the sky as I searched for my Cross In The Sky; but as I looked, two or three tiny clouds would appear, form a cross and then disappear, causing me much joy.

These crosses in the sky were most unusual. After I no longer saw them, I would look for a cross and I never saw one. I have looked ever since 1942-1943 and never once saw a cross in the sky as I had seen at that time. Surely, the Lord used this as another way to bind our two hearts together.

It was also at this time when I "found" Mary. I had thought that my love for God had been complete. Then, one day in church, I found Mary. Even though I knew almost nothing about her, suddenly love for her was infused into my heart. When that happened, my love for God increased a great deal and I knew that Mary had to be part of my love for God.

Then I received another great sign from my God.

One day when I was walking home from downtown Meriden to the West side of town where I lived, I walked up the little hill near St. Joseph's Church. As the church came in view, I stopped in amazement. By the side of the church, in the sky in rows of steps, were the most beautiful clouds I had ever seen. They formed huge steps across the sky. The edges of each step were pink and gold.

I stood frozen in awe and delight. I knew the clouds were from Heaven. I knew I had seen Heaven in the clouds. My soul was transformed to the place where my God and Mary lived. I did not want to leave the spot I stood on as I gazed at the wonder before me.

Then a man was walking down the hill towards me. I pointed to the sky and I said to him as he passed: "Look, look at the clouds, they are so beautiful."

He turned around to look and said coldly: "Clouds? What clouds? I don't see any clouds." With that remark, he walked away. The clouds disappeared, but I never forgot them. I knew I had seen a part of Heaven and from that moment on, there came into my heart a deep longing for Heaven which never left me. I would walk along city streets, look down on worn or dirty sidewalks and long to walk the beautiful streets of Heaven. This became one of my greatest sufferings; this longing for Heaven while I still walked the streets of earth.

In spite of all the favors and signs which God bestowed upon me, I still had a great deal more to learn from Him and my Lady.

Just before I left Meriden, I was taught another lesson about my life and faith which was not a very pleasant experience.

I had already planned to move to New York where I could skate all year at the indoor rink I had often gone to. I felt that I could learn much more and become a better skater if I was able to skate every day and not just on weekends.

At that time I had another love. It was horseback riding. I became an excellent rider and I loved to go to the stables almost as much as I loved to go to the skating rinks. My brother had introduced me to the sport.

One morning I was most anxious to go to the stable because there was a new horse I was interested in buying. I wanted to ride him. The horse was very frisky but that only made me want to ride him more.

I knelt to pray, but I jumped up and I said: "God will understand that I have no time for prayer." Then I hurried off to the stables.

I was soon riding the horse, in "all my glory" down a highway. I felt proud of myself because I was able to handle the horse.

Suddenly the horse took the bit between his teeth and started to run as fast as he could. He ran away with me.

I tried to stop him but it was impossible. Then he went around a corner, slipped and fell and threw me to the ground. I landed in some hedges which broke my fall. Otherwise I would have been killed.

Just before the horse fell, I screamed: "God help me! God help me!"

That was all I remembered. I don't know how I ended up in a doctor's office, but I was there. I was told that I had walked back to the stables but I did not remember doing that. I don't know what happened to the horse.

I was badly hurt, but not seriously and I had no broken bones. I did injure my neck so that for months I could not raise my head to look up at anything above me. I had to keep my head down. Needless to say, I never rode another horse.

The accident did not change my plans to move to New York City, but something changed deep within my being.

For weeks I thought about the fact that I had called on God to help me and He did not. I would say over and over to myself: "I asked God to help me but He did not. Why?"

Then, one day I found the answer. I said to myself: "God did not help me because I never did anything for Him." From that moment on, I told myself that I had to do something for God. I called this my second conversion.

The injured neck also became a lesson for me to learn. I accepted it as the way God taught me to be humble. I would think about the fact that I could not hold my head up, only down in humility.

I never again told God that I had no time for prayer.

Before I close this chapter, I will mention the fact that I did not mention any boyfriend in the story of my youth because I never had one. I was not interested in boys because my only interest was to become the second Sonja Henie.

Boyfriends, even marriage were the furthermost thing from my mind.

As I said, I found it very difficult to make friends. But that did not bother me because I had my ice skating and my dream of becoming a second Sonja Henie.

There is one thing more I would like to mention before I explain about my life in the big city. Before I left Meriden, I wrote my very first article about God. I had heard it said that God was an angry God, one to be afraid of, always looking stern; waiting to punish a person for his or her faults and sins.

I did not perceive God in that manner. So, I wrote an article and called it, "God Can Smile" or "God Can Laugh."

I did not know it at that time but I had been chosen to bring a tender, loving God to His children. That article was to be followed by thousands of pages which I later wrote including many books and articles for newspapers and magazines about God and His love for His poor, suffering children.

This picture shows Louise skating on a lake in a huge park called Hubbard Park in Meriden. This park was only a short distance from the place where Our Lady wanted her shrine.

Louise is shown with one of the horses she fell in love with. She went often to the stables. She was even planning to buy a horse. Then she had a disastrous fall from that horse. This fall caused her to focus upon God and her relationship with Him.

Saint Joseph's Church in Meriden. In this church Louise began to sit quietly in the back of the church on her way home from school in 1942. And where Christ began to slowly draw her soul toward His Heart.

This is the statue before which Louise was praying when the statue became alive and Christ lifted His head and looked out above and beyond her.

This picture shows the altar rail Louise knelt at in St. Joseph's Church where the statue of the Sacred Heart came alive.

This picture shows the exact spot Louise was on when, walking home from downtown Meriden, to the West, as soon as St. Joseph's Church came into view, she suddenly froze because Louise saw, in the sky, the magnificent steps of clouds. That was in 1943.

Part 4

I Move to New York City
God's Plans For Me
Start To Unfold
First Visions: Years 1944-1945

— 1 —

I MOVE TO NEW YORK CITY

While I still worked in a defense factory, I planned to leave Meriden and move to New York. That was shortly after I graduated from High School in 1942, at the age of 18. It took me about a year to finalize such plans. When I left Meriden, I was not going into a big, frightful far-away city. I knew the place quite well. To me, it was my second home because what I loved the most was there: ice skating. I had gone many times to skate at the rink which was on top of Madison Square Garden before that building was torn down. That put me right in the heart of Manhattan next to Broadway where all the famous shows played. Once in a while, I would stop in to see one. The matinee did not cost very much and I enjoyed such shows as: "The King and I," "Banjo Eyes," South Pacific" and a couple of others.

Also, I was quite capable of taking care of my life. Being away from my mother and on my own most of childhood did have one good result. I had learned to make my own decisions and I was not afraid to face the daily problems which, perhaps, other children would have had to run to their parents for help with. I had no parents to run to.

No one helped me with my ambition to become the second Sonja Henie. I arranged everything myself knowing exactly what I wanted.

When I found out about the New Haven Arena, I arranged to go there to skate. I traveled by bus or got a ride with whomever was going there.

When I learned that one could skate in the summer in New York, I made my own plans to do just that. I would take a train or a Greyhound bus to New York. I worked in a store to pay for the trips.

When I needed new skates, I found the shop in New York

127

where the boots were made and the store where I could buy the blades.

I made my own skating outfits and some of my other clothes.

I found the place where I wanted to live in New York and the nearby restaurants where I ate my meals.

I even taught myself how to sharpen my own blades. Later, when I was in a show, it was soon discovered that I was the only one who knew how to do that. I was kept busy sharpening the skates of everyone in the show, which I did for nothing. No one else had the tools I had which I had bought years before.

I was most efficient in all I did, never doing things halfway. That was, no doubt, a grace from God which I would need when I wrote notes or books or started the Maryheart Evangelization Center in Meriden, Connecticut.

In addition, God blessed me with common sense and a very excellent memory. I could analyze situations or remember things in a way that others could not and I would wonder why others would have difficulties in such areas.

Sometimes my abilities to remember would frighten me. If, for example, someone brought up a subject, I would say: "I remember something like that." Then I would repeat what I knew or what I had read, word for word, much to my own amazement. Later, I would say to myself: "How did I know that?"

Such graces greatly helped me as I spent my life carrying out God's holy will for me; and as I struggled to improve my spiritual life.

The greatest help was when I taught religion or wrote about it. I could remember a great deal of what I read or heard. I often quoted the Bible even before I ever read it, then wonder how I knew such words were in the Bible.

But that would come later. Meanwhile back to New York. I made my plans carefully. I kept working in the defense factory until I had enough money for my expenses in New York before I could find a job there. I chose to leave at the end of 1943. I was nineteen years old.

My mother had no objections to my going to New York. She had become so used to being without me and so disinterested in whatever I did, that she did not even miss me. She had formed her own social life which I did not fit into. Yet, I must say this about her. Although my mother was not interested in what I did or where I went, she never interfered with my plans to become a professional ice skater. She, at one time in my childhood, arranged for me to take ballet lessons which greatly helped me when I improved my skating ability.

In 1941, she gave me a book on figure skating for my birthday. I had already bought Sonja Henie's book called "Wings On My Feet."

I did not have any skating teacher but I learned a great deal about ice skating from these two books, as I practiced very hard to follow the instructions I read. My Sonja Henie book is much-used and very worn.

I loved the famous skater for another reason other than her skating. To me, as her pictures show, she was filled with sweetness and love. She seemed to be the example of everything I wanted to be, but was not: sweet, gentle, loving, and loved by everyone. I felt that if I were to become the second Sonja Henie, I would automatically become just like her: sweet, gentle, loving, and loved by everyone.

My mother not only allowed me to move to New York on my own, she came with me to see the room where I was going to live and she brought my things to New York in her car. I had found the rent by reading the New York papers.

I did not go to New York alone. I had met a girl at work, named Gloria, who was also interested in ice skating. She wanted to come to New York with me. I, at first, thought it was a good idea. It was not.

The short time that she roomed with me she caused much turmoil. She was very shy and she could never make up her mind about anything; whereas I could.

She had no talent for skating and would stand on the side of the rink waiting for me to take her by the hand and teach her how to skate.

I soon got tired of doing that and she would complain that I left her alone.

We simply were not compatible and we soon got separate rooms in another rooming house.

The thing which most annoyed me about Gloria was that she constantly was undecided as to whether she should or should not go home. Whenever we were together that was all she talked about. One day, I could take it no longer. I packed her things and made her go to the train station with me where I put her on a train and sent her back to Connecticut. That ended our brief friendship.

However, Gloria did play a part in my spiritual growth.

I did not go to New York because I thought I could be more religious there. I went because I wanted to improve my skating and join some kind of a professional ice show. I looked forward to skating every day. My ill health, which had plagued me from childhood interfered with my desires to become a better skater and to skate every day. When I skated, I was often weak, tired and out of breath. I could not jump as high as I wanted to. I soon found out that my desire to skate every day was not to come true. After working at the job I found in New York, I was often too tired to go to the rink in the evening.

I had had many illnesses. One was, as a child of 8 or 9, I had ruptured appendicitis and needed an emergency operation. I always attributed my ill health to that operation. But that was not the cause. As I said, I had a hole in my heart which I was born with. I also had rheumatic fever as a child which damaged the mitral valve. The hole in my heart and the damaged valve were repaired by open-heart surgery which I had when I was 68 years old. One doctor said that I was a living miracle because of the hole in my heart.

However, when I was 18 then 19, trying hard to become the second Sonja Henie, I knew nothing about holes in hearts or mitral valves. I only knew that all my life I was always weak, tired and often ill with other ailments.

Still I would not give up. As I said I always had a great

determination. I continued to do all I could to make my dream for material success come true.

God had other plans for me.

As I said, Gloria played a part in my spiritual growth while she was still with me in New York.

She was a practicing Catholic so we went to Mass together at a church a few blocks from where we lived in the rooming house. I considered her to be the kind Of Catholic I wanted to become. I did admire her for that reason. I sort of put her on a pedestal as I tried to be like her in that respect as I saw myself as a person filled with faults and weaknesses and I saw Gloria as the holy, almost perfect, Catholic I wanted to be, but was not.

Each time we went to Mass, I would walk in back of her because I felt too unworthy to walk ahead of her into the church. I was not attempting to pretend that I was humble by doing that. I honestly believed that I was not worthy to walk in front of her. That was part of my self evaluation since I was a child when I saw myself filled with faults and weaknesses and I tried to become a better person.

In any self examination of my faults and virtues which I made, I would find more faults than virtues. I could never understand why the good Lord found me so attractive.

When He or my Lady praised me, as they often did, such praises did not bring me comfort or joy. They added to my sufferings because I could not understand why they would praise a big "nothing," or a "stupid child," as my Lady once called me, who made so many mistakes.

Such praises remained in my notes for years unread by me even in my darkest spiritual moments, I could not use them for comfort because they only added to my torments.

It always puzzled me why I was given the job (I did not like to call it a mission) to do for God and my Lady when others could have done a much better job—someone like a saint.

Sometimes, I would start to pray and say: "Dearest Lord, I am sure you can find someone else to do this job. They could do a better job than I am doing."

Years later when some people attempted to take my job away from me, I would say: "They can have it—for nothing." (When they saw all the work I had to do, they changed their minds.) Yet, in spite of how unworthy I felt about praises and the job God gave me to do, I would not give up. God blessed me with another grace: love for His holy will. And part of accepting His will was to accept all the praises as well as all the suffering.

I had always, as a child, had a calm way of accepting whatever happened to me even though it caused suffering and tears.

If, for example, a child took my pencil or paper during class, I would say: "That is all right."

If something I had was destroyed or damaged, I would say: "That is all right."

So, when God gave me the job He wanted me to do for Him and the world, I accepted it and said: "That is all right, I so love Your holy will."

No matter how unworthy I felt about being chosen by God for the role He placed me in, I would say: "I so love Your holy will, do with me what You want."

I also dearly loved what I called "my world" and God's suffering children and I truly wanted them to find peace, joy and happiness.

One more remark about Gloria. She always wore around her neck an assortment of medals and chains. I did not know anything about saints or medals, but I longed to have one of hers. So, one day I shyly asked her if I could have one of her chains and medals. She refused.

I was deeply hurt. I did not know that I could go into a religious store and buy any medal I wanted. When she left New York I forgot about the medals so I did not try to find any for myself.

I lived in New York only a short time before God and Our Lady placed me upon the path which led to The Golden Lady of Happiness and my role in her triumph.

Louise graduated from high school June 1942. This is her picture, age 17¹/₂.

2

THE CIRCUMSTANCES OF MY LIFE
WHEN I FIRST SAW AND HEARD
JESUS AND MARY STARTING IN 1944

Another thing to be taken into consideration when reading my secret notes is the circumstances of my life when such revelations were first given to me and the daily life I led at that time in 1944 when I was only twenty years old.

I was living in New York City where I had gone to become a professional ice skater. I had at that time, before my Lady and Our Lord began to reveal God's plans for me, no intentions of doing anything for God or suffering humanity. My dream was to become a second Sonja Henie. In other words, I could not have produced visions or messages because I was far removed from them.

Next to be considered is my education. I had only a high school education. I had been a good student, but I definitely was not a learned teenager. Math and Spelling were my worst subjects. I received only a very basic high school education.

In addition to having only a high school education (which in the 40's did not consist of any advanced knowledge unless a student planned to go to college, which was never my intention; mainly, because only children born into wealthy families went to college) I had no special talents except perhaps a bit of an artistic ability. However, I was very conscientious about my school studies, always doing homework as assigned. That special quality, no doubt, played an important part in the fact that when I heard the words of Jesus and Mary, I recorded them exactly as I heard them, never changing one word or vision which I saw.

Also, I knew next to nothing about Catholic teachings or doctrines. I had no religious education except for the few lessons I learned in my First Communion class. The only thing

I remembered was to go to Mass and how to confess one's sins. All else had been forgotten. I did go to Confirmation classes before I was confirmed, but all I remembered about what I must have been taught was that you had to have a confirmation name. I chose Veronica. Needless to say, I never went to any Catholic schools, just local schools.

As I have explained in this book, before I moved to New York City in the Fall of 1943, I had some religious experiences which I called "my conversions" however, my main goal in life, or ambition, centered around my ice skating and not around religion. When I moved to New York, my "conversions" had been forgotten.

After I had suffered through an unhappy childhood, I wanted to go into show business thinking that was the only way I could bring joy and happiness to others. I had chosen to become an ice skater. This ice skating career had nothing to do with religion.

When Jesus and Mary began to appear to me and speak to me in 1944, I knew so little about my Catholic faith that I just assumed that was part of my faith and "everyone" saw and heard them as I did.

I was completely ignorant of most of what I was told. I would merely say as I wrote: "Well, if that is what Jesus and Mary say, it is all right with me." That was the main reason why I wanted Monsignor Hayes (my spiritual director) to tell me that all was from God. He had the expert knowledge to do just that.

When I was told about Mary's heart, I did not even know what the Immaculate Heart of Mary was. I had no idea what plans God had which connected me with Mary's heart and her shrine of triumph.

When I was told that I would become a writer and my writings would be read all over the world, not only did I not have any writings, but I had no intentions of becoming a writer.

As I said, I had only a basic childhood education which did not include any training to become a writer whose books would be read all over the world; and I really did not have any special intelligence. The fact is, my Lady had called me "stupid" and I readily agreed with her:

May 5, 1944: "You, Louise a simple, stupid child, with many, many faults, a child who was once lured away by earthly pleasures (my fondness for ice skating) has been chosen to do a great job for Our Lord."

Also: "So, my child, you who are so simple and so stupid (she had to use a word I would understand) that you cannot remember things . . ." Later my memory amazed me.

Remember, as you read my secret notes, that Our Lord and Our Lady spoke to me in words I would understand. They had to come down to my level of my lack of education and my ignorance of Church doctrine and teaching.

Yet, hidden within the messages are profound teachings of my Catholic Church; even if I was called "stupid."

For example:

I knew nothing about free-will yet, I was told to use my free-will to fight the devil and to choose God's ways and not the devil's. I knew less about grace. One day at Mass, a priest said it was a very serious sin to go to Holy Communion without first going to confession, if a mortal sin had been committed, to return the soul to the "state of grace."

I had no idea what was meant by the words "state of grace" and I panicked. I did not know if I had been in the state of grace when I received Communion. I sought out a priest for confession. After I asked him what being in the state of grace meant and after he questioned me, he assured me that I had been in the state of grace when I received the Eucharist.

But I will say that although I did not understand my role in God's plans, I accepted it with much trust, faith and total love for God's holy will for me. There can be no question about that.

However, my ignorance was a blessing, not only because it proved I could not possibly make up the words I heard; but years later when I wrote my books and articles, I understood the spiritual needs of the average Catholic lay person because of my own experiences as I journeyed to a closer union with Christ.

— 3 —

FIRST RELIGIOUS EXPERIENCE
IN NEW YORK
MARY'S VOICE
FIRST VISION

As I said, I had not gone to New York City to become more religious. I went there to become a better ice skater and to join a professional ice show. At that time, there was a show on national tour. In addition, there were a couple of smaller shows. The grandest show of all was in Hollywood. That was in a Sonja Henie movie. That was my goal: to one day go to Hollywood and skate in a Sonja Henie movie. The good Lord had other plans for me; although I did join a small traveling ice show, I did become a professional skater . . . but not for long.

As soon as I had arrived in the big city, God began to change the direction of my life.

While I still lived in Meriden, I had found a wondrous feeling of peace whenever I paid a visit to my parish church on the way home from school or work. (This was my first conversion.) In the excitement of planning my move to New York and of actually going there to live, I forgot about these feelings of closeness to God. My only thought was that I would, at last, be able to skate every day, winter and summer. What joy!

However, I did not forget God, Mass, Confession, prayer or the Eucharist.

I was in New York, settled in my room, at a rooming house, for only a few days when I began to notice that as I knelt to pray before I went to sleep, a wondrous feeling of peace and heavenly sweetness would cover my soul. This was the same feeling I had received when, in Meriden, I sat in the dim light of my parish church and told God that I loved Him.

The feelings of being close to God in His light and love seemed to raise my soul to Heaven; although, I had no idea what that meant or why I experienced such closeness to God.

When I said my evening prayers, I would close my eyes and tell my Jesus that I loved Him and the feelings of peace and sweetness would cover my soul. I began to look forward to my evening prayers just so I could feel the heavenly joys of being so close to God. I also began to have a desire to learn more about my Catholic faith.

That was not too difficult to do. I had gotten a job running an elevator in an apartment house not far from Saint Patrick's Cathedral. This work was very difficult, and the reason why I soon discovered that I was often too exhausted to skate every evening as I had planned to do.

The job had always been done by men, but due to the war (World War II), there was a shortage of men and so the owners hired women. My roommate Gloria and I were the first women hired for the job. (We worked different shifts). The reason the work was so difficult and exhausting was the way the elevator had been built. One did not just push a button to make the elevator go from floor to floor. This one was operated by water power and there was a very large lever which had to be pushed back and forth to make the contraption move. Also, in order to make it stop, this lever had to be pushed back and forth which required a great deal of strength, a strength I did not have. When I left work, I would often be so exhausted I could only go to my room to rest. My skating would have to wait for days off or when it was not too busy at the place where I worked.

The name of the place where I worked was The Carlton House. This was connected to a hotel called The Ritz Carlton. It has since been torn down, but it was located at 44th or 46th Street and Madison Avenue when I worked there. The hotel side was for guests (very wealthy guests) and The Carlton House, where I worked, was for permanent residents (very wealthy residents).

I saw many a famous person walk into the building, and I

delivered mail, etc. to other famous people who lived in the building. But their fame and wealth did not impress me.

I was more interested in learning about my Catholic faith. As I said, that was not too difficult to do.

I soon discovered, when I visited St. Patrick's that in the back of the church there was a tiny gift shop with many booklets in racks on the wall. These booklets were about the Catholic faith, little prayer books, Novenas, and short stories of the saints. They were not about theology, but they were what I wanted to read.

As I sat in my elevator waiting for a call or waiting to take someone to a floor, I would sit on a little seat and read these booklets. I was happy knowing I was learning more about my faith and how to pray.

In reading these booklets, I finally learned why the Stations of The Cross were in churches. I also read and learned about Purgatory, The Holy Spirit (The Holy Ghost as He was called then), the Holy Mother of God, Heaven and Hell. This began my daily spiritual readings which I continued for the rest of my life. These little booklets were the foundation for my future books and articles about my Catholic faith, which I wrote years later.

But as I sat reading the little booklets, a most remarkable thing began to happen. Suddenly, as I was reading about prayer to the Crucified Christ, I would hear the voice of the Holy Mother of God. There was no mistake about it. I clearly heard the voice and the words. The voice was the sweetest voice I had ever heard and the words were: "It is I, Mary, Mother of God, talking to you." "Listen, for it is I, Mary, Mother of God, talking to you." "Listen, to me. It is I, Mary, Mother of God, talking to you."

Perhaps someone would say that it was my own mind playing tricks on me because I was reading religious booklets, but that was not the case.

At first, I did not pay too much attention to the voice I heard, and I certainly did not want any heavenly voice talking to me. I still wanted to be a skating star and I read my skating books as much as I read the little religious booklets. But Our Lady kept speaking to me very often as I sat in the elevator. The words were the same: "It is I, Mary, Mother of God, speaking to you. Listen because I have much to tell you." "Hear my voice for it is I, Mary, Mother of God, talking to you."

It was as if Our Lady wanted me to recognize her voice and to become accustomed with her voice. Later when I actually saw her and she spoke to me, I instantly recognized the voice I had heard in the elevator.

Then, one day while I was working at The Carlton House waiting in the elevator for a call, much to my amazement, I saw my first vision. Although that happened over fifty years ago, I can clearly remember what I saw and where I was when this happened.

The elevator was at the main lobby. I was sitting in it reading one of the booklets. A bellboy, in his uniform, was standing next to the main entrance door.

Suddenly, I looked up and I noticed a brilliant light where the main door and the bellboy should have been. They had completely vanished from my sight. Then, within the brilliant light, I saw an object which I did not recognize. I knew only that it had something to do with God; but I had no idea what it was. The light and the object in it were very clear to me. I stared at them unable to move. But I had no idea what I was looking at.

Then just as sudden as the vision had appeared, it vanished and the door and bellboy were there as before.

I could not remove the object from my mind. I had to find out what I had seen. I searched to find a picture of what I had seen for weeks. I looked through prayer books, even the booklets I had bought and I could not find anything which resembled what I had seen.

Finally, one day, when I had stopped looking through prayer books for the object, as I began to read a new booklet, much to my amazement, as I turned a page, there on top of the page was the object I had seen in the vision. But I still did not know what the object was; but I had been correct. It was something that was connected with God.

I can't remember exactly when I found out what the object was, but I did. It was a Monstrance that I had seen, used to expose the Blessed Sacrament. I had seen the outline of a Monstrance with rays of light coming out of points. This was upon a stand, as are all Monstrances.

This first vision of a Monstrance was very significant. My whole future spiritual program centered around the Mass and the Eucharist as well as prayer and devotion to the Holy Mother of God: the Mother of the Eucharistic King; the Mother who had talked to me and said: "Listen, it is I, Mary, Mother of God, talking to you. I have much to tell you."

This vision made such a deep, lasting impression on me, that as I said, I never forgot it.

— 4 —

MY LOVE FOR MY FAITH EXPANDS

As soon as I found the little booklets in Saint Patrick's, I began to take seriously the little lessons I learned about my faith from these readings.

The more booklets I read about my faith (there were no catechisms just little booklets and pamphlets) the more I wanted to learn. I began to fall in love with my Catholic faith as well as with Christ and Mary.

I found such joy in learning about my faith and God that I soon discovered that this new-found joy and happiness far outweighed the happiness I had always thought was as great as happiness could get when I skated.

The joys I had felt when I skated were, to me, nothing compared with the ones I began to find learning about the treasures of my Catholic faith. I wanted to learn all I could.

That began my quest for knowledge about my faith which never ended. At that time, I read no books about my faith, nor the Bible. The fact is, I did not even know that the Bible existed. I did hear the readings and sermons during Mass, but I did not understand them nor did I realize that the readings in the Liturgy were from the Bible. The only thing I remember from a sermon I heard in New York (at Saint Patrick's) was when the priest said about Adam and Eve that they would have to work "by the sweat of their brow," but I did not know who Adam and Eve were.

During that time, when I ran the elevator at the Carlton House, I began to form new goals for my life. I had always wanted to do something to make people happy and to stop crying since I was so sad when I was a child. I had chosen to be an ice skater so that I could bring joy to people where they saw me skate.

Suddenly, when I discovered the treasures of my faith, I

wanted to bring joy and happiness to others, not through my skating, but through my faith. I would repeat over and over: "Dear Jesus, I want to bring peace, joy and happiness to others and to the world."

The following is a little article I wrote at that time after I started to write for God in 1944.

TEARS

Dear ones, where are your greatest examples to follow if they are not in the ways of the Mother of God? Little indeed are your sorrows compared to hers. But find such sorrows and she is ready to wipe away your tear drops and put new joy in your heart.

Dear ones, Mary your Mother, knows what tear drops are and hers she shed in so great a number. But I think that there is a rainbow in each drop if you look for it. Then you will smile.

I also wrote: I am now going out into a new life with Mary's words forever in my ear. And I must wander in amongst lost souls and slowly but surely tell each and everyone how to find their home again and their kind, loving, forgiving Father.

Of course, when I prayed to bring peace, joy and happiness to the world, I did not know the plans which God had for me and for my Lady's shrine; but I was "on fire" to give to others the joys and happiness I had found in my faith. I called this discovery my third (and last) conversion. (The first being when I was a teenager and found such peace in my visits to church. The second being my fall from the horse.)

At the place where I worked, I began, what I thought was the way to "convert the whole world" so that everyone could find the happiness I found in my Catholic faith. I wanted to share what I was learning with everyone.

This enthusiasm soon came to an end. The people I worked with and met were not the least bit interested in my efforts to bring them joy and happiness through my faith. They completely ignored me, even Gloria, who was an excellent Catholic.

She did not want to know any more than she already knew about the Catholic faith. She thought that I was overdoing things a bit much.

I, very soon, became discouraged in my attempts to "convert the whole world" and retreated into my own little world of love for my Catholic faith.

A short time later, when the Holy Mother of God began appearing to me, one of the things she told me was: "Do not expect to conquer the world; but do start a landslide that will make people stand up and take notice" (March 31, 1944).

I, of course, had no idea what this "landslide" would be. After I made my Lady known in 1960, I found out. This message, by the way, was one of the very few secrets which I revealed after I did make my Lady known.

As my studies of my faith continued, I fell deeper in love with Christ and Mary. I was especially drawn to my Crucified Savior. I remembered that I had chosen, for my confirmation name Veronica because it was the only woman's name on the Stations. I became a "Veronica" feeling great love and pity for my Jesus who died upon that cross for my sins. Many a time, I would kneel before the huge crucifix which was in Saint Patrick's. At that time, there was no kneeler in front of that crucifix and so I would kneel on the hard, marble floor, pouring out my love for my Savior. Many people who walked by me would stare or give me a "dirty look" of displeasure as if to say: "Who do you think you are acting like that?"

But their looks did not bother me. I continued to kneel on the floor. At that time, I did not know what penance was, but I did do a lot of penance as I knelt until my knees hurt. To me, that meant that I loved my Christ.

Then the time came when my sojourn ended at the Carlton House and Saint Patrick's (which was only a couple of blocks from where I worked). My health (what little I had) completely gave out. I was forced to quit my job.

Part 5

The Foundation For
My Role in My Lady's
Triumph:
Year 1944

— INTRODUCTION —

Before I saw the visions of The Golden Lady of Happiness and heard her promises in 1948, I was being prepared for that event. I, of course, did not know that fact, but as I review my first notes, I can clearly see this preparation and the events and messages which led up to the visions in 1948. In other words, the job I had to do and the role I was to play in my Lady's triumph were slowly being revealed to me years before I knew that there would be The Golden Lady and her promises. The following chapters explain these early revelations.

— 1 —

FIRST WORDS OF MARY: YEAR 1944

In the year 1944, when I was struggling so hard to become the world's greatest ice skater (except, of course, for Sonja Henie) suddenly the good Lord began to show me that He had other plans for me.

Gradually, He began to prepare me for my future role for Him and my Lady. But, of course I did not know that when this slow transformation occurred. However, all the signs were there.

One of the first prayers that I taught myself in 1944, was: "Dearest God do whatever You want with me, I don't mind." I formed a great love for God's holy will in my heart, and I prepared myself to accept His will. I would say over and over: "Your will is mine, and my will is Yours." I was practicing Holy Abandonment even though I did not know what it meant.

This love for God's will became a major factor in my job for God. Because, I not only accepted God's will in my material life but I also accepted it in my spiritual life; and by doing that, I accepted without question whatever favors He desired to bestow upon me. Very often His favors or words would puzzle and confuse me, but I would look at my God and say: "Well, if that is the way You want things, then that is all right with me. I accept all You want to give me."

And the good Lord desired to bestow many favors upon my poor soul—favors which even today I do not fully understand. But one thing I do understand: these favors will enable me to raise this fallen world and to lead God's children to the heart of the Golden Queen of Peace and Happiness.

In 1944, when I first learned how to love God, I also had in my heart a deep love for suffering humanity. I would pray asking God to allow me to become a Refuge for Suffering Souls.

151

When my Lady began to talk to me in March 1944, she said that my prayer had been answered and I would become this Refuge for Suffering Souls.

This title of Refuge was one of three given to me in 1944. My Lady also said, as I recorded:

"She said that I would have all the strength and knowledge and courage that I need to carry on God's will of being a Refuge for Suffering Souls and to set an example that the whole world would follow" (March 27, 1944).

I would also pray: "Dearest God, let me bring peace, joy and happiness to suffering mankind." Little did I know that such words spoke of future events.

Then in that same year, a most dramatic event changed my life forever.

I became so ill because of the difficult strenuous work I had done running the elevator at The Carlton House that I was forced to leave the job. I was so ill that I could no longer skate. I could hardly leave my room. My roommate, Gloria, was very kind to me. She continued to work and she brought my meals to me. I thought surely I would die. That thought caused me great joy because of the longing I had to go to Heaven to be with my beloved Christ and His Mother; but, suddenly, I recovered.

When I felt better, I still did not leave my room hoping my illness would return. It did not.

I stayed in my room for two days more going out only to eat. The third day I felt better. That made me disappointed. I thought that God did not want me, that was why I had gotten better. I left my room and started to walk down the street. I was crying because I thought that I would never be good enough for God to want me.

All the trauma I had suffered in my childhood when I thought surely no one wanted me returned.

I walked around the neighborhood, where I lived in a rooming house, not caring where I went. Suddenly, I discovered I was in front of my parish church, the one I went to for daily and Sunday Mass. This was the Church of the Blessed Sacrament on the West side near 68th or 70th Street.

I was surprised to find myself in front of the church. I went in to try to find some comfort and encouragement. I walked to the altar rail and knelt down. Tears were still in my eyes when suddenly, I heard my Lady's gentle, sweet voice.

I found myself kneeling in front of her statue and her sweet voice began to explain to me my future life.

I instantly recognized her voice for I had heard it often when I ran the elevator: "It is I, Mary, Mother of God talking to you. Listen for I have much to tell you." And I listened as she began to explain to me things which were impossible for me to know.

I recorded the words I heard, dated March 27, 1944 (I was still only 19 when I heard the first words of Mary.):

I wanted to die very much. I went into the church and Mary started to talk to me.

Then I felt myself "come back" (from my disappointment). I could almost see her standing in front of me. (I did not see her). I could hear her voice talking to me.

Mary started to talk to me and since then she has been talking to me and telling me hundreds of things. Here are the first things she said to me.

The first thing she told me was that everything was all right. She told me that all I went through because of my death, thinking that I was to die was a test. The Sacred Heart of Jesus was putting my love for Him through a very hard test. Mary said that I had passed this test 100% because I had been willing to give up everything for God. She told me that I had proven my love for God completely and that I had proven myself worthy of the job Jesus had for me to do.

Then Mary said that Jesus had chosen me to do a job of teaching His children things that He wanted them to know.

She told me to write down all the things Jesus tells me to write down because they are to be used after my death.

Mary told me that I had made myself fit for the job of carrying her name to her children. She told me that she wants me to teach her name to all children because she is interested in all her children.

Then, one by one, she took my daily prayers and answered them. She said that I was to make a light shine on dark paths so that God's children could see the light and find peace and happiness.

When Mary told me that, I was deeply puzzled for I knew not how such could ever happen. I repeated the words over and over so that I would remember them.

My Lady Mary told me many things that year, 1944. Many of them I have or will mention in this book. For example: She told me that I was part of Jesus' army from Heaven on earth and that I must teach His children what He wanted me to teach them.

She told me many other things (recorded elsewhere in this book).

After I heard her words, my heart was so filled with joy that I wrote: I am now going out into a new life with Mary's words forever in my ear. And I must wander in amongst lost souls and slowly but surely tell each and everyone how to find their home again and in it their kind, loving, forgiving Father.

Later, I wrote that these words were "too ambitious"; however, I never turned away from the path my Lady placed my feet upon in 1944.

These first messages, which I carefully recorded in my first note book continued from March 1944 to June 1944. At that time I was only 19 years old, still a teenager.

One of the last things I wrote in 1944 was (June 1, 1944): I said: "Mary who am I?" She replied: "You are a servant of God who shall do His job according to His will."

— 2 —

JESUS' FIRST WORDS TO ME
FIRST VISIONS

In 1944 when Mary spoke to me in my parish church, my Lady's role in God's plans was being revealed—and that role would blossom forth as being The Golden Lady of Happiness, the one who would bring peace, joy and happiness to the world. At the same time, God was preparing me for the part I would play in His great plans. I saw the following visions in 1944. All of them concerned the world and God's plans to bring peace, joy and happiness to the world.

One evening after I retired, I was laying in bed trying to sleep. Suddenly I saw, what I always called: "A flash vision." In one brilliant flash of light a vision is seen in the mind or intellect. The flash vision is instant; but is real, so clear so vivid that never is it forgotten. The message of the vision is seen and lingers long after the flash of light disappears.

The first time that happened to me, I became frightened; however, I never forgot what I saw: God the Father dressed in long, white robes and upon the robes were tiny black crosses. I knew that the crosses represented the sins of mankind which were being constantly "thrown" up to God.

Soon after I saw that vision, I heard the voice of Christ for the first time. I was told the following:

Jesus said to me: "Know My child that you will suffer greatly, mentally, physically and spiritually. I will place the weight of suffering humanity upon your shoulders and you will be made to bear such a weight."

So, my job for God was definitely linked to suffering humanity.

Then, I received another title, this time from Jesus; and this time I not only heard His voice I saw Him appear before me. I recorded the following notes to explain how I was called The

155

Mighty Warrior of Truth and Righteousness in the year 1944.

(I copy these notes from a manuscript I wrote in 1963):
I received that title in the following manner. I was in a church in New York City. It was the Church of The Blessed Sacrament on the West Side near 68th or 70th Street. It was in this church where I received the first of many special favors and graces from God and from the Blessed Virgin.

Suddenly, when I was kneeling before the altar rail, Jesus appeared to me. He showed me a vision of an army of angels and told me that I was The Mighty Warrior of Truth and Righteousness.

This was the Mighty Warrior who, years later accepted and won what is called The Devil's Challenge. That challenge, which, I explain in later chapters of this book, was part of the role I was to play in my Lady's triumph; but, of course, I did not know that in 1944 when I was given this title.

Christ hinted that there would be this challenge when He said to me on May 4, 1944 (which was one of His first messages to me): "Fear nothing but Hell, My child and fear Hell because it is there you shall go if you lose your grip on Heaven. And your grip on Heaven is the love you have in your heart for God the Father, Me and My Mother.

"But, do not fear the devil for he has no power over you, unless you let him; and you shall not let him have any power as long as you hold God's hand."

At the same time (May 1944) I saw another vision of Jesus. This time I saw Him weeping because His children did not love Him. I wrote: My sweet Jesus in the glory of His kingdom was crying bitterly because His children did not love Him and He sees them possessed by the devil . . . He desires me to help Him and to help His lost children find Him so He can hold them very close. He desires to help me in every way possible and to make Him laugh and sing again.

Tonight I wrote: "I must help You, dear Jesus, so that You shall not cry again:"

Here could be seen my future role of founding my organization, The Maryheart Crusaders, and of my writings which was done to help bring back fallen-away Catholics to the practice of their faith.

I continued, in 1944, to hear the words of Jesus and Mary. I had seen Jesus, but I had not as yet seen a vision of Mary. I only heard her voice.

Jesus also said other things to me in May 1944: Jesus said to me: "You are nothing, My child, teach others that they are nothing but a creature of God's and they have no right to think they own the world or themselves because the world and they belong to God. . . ."

On May 2, 1944, Jesus told me that I wasn't meant to be faithful to anyone but God and His will. I was meant to do only God's will forever.

Our Lord was telling me, which is one of our Church's teachings, loving the will of God and doing the will of God was to be my whole life as I carried out the job which God gave me to do.

It was also at this same time when I was given the title of Child of Love (my third title). I wrote in 1963: My Jesus also gave me another name in 1944.

In 1944, when Jesus and Mary first started to talk to me and to appear to me, they began to call me their Child of Love. I received that title in the following manner: When ever I would say to Jesus or to Mary: "I love you," they would answer: "And I love you, My Child of Love"

So I had been given three titles by God:

1. God's Child of Love
2. The Refuge For Suffering Souls
3. The Mighty Warrior of Truth and Righteousness.

Such titles would have been meaningless if I had not been given a special job to do for God and Our Lady. Of course, in 1944, I had no idea what that job would be or my role in my Lady's triumph. At that period in my life, I knew nothing about this triumph; however, my three titles became a very important part of the story of my Lady's triumph.

The three titles meant a great deal to me; although, I often did not feel like any Mighty Warrior. I would say to Jesus or Mary: "All right, I can accept the titles of Child of Love and Refuge for Suffering Souls; however, I think You made a mistake about the one for Mighty Warrior."

Yet, no mistake was made as was proven when I worked for years, as a Mighty Warrior, fighting against false visions, cults and the teachings of Biblical Fundamentalism which attempted to take Catholics away from their faith, and the role I played in The Devil's Challenge.

Ever since 1944 (over 50 years ago as I write these words), these three titles have been mentioned in my daily note books and manuscripts. The one title which is used more than the others is Child of Love, which Jesus and Mary constantly called me as the following example shows.

This happened also in the year 1944. This vision not only showed the way I was called Child of Love, but also it was a sign of my future role in my Lady's triumph. I wrote about this vision in my 1963 manuscript:

So my job for God was definitely linked with suffering humanity. Jesus linked it further by showing me this vision. I saw myself in the middle of a destroyed world. It was torn apart not only by war but by sin and corruption. Jesus looked at me and said: "Raise this fallen world, Child of Love."

I replied: "But how can I do that, my Jesus!

He answered: "With love, My Child of Love, with love."

Ever since Christ told me that, I have considered the world "my world" and I have dearly loved my poor, suffering world in spite of all its ills, problems and evil. When people (and there were many of them) fueled by their belief in false visions which spoke only of death, doom and destruction for the world came to me and told me how evil the world was and it had to be destroyed, I would feel so sorry for my poor world and I would smile and say: "I don't believe the whole world should be destroyed, I want to make it into a better place to live in."

THE DIAMOND ROSARY
THE FIVE BEAMS OF LIGHT

The first time I saw Christ, He was dressed in beautiful garments and held in His hands a diamond Rosary. Up to that point, I had not seen Mary. I had only heard her sweet, gentle voice. It was Christ who had the Rosary, not Mary.

Then the following event took place which I did not understand at that time. I wrote about it in 1951, also in 1963:

One day, while I lived in New York in 1944 (I left there the beginning of 1945) this happened: I went to church (The Church of the Blessed Sacrament) and I paused in the hall to look at the book rack. I glanced up through the little round windows in the swinging doors and looked inside of the church. I saw suspended in the air, coming from the top of the ceiling, beams of light. I did not, at first, pay too much attention to them. I continued to read the booklet which I had chosen.

I finally walked into the church and I walked down the side aisle. But I stopped short. For there, coming from the top of the church and suspended above the floor were beautiful, bright beams of light. I had never seen anything like it before (or since) the beams were evenly spaced from the front of the church to the rear. I could clearly see them with my naked eyes; but my whole being told me that they were unusual and "from Heaven."

When I could move, I slowly walked down towards the altar. And as I did, I noticed that everything, even the people in church, seemed far away and they faded into the background.

I walked through each beam of light and I was deeply affected. When I reached the altar rail, I instantly turned around; but the beams had vanished! Then I heard Jesus say to me: "Count the beams of light and remember how many there were."

I saw the beams again; but very faintly and I counted five beams of light when I walked out of church through each beam again. I never forgot that number: five. Before I left the church, I glanced through the little round windows and I saw the beams once again bright and clear.

For years I tried to figure out what the beams of light meant. First of all, I thought that they meant that the war would go on for five more years. Later, I connected the five beams with the five wounds of Christ, but such thoughts were not correct. For one thing I saw this vision at about the same time I saw one of the very first visions I had seen of Jesus. He appeared to me dressed in red and white garments. He held in His hands a diamond Rosary. He held the Rosary out and said that it was for me. Five beams of light came from the diamond Rosary and covered me. That could only mean that there would be some connection between me and the Blessed Virgin.

There are two extremely remarkable things about this diamond Rosary and the five beams of light. The Rosary gave forth five beams of light which covered me. I walked through the five beams of light I had seen in the church. I never saw such beams before and I never again saw them at the church.

The two events took place at the same time; and this was four years before I first saw my Lady on the rock in 1948 when she gave me her five promises.

As I said, I tried for years to figure out the five beams of light and why I had walked through them. I could not, but without a doubt, they were connected with the five promises of The Golden Lady of Happiness and my job for God.

When Jesus showed me the diamond Rosary, He said it was for me. After I had walked through the five beams of light, Our Lord told me that the five beams of light I had walked through were the five decades of the diamond Rosary which also had five beams of light which emanated outward to cover me. In 1944, I had no idea how these two visions were connected. The fact is I never even tried to connect these two events.

I wish I could fully explain the way I acted or thought in 1944 when I heard Mary's voice and saw the remarkable visions which I have just recorded. I never tried to figure out why I was told such things or why I saw the visions I did see. To me, it was simply "God's holy will" and I accepted all like a child accepts candy from her parents. I merely recorded all, never thinking about future events or how the things I recorded would be fulfilled or what connection there could be between what I saw and heard and my life in the future. The fact is, I still loved my ice skating and the plans I had made for my future life.

It is only now, as I write this book and review my early notes so as to fit each one into its proper place, when I see the full significance of past visions and messages. It never ceases to amaze me when I do that thinking that in my notes were secrets which I had hidden for 50 years which only now can shine forth and reveal the great peace plan which God created to bring peace, joy and happiness to suffering mankind, this peace plan which revolved around the role I had been given as well as around my Lady's triumph.

Now, as I write this book, I can see the connection between the diamond Rosary and the five beams of light and my job for God and my Lady's triumph by the explanation Christ gave me when He told me what each beam of light symbolized: He said (written in 1951 and 1963 autobiographies):

> "One beam was for love.
> One beam was for truth and righteousness.
> One beam was the power to plant
> the love of God in the hearts of men.
> One beam was for the power of
> God to work through me.
> And the last beam was for peace,
> joy and happiness."

In 1944, I would never have had the knowledge of future events to invent such an explanation. I can now plainly see that each beam represented my life's work for God and for souls as well as the shrine of The Golden Lady of Happiness.

The first beam was for love. Not only was I called Child of Love, not only did I write thousands of pages about God and Our Lady's love for their children, but my Lady's shrine is a shrine of love.

The second beam was for truth and righteousness. Surely, that foretold my role as The Mighty Warrior of Truth and Righteousness when I used all the skills I had been blessed with to fight to defend the truths and teachings of our Catholic faith; and to accept and win The Devil's Challenge.

The third beam was the power to plant the love of God into the hearts of men. This referred to my ability to write books, articles and to give lectures all the intentions of doing just that.

The fourth beam was for the power of God to work through me. This took place for the rest of my life when I allowed God to use me in any way He wanted to for the good of my own soul and the souls of others. In other words, to follow His will for me and to love that will no matter what He wanted me to do for Him.

The fifth beam was for peace, joy and happiness. This refers to my Lady's shrine and to her title of The Golden Lady of Happiness which she would tell me about years later.

Finally, all five beams together, covering me placed my Golden Lady, her shrine, my work for God and my role in her triumph together as one.

In the manuscript I wrote in 1963, I added these words after I had recorded these two events, the diamond Rosary and the five beams of light I walked through in that church:

Thus you see how Jesus weaved my life and my heart around the Blessed virgin and her heart. But I could not have ever begun my job for God if I had not had my Lady to guide me every moment of the day and night.

Up to this point, although I had heard my Lady speak to me, I had never seen her. That was to change.

FIRST VISION OF MARY: YEAR 1944
THE GARDENIA OF LOVE

As can be clearly seen by what I saw and heard in 1944, the good Lord laid before me my whole future life and the work I was to do for Him and for souls. One will see, as this book is being read, more words or messages from Jesus and Mary which I heard in the year 1944 which show that.

After the visions and messages began in 1944, they never stopped. They continued as my job for God unfolded in my daily life. I will also add, that such revelations continued as I watched the world, which I called "my world," fall and rise again from the rubble of wars and human desires of materialistic, selfish goals and aims: all of which revealed mankind's quest for a lasting happiness.

In 1995, I wrote the following article about the world I lived in.

MY WORLD

As I sit by my window this first day of May 1995, I look out beyond the flowering trees which grow so well in my yard. I look further beyond the limits of the man-made boundaries of my state and I see the world: my world.

The world I was born into was not a pleasant-filled-with-laughter type of world. It was one where dark war clouds seem to be hanging over mankind far more than carefree days of sunny brightness.

I When I was born, June 13, 1924, the first world war was still fresh in the memories of all who lived and suffered through it, including my father.

Then came dreadful days of The Great Depression followed, not too many years later, by the second world war.

As time marched on, my country saw one war after another, Vietnam, Korea and a host of other little conflicts which erupted on all continents calling for the help of the resources of my country which often included our armed forces.

Meanwhile, in between the wars and the conflicts, people tried to live as normal a life as possible carrying out daily duties and obligations.

The world, at times, seemed to become engulfed in its own instabilities as it struggled towards an uncertain future; however, life went on, new generations were born and old ones slowly died out.

As I marched along with the rest of humanity, day by day watching my world live and then die only to be reborn again, I saw not so much the dark clouds or the mechanisms of war, but I saw people. I saw suffering humanity and I carried upon my shoulders its pain and sorrow.

But I saw something else. I saw in my world, among all the ups and downs, the falls and risings, the silent glow of God's love for that suffering humanity.

That was one light that I knew would never fade or grow dim no matter how dark the clouds were because I had a beautiful story of that love to tell. So now I can, at last, tell that story: the story of The Golden Lady of Happiness and her glorious triumph.

In the year 1944, my Lady and my Lord were formulating not only my future life but hope and encouragement for poor suffering humanity as well. They designed that around the job I would do and the love and care of the Holy Mother of God expressed in her triumph.

Right from the beginning of my job for God and Our Lady that was clearly seen. The two, her job and mine, were to become as one.

In one of the first visions I saw of Jesus, He showed me a beautiful diamond ring. He told me that Mary was the stone and I was the setting. He explained that alone and separate we would be beautiful, but together we would be precious and priceless and so we could never be separated (1951 autobiography).

I am writing such words (and more later) not to want everyone to think that I am so important or great. That is not my intention. Remember I hid such words for over 50 years. They are what I always called my most precious secrets. I reveal them now under obedience to my spiritual director, Father Brad. When he insisted that I reveal my role in my Lady's triumph, he kept telling me about this diamond and setting which could not be separated.

It was my Lady who told me in 1944, that I had a great important job to do for God and her. On March 31, 1944, she, had said to me: "You must know how important you are to Jesus and me. You must know what a big job we have for you so that you must realize how much you mean to Jesus and me. Your job is big and great for God wanted it to be so. You have a tremendous job to do and do it well for it is so very important to God."

When I objected to such words, fearing I would get "swell headed," as I called it, my Lady said to me May 5, 1944: "Fear not, my child, for God makes no one important to themselves. Their job is only important if it is important to God because He is the only important one."

I wrote under these words:

Mary said that to me because I started to worry as the devil was getting after me, that I might get a big head because she tells me how important my job is. I don't want to get conceited because I know it is wrong and Jesus would not like it.

Then in May of 1946, when Christ was praising me, He told me something that I have mentioned often. I wrote: "But Jesus, I can't hear anymore, my Christ. I am nothing. You told me yourself that I am nothing. Please don't say anymore! Please!"

Christ sweetly replied: "Ah! dear one, is it not I who has the power to make something out of nothing? But, dear one, ease the pain by knowing that as long as I praise you and your love, I will put to shame the great ones of the world who think they love me, but only love themselves."

The "greatness" of my job for God was always far removed from me; except when, at times, God permitted me to catch a glimpse of it. Then the "greatness" would crash down upon me and almost smother me. I would become weak, even frightened. Still, on the other hand, I had to know and to understand at least part of that greatness or else I would never have been able to carry out my role of The Mighty Warrior who used her "greatness" to defeat the devil.

But most of the time, I never once thought about my job as being so tremendous and great. I merely accepted it like a child accepts a priceless jewel unaware of its great value. Others will see the greatness of my job; but I prefer to remain the little child who hides away from the greatness behind the coverings of littleness.

Our Lady also connected my job with hers, which became one, when I saw her for the first time in 1944. Up to the time of this first vision, I had only heard her voice. I had heard and seen Christ, but not Mary.

Then, one day as I knelt before her statue, in the church where I had heard so many wonderful words from her, I suddenly saw her standing before me.

She was resplendent, filled with beauty and light. She was dressed all in white (I usually saw her, after that first time, dressed in white. I did not see her dressed in her garments of gold until I saw her on the rock in 1948, as The Golden Lady of Happiness.) I noticed immediately that she had two gardenias on her feet, one on each foot.

I had no idea what the flowers meant or stood for; but she told me that the flower was the Gardenia of Love and she said she would give me this Gardenia of Love. She also said that this flower would bloom forever. I waited two years to find out how she would give me such an everlasting flower. She finally told me on August 15, 1946: I wrote: After I went back to my seat, after I had received my beloved Lord in Holy Communion, suddenly, I saw my Lady Mary sitting on a throne with hundreds of angels around her. She was so very beautiful. I knew that Mary would tell me what the Gardenia of Love was because I asked her to tell me before Mass. She did tell me and it surprised me at what she said for she said that I was the Gardenia of Love to be placed next to the "gold leaf" (the one I had put in a locket and left with Father Shea when I left New York in 1945. However, the "gold leaf" was in fact my Golden Lady) for all eternity and we will never be separated.

Here is what I wrote in my 1963 manuscript (my notes dated August 15, 1946):

She said: "See how frail and delicate the gardenia is, yet so strong are its petals that it takes a hard pull to separate them from the stem. Such are you, my child, frail and delicate as the little child, yet strong and mighty as the warrior you are. See how pure white the flower is? This is your pure white soul, and your purest heart of love.

"Smell the fragrant odor! Oh! dear child! this fragrance, which is your sweet love, will encircle the earth and all who breathe in this love and remain within sight of this pure flower shall be saved and have life everlasting.

"For all who follow you and love you will not perish for they, who see you, cannot fail to see God. For where you are so is their God and His beauty that shines forth.

"This I say to you, my sweet child, that this flower shall become more than a symbol to God's children. It shall become part of them so that never could they go anywhere without it.

"And this pure flower shall grow where all others have withered and died, for this flower is love and this love is you. And you, dear child, shall be planted in these places and soon the brightness that is yours will light the places and no longer will it be dark. For your words and your examples will become so implanted on the earth that you and you alone will save millions of souls from eternal damnation." (Here my Lady refers to my writings and how I teach, in these writings, the truths of God as taught by the Catholic Church. Also, I teach others to receive the sacraments. This has already started to happen. My published books and lectures have helped thousands to return to God and the practice of their faith.) "And your influence will be felt throughout the world so greatly that nations will become peaceful and great powers will become meek and humble and Jesus' cross will be planted on the soil and in the hearts of men, so that through you, the fallen world will rise with banners of God and of His Holy Mother flying high. And your name will never be blotted out but shall be a guide to God's children from now until the end of time.

"You alone will so shake the foundations of the world that never will they forget you or what you stand for."

I was so upset by these words that I wrote: "Oh! my goodness! What can I say to this? It is so very great! I don't know what to say. I can only do God's will to the best of my knowledge."

There is another very remarkable fact about this revelation when my Lady told me that I was the Gardenia of Love. Long after I forgot these words, in the year 1987, they were jolted back into my memory by what Jacinta told me the first time I visited Fatima 41 years later as explained in the chapters on Fatima (date 7/15/87):

I bowed my head in prayer as soon as the Mass started and suddenly Jacinta appeared to me . . . Suddenly, I saw her raise her arms high and from her hands there fell a shower of rose petals as if floating in a gentle breeze.

Then she smiled sweetly and said to me: "I am just a tiny, gentle breeze blowing in the wind of God's love for mankind. You, dearest Child of Love are like a roaring storm which will shake the foundations of the world."

I was absolutely amazed by what the child said to me and I knew my Lady had said the same thing years ago. As soon as I returned home, I looked through my note books until I found the message of August 15, 1946. However, I did not find that message until 6/30/90, three years later.

In a short autobiography written in 1951, I wrote about this revelation: Such words I can now read and not suffer from their power and greatness. When my Lady first spoke them in 1946, I trembled with fear and I suffered greatly to think that she had dared to speak to me in such a way. I became weak and sick and I could not say anything.

Now I can look back upon the sufferings I have endured for the love of God and from the battles with the devil and I see before me a beautiful picture of the truth of God. No longer do I tremble in my armour of love. For God has well prepared me for the coming battles. I feel power and strength because I fight for God and with God. I feel like The Mighty Warrior that God made me and I know that no force could destroy me or the truth that I represent (for this truth is God's truth as taught to me by my beloved Catholic Church).

Never could we be separated for our hearts are one. Love has opened the doors of light. The darkness is gone and I clearly see, not only the love of God, but the holy will of God.

The light that now surrounds me, and the love that is mine alone is for the world! And soon after I die, the world will see this light and this love. I will gather my world into the arms of love and until the end of time, never will I let my world fall back into the arms of the devil.

But that was written in 1951. In 1944, I still had a great deal to learn about the ways and the love of God; and the ways and the power of the devil.

By the end of 1944, I was filled with ambition, ready to convert the whole world and to bring peace and happiness to suffering humanity; but such was not the plans of God. I had no way of knowing that. Even though, a great deal had happened, it was only the beginning!

On March 31, 1944, my Lady told me as if to hold back my enthusiasm: "Do not expect to conquer the world. Do not expect to convert millions. But do start the landslide that will make people stand up and take notice. Cause an avalanche of love, happiness and joy and show the world how to find their own happiness, love and joy.

"Teach a few and a great many will seek you out to find what you have taught others."

That I did do as the years went by and I silently wrote and worked for God, my Lady and my Church.

My main goal in all the work I did was to save souls and to lead lost, lonely, bewildered souls to the loving arms of their Saviour and His gentle Mother. My love for my Catholic faith is clearly expressed in all my writings which now number thousands and thousands of pages; and as in 1944, I wanted to share that faith with "my world" and poor, suffering humanity.

Once I found the path which God and Our Lady wanted me to walk upon, I never left that path. Oh, I did fall through human weaknesses but I always rose again with the help of God's graces to continue the journey I had started in 1944.

On November 5, 1987, I wrote the following prayer:

PRAYER OF TOTAL LOVE

Dearest God: May each breath I take today be an act of pure love for the Holy Trinity, Mary and all the saints. May I walk, each second of the day, in the sun-rays of Your pure love for me. May all I do today be done with total love for Your will and become an act of love for Your honor and glory. May I feel, in each and every cross You care to send me today, the gentle touch of Your hand as You stay so close to me helping me rise whenever I fall. May I end my day filled with the satisfaction that I, in all I did, said or thought did not detour from the paths of holiness which You have placed me upon. Amen

Louise

This picture shows Mary's altar in the Church of The Blessed Sacrament in New York City which was my parish church when I lived there, a few blocks from the church. I was kneeling before this statue when Mary spoke the words which I heard in 1944. At first I did not see her. Then one day, as I knelt here, Christ appeared to me. Later, I saw my first vision of Mary as I knelt before this statue

This is the crucifix in The Church of The Blessed Sacrament which I often knelt before to pray. On the left-hand side, you can see part of the votive light stand. It was in such a stand, placed there (I don't know if the original one is the same as this one) where I put out the fire, in the bottom of the stand with my bare hand. (See next chapter)

— 4 —

A CLOSER LOOK AT MY TITLES

In 1944, I was given three titles. At that time, such did not mean anything to me. But now, being 73 years old, I can look back at my life and understand what each title or name means. Surely, these names were predictions which came true. The three were:

1. Child of Love
2. Refuge For Suffering Souls
3. Mighty Warrior of Truth
   and Righteousness.

I will attempt to explain each title as follows:

CHILD OF LOVE

This title I was able to understand first. I wanted to love The Blessed Trinity, Christ my Saviour and Mary with my whole heart and soul.

However, Child of Love was not just referring to the love which I had in my heart for The Trinity, Christ and Mary. I had a very deep love for what I called "my world" and poor, suffering humanity. In addition, I had a very profound love for souls.

Even as a child, I had a concern for souls. Whenever I heard of the death of someone, I would say: "What about his (or her) soul?" I did not know what a soul was but to me it was connected with death.

I remember that, as a child of ten or eleven, I would go to the movies with my brother to see all the cowboys and Indian movies. These usually showed the Indians being killed on the battlefields. My brother would enjoy these movies, I would not. I would leave the theater and say over and over: "What about their souls?" The movies never explained what happened to the souls of the dead warriors. I could not explain that to myself.

The love which I had for suffering humanity and souls inspired all my writings: books, articles and all my lectures. I worked day and night for long years (with no pay) writing to teach people how to find peace, joy and happiness within their love for God and His love for them, repeating in my writings and lectures the teachings and doctrine of my beloved Catholic Church. I knew that within such teachings and doctrines they could not only find their joy and happiness but their eternal salvation as well.

I started my organization called The Maryheart Crusaders which has as its goal the reuniting of fallen-away Catholics with their faith.

I knew that my Lady's shrine was a shrine of love for God's suffering children.

I have such compassion and love for God's poor, suffering children that I often said: "Even if I had messages of death, doom and destruction (as are given by false visionaries) I would not give such messages to the world, God's children are suffering enough. They don't need any words which would increase such sufferings. They also need to be shown the way to God's Heart of love."

As if to verify such thoughts, I recently read in an issue of "Our Sunday Visitor" (October 1996) the following words spoken by Cardinal Joseph Ratzinger, the Vatican's top doctrinal official: "The Virgin does not engage in sensationalism; she does not create fear. She does not present apocalyptic visions, but guides people to her Son."

As far back as 1944, I was attempting to bring hope, encouragement and God and Our Lady's love to suffering humanity. I started to write (as I was told to do) articles and even poems which expressed my desires to show people how to find love for God, His and Mary's love for them and their peace, joy and happiness.

Here is a sample of the articles and poems I wrote between 1944 and 1945. I also put into these first articles words about my visions because I was constantly being told to make myself known and to make Mary and Our Lord's words known.

This article (not complete) I called "My Lady's Voice" was written at the end of 1944 or the beginning of 1945.

MY LADY'S VOICE

Ave Maria my heart sings with love. What a beautiful song that is! and how pleased Jesus is when He hears His children sing this song to His dear Mother.

My children of God, gather around me and I shall tell you about your heavenly Mother and how she loves you and wants you to love her.

How well I know what Our Lady desires for you, to whom she sends her messages. She asks me to talk to you and to give you these messages that she sends through her humble servant.If you could only hear her voice, how your heart would sing, and how you would forget all else except the sweet music of her tender words.

My Lady speaks to me and her messages to you are filled with joy and bliss, the joy and bliss that she so gladly gives to those who love her.

SELF-LOVE

Don't you love to please the ones you love? Don't you want to do just what they want to do? You must feel that way if you really love them instead of yourself.

To love yourself is to always do things that please you and to have others do things that please only you. To love others, you give all for them and care not how much you suffer as long as they are happy and pleased. Now to really love God is to do all for Him. Suffering is a marvelous test that God gives you and it proves if you love Him and His will or just yourself and how you feel.

Oh! to please God! What joy is there to please Him. It is the joy of real love for Him and His children. Would you present a child in front of God and hear His praises for this child? Would you desire to have God also praise you and place you by the child or maybe in front of that child? Please don't do that. Please bring the child to God and then run away. Because you brought this child to God, you have made Him happy. That is enough. He does not have to make you happy in return. He might even make you suffer. But don't mind because each cross may be your only reward and praise. But you will be so very glad that your God is happy and even if He seems to ignore you, you shouldn't mind because as long as He is happy then that is all that matters. Then, indeed, will you lose all self-love for the total wondrous love of God alone.

When I reread such articles today, I am amazed at the insight I had when I was only 20 years old.

Here are some poems I wrote in 1944-1945.

LOVE AND TEARS

I love each pain You care to send,
I love my cross that makes me bend.
I love the tears I shed for Thee,
I love the sufferings You give to me.
I love them all because of You,
For me, You had great sorrows, too.
But You loved Your cross and nails,
So I, too, love my storms and gales.
Love can make all things seem mild,
And strengthens such a small, weak child.
And I do so hope and pray,
That I can die for love, one day.

I wrote this article to go with. this poem:

At times, it seems like it is much easier to continue to the end of some deed that is of sin rather of good deeds that will increase your holiness. That is because the devil is so strong and he puts, in your pathway, aids to his sin.

I myself, found that the closer I attempted to get to God's love, the harder the climb became and the more barriers the devil put in my way.

The way to perfection is not over a rose-covered path. Yes, the rose bushes are there, but the flowers have been gathered and the thorns are left for your bare feet to trod. Such is the way of the saints.

You will see as you walk onward many roads that lead off the narrow, thorn-covered road that you walk on. These roads are filled with soft grass and you are so tempted to turn your footsteps to follow them.

Ah! but beware for these roads were built by the devil and lead to his Hell. No! you must not leave your road. You must go on and on, even if you fall to your knees and must crawl. But alas, so few saints there are for the price is high. So many turn off because they see only thorns ahead on their road.

The beginning is easy for you have strength and courage. You have not been tested. You think yourself brave and you go forward and say: I can do it! Ah, but how soon you fail when God tests you. You failed, dear ones, because you did not say: "I can't do anything alone, dear Lord, You must help me."

ALWAYS A TOMORROW

Today the sky is very gray,
But tomorrow is another day.
This day's toil will soon end,
And a tomorrow God will send.
All things of deep, dark, despair,
Will vanish in the morning air.
A rose will surely take the place,
Of a thorn's sharp, ugly face.
A wondrous part of our life,
With all its trouble and strife,
Is that the dawn ever bright,
Always follows a dark night.

MARY, MOTHER OF ALL

Send your tender prayer to me,
A little song of love.
I will always be with you,
And bless you from above.

Keep within your heart my name,
Let me hear you say,
"Mary, Mother be with me,
Each moment of the day."

When unhappy hours are yours,
Trust in me, my dear.
Remember that you're not alone,
For I am always near.

If joy comes along the way,
Please say a little line,
A "thank you" means so very much
For a gift of mine.

Keep the name of Jesus Christ
Forever in your mind.
For the love of your dear Lord,
Be always good and kind.

Praise, adore and love your God,
Kiss His cross each hour,
And from Heaven's heights
I'll send graces in a shower.

When the evening shadows fall,
And the night is due,
Sleep, my child, a sleep of peace,
For I am watching you.

When your busy life is past,
And your job is done,
Follow me in holy light,
I'll lead you to my Son.

THE REFUGE FOR SUFFERING SOULS

This title goes with the one called Child of Love. As I said, in 1944, I had no idea what the three titles meant, however, I started this job of being a Refuge for Suffering Souls then; even though I did not know that at that time.

My Lady had referred to that title when she told me in 1944: She said I am to make a light shine on dark paths so that God's children can see that light and find peace and happiness.

On March 27,1944, I was told: She said that I would have all the strength and knowledge and courage that I need to carry on God's will of being a Refuge for Suffering Souls . . . She said that I would have the knowledge and courage to meet up with any situation so that I can aid any suffering child of God in any way possible.

Not only was I to bring encouragement, hope and love to God's suffering children as the Refuge for Suffering Souls, I was to share these sufferings. In 1944, Our Lord said to me: "I shall place the sufferings of humanity upon your shoulders and you will be made to bear that weight."

It was this weight of the sufferings of humanity which Christ place upon my shoulders which constantly gave me the strength and courage I needed to go on with the job the Lord gave me to bring peace, joy, comfort, encouragement to suffering humanity. I felt so sorry for the ones who had heavy crosses to carry, who were alone and crying with no one near to hold them and kiss away their tears.

If I woke up at night, I would say to my Lord: "Dearest Jesus, I know there are so many of Your children who, at this very moment, are filled with pain and sorrow because they have such heavy crosses to carry. If only I could go to them to hold them close and comfort them."

I knew I could not do that, but I could write and so I wrote words of hope and comfort and love as I had been told to do on November 13, 1945: "Write! Wrote long and hard!" (At that time I had no idea I would write "long and hard") "Write My love and My Mother's love and give to the world that which I want them to have. Write as only My Child of Love could write!"

I began to fulfill my role as a Refuge for Suffering Souls almost as soon as I was told I was that refuge. But I did not know, at that time, that I was doing that.

I can remember three incidents which occurred at that time, in 1944, when I lived in New York City. The first one involved a child, a boy, who was about seven or eight years old.

I was in a store which sold candy, papers and magazines making a purchase. Suddenly, this little boy ran into the store with tears streaming down his face. He held in his hands an empty Easter basket. He was completely distraught. He was crying.

I went to him, bent down and tried to get him to tell me what was wrong. He finally told me between sobs, that the teacher at school had given him candy in the basket to take home to his mother. His little heart was filled with joy; however, on the way home some older boys had taken the candy and he had no candy to give to his mother.

I did not have very much money in my pocket, but I bought him enough candy to fill the little basket. He exploded with joy and as soon as the basket was full, he ran home to give the candy to his mother. He did not even wait to thank me; however, the clerk in the store said: "God bless you." The joy in the child's heart was all the thanks I needed.

Another incident involved a man who lived in the rooming house next to the room I rented. He had moved in with a woman. I thought they were married. One day, I met the man on the stairs. He looked terrible with dark circles under his eyes as if he had not had a good night's sleep in weeks.

I don't know why he confided in me but he stopped me and told me that the woman who shared his room was not his wife.

She was someone he had met and she refused to give him up. They had moved from place to place. He wanted desperately to leave her, but she always threatened to kill herself if he left her. He was afraid to move out.

I looked at his sad face and said: "I will pray for you. Just move out. She won't kill herself. Free yourself from her hold."

I thought no more about the situation until a few days later. As I sat in my room, I heard someone at my door. The person was trying to put a note under my door. I became frightened, but I opened the door. There to my amazement was this man (I never found out what his name was) standing outside my door, smiling, with a suitcase in his hand.

He said the note was to thank me for giving him the courage to leave the woman, who had gone out to shop. He thanked me in person and left. I never saw him again. The following day, I saw the woman leave with her suitcase. The threats to kill herself never became a reality.

I was very surprised because this had happened, but happy that he had freed himself from this woman.

The third incident had to be one in which My Lady had said: "She said that I would have the strength, knowledge and courage that I need to carry on God's will of being a Refuge for Suffering Souls. . . ."

I was in church praying one day when a woman came forth to light a candle in one of the candle stands. She lit the candle and then tried to put out the wick she had in her hand in the sand on the bottom of the votive stand. As she placed her wick into the sand, suddenly, all the wicks in the stand caught fire and a flame shot up. The fire was rather large and covered most of the sand in the stand.

The woman moved backward in fear and a look of horror came upon her face. I looked at her and thought: "Here is a suffering child of God who needs my help." I stood in front of the stand and slowly put my hand into the fire and patted out the flames. The look of horror on the woman's face turned to one of absolute amazement. I only smiled at her. She was so shaken by what I had done that she ran out of the church.

Then it was my turn to start shaking. I could not believe what I had done or the results of my action. I looked at my hand and there were no burn marks on it. I had felt no pain as I put out the fire with my bare hand. I looked at the blackened wicks in the stand and said out loud: "Did I do that?" I was thankful that no one had been in the church with the woman and me to see what I had done.

When I put my hand into the fire, I never thought that I could have been badly injured. My only thought was that a poor, suffering child of God's needed my help and so I helped her. I also knew that my Lady had worked this "miracle" to show me how I would help other suffering children of God's in the future.

Through all the years of my work for God, I did not count the cost of what I suffered in order to help someone.

Numerous people came to me for help, advice, prayers, comfort and understanding after I made my Lady known in 1960. I welcomed everyone and tried to help each one. They said that I did help them. I often went to places to meet them if they could not come to see me. My husband would drive me to their homes or even to a hospital where someone needed me.

When I started my organization The Maryheart Crusaders in 1964, I called it a Refuge for Suffering Souls. I did that without thinking about the title I had been given in 1944.

To me, it was only natural to call the organization the Refuge for Suffering Souls.

When we had our store and chapel where daily Mass was said and confessions heard (with the approval of our Archbishop), I called the chapel a Refuge for Suffering Souls. Hundreds of suffering souls found comfort and hope in that chapel. It truly was a refuge for their suffering souls.

THE MIGHTY WARRIOR OF
TRUTH AND RIGHTEOUSNESS

This was the one title which I had the most difficulty accepting. For years I could not see myself as this Mighty Warrior.

Often I would say to Christ or Mary: "I can accept the role as The Child of Love and Refuge for Suffering Souls, but this business of being a Mighty Warrior, forget it. I think You made a mistake here. I think someone else could do a much better job than I am doing being this Mighty Warrior." But I was.

In 1944, My Lady had said to me: She said that I was part of Jesus' army on earth and that I must teach His children what He wants me to teach them (March 31, 1944).

When my own spiritual journey was having all its ups and downs as I struggled to reach a more perfect union with God, I seldom felt like any Mighty Warrior. I did not know what this Mighty Warrior was suppose to do or be. Then I found out.

I began to see the role of this Mighty Warrior when I became more involved in the work I did for The Maryheart Crusaders. It took me some time to settle upon the name for the organization I had founded; and when I chose that name I was already on the battlefields fighting as a warrior to defend the Catholic faith against the fallen-away Catholics, the cults and sects which attempted to destroy the doctrines and teachings of our faith causing lay people to leave their Church.

No matter where I went, I was confronted by someone who challenged me with their own ideas, reasoning and religious convictions; and I accepted the challenge. As time went on, I wrote three published books showing the way God's Mighty Warrior would not back off when she came face to face with religious battles. These three published books are:

TOO BUSY FOR GOD THINK AGAIN

COME HOME THE DOOR IS OPEN

THE CATHOLIC ANSWER TO
THE JEHOVAH'S WITNESSES

I also have written other books and articles doing battle with cults and fallen-away Catholics and their confused, mixed-up ideas. Each time I saw a problem in their way of reasoning, I wrote an article revealing, the true teachings of Christ and our Church.

For example, one of the first persons I met who surprised me with her mixed-up ideas (I was surprised because I thought everyone believed as strongly as I do in my Catholic faith), told me that she doesn't care how many sins she committed or what kind of a life she led because God was so merciful, He would allow her to confess her sins on her deathbed and thus be saved.

I answered her: "What if you are not given time on your deathbed to repent?"

She looked at me and said: "I never thought about that."

I went home and wrote an article on that subject.

Each time I learned about someone's spiritual problem, I would write an article helping to solve such a problem.

One day I went to visit a sick woman. Suddenly, her son and two of his friends surrounded me and started to tell me what was wrong with our Church's teachings. I would not turn away. I talked for an hour explaining how wrong they were. I don't know if they were converted, but at least I gave them something to think about.

Such conversations left me completely exhausted because of my poor health. But I would not give up.

I travelled thousands of miles with my husband, some of my friends and my helper, Donald D'Efemia, to help someone with a spiritual problem or to give a lecture explaining the teachings of our faith. I never relished the idea of doing that. I dreaded the thought of giving a lecture. I often started the talk in such a weak, low voice that people could not hear me until the Crusaders bought a P.A. system for me.

It is to be noted that when I gave these talks and lectures, I never mentioned the visions or the job given to me connected with the visions. Most people who heard my talks did not even know I saw visions. That part of my job for God was completely separated from the visions. That was my role as The Mighty Warrior of Truth and Righteousness.

I was merely doing what I was told to do in March 1944:

"Teach a few and a great many will seek you out to find what you have taught others."

April 2, 1944: My Lady said to me: "Teach the world to carry its crosses as well as Jesus carried His.'"

March 31, 1944: "You must go forth and teach the world the things Jesus wants them to know."

March 31, 1944: "Your job is to go forth into the dark hills and gather up all of God's stray, bewildered children and bring them home before they die from hunger."

Then there is The Devil's Challenge. That definitely revealed my role as The Mighty Warrior. This consisted of my own personal fights with the devil as I journeyed to my union with God and as I fulfilled my role which God and my Lady had given to me in connection with her triumph.

I was told that this battle would be there and it would be never ending. March 31, 1944: "Your job will be hard, Louise, very hard. It is true, Jesus is on one side of you, but also on your other side is the devil. They are both pouring words into your ears and it is up to you to use your free will to believe whom you want to believe. The devil hates you, Louise, because you belong to us. Always he will be by you telling you lies and tempting you. You must be strong."

March 31, 1944: "God has chosen you to make known to the dark world many things which would otherwise not be known. You have a great, hard, important job to do. You will meet opposition and hate for the devil will be strong. But slowly and surely you will win because God wants His children back."

That summarizes the role I was given as The Mighty Warrior of Truth and Righteousness.

5

I BECAME A PROFESSIONAL
ICE SKATER
1944-1945

By this time, the reader might wonder whatever happened to my dreams of becoming the second Sonja Henie? Also, how could such desires and ambitions be part of my job for God and my Lady's triumph? After I started to hear my Lady and my Lord and see visions telling me what my future life would become, was ice skating and show business part of that future? How could the two be compatible? Was there not too much difference between them? How could both be in the same life?

In 1944, all the while my Lady and Christ spoke to me, I was still training to become a professional ice skater. That was why I had moved to New York City. When I did move there, I never expected or even imagined what happened would happen concerning visions and a job to do for God.

As the foundation for my work for God was being built by Christ and Mary, I still had to work in offices to earn a living and I still ice skated atop the old Madison Square building where there was an ice skating rink called "Ice Land."

However, as can be expected, the more love I found in my heart for God, my Lady and suffering humanity, the more I was faced with the conflict of asking myself: should I give up my skating to become a nun? I was most willing to face that problem, and I became more and more convinced that was indeed what the good Lord wanted me to do. I was willing to make this supreme sacrifice to show my Lord how much I loved Him and His Mother. In spite of the visions and my love for God and my Lady, I still greatly loved ice skating. My heart would fill with joy just by stepping on to the ice. If I did a jump or a spin well, I would be thrilled.

By that time, in 1944, I had become an excellent skater, far better than the average skater who came to the rink. I never had the abilities of the skaters in the '90s with all their triple jumps and elegant spins; however, when I skated, such achievements were not the norm. If a person could skate forward and backward, that person could be hired for a show; and I was far better than that; so much so that I was asked to join a show that was preparing to travel around the country. This was my "dream come true" so I accepted the offer and soon I found myself rehearsing with the other members of the show.

That was in January of 1945. The show was called "Hollywood Ice Review" and was to open in the Spring of 1945.

This was actually the second professional ice show I was in. The first one was a small show put on by The Hartford Skating Club in 1942. It opened Christmas night and ran to New Year's 1943. I was paid a small amount of money for that show. It was nothing extraordinary, but, in a sense, it started my career as a professional ice skater.

I was thrilled to be rehearsing for a real ice show. But what about my doubts about giving up ice skating because of the visions and the work I was told I would do for God and my Lady?

These doubts were taken away after I accepted this job as an ice skater.

By that time, I had met a priest whom I considered my first spiritual director. His name was Father Shea. He was secretary to Cardinal Francis Spellman, Archbishop of the New York, N.Y. archdiocese (1939-1967). As I explained in the following chapter about my spiritual director, Father Shea was most interested in me and my visions.

After I saw my first visions, I knew that I had to have a priest review them and give me prudent advice. I decided to go "right to the top." So, one day, I rang the bell at Saint Patrick's rectory and asked to speak to the Cardinal.

Naturally, I was not allowed to walk into the Cardinal's office to tell him what was on my mind. Instead I met his secretary, Father Shea, who came to see me and greeted me warmly.

As soon as we met, we established a friendship which

endured until 1947 when I met my second spiritual director, Monsignor John J. Hayes. (I believe Father Shea left New York after that.)

Father Shea was most kind to me as he listened to my story of visions and words from Jesus and Mary. He knew I was most sincere and honest. I also let him read some of my writings.

I do not know if he ever had anyone else tell him that he or she saw visions, but I do know that he became most interested in all I told him; and when I finished my story, he wanted to see me again.

When I wrote him a letter from Akron, Ohio while traveling with the show, he wrote back: "We are praying for you here and wish you well. Our Lady's blessings."

When it came time for me to consider joining a show, or to become a nun, I took the problem to Father Shea. At that time, I was ready to give up ice skating and join a convent. I told that fact to Father Shea. I really thought he would agree with me, however, he did not.

He wisely said: "I think you should keep skating, even join a show. If the visions are true, they will continue no matter where you are. If not, the convent would be the worst place on earth for you."

I was actually keenly disappointed. I began to feel that I was willing to give up all for God, but He did not want me; once again I felt no one wanted me.

I went back to my room very upset. But then my Lady explained to me why it was God's will that I go into show business. Suddenly, I heard her speaking to me.

I dated this message May 5, 1944. My Lady said:

"There are more souls lost to eternal Hell because they have found what earthly pleasure and gain and fortune can be had from a successful life in show business than any other ways of sin.

"These people know only the lure of fame and fortune and forget the simple life of the love of God.

"They go around in their seemingly glory and live only for what life can give them as far as earthly wealth is concerned.

I need not say more about that. You understand what I am talking about.

"You, Louise, a simple, stupid child, with many, many faults; a child who was once lured away by earthly pleasures has been chosen to do a great job for Our Lord.

"You are wanted only by God to go forth and teach the world the things God wants you to teach them.

"You must go forth into this show business that has gotten so far away from the Church that it needs missionaries to bring it back.

"True, there are many good Catholic show people, but on the whole, their world is very far away from the Church.

"So, my child, you who are so simple and so stupid that you cannot remember things; that you cannot pronounce certain simple words; that you cannot spell words that a child could spell. You, who are really very, very stupid, have been chosen to go forth into that world apart from God and bring it back—ever so slowly but surely—to God and peace and joy.

"This will serve as an example that others will follow for the show business is that great on earth that many will follow its lead.

"You must teach them love for God and love for Him alone. You must teach them a simple life, a life of hardships and sufferings.

"You, my child, will suffer greatly.

"You must teach these people the nothingness of this earth, the greatness of Heaven, the shortness of time and the length of eternity.

"You must teach them many other things that God wants you to teach them.

"You do not know how now. But after the Holy Spirit comes to you to inflame you with the gift of tongue and knowledge, you will know."

This rather long discourse on the subject of my going into show business, or the entertainment world, has many surprising aspects about it which I did not see when my Lady told me that in 1944.

When she spoke to me about show business, I was thinking only about the people who lived and worked in Hollywood making movies. That to me was "show business."

Yet, my Lady's words expanded far beyond the Hollywood I knew in 1944. She saw the future concerning all the forms and types of the Arts and Entertainment commercial enterprises; especially when she said: ". . . this show business that has gotten so far away from the Church that it needs missionaries to bring it back."

My own life as a professional ice skater was not that great nor that long.

I joined an ice skating show in New York City which went on tour in the Spring of 1945. Before I left New York, I went to see my spiritual director, Father Shea. It was then when I gave him my precious locket which contained the "gold leaf" as I called it. I gave it to him to hold so that nothing would happen to it while I was with the show. I received a letter from him dated: Feast of Saint Rose of Lima, 1945. In this letter, he said: "Your book "Hope" is here; your chain and all the rest."

The show I had joined was not a "roaring success." The fact is it was more of a failure. It was so poorly organized that after we opened in Trenton, New Jersey and went on to Baltimore, Maryland, we had to return to New York to try and repair the obvious flaws. That was done and we opened again in Rochester, New York in April 1945.

We traveled across the country to several states, all of which made matters worse. We had to travel long distances between shows and often had no sleep until the next performance: again poor management. That system greatly affected my health, which was poor all my life. (In 1993, the doctors found that I had a hole in my heart which I was born with as well as a defective Mitral valve.)

This show "Hollywood Ice Review" was doomed from the start. it lasted only until June 1945.

After the show closed, I returned to my home where my mother lived at 517 West Main Street in Meriden, Connecticut.

When the promoters of "Hollywood Ice Review" wanted to try again, they sent me word that they were starting a new show; and they begged me to join. I really did not want to because I had had enough of show business, but I felt sorry for them and so I again left Meriden to join the new show and go on tour. This show ended up to be worse than the first one, due once again, to poor management. It started in October 1945 and quickly ended in November 1945.

Part of the two shows' problems was the fact that the show was not put on in existing rinks around the country, which were very few and far between. The show carried with it a portable rink consisting of large metal plates which had to be put together, then flooded and a truck, with freezing equipment, had to be hooked up to the metal plates. Often the water leaked out of the plates or else there had not been time enough to have the water freeze and our skates would produce sparks as we glided over the plates during the numbers of the show.

When the show ended, we went to Chicago, Illinois. There, I made one of the most important decisions of my life. After the show broke up, some of the skaters were going to Hollywood to skate in Sonya Henie movies. They wanted me to go with them.

Here was my chance to make my "dream of all dreams" come true. Not only would I meet my Sonja Henie, I would actually be able to skate in one of her movies. What joy! What would I choose? Would I go running off to Hollywood or would I return home to do my work for God, which was to write.

I chose God and my writings. I left the group and returned to Connecticut.

By that time, I had learned that show business was not for me. I was not only seriously ill, but Christ had told me that my role in show business was not, to skate. However, I did go into show business. I did become a professional ice skater. That part of the dream I had as a child came true. There was no question about that fact.

Also, my visions continued while I was on tour with the two shows. I remember, especially, the following incident.

One day as I was walking towards a church in one of the cities where we had a show, I looked up and in the sky next to this beautiful church, I saw a vision of Our Lady of Grace. Surrounding the figure, there were brilliant rays of light; and it seemed to me that each ray was more or less pointed and separate from the others.

When I entered the church, I was amazed. The exact same vision I had seen was a statue of Our Lady of Grace in that church, complete with metal rays of light surrounding the statue.

While I was on tour, I never missed Mass on Sunday or Holy Days; and I also continued to write.

One reason why I no longer wanted a career in show business was the fact that I found backstage not as glamorous as I had imagined. There was constant turmoil among the members of the cast. There were arguments and even acts of jealousy. Not everyone acted like that, but many did. Once someone put cold cream and lipstick marks in a star's skates to show an act of hate. Once one of the girls came to me and told me she thought she was pregnant. I didn't know what to say except: "I will pray for you."

Often the members of the show were so wild that they caused problems at hotels. Once the hotel reservations were cancelled after the management found out who or what was coming to the hotel. Often I would find a different hotel to stay apart from the group.

But the thing I disliked the most about the two shows I had been in was the way I felt completely isolated from the rest of humanity—my suffering humanity.

I felt that a city and all its inhabitants came into existence only for the days our show played in the city. Then after we left, the city and everyone who lived there simply ceased to exist. I did not like that feeling.

Everyone in the show was completely caught up with the show: the music, the different numbers, etc. That was all we talked about. No one mentioned the war or what was happening in the rest of the world. I went to newspaper offices in each city to find out what the news was all about. That was good in one way. I was able to collect our ads which were in the local papers. (I still have them.)

Now to return to my Lady's words to me on May 5, 1944: "There are more souls lost to eternal Hell because they have found what earthly pleasure and gain and fortune can be had from a successful life in show business than by any other ways of sin."

Such words did not refer only to my limited knowledge in 1944, when I thought the term show business meant only Hollywood and its stars. My Lady clearly was looking into the future when, indeed, the whole world of Arts and Entertainment would need missionaries to bring this industry back to God and simple living.

Although there were, no doubt, many stars (not all) in show business in 1944, who did indeed fit my Lady's descriptions of sinners walking the paths to eternal separation from God, Hollywood and its stars were not the whole of show business. Nor was it to stay the most important symbol of glamour drawing attention to that way of life filled with riches and fame.

In 1944, stars of the screen did all in their power to stay out of the scandals and disgraceful situations which could cause public condemnation. They made efforts to place before the adoring public illusions of decent living. The wrong publicity could destroy one's career.

But by the '90s, the public was more forgiving and accepted whatever any star wanted to do with his or her life. And that was where the spiritual danger laid. (There were, however, many stars who lived decent, even holy lives.)

When my Lady mentioned the stars of show business falling into grave sin, she was also thinking of the millions of fans who would not only accept the corrupt ways of some of these celebrities but who would want to and try to follow these unholy examples.

Show business turned not into the Arts and Entertainment profession it was intended to be, but into a way and the means to push upon the public vicious acts of violence and sexual situations which were intended to "teach" the public about the facts of life.

Counting all the millions of people in this profession as well as the millions who are influenced by the ones in show business, you have half the world caught up in this web of temptations which could lead to the tragic loss of souls: temptations and examples which come directly from show business.

You can see what I mean when I list the various forms of show business which developed since 1944 or which continued to exist as the years went by.

First of all, there remained Hollywood and its movies. But the focus of the end results changed from wholesome entertainment, such as the beautiful musicals of the '40s and '50s into movies which were unfit for children and young adults to see.

Added to these disgraceful movies, there emerged television which became a new way to show more violence and sexual situations: this time in the family home. Add to that "entertainment" startling talk shows which presented to the public all sorts of lurid, gruesome stories about people caught up in their own abnormal, dysfunctional fantasies. These became so popular and so many in number that they were presented as the average, "normal" way to live.

Everywhere, all over the world, there was show business in one form or another:

Opera
Broadway
Cruise Ships
Night Clubs
Gambling Casinos
Radio Shows
Movies
T.V.Productions
Ballets
Amateur Shows
Shows on Tour

Shows in Fair Grounds
Ice Skating Shows
Shows in Colleges

In addition, there are hundreds of books, magazines and newspapers all devoted to show business and its stars and the scandals which millions love to read about.

Add to that list the tremendous influence of Rock stars and Rock concerts which attracted hundreds of thousands of fans most of them youngsters. Some of these acts with their horrendous "messages" were nothing more than glorification of sex, drugs, rebellion, murder and even suicide leading countless souls into the devil's play grounds.

Now you can see the millions of people who could walk the paths to everlasting separation from God; who were blindly led to that sad walk by show business and the unholy examples given to the public by notorious stars and money-hungry producers who cared little about the fall out from their actions, words and deeds.

Of course, not all stars, movies or productions are evil examples of sin and corruptions. There still are a few wholesome entertainers and entertainments.

However, all of show business projects a picture of fame, wealth, riches to be found and a life of worldly pleasures. These end results cause millions of people to lose numerous spiritual treasures as they dream about someday finding their own fame and riches.

How can all these millions of people see the emptiness of all that show business stands for? How can they remove the blinders from their eyes, their hearts, their dreams so that they can see the wondrous peace, joy and happiness found in staying close to the Hearts of Jesus and Mary as they daily carry out their duties and obligations? How?

I can teach them. I know. I was in show business. I saw its darkness. I can light a path that leads, not to fame and fortune but to God's own Heaven of love.

Louise as a professional ice skater in a show called "Hollywood Ice Time" October 1945

Louise in full stage make-up in ice show. Picture taken in Dayton, Ohio (Lawrence Hollifield) 1945

6

FATHER F. X. SHEA SECRETARY TO CARDINAL F. SPELLMAN NEW YORK FIRST SPIRITUAL DIRECTOR

When I found my first director, I was living in New York City where I had gone to become a professional ice skater, a career I had chosen in my youth. It was while I lived in New York, in 1944, when the visions started.

I sought some sort of spiritual direction when I realized that what I was experiencing was part of or belonged to my Catholic faith.

Then, after the visions and revelations continued, in 1944, I knew I wanted to talk to a priest about what was happening other than the ones I went to confession to.

When I went looking for a priest I could talk to, I went right to the top. I wanted to see the Cardinal whose residence was in the rectory behind St. Patrick's cathedral. I felt sure that he could help me understand what I was writing in my daily note books.

So, one day, I went to the rectory and shyly rang the bell. The Cardinal, of course, did not answer the door bell and I never met him, but his secretary who had answered the bell led me into a waiting room.

He asked me why I wanted to see the Cardinal, and I told him a little about my religious experiences.

The priest, whose name was Father Shea, was extremely kind to me. He listened carefully. He did not scold me or tell me to stop saying things like that. I think he was impressed with my sincerity and honesty. He agreed to give me spiritual advice and I always regarded him as one of my spiritual directors. I saw him several times before I left New York.

After I left New York, I wrote him many letters. I saw Father Shea or corresponded with him from 1944 to 1946. Later, he left New York, and I wrote letters to Father Shea, but I soon lost track of him.

He, as can be seen from his letters to me, believed in my visions and did all he could to encourage me.

I allowed him to see some of my writings, which impressed him. Needless to say, he was very capable of judging my visions and my work for God being the secretary to Cardinal F. Spellman (who was in New York from 1939). Father Shea being such an important person would never have allowed me to continue to see him and he would never have written me encouraging letters if he thought I was a fraud or I had deceived myself. Of course in 1944, I did not realize what a distinguished priest God had chosen to be my first spiritual director. I just knew that he was my friend who encouraged me and was very kind to me.

When I met Father Shea, the greatest problem I had was whether or not I should continue with my dreams of becoming the second Sonja Henie or to give up everything for God and join a convent.

Because of my love for God, I thought I should give up all my dreams and become a nun. Father Shea did not agree.

After he heard what my problem was, Father Shea wisely said to me: "Continue with your ice skating. If your visions are true, they will continue no matter where you go or what you do. If your visions are not true, the convent will be the worst place for you."

I had already signed a contract to go on tour with a small ice show. After Father Shea told me that, I felt free of the problem and I left with the show in the Spring of 1945.

Before I left New York, I entrusted Father Shea with my most precious possession. That was what I called The Gold Leaf. This was a tiny gold leaf that had fallen upon my coat one day when I prayed in my church in Meriden. I had picked it up and put it in a locket. When I did, it broke in two pieces. I soon noticed that if I did something which pleased God, the two pieces would join. If I did or said something which displeased God, the two pieces would separate.

I gave this locket to Father Shea thinking I might lose it when traveling with the show.

I also left with Father Shea a little book I had written containing my first articles which I called "Hope."

On August 23, 1945, he wrote me a letter (I was home in Meriden at that time), saying: "Your book "Hope" is here. Your chain and all the rest."

Again, I will say that he believed in my visions and encouraged me in them. If he had not, he would have never kept my "treasures." He also answered many of my letters. Nor would he have welcomed my visits after I left New York, but be did.

When I traveled with the show from state to state, and after I returned home in Meriden when this show closed in June 1945, I wrote letters to Father Shea whom I still considered my director.

The first letter I wrote was from a hotel in Akron, Ohio where the show stayed for about two weeks. I explained about the show. Father Shea wrote me a short note saying: "We are praying for you here and wish you well. Everything is fine."

Our Lady's Blessings
F.X.S.

On August 23, 1945, after I had returned to Meriden, I received another letter from Father Shea. (I lost the one I had sent to him.) He assured me that my book "Hope" and my locket was safe in his possession. Then he added; "Come in when you can"; stating "Keep steady and be an obedient child of the Church."

On September 11, 1945, I wrote to Father Shea a long letter giving him more details about my job for God. I wrote: "This is hard for me to write to you for I cannot fully understand what this job may lead to."

I explained how I ". . . must write . . . I have been taught many things by Jesus and Mary and The Holy Ghost and God my Father and even the saints . . . These are lessons."

Then I wrote about the many things I had been told in 1944.

I added: "As long as I have this God-given desire to write what I know deep in my heart all else must be forgotten . . . God calls me His Child of Love and so I can bring love to the world and thus bring the world back to the source of all love: Jesus' Sacred Heart."

I asked Father to send my articles to a catholic paper.

On September 18, 1945, Father wrote to me and gave me the address of a newspaper, saying I was not to connect his name with my articles by trying to get them published. I followed his instructions. They were not published.

On December 13, 1945, I wrote to Father again and said among other things:

"I know that you are my confessor and advisor and I won't want anyone else to be. No matter what happens, I only want you to be my advisor. I will do anything you say in regard to my religion and visions. You told me that you believe me and I never want you to say that you don't believe me anymore. I would cry so much if you did."

On December 15, 1945, Father Shea wrote and told me to contact a Reverend George F. Johnson, S.J. in Jersey City, New Jersey and told me to use his name, Father Shea. I did write to him, but I never received an answer.

I continued to write to Father Shea. I have a letter I wrote dated February 20, 1946. When I wrote that, I was very discouraged because no one would publish my articles.

I wrote: "I guess the world doesn't want my writings now. I feel that none of my articles will be published until after I die."

I also mentioned: "I would like so very much to go into a convent to be a nun; but then I might feel better (my health) and then I would have to go back into a show because Jesus said that I belonged in show business."

On March 25, 1946, I again wrote to Father and spoke about becoming a nun: "Dear Father, the desire to become a nun has taken hold of me so strong that I suffer greatly from the fact that I am not a nun."

Father sent me holy pictures to encourage me. I continued

to write to him and on April 25, 1946, He asked me to visit him in New York.

It was about this time, in May or June of 1946 when Father Shea finally gave in to my desires to become a nun. He began to feel that I might have a vocation because I had willingly given up ice skating. I had been asked to join two shows, but I refused because I wanted to spend all my time writing for God and my Lady.

As a result, Father Shea arranged for me to talk to a nun who was in charge of a convent in New York City. The name of the order or community was Saint Zita. (I think that was the name.)

Father told me how to reach the convent and I shyly rang the bell at the door. I was welcomed into the convent by a nun who said the Mother would see me soon. She suggested that I wait in the chapel. When I walked in, there were a few nuns praying. The silence and the whole atmosphere of holiness overwhelmed me. I felt as if I were in Heaven surrounded by saints; and a strong feeling of unworthiness came over me. I felt like I wanted to kiss each nun's feet. Did I belong with them?

When the Mother came to get me to talk to me, I was utterly confused unable to think that a convent was where I belonged.

Mother was kind to me and gentle, but I could not answer her questions as to why I wanted to join her community. I finally said: "Because Father Shea wanted me to" which, of course, was not the proper answer.

I simply was not able to pour out my heart and soul to her or tell her of my love for God and Our Lady.

Mother finally went to the phone and called Father Shea saying she was sending me back to him. Later; I wrote to this superior and told her that Father Shea and I agreed that I should try to enter an order in Hartford. Mother agreed that was what I should do; however, I could not enter that order because of my poor health. I had health problems all of my life because of a hole in my heart which I was born with. This hole was not discovered until I had open heart surgery in 1993. Up to that time, no doctor could find out what my health problems were. This illness was the main reason I did not become a nun.

I kept up my spiritual relationship with Father Shea until I found my second spiritual director: Monsignor John J. Hayes. Also, Father Shea left New York.

The last letter I received from him was July 25, 1946 when he said I could visit him to get all the books which I had given to him at various times. I wanted them back because I had no copy of them. These included my very first note books. I am thankful I got them back.

Father Shea greeted me warmly and assured me of his prayers and blessings. He still believed in my visions; however, he thought I needed spiritual help closer to home. He was too far away in New York and I could not see him very often.

Our spiritual relationship ended on a warm note and I never forgot his kindness to me and his encouragement when I had just started the job God gave me to do.

Father Shea was my first spiritual director and he believed in my visions. In the years which followed, all my spiritual directors and confessors accepted the visions and my job for God as genuine after talking to me and reading my writings for years.

I needed such encouragement as the years went by because my greatest temptation for years was the way the devil tried to make me give up my job and to believe that the visions were false.

An example of that is what I wrote in a letter to Father Shea dated September 11, 1945: "This is hard for me to write to you for I cannot fully understand what this job may lead to. But if I know that you believe in my work for God, no matter what happens and you stick by me, then I shall be able to continue with the knowledge that if the whole world is against me then you shall not be." Also, December 13, 1945: "You told me that you believe me and I never want you to say that you don't believe me anymore. I would cry so much if you did."

He never stopped believing that my visions were true.

Part 6

The Gifts of The Holy Spirit
Suffering Humanity
and My Writings:
Years 1944-1945

— 1 —

THE GIFTS OF THE HOLY SPIRIT
MY WRITINGS MY WORK FOR GOD
YEARS 1944-1945

My writings were to play a most important part in my job for God and in my Lady's triumph: also in my own personal triumph. One of the most difficult, ongoing battles which I had with the devil was the constant struggle to keep writing daily notes, articles (which were published in national newspapers and magazines), published books and writing numerous lectures (which I gave for over 30 years).

But I would not give up because I knew that my writings would bring comfort to suffering humanity and help raise and rebuild a fallen world. Also, I knew that my writings would show the pathway so that lonely, lost souls will be able to find their way to the Hearts of Jesus and Mary by reminding them of the wondrous teachings of the Church. I knew that the voice of the Church was the voice of Christ.

When a modern world (especially some Catholics) was going "wild" throwing out the moral standards and ethical teachings of society, I wrote to defend such teachings. When Catholics became confused and upset by articles they read or words they heard against the Church, I wrote or gave lectures calming their fears and teaching them the truths taught by their Church.

My writings, as I said, became my triumph as I struggled for over 50 years against weariness, fatigue, serious illnesses (which I had all of my life) working full-time jobs as a working-wife, lack of time, numerous interruptions, etc. any one of which was reason enough to stop my writings and doing my work for God.

But I did not stop and when the bulk of my writings was finished, that became not only my triumph, but my Lady's as well; for I faithfully did what she and Christ told me to do in 1944.

207

What was it that they told me to do and what happened in 1944 which gave me the unshakable impetus to keep writing? Even the devil's traps, tricks and attacks could not stop me from writing.

And I had no intentions of becoming a writer in the first place.

Although when I was in school I found it very easy to compose an essay as a class assignment, I never was drawn to any literary career or vocation. I was not the least bit interested in writing class essays or anything else. My main interest which actually consumed my every waking hour was ice skating.

If I had a talent for writing (which several teachers told me I had) that never impressed me. I was filled with joy not being told I could write essays which were so good I had to read them in front of the class (which I thought was a punishment) but if I had finally made a perfect figure eight on the ice.

The fact is, I may have written well, but I hated spelling. That was perhaps what made me such a poor speller. My Lady mentioned that when she told me I could not spell words that a child could spell: (May 5, 1944) "So, my child, you who are so simple and so stupid that you cannot remember things, that you cannot pronounce certain words, that you cannot spell words that a child could spell . . . have been chosen. . . ."

(Remember that when my Lady used the word stupid, she was using a word which I could easily understand. I was not a well-educated person with any college degree. She had to talk in the way I would best understand, and I knew very well what she meant when she called me stupid. I definitely was not intelligent, the opposite of the word stupid.)

That was more than true. Once, I was on a plane heading towards Lisbon, Portugal. I sat next to a child age about ten. I was showing her a little spelling computer I had with me (which greatly improved my spelling ability). I would think of a word to put into the computer and before it told me I had spelled it wrong, my little friend would tell me the correct spelling much to my embarrassment. I soon stopped playing that game with her.

Yet, in spite of my poor spelling, writing was to become a most important part of my life from 1944 onward. I was to write long and hard and write not only notes, but numerous articles as well as published books. Writing actually became my career instead of ice skating. How did such a thing happen?

It began in 1944 when Our Lord and Our Lady told me what my life would become. They told me exactly what my job for God would be and writing was to become an important part of that job. But how could I write when I had no desires to do so; and what would I write?

The answer came as soon as I started to hear and see Christ and Mary in 1944. At that time, I had no writings.

My writings were to teach God's children what He wanted me to teach them. I was told, as follows:

March 27, 1944: "Mary said that Jesus chose me to do a job of teaching His children things that He wants them to know."

My writings would also include my numerous daily notes:

March 27, 1944: She told me to write down all the things Jesus tells me to write down because they are to be used after my death. She said that I am "to make a light shine on dark paths so that God's children can see the light and find peace and happiness."

She said that I would have all the strength and knowledge and courage that I need to carry on God's will of being a Refuge for Suffering Souls and to set an example that the whole world will follow.

She said that I will have the things I need to teach the world what Jesus wants me to teach them and that I need never fear anything.

She said that I will have the knowledge, strength and courage to meet up with any situation so that I can aid any way possible.

She said that I was part of Jesus' army from Heaven on earth and that I must teach His children what He wants me to teach them.

She said that I must go forth and get others to love them (God The Father, Christ and Mary) because they desire so for the love of their children. She said that all the love of all the children that do love them is very precious but they desire to be loved more.

On March 31, 1944, I wrote:

Mary said: "You must go forth and teach the world the things Jesus wants them to know. You must go out and bring all of God's lost children to Him. We must protect you, Louise, because of the job you must do for God. You will know what that job is. Most of all, you must bring Jesus' and my name into the hearts and homes of people who do not know us, who do not want to know us or who do not know us as we desire to be known.

"Your job is to go forth into the dark hills and gather up all of God's stray, bewildered children and bring them home before they die from hunger.

"Your writings will be left for the world so that others can understand and follow your examples.

"You are part of God's great army. You are on earth and you shall be sent where you are most needed.

"God has chosen you to make known to the dark world many things which would otherwise not be known. You have a great, hard important job to do. You will meet opposition and hate for the devil will be strong. But, slowly and surely you will win because God wants His children back.

"Do not expect to conquer the world. Do not expect to convert millions. But do start the landslide that will make people stand up and take notice. Cause an avalanche of love, happiness and joy and show the world how to find their own happiness, love and joy. Teach a few and a great many will seek you out to find what you have taught others. if you die and have reached only one person (converted), that person and your writings will be enough to start a second crusade and to end up with many people walking the right road to God."

On April 2, 1944, I was told: "Teach the world to carry its crosses as well as my Jesus carried His."

On April 24, 1944, Our Lady said to me: "Teach people that I am stronger than the devil and all the evil spirits and teach them that if they learn to love me and trust me and to have faith and hope in me, then they should fear nothing."

On May 5, 1944, Mary said to me: "Jesus will not give you an assignment unless He makes you capable of handling it. You are wanted only by God to go forth and teach the world the things God wants you to teach them."

November 13, 1945: "But, my little one, write. Write long and hard. Write my love and my Mother's love and give to the world that which I want them to have. Write as only my Child of Love could write. I promise you, little one, that before your death the world will know of you."

I was also told on February 6, 1946: "Pearl-like words will come from your lips." That, without a doubt, referred to the lectures I gave for over thirty years.

On May 17, 1946, Our Lord said to me: "Know, my little one, that for all time your writings will be read as you wrote them. Not one single word will be lost by any force or power. Your writings and my messages will be spread over the whole world. My children shall read not only the messages from Heaven, but the love you wrote in your articles and writings."

On June 4, 1946, I heard these words from my Lord: "If the world comes to your door, do not run and hide, but let them in for you have much to give them."

I wrote these words after hearing that statement: "I don't want people to come, oh! I don't! I want to be alone and unknown. I want to run away. (but) I will face them and give them what Jesus wants me to give them if He wants it that way."

I was also told in 1944, 1945 and 1946 to make myself known to the world and make Jesus and Mary's words known to the world.

SUMMARY

Now to make a summary of what I was told about my writings and how I would not only teach people, but bring them much comfort and love.

One of the first things I was told by Mary in 1944 was that I would teach God's children what He wanted them to know.

Then I was told to write down all the things Jesus (and Mary) tell me to write down.

I was told I would have the knowledge to carry out the will of God.

Again, I was told to teach God's children what He wants me to teach them.

I was to find God's lost children and bring them home. I was to gather up all of God's stray, bewildered children and bring them home.

I was told to teach a few and others would seek me out to find what I had taught the few.

I was told that my writings would be preserved.

I was told that pearl-like words would come from my lips.

I was told that the world will come to my door and I would have a great deal to tell them.

I was told to make myself known and to make the words of Jesus and Mary known.

Finally: my writings (which I did not even have at that time) would be spread and read all over the world.

As the years went by, all these things which had been foretold came true. How did they come true? What events happened which made me the writer and the lecturer God wanted me to become?

As I said, when I was told all these things about my writings, I not only had no writings, but I had no intentions of becoming a writer. How could I teach God's children what He wanted me to teach them?

Not only that, but what was I to teach them? At that time, I knew next to nothing about my Catholic faith, the teachings of the Church, the doctrines or even about the Bible.

How could my writings be read all over the world when I had no writings? I am sure there are millions of would be writers who never get anything published; how could I?

I was told what would happen concerning my writings and lectures at a time when all I wanted to be was an ice skater.

What events happened which made me the writer and the lecturer and the Refuge for Suffering Souls which God wanted me to become?

THE HOLY SPIRIT APPEARS AND GIVES ME KNOWLEDGE AND A GIFT OF WORDS

The first event which happened, concerning my writings and my lectures, was direct action from The Holy Spirit, this Holy Spirit which had entered my life in such a dramatic and mysterious way when I was confirmed as a child on September 26, 1939 at age 15.

In 1944, when I was being told about my life's work, Our Lady said to me on March 27, 1944: She said that the Holy Ghost (Spirit) will come to me and really inflame my heart with the love for Jesus and her and God. And that He will give me the gift of words and the knowledge that I need to do God's will perfectly (also on May 5, 1944).

She said that I would have all the strength and knowledge and courage that I need to carry on God's will of being a Refuge for Suffering Souls and to set an example that the whole world will follow. She said that I will have the things I need to teach the world what Jesus wants me to teach them and that I need fear anything (March 27, 1944).

I, of course, had no idea how or when the Holy Spirit would come to me, but I knew He would come just as Mary said.

After my Lady told me that the Holy Spirit would come to me, I wrote in my notes on March 27, 1944:

"I love you so, Mary. Thank you a million for coming to me and telling me all these things. I can hardly wait, until the Holy Ghost comes to me. I don't know when or where He will come, but Mary said He will and I'll know it very well."

And the Holy Spirit did come to me. As I explained in the autobiography I wrote in 1963, the following happened:

A few days after my Lady told me that, I was kneeling in my little room in New York City, praying. Suddenly, as I prayed, my room filled with a brilliant light and I beheld the Holy

Spirit, in the form of a magnificent white dove coming towards me, which was visible to my naked eyes. However, the vision was not just visible to my eyes. My whole soul and being were affected by the vision. I could actually feel some kind of magnificent power being given to me; one that I could not understand. My whole being rose to Heaven and I felt united to God in a wondrous, unexplainable way.

After that, my heart was on fire with love for God the Father, God the Son, God the Holy Ghost and also for Mary. Not only that, but I had been given the knowledge and the words which I used throughout the years in my spiritual writings.

At that time, 1963, I had very few spiritual writings. These would become part of the writings I was told to create so that I could teach people what God wanted me to teach them; but these writings (letters I wrote) were only the beginning of my writings.

I was told that I would receive the gift of words and knowledge from the Holy Ghost . . . (The Holy Spirit as He is now called).

The gift of words and knowledge from The Holy Ghost! Now as I write these words in 1996, I find that expression most remarkable.

Today, there is the Charismatic Movement within the Catholic Church wherein individuals claim to receive a gift of the Holy Spirit. I, myself was never involved in these prayer groups which developed decades later. There were no common, outward expressions such as the "gifts of the Holy Spirit" in 1944.

The Church has always taught that the Holy Spirit does give gifts to the Church and to individuals. There are many beautiful writings about the gifts of the Holy Spirit such as can be found in the "Catechism of the Catholic Church" (copyrighted in 1994 United States Catholic Conference, Inc.). These words are on page 211-212:

> For where the Church is, there also is God's
> Spirit; where God's Spirit is, there is the Church

and every grace . . . The Holy Spirit is the principle of every vital and truly saving action in
each part of the Body (of Christ) . . . finally,
by the many special graces (called "charisms")
by which He makes the faithful "fit and ready
to undertake various tasks and offices for the
renewal and building up of the Church."

Whether extraordinary or simple and humble,
charisms (or gifts) are graces of the Holy Spirit
which directly or indirectly benefit the Church,
ordered as they are to her building up, to the
good of men and to the needs of the world.

However, I knew nothing about such a teaching in 1944. I
did not even know who the Holy Spirit was other than the
third person of the Blessed Trinity; and I knew less about the
Trinity.

When my Lady told me, in 1944, that I would receive gifts
from the Holy Spirit of words and knowledge about God and
His love, that statement was a direct reference to one of the
basic teachings of our faith; the power of the Holy Spirit to
bestow His gifts upon our Church and individuals.

Needless to say, in 1944, I had no idea that her words to
me referred to that truth.

When the Holy Spirit did give me the gifts of words and
knowledge, my simple uneducated mind was transformed into
one filled with the knowledge of God's love and how to teach
people about that wondrous love.

I am not saying that I was changed into a writer as to how
to write or even how to spell words correctly. That I had to
teach myself. But I was given a knowledge about God, Our
Lady, Christ's teachings, the ways of God and a gift of words
which I could never have learned in any way other than by a
direct action of the Holy Spirit.

When I did study my beloved Catholic faith, reading many
excellent books, I was able to clearly understand all I read.

When I talked to others about our religion, I could remember what I read in a way that would amaze me. I knew many things which were in the Bible even before I read the Bible. I would say: "I know that is in the Bible" and I would search to find what I was looking for. I could explain God, Mary, Christ's ways and the teachings of the Church in a way that not only amazed others, but also amazed me. When people would ask me questions about the faith, I would often say: "Everyone knows the answer," but they did not, I did.

I will say that I, myself, studied my Catholic faith for years. I gathered much information from my confessors and spiritual directors which I used in my books. I even studied English and books about punctuation; however, such lessons learned were only half the reason I could teach others what God wanted me to teach them. There was a much deeper, more profound reason why I was able to do the work or job God and my Lady wanted me to do. The reason was the direct action of the Holy Spirit. To read about the doctrines of our faith is one thing. To be able to understand what one reads and to be able to explain to others what one has read is another thing altogether. That was very easy for me to do.

The first time my second spiritual director, Monsignor John Hayes, (who read my writings for 10 years and approved all I wrote) read my note books and my very first articles, he said: "It seems to me that you understand God's love for His children."

Truly, the Holy Spirit gave me a gift of words and knowledge so that I could do the work God wanted me to do.

MY BOOKS AND ARTICLES

As the years went by, I wrote numerous articles and books, all written to teach people about their beautiful Catholic faith. The very first book I submitted to a publisher—"Our Sunday Visitor"—was accepted and published. It was called "Too Busy For God? Think Again." The second book I wrote was also published by "Our Sunday Visitor." That was called: "Come

Home The Door Is Open." I later bought back my rights to these two books.

My articles appeared in national publications such as "The Marian Helpers Bulletin," "Our Sunday Visitor" and "The Catholic Transcript."

For a while I even had my own little newspaper filled with my articles.

Then I wrote my book against cults: "The Catholic Answer To The Jehovah's Witnesses." This book became a best-seller and was read all over the world. I wrote two published books about the spiritual life: "Come Climb The Ladder And Rejoice" Volume I and Volume II, the prayer life.

I also have several unpublished books all written to teach people what God said I would teach them.

THE MARYHEART CRUSADERS

In 1964, I started a Catholic lay organization (approved by our Archbishop) called The Maryheart Crusaders. This was a direct fulfillment of what had also been told to me in 1944. For one thing, I called this organization A Refuge For Suffering Souls, not thinking that I had been given such a name. I also founded the organization to bring back to the Church fallen-away Catholics.

Thousands of people came to me by and through the work I did for The Crusaders to seek knowledge about their faith or to be consoled and to learn how to carry their daily crosses.

I organized meetings in different cities and states and gave lectures to teach the beautiful truths about our faith. I was told that pearl-like words came from my lips.

The words I spoke, I was told, profoundly affected and touched the hearts and souls of all who heard me speak. Then I would wonder what I said that caused such a reaction.

My words would bring tears to the eyes of the people who came to my lectures, and I would whisper to a friend of mine: "What did I say?"

When I finished speaking at one of my first lectures, no one applauded. I had expected, maybe a little reaction from my audience. I became very nervous thinking I had said something wrong. When I asked a friend of mine, who sat with the others in attendance, what I had said wrong, she replied: "Wrong! Nothing you said was wrong. The talk was so beautiful, we could not move when it was over. We never heard anyone talk like that before."

I will add that my writings and lectures were not about my visions Maybe I could have attracted a world-wide audience if I had talked and written about my visions and my Lady's shrine. But I chose not to do that in obedience to my bishop. I had told him that I would not promote the visions and I did not.

After I made my Lady known in 1960, hundreds of people began to come to see me or to write, not asking about the visions, but to tell me their problems or to ask questions about our faith. I wrote hundreds of spiritual letters of comfort, encouragement or sympathy. I wrote about God and Our Lady's love. I wrote letters explaining the teachings and doctrines of our faith (these letters became the foundation for my future books).

I helped hundreds of people who came to see me, not talking about visions, but who needed my comfort and spiritual knowledge in order to face the numerous problems of daily living.

I was called to be a Refuge for Suffering Souls, and that I did become.

I was also called A Mighty Warrior of Truth and Righteousness. That also became part of my job for God as I wrote and spoke against cults and as I straightened out confusion and wrong ideas among the laity.

Although some people who came to my meetings to hear my lectures or who read my books knew about my Lady and her shrine, most who heard me speak or who read my books never knew that I saw visions.

I would often say that I was so glad that I became a writer with published books and articles (many in national publications) before people knew I saw visions. That shows I became such a writer on my own without mentioning visions and I had talent as a writer.

I was thrilled when one day a woman, who knew about the visions, said to me: "We come to learn about our faith not to hear about visions."

Yes, all that I was told about my writings and teaching people what God wanted me to teach them, all that I recorded so long ago in 1944 came true.

My early notes and writings were preserved as I had been told they would be, in spite of the many moves in my life. I use them now as reference.

My books as I said, are read all over the world in places like Japan, China, England, Africa, Malta, Australia, etc.

It was not easy to do all this writing and to give so many lectures, but I would not give up because I so loved my world and souls; and I so loved my Lord. I did it all for Him and my Lady asking nothing in return, not even any fees or royalties.

I did all because this was God's holy will for me; and that became my triumph and my Lady's triumph because it was a victory of grace.

What ever I accomplished, as I carried out God's holy will for me was done using grace. The power of that grace enabled me to continue upon that most difficult path. My writings and work I did for God, my Lady and the Church reveal not only the gifts I received from the Holy Spirit, but the power of grace when grace is accepted and used: the power obtained and preserved through prayer and the sacraments, the power to bring forth wondrous deeds for God and to raise a fallen world. The power to touch hearts and souls with the kiss of God's pure love. All that comes from grace.

On December 10, 1986 I wrote the following prayer:

> Dearest God, my most beloved Trinity, surround
> me at all times, with your presence, your grace,
> your love. I cannot exist outside of your pres-
> ence, your grace, your love. Where ever I go,

let me bring your love, your ways, your total presence. Let me walk among all the darkness and sorrows of life and become a ray of pure light shining forth for all to see. Let people say: "Wherever Louise is, there is God, His ways and His love." Let people see you in me for I wish at all times to reach out and touch souls with your light, your grace and your love. Amen

My Lady could say "My triumph is yours and your triumph is mine" (September 7, 1982) because by doing all that God wanted me to do, she could show the world the power of grace and the way grace can defeat all the forces of the devil and his demons as they tried, with all their power, to stop me from doing the work God had chosen for me to do.

One of the greatest signs which prove that my work or job for God came from Him and my Lady is the sign of the power of grace: this grace which is far more powerful than the combined power of Satan and all his evil spirits.

On April 24, 1944 Mary said to me: "Teach people that I am stronger than the devil and all his evil spirits."

She also said, on April 9, 1944 that my life is an example for the world to follow. That is the things I go through, the torments of my mind, the fights with the devil and myself and the final outcome of great undying love.

My writings and all my work, which I so lovingly did for God, my Church and souls, prove that grace, Mary and God's grace, is indeed more powerful than all the combined power of Satan and his evil forces.

That is, as I said, my triumph and Mary's.

— 2 —

SUFFERING HUMANITY
MY FIRST ARTICLES AND POEMS

In addition to what I had been told about my writings in 1944, Our Lord also told me that He shall place the weight of the sufferings of humanity upon my shoulders and I would be made to bear that weight. He also told me to raise a fallen world with love.

Ever since then, I have considered the world "my world" and suffering humanity "my poor suffering humanity"; and I was filled with desires to do all I could to make the world a better place to live in.

When false visionaries and their followers loudly shouted that the world had to be destroyed because of all the "sin and corruption," I wanted to try and do something to ease the pain of people caught up in situations they did not create which caused them so much misery and anguish. When people would tell me how evil "everyone" was and they should be punished, I would answer: "But there are millions of decent, good folks all over the world doing their best to work and raise families in spite of the problems they face."

I had tremendous compassion for suffering humanity. That was one reason why I accepted The Devil's Challenge (as explained in another part of this book). This compassion and love for suffering humanity never left me.

Throughout the years, I suffered along with suffering humanity as wars and natural disasters caused much heartache, tears and pain. I did not want to run away from such human misery. When I read a story of a saint who had hidden herself or himself in a convent or monastery because they did not want to be tainted by the corruption of the world. I would sadly say to myself: "But what about all the poor, suffering people in the world who need so much compassion and love?"

221

On July 20, 1952, I drew a picture of a tree with its branches protecting the world, and a snake (the devil) entwined in its roots.

I wrote underneath that picture: I am a tree that spreads its protecting mantle of love over my world. It need never fear the devil for he is trapped beneath the roots of this tree.

I wrote on February 1, 1958: I am living in a most frightening age. Indeed, it is the age of fear. Yet, it is also a wondrous age of doing unheard of things with a promise of more fantastic dreams that will come true.

It is a most restless age filled with millions of restless human beings. It is a fast and furious age with a race between nations; a race that could offer peace or war as its goal.

Such an age has a great affect upon the people of all nations. Mothers and fathers are afraid of the future world that will be given over to their children.

But the most tragic outcome or effect of this age is the sin and corruption it daily brings to restless people who have no faith to use to calm their fears.

Now more than ever God is needed in this world. We are growing more powerful every day, but more than ever, we need the guiding hand of God to lead us through this tremendous materialistic world of materialistic demands and ambitions that surrounds us, in a most crushing way, to our eternal salvation.

Too many are being lead astray by false notions that come from others that tell a person and a soul to fight only for a worldly place in a worldly society filled with material possessions that one feels one cannot live without.

The fear that most people have in this fear-filled world is nothing more than the dreaded thoughts of losing material possessions.

If people could learn to live for their God and their souls, much of the fear would vanish. For truly, the only really great loss is a soul that will not be with God for all eternity.

On May 16, 1958, I wrote: I feel so happy knowing that I have saved my world. Yet, I must still remain silent and live only a plain, ordinary life. That is good.

But sometimes it is hard to see so much suffering, unrest and sin in this fallen world. Things seem to get worse. Every day a new kind of war seems to break out somewhere in the world. And there are so many public appeals for food and such for millions of homeless people all over the world. I wish that I could be like Joan of Arc leading an army against all the evils of our modern times. I wish that I could feed all who are hungry, clothe all who are so cold and help the millions who know only war, hunger, disease and suffering.

But I cannot make such dreams come true. I can only live a silent, hidden life.

On October 15, 1958, I wrote:

I pray so very often for my world. I ask God, especially, to put His mantle around my country and protect it from invasion. (At that time Russia was a threat to my country.)

On November 27, 1958, I wrote:

I want to help people through a book and someday I will succeed. I know one thing for sure—I know that my fullest and deepest happiness will come to me only when I have helped others—a great many others. For I see before me a world filled with lonely, unhappy, unloved people who are crying. It is my desire to dry their tears and to bring sunshine into their lives.

I guess that I am still growing up. I have so many things to learn. After I learn them—then I can give help and happiness to others as God so wills.

I keep thinking about something that Jesus told me years ago when I think about this book. He said on November 13, 1945:

"Write long and hard. Write my love and my Mother's love and give to the world that which I want them to have. Write as only my Child of Love can write.

Every night I pray for this poor, sick world, especially for my country. I ask Jesus to spread His mantle of love around my world.

I continued to carry the sufferings of humanity upon my shoulders as the years went by. I longed to give this suffering humanity words of hope and encouragement and love. I knew

I had such words in my visions; however, I had placed these words and the shrine my Lady wanted into the hands of my spiritual director, Monsignor Hayes, and I would not act unless he told me to.

On January 20, 1959, I wrote:

I have a great desire to help people in a great way. When I read about people being enslaved all over the world, I want to free them and make them happy. It bothers me so to know that all these people, thousands of them, are unhappy and crying. I want to go to them and tell them to be happy and at peace.

Again on May 7, 1959:

I always think about my world and my job for God and how my love can cover this earth like a warm, soothing blanket. I see the way things are and I long to give everyone hope, courage, love and peace.

On October 22, 1981, I wrote:

In 1944, I was told by Our Lord: "I shall place the weight of the sufferings of humanity upon your shoulders and you will be made to bear that weight."

As the sufferings of humanity increased, so did that weight upon my shoulders.

My job for God involved much more than seeing visions, because I also saw my world, its ills, its faults, its needs and all its desires.

One has to see and fully understand the world from 1944 to see and fully understand my job for God and my Lady's triumph.

On July 10, 1984, I wrote an article called "The World I Live In." At the end of this article, I wrote:

I carried the weight of the sufferings of humanity upon my shoulders, as I was told I would. Then there was The Devil's Challenge, and I won (with my Lady and grace). This was the age that truly needed The Devil's Challenge and I was asked to do that.

So, what so ever has happened in my world (which I saved by and through The Devil's Challenge from falling into the evil traps set by Satan), was not unknown to me as I lived through all its joys, fears, sorrows, pains and changes.

In 1990, I wrote an article about another need of my poor, suffering world, other than food, shelter and clothing. I wrote:

Still, where I am, I find a tremendous need among the people of my social group and even among the wealthy people who have far more material things than I would ever have or want. I find also that there is a neglect of the spiritual needs of the people who are not in want, needing food, clothing or shelter.

Daily, I come in contact with or hear about people who are well taken care of on the "outside" but who are spiritually poor and crying within. They are all around me, thousands, millions of them who have comfortable lives, but who desperately need spiritual food for their souls. They are spiritually hungry, homeless, in need of something which no social agency, food kitchen or shelter could give them. They are lost, even though they have a comfortable life style. They are ever searching to find something and they don't even know what that something is that they are searching to find. They cannot carry daily crosses. They may even go to Mass faithfully, but they still have not found what they are searching to find. They hunger for God, but they don't understand such a hunger or even if they knew what they want, they are at a loss to know how to find it.

When I look into their souls, I see hungry souls, empty souls, souls in need of comfort, knowledge, grace, holiness. These I so long to help, these *I can help*.

Yes, I can help with my writings, giving them the spiritual help which they are so in need of.

On December 30, 1990, as I was thinking about all the Problems which we have to face in running The Maryheart Crusaders' store and center, where we have daily Mass, Our Lord suddenly appeared to me and sweetly said: "But your world is not just your center where you work so hard to save souls. Look outward at your world, now dark and crying, yet, it does not know what it cries for. It is crying for your love, your words, your light, which shall light up the dark paths and with your light to guide them, my children shall find me and my saving grace and love." I was deeply touched by my Lord's words to me. On January 1, 1992, I wrote:

I carry on my daily life as God's holy will for me, but that does not mean that I am not interested in humanity or my poor, fallen world and all its problems because my whole job for God revolves around them and my Lady's triumph.

On November 4, 1986, I wrote a prayer in my daily prayer book, which I constantly say for poor, suffering humanity:

> Dearest God! Accept my prayer of love, accept my heart of love for my heart is your Heart. Let me walk through this darkness called life and hold high a lantern of light for all to see. Let me wander among the lost, the lonely, the sad, the poor and show them that the light of your love, which I carry, can lead them into a joy, happiness and peace which they never knew existed. I will walk among the darkness and find the ones who need me and your Heart of Love. Then they can rejoice and praise the God who never stopped wanting and loving them.

Throughout my entire life, since 1944, I had a great compassion for the millions who lost homes, friends and families because of wars or disasters. I wanted to hug each and every one of these poor, unfortunate people and allow them to cry in my arms.

Often at night when I could not sleep, I would lie awake and say: "I have such compassion for the ones who at this very hour are carrying tremendous crosses."

I longed to help ease the pain of my poor suffering world, but like Saint Peter who came upon the crippled man at the gate of the temple, I had "neither silver nor gold" (Acts 3:3-6) to help ease the sorrows of "my crippled world."

But I did have something which I could give. That was my writings and my love.

With my writings, I could give to the world words of hope, encouragement and love.

I did not have to wait to see and be part of suffering humanity when my work for God and Mary began in 1944. I was already part of that suffering humanity. The war called World War II had torn apart my family as well as the families of millions of people all over the world.

I remember, so well, my mother and I crying, clinging to each other at the railroad station as we said good-bye to my brother as he left to go to the war.

MY FIRST ARTICLES FOR SUFFERING HUMANITY

As soon as I was inspired by the Holy Spirit to write, and with His gifts which He bestowed upon me of words and the knowledge needed for my writings and work for God and my Church, I began to write without stopping. I, desperately, wanted to help my poor suffering world and to bring comfort and God's love to lost, bewildered souls.

My first thoughts, after the Holy Spirit appeared to me, were to use my writings to help suffering humanity.

I was not a very good writer, but what I wrote was truly inspired by the Holy Spirit. Remember, up to that time, when the Holy Spirit appeared to me, my one interest in life had been ice skating. Surely, there was nothing in the books I read about ice skating which gave me the knowledge I had after the Holy Spirit appeared to me.

The very first article I wrote after the Holy Spirit appeared to me, I recorded in my 1944 notes. Part of it reads:

You don't need anything—nothing at all—than the love of God and Mary and Jesus and the Holy Spirit and the knowledge that you are doing God's will to find all the peace, joy and happiness that you would ever need in your life.

I knew that is all I have and I have perfect, peace, joy and happiness. And, you too, can have it if you put down all earthly pleasures, as I have, and look up into Heaven and ask God to send you the grace that you need to love Him more and to have the courage to lay aside all for the love of God.

I also began, much to my own amazement, to write poems. I wrote them very fast, one after the other. I never knew that I was a poet until I began this series of poems.

And the very first poem I wrote after the Holy Spirit appeared to me reflects my deep love for poor, suffering souls and how I wanted to give them hope, encouragement and love. This poem also reveals the gifts I had been given by the Holy Spirit because I was only 20 years old when I wrote it.

GOD'S GIFT OF TEARS

What is a tear that is silvery white,
And falls from pain filled eyes?
What is a heart that has died yet lives,
Or a soul that mournfully cries?

What is to be found in the ways of one,
Who walked the thorn filled road,
What is to be seen in future dreams,
When they all have been lost or sold?

What has become of the hope of the day,
Or the trust you need in the night?
What has become of the love in your heart?
And the peace that made life seem right?

When does the lonely road end at last,
So that you can rest a while?
When shall you see new joy for yourself,
And upon your lips a smile?

When can you kneel and pray once more,
With sincerity and true love?
When can you make yourself believe,
God answers your prayers from above?

When can you greet the very next hour,
With a cheery, sunny song?
When will this endless sorrow depart,
And your bitter heart cease to long?

As one voice crying in an empty space,
And the echoes rebound and rebound,
Then up from the place God calls His earth,
Comes the wailing, sobbing sound.

His ears aren't deaf to the questions you ask,
He knows of your heartbreak and care,
He knows of your deep, desolate pain,
Of your crushing, sad despair.

He knows of your tears for each one He does count,
He knows of the thorns in your way,
He knows you can't find the trust in the night,
Or the hope you need in the day.

He knows that your dreams will never come true,
Not the dreams that weren't to be.
He knows of your soul that mournfully cries,
Of your unanswered kneeling plea.

He knows of the peace you lost on the road,
That was lonely and so very long.
He knows that the next hour that will come,
Won't hear your cheery song.

Yes, my dear child, God knows all things,
That enter into your life.
Yet why you ask, does He will it so
That your days are filled with strife?

I can't really explain the ways of God,
They are strange a puzzle to me,

I don't know why God in all His great love,
Allows such sad things to be.

But think of the flowers that need the rain,
Or else they would wither and die.
And sorrows as rain are needed in life,
It's a gift from God on high.

Think of it this way, that God bestows,
A blessing with each cross you bear.
And then adds them up as merits so great,,
For a high place in Heaven you'll share.

Each silvery tear that falls from your eye,
When pain and sorrow you feel,
Becomes a bright jewel, an offering to God,
Which no one on earth can steal.

A heart that has died remains in its place,
And becomes the base of the cross.
The one on which Our Lord suffered and died,
Such a heart cannot be a loss.

God hears a soul that mournfully cries,
And sees it helpless and wild,
If you will believe, you'll hear His soft voice,
As He holds to His Heart this child.

The ways of someone who walked the long road,
Where at each step was placed a thorn,
Can change to be near the Consoler of all,
And a son of God is thus born.

For each dream that was lost as the will of God,
In its place there will be found,
One dream of great joy that God gives to all,
The gentlest, loving sound.

The sound of the glory that God has above,
Like the flip of His angels' wings.
Or the stories of bliss and the happiness there,
In paradise where each saint sings.

The hope of the day and the trust of the night
Is hidden deep down in your heart.
Then smile at the world and be thankful and glad,
From this source of strength you didn't part.

This love that you had, God took for a time,
But He's ready to give it all back.
And right by yours, is the sweet love of His,
That brings you the peace you did lack.

When you find the things God planned for you,
You'll be able to kneel and to pray.
Your sorrow will depart, your heart cease to long
And the greatest of joy come your way.

For the children of God that He loves the best,
Receive the greatest grace,
That He lovingly hides from the rest of the world,
By the tears that fall down your face.

So cherish each cross, hold it to your heart,
And soon your long road will end.
And in Heaven is your throne of purest gold,
You won by the tears He did send.

After I wrote that first poem, I continued, without stopping, to write others, as follows:

ALWAYS A TOMORROW

Today the sky is very gray,
But tomorrow is another day.

This day's toil will soon end,
And a tomorrow God will send.

All things of deep dark despair,
Will vanish in the morning air.
A rose will surely take the place,
Of a thorn's sharp, ugly face.

A wondrous part of our life,
With all its trouble and strife,
Is that the dawn ever bright,
Always follows a dark night.

At that time (1944) all in all, I wrote over 20 poems; and in addition, I wrote short articles.

I wanted to teach God's children what He wanted me to teach them. I wanted to bring back lost souls to the safe harbor of the sacraments and God's Heart of love. However, in my simplicity, and I will add my ignorance, I thought that when the war ended, there would automatically be peace, joy and happiness for suffering mankind and there would be no need for my writings. So, I thought that the world had to have my writings before the war ended or else my writings would be useless after the war ended.

As a result of such thinking, I not only began to write article after article, but when they were finished I sent them to magazines and newspapers so they could be published before the war ended.

Also, in my simplicity and ignorance, I thought that if I told the world about the beautiful words of Jesus and Mary, they would find much comfort, encouragement, hope and joy. So, the very first article I wrote included such words. I called it: "My Lady's Voice."

I included in this article, a message from Mary which I had not recorded in my note books.

MY LADY'S VOICE

Ave Maria my heart sings with love. What a beautiful song that is! and how pleased Jesus is when He hears His children sing this song to His dear Mother.

My children of God, gather around me and I shall tell you about your heavenly Mother and how she loves you and wants you to love her.

How well I know what Our Lady desires for you, to whom she sends her messages. She asks me to talk to you and to give you these messages that she sends through her humble servant. If you could only hear her voice, how your heart would sing, and how you would forget all else except the sweet music of her tender words.

My Lady speaks to me and her messages to you are filled with joy and bliss, the joy and bliss that she so gladly gives to those who love her.

It is so wonderful to be able to tell you what Mary wants and how grand it is that I am chosen to do this great job for Mary and God. Listen when my Lady says: "As I am the light of my Son's Heart, so also I am the light that is given to you to see your way over the dark paths that the devil puts in your way. There is no corner of the earth dark enough to prevent my light from showing and guiding my poor, lost children who call on me to guide them.

"Today you see the shadows fall. Tomorrow you walk in the pure sunlight, if you walk with love for me in your hearts, and if you whisper my name. For all who whisper my name are heard by my Son, who gives me the power to aid all who call out in the blinding darkness. Then the blindness is lifted, for your hearts will be lifted and light shall be put into your hearts and in turn it will radiate forth and form the light to guide you.

"Stay in the light. The beam is very small and narrow, but bright. All around you, there are pitfalls and evils that lurk in the darkness to grab straying souls."

I wrote in 1963 when I recorded that message in my autobiography:

Such words remind one of these words of Christ in the Bible. But in 1944, I did not know anything about the words of Christ in the Bible for I had not read the Bible at that time.

"Enter by the narrow gate; for wide is the gate and broad is the way that leads to destruction" (Matt. 7:13).

To continue with Mary's words:

"Keep within your hearts the Light that is yours to have and let it light up your life and your death."

Dear children of God, I can give you that light, so that you can see it and follow it to Jesus and Mary. I can bring to you that light of Mary's and I can show you how to follow it so that you will not fall into the pits that are on all sides of you and have been put there by the devil. I can do this because Mary has shown this light to me and the way to show it to you.

I wrote that article 16 years before my Golden Lady of Happiness appeared to me in 1960 and said:

"The rays from my golden gown will encircle this world and mankind will find within these rays, the peace, joy and happiness that it longs for. Every dark corner of this world shall see my splendor. I am the Golden Lady of Peace and Light."

As I wrote articles and poems which I thought could help suffering humanity, these sufferings did, as I had been told, become a burden upon my shoulders; and I longed for the war to end. I would walk the streets of New York and say to myself: "My poor, suffering world. If only I could help you now. But wait a little longer and soon I can make known the messages of Jesus and Mary. Then you will find your peace and joy."

MY CHOIR OF LOVE

I began, in 1944, and continued into 1945, to write a series of articles which I called "My Choir of Love."

I was most anxious to have these articles published before the war ended.

As soon as I could, I sent these articles to newspapers and magazines thinking that they had to be published at once because after the war ended, they would be useless. I included in the 10 articles the first one I wrote called: "My Lady's Voice." Needless to say, no one would publish the articles which caused me much grief. I felt I had failed God and my Lady.

The war ended in Europe on May 7, 1945 and in the Pacific on August 14, 1945. My writings, wherein Jesus and Mary spoke about bringing peace, joy and happiness to suffering mankind, had not been published. That was *not* because I did not try to get them published before and even after the war ended. Now, of course, I know why such articles could not be published. They did mention the visions and also the messages I received from Jesus and Mary. Editors of Catholic newspapers and magazines were not the least bit interested in someone's private revelations. But there were other reasons why such articles could not be published at that time. The reason was that my job for God had just begun, even though I thought it ended when the war ended.

I have in my possession some of the rejection letters I got when the editors returned the articles. Even after I poured out my heart and my love for suffering humanity in my letters to the editors, I received such answers as:

"Sorry, I cannot use the enclosed manuscript," Or: "I regret The Catholic News is not in a position to use the articles you were good enough to allow us to see." Or: "We do not find it (the manuscript) available for publication in The Messenger of The Sacred Heart."

Following are samples of the articles I wrote in "My Choir of Love":

THE THORNY PATH

At times it seems like it is much easier to continue to the end of some deed that is of sin rather than of good that will increase your holiness. That is because the devil is so strong and he puts in your pathway aids to his sin. The closer you attempt to get to God's love, the harder the climb is because the more barriers the devil puts in your way.

The way to perfection is not over a rose-covered path. Yes, the rose bushes are there, but the flowers have been gathered and the thorns are left for your bare feet to trod. Such is the way of the saints.

You will see, as you walk onward, many roads that lead off the narrow thorn-covered road that you walk on. These roads are filled with soft grass and you are tempted to turn your footsteps to follow them.

Ah! but beware for these roads were built by the devil and lead to his Hell.

No! you must not leave your road. You must go on and on, even if you fall to your knees and must crawl. But alas! few saints there are, for the price is high. So many turn off because they see only thorns ahead on their road.

The beginning is easy for you have strength and courage. You have not been tested. You think yourself brave and you go forward and say, "I can do it." Ah, but how soon you fail when God tests you. You failed, dear ones, because you did not say, "I can't do anything alone, dear Lord, You must help me."

SELF-LOVE

Don't you love to please the ones you love? Don't you want to do just what they want to do? You must feel that way if you really love them instead of yourself.

To love yourself is to always do things that please you and to have others do things that please only you. To love others, you give all for them and care not how much you suffer as long as they are happy and pleased. Now, to really love God is to do all for Him. Suffering is a marvelous test that God gives you and it proves if you love Him and His will or just yourself and how you feel.

Oh! to please God! What joy is there to please Him. It is the joy of real love for Him and His children. Would you pressent a child in front of God and hear His praises for this child. Would you desire to have God also praise you and place you by the child or maybe in front of that child? Please don't do that. Please bring the child to God and then run away. Because you brought this child to God, you have made Him happy in return. He might even make you suffer. But don't mind because each cross may be your only reward and praise. But you will be very glad that your God is happy and even if He seems to ignore you. you shouldn't mind because as long as He is happy then, that is all that matters. Then, indeed will you lose all self love for the total wondrous love of God alone.

A CHILD'S PLAYGROUND

I want to talk to you for a little while. I am your friend and you know what? I am going to make you smile. Oh! yes, you are because you will just have to smile when I talk to you because I don't like to see tears in your eyes. You are going to smile and sing. I am going to teach you the song. It is a child's song but even if you are 100 years old, you will smile when you sing it.

If you can't talk, you can sing and if you can't hear, you'll hear this song and if you can't walk, you'll be able to dance to this song. And if you can't see, well, my goodness, you can look all around and what fun you will have, when you try and figure out noises and objects. It is such a delightful game that you'll enjoy it as children enjoy their games.

So, you know how you can dance if you can't walk? Well, you can dance with your fingers. They can go all different ways and always with the music. Music is so wonderful. It is such a grand game. Life is such a wonderful game. We can all play at it.

And tears! well, they are just the showers that give life to the beautiful roses. But they can't always have showers. They must have sunshine to smile at you so you must smile at them and bring them the sunshine that they need.

You know if you can't talk, you can sing way down in your

ear and no one will laugh when you go off key. You think no one is listening? My goodness, you are wrong. Why God, Himself, is listening and His angels and saints, but they won't laugh when you go off key because they are too pleased with your song.

And you who can't hear, now don't you think that there is just silence around you. Why, you can hear things that others could never hear. You can hear the sound of the angel's wings. You can hear the songs they play on their harps. You will be able to hear my song in the words I write. You can hear so many wonderful things. And you can look like a child who just did a trick and is hiding it because you can hear what others can't.

You who are deaf and blind will be able to see and hear hundreds of things that others can't see and hear because you will learn my little song. It is not a great secret. It is only love.

For love is the song I am teaching you and with love you can do anything. Funny though, you'll find that when you have this love of God, you just don't want anything else and you won't care how you feel or if you can't walk or talk or see or hear, as long as you have love, you have everything. No matter what your cross is, you can have love and when you have it, you'll see how unimportant other things are because you'll have the greatest treasure in the world.

Now I see you smile. Oh! yes, I do. You can't hide it from me. You are smiling because you are playing my game now. We make such wonderful playmates. we can laugh so much. Laugh like little children at play.

I wrote the following poem to go with this article:

PLAYMATES

Let's be playmates you and I,
I'll make you laugh instead of cry,
I'll chase all your blues away,
I'll make you smile all the day.

I'll bring to you my favorite toys,
That will bring you added joys.
I'll let you play with what I own,
Soon all your cares will be gone.
The world is our huge playground,
With toys for children all around
And under Mother's watchful eye,
We'll play till the sun leaves the sky,
We'll find the many treasures rare,
That God made will loving care.
We'll dance and sing and play so gay,
Dark clouds and shadows will fade away,
Playmates of God's love we will be,
Please, come, dear ones and play with me.

THE LAST RAYS OF A GOLDEN SUNSET

How many of you fear death? Gather around me, dear ones, and I will teach you love instead of fear. Here is a wonderful way to describe death: the last rays of a golden sunset fade from the evening sky. The trees bend forth in weariness. All is peaceful and calm. Such a beautiful picture that is. Dear ones, that is a picture of love; a picture of God's love for you and your love for Him. His love enables you to rest after your hard day. Your love for God enables you to be peaceful and calm.

Yes, dear children, love can do wondrous things for with God's love all ways are opened to those who seek to gather up graces and virtues. Such is a wonderful grace, to be able to close your eyes on this day and open them again in the eternal day without fear or distress or worry.

But you must build up for that moment of eternal bliss. You must gather up your graces and love them and hold them close so that you can smile on your deathbed and die as saints do, with love.

Once I heard a priest talk about Holy Communion. He said that the altar rail was not a separation between you and the

Blessed Sacrament. It was the table at which you received the divine food. It was the gateway to divine grace. It was there in church so that you can go to Jesus and Jesus can come to you. It was not there to keep Jesus away from you.

Little ones, fear not death for it is the gateway to eternal bliss. It is that divine moment when Jesus can gather His little child and hold her close with love.

I think that in Heaven one considers death the happiest moment they knew. For the happiness at the first sight of Heaven will never be surpassed. In that second, such joy and bliss will fill your soul and throughout eternity, you will treasure that moment and find added bliss when you think of it.

Death is when your Jesus comes to you and you go to Him. Death is hardly the separation, it is the uniting. Even if from your dear ones you separate, you will become closely united to them because you will be better able to help them than you ever were before.

Now, dear ones, why do you fear? Would you fear to run into the arms of your mother and father with love? Then, you should rejoice for through death, you can run into the arms of your Father and He will hold you close forever.

I am always amazed when I reread my earliest writings to find in them the spiritual insights which I had in my articles. I would write the same things today (after 50 years). such insights have to be attributed to the direct action of the Holy Spirit.

Although I was disappointed because my articles had not been published before the war ended, I continued to write, as I had been told to do.

Although the spiritual insights which I wrote in my articles were a proof of the Holy Spirit's direct action upon me and my work for God, I was definitely not a polished writer. I had yet years of writing experience to go through. I also had to teach myself sentence structure and a great deal of English grammar before I could write my published books. I will say that my poor spelling never improved. Today, I am helped in that department with a little spelling computer.

In May of 1946, I gave a nun, whom I knew, some of my writings to read. She did not encourage me. She told me my writings were very poor (she being a teacher) and that I should study English and I should read the classics of well-known writers before I attempted to write. She also told me to learn how to spell correctly. She said that if I wanted to write for God, He expects me to be perfect.

I thought sure that this nun whom, I had greatly admired, would understand what this "child" was trying to tell the world about God and Mary's love for their children. Instead, she read my writings, as a teacher would, searching only for mistakes— which were easy to find. I was completely discouraged. I did not even know what these classics were which she told me I had to read.

I was crying when I told my Lord how sorry I was because I was such a poor writer.

I wrote in my notes (May 23, 1946):

No one else could write so bad or so poorly about Our Lord because no one could be as stupid as I am. Mary called me stupid and I don't mind. I want to be just a little child. I am sorry if you don't like my writings, but please love the messages from Jesus and Mary, not about me, but others. They are beautiful.

Suddenly, as I was writing such words, and crying, my dear Lord said so sweetly: "Dear little one, know my child that I say to the world, if I wanted you to write great words would not I have given you the power and ability to write them? No, my little one, I wanted a child to write so I made you write, my little Child of Love. For I want a child to teach the wise and to bring to the intelligent the knowledge they lack.

"I want a child to teach them because indeed I say to all unless you become as little children, you cannot enter the kingdom of Heaven.

"And your words will live for the words of the brilliant contain not what your words do and they shall die. And where do you find such pure, holy love as you do on the innocent face of a child? And where are truer words spoken than those that come from the stainless heart of a child? Such a child cannot lie for the grace I give prevents lying.

"It is the child's way of trust, faith, hope and love that I bring to my children through your pen."

I am a tree that spreads its protecting mantle of Love over my world! It need never fear the devil for he is trapped beneath the roots of this tree.

Z. W.
July 20, 1952

This is a picture I drew on July 20, 1952 to show the way I would protect the world "my world" from the devil.

Part 7

The Devil's Challenge:
The Pathway To
My Lady's Triumph
April 5, 1946

INTRODUCTION

On January 20, 1990, as I prayed to God the Father, He suddenly appeared to me and sweetly said: ". . . you are the one who accepted and then won The Devil's Challenge; and by doing so, you pathed the way and opened the path for the triumph of Mary, the Mother of My Son."

What was this challenge which God the Father mentioned? And how was it connected with my Lady's triumph? That will be explained in the following chapters in this book.

The words I have quoted in these chapters about The Devil's Challenge have been in my private note books since I wrote them on the dates mentioned (most over 50 years ago). To me, they were the most precious of all my secret notes. The challenge and the praises, which I heard about myself from the lips of Christ, Mary and God The Father were so unusual (I never read such things in the lives of the saints) that I carefully hid such from people including my own mother and brother. Then I knew I had to allow my spiritual director, Monsignor Hayes, to read them. I would not allow that until almost one year after I let him read my other notes. When I did finally give him these secrets, I handed him the note book and then ran away. I was sure he was going to say all was false even though I believed all. I even began to plan what kind of a life I wanted when my writings were ended.

However, the opposite happened. Monsignor Hayes told me that all was true and from God. Then I was able to go on with my job for God, my writings and my Devil's Challenge. Throughout the ten years he was my director, he read all my notes and other writings and approved everything.

My writings were also read by my confessor, Father Lyddy, and he approved them.

When Father Bradley Pierce became my confessor and spiritual director in 1984, be also read about The Devil's Challenge and the praises and insisted that I explain them in this book because, as he also told me, all was true and from God and were an important part of my Lady's story.

When Father Bradley Pierce first told me that I had to put into this book my secret notes, which revealed many things I was told, he did mention The Devil's Challenge. While I was willing to obey my spiritual director and to add to the story of my Lady, many things which I had previously left out of other manuscripts about my Lady, I made up my mind that I would simply not mention The Devil's Challenge. That, to me, was too personal. The Challenge only concerned my own struggles to reach a closer union with God, so I thought. But Father Brad, who had read most of my writings saw what I could not see; that was, how necessary it was to include the challenge in the story of my Lady and her triumph.

Father Brad was not the only one who knew about The Devil's Challenge. Two of my closest friends also knew, one was Donald and the other was Estelle. When they found out that Father Brad had told me to include The Devil's Challenge in my book, both Donald and Estelle were delighted. They also thought that the story of my Lady and her triumph had to include the story of my challenge.

Estelle, who had typed the first manuscript (1995) which did not include my secrets, said that as beautiful as what I had written was, she felt that I was not telling the complete story because I had hidden so many facts about myself and my own spiritual life. When I told her that I wanted the public to see my Lady and not me, she replied: "How can you tell the story of Christ without telling the story of Mary?"

My friend, Donald, also said the same thing. He insisted that I not only reveal many of my most precious secrets, but I had to include The Devil's Challenge.

On January 14, 1996, 1 wrote these notes: "Donald and Father Brad and The Devil's Challenge . . ." They insist that I add that to the book . . . But I don't want to add the challenge. Father Brad replied: "How can you tell the story of your Lady's triumph if you don't put in The Devil's Challenge?" Their arguments were so strong that day that I added:

Now, The Devil's Challenge is in.

But in my heart and mind, I still did not want to reveal the challenge in this book.

After I had thought about it for a few days, I called Donald and had a long conversation with him telling him why I did not want to include The Devil's Challenge in this book. The result was that both Donald and I agreed that the challenge should be left out.

Now, I had to convince my spiritual director. I thought I had won the argument with Donald on my side. As I said, I was extremely reluctant to reveal all the struggles and spiritual battles I had during a lifetime of living with the challenge.

So, the next time I saw Father Brad, I told him that I had decided not to include the challenge in my book. I explained what happened in the notes I wrote on January 13, 1996:

Father Brad, on the other hand, saw my role in a far more profound way; and at times attempted to make me understand my complete role in my Lady's triumph. At such times, when I could not understand all he was telling me, he would just give up.

When I told him that I had finally decided not to include the challenge, when he knew I was not really following his way of thinking, he threw up his arms in frustration and said (in a loud voice)! "You really don't know who you are or what-you have done!"

I replied in a weak voice: "I guess I don't know."

He asked: "Do you really know your role in Our Lady's triumph?"

I said: "I guess not?"

He calmed down and replied: "Well, I do. You have to include the challenge. There is no way you can tell the story of your Lady's triumph and not mention the challenge. The challenge and how you fought and won the challenge reveals the way God's plans to bring peace, joy and happiness to mankind revolves around your accepting and winning this challenge. That led to Our Lady's triumph."

So, now The Devil's Challenge is in and I explain that in the following chapters.

— 1 —

WHAT IS THE DEVIL'S CHALLENGE?

In 1996 after I wrote the first pages about The Devil's Challenge, I read them aloud to Father Brad and Donald thinking I had given a rather good explanation. But, Father Brad was not satisfied. He saw many missing parts and he and Donald began to ask questions in such a way that I began to cry. One of the questions was: "Who called that The Devil's Challenge? Who named it? You or Mary or Our Lord?"

I did not know.

For over fifty years, I had called this: My Devil's Challenge. It never once occurred to me that by saying that it would seem as if I had named the challenge.

When Father Brad, along with the words of Donald, insisted that I tell them who named the challenge, The Devil's Challenge, I was thrown into a state of confusion. Tears filled my eyes.

Throughout the years, I had written hundreds of pages about the challenge, yet, I never wondered who had named it. I never asked myself how I knew to call the challenge The Devil's Challenge.

The following day I knew I had to do more research into my early note books. I asked myself the same questions Father Brad had asked me: Yes, who first called the challenge, The Devil's Challenge? Did I invent that name or was I told it by Christ or Mary?

As I write this book, now I can understand how important the answers to the questions were. Once again, Father Brad unlocked the door to my hidden secrets which had kept from my view a great many important facts about my role in my Lady's triumph. This was one of them.

I was first told about the challenge on April 5, 1946. I began to carefully read the notes I had written after that date. The notes I had written one month later on May 3, 1946 provided the answer I was seeking. Our Lord had said to me: ". . . long have I waited for you to accept The Devil's Challenge."

Then on May 7, 1946, I was told by God the Father: "If you had refused The Devil's Challenge."

So, when I mention the challenge in these pages, one can know that I did not invent the name for the challenge. It was told to me first by Christ, then by God the Father.

That is a very important fact, one that I never realized before, because the challenge itself was made, not to me but to God! I was only asked to accept it.

My whole role in The Devil's Challenge revolved around that one fact that when I was offered the challenge I accepted it.

When I was first offered the challenge on April 5, 1946, I accepted it in a very simplistic way as I tried to explain to myself what it meant in terms of how this challenge would be carried out in my life. I understood that it would entail great sufferings on my part; but I wasn't sure how and when the sufferings would come about. As the years went by, as I wrote many pages about the challenge, I was given more insight into it and I was able to express it in a different way. However, as can be seen by the first glimpse I had, it did not reveal its full contents or meaning. However, I did understand about my sufferings from the challenge, the temptations of the devil and how he and his evil ones use their power to capture souls.

This is the way I explained the challenge on April 5, 1946:

Here begins a new chapter in my life and one of the most unusual chapters I have ever written. But I am so stupid, I can't really explain all this; yet, I seem to see it clearly . . . Maybe you won't believe it . . . then I can't blame you . . . yet, I must believe it . . . never have I read or heard anything along this line. Never could I have imagined this for I am too stupid.

I have written much as God's Child of Love and the Refuge for Suffering Souls. But I am the Mighty Warrior with all the strength I need . . . I shall fight Satan and his devils until the

Last Day, but I shall do even more than that.

I could fight his evil ones but they would come back and still roam the earth and tempt people to sin. Now, however, God offered to me a way to keep them locked up in Hell, so they can't get out to tempt people. I will fight them and I will wound them so severely that they will never leave Hell because in Hell there will be no one to heal their wounds.

Right here I must stop to explain how a demon or evil one can be wounded. After one year of severe attacks by the devil and his evil ones, Christ gave me the weapons I would need on the battlefields. When He told me about the weapons, He also explained how I would wound the evil ones. Christ said to me, (April 9, 1947): "Now, sweet Child of Love, I give you your weapons to use upon the battlefields. I give you extraordinary graces which I have given to no other person, except My most beloved Mother. I give to you an increase in your love for Me and souls. You will wound the demons with your faith, your trust, your confidence, your love and especially your love for Me and My holy will for you."

Thus, it can be plainly seen that the demons who come with severe temptations can be wounded by grace and love. If you conquer such temptations and the evil ones or Satan lose a battle, what is wounded? Their pride. To continue with my explanation of the challenge:

It seems, as it was revealed to me, that centuries ago, God and the devil talked. The devil said that if God would send into the battlefields someone who will be wounded, then this person could wound the evil spirits and each spirit or evil one that is wounded by this person will be locked up in Hell and will never again roam the earth to tempt souls to leave God. But the one who fights these evil spirits, the one who wounds them must suffer greater than the greatest pain of Hell! That will be in order to have the devil lock his wounded evil spirits up for all time. God must pay a price, so to say, and the price is to let the person who wounded the spirits be wounded and suffer the greatest possible torment and agony . . .

The price is so high that many have refused to do this when

God asked them.

Jesus can heal His wounded one, but the devil's wounded will no longer roam the earth to tempt people . . .

This was revealed to me and Jesus offered me the job of this warrior: the one to be wounded, the one to suffer so that evil ones can vanish from the earth.

That was the very first explanation I gave of The Devil's Challenge. Little did I know that was preparing me for my role in my Lady's triumph.

I did not even discover, until now, that wrapped in the words I wrote on April 5, 1946 is one of the promises of The Golden Lady: "much sin will vanish from the world" (third promise).

My devil's challenge would become a very important part of my Lady's triumph.

Our Lady did not need me or anyone else in order to have her Immaculate Heart triumph. She has enough power to do that without anyone's help, let alone mine. But what she needed was for someone on earth, a warrior, to be wounded on the battlefields. She had said:

". . . the devil and his evil ones will be pushed back into Hell and much sin shall vanish from the world . . . (third promise)."

One might visualize Our Lady leaving Heaven to come down to literally push the devil and his evil ones back into Hell. Such would never happen. Throughout the years, when I was asked how the devil and his evil ones would be pushed back into Hell, I always answered: "With grace. Where grace is, then sin disappears."

The Devil's Challenge then becomes a prime example of the power of grace when grace is used to fight the devil and temptations. In order for God and Our Lady to show this example, there had to be a challenge for someone to fight; and with weapons of love and grace, to prove that such grace and love are strong enough to fight all the might of the devil and his evil ones, that person could prove how powerful grace and love are.

Such an example is not unusual. Everyone has his or her

own Devil's Challenge. Always within these challenges, there rages the battle between temptation, the power of the devil and grace, the power given by God and Our Lady to win battles. In addition, Our Lady and God need another example which only a Mighty Warrior on the battlefields could give. Grace, even when given to a person to aid in daily battles between temptations and virtues, can be accepted and used or rejected and abused. If I won The Devil's Challenge, and I did, the triumph I found was an example of the power of grace and how this grace was accepted and used upon the battlefields.

As can be seen by the very first words I wrote about the challenge when I mentioned evil ones vanishing from the earth, I did not know about the promises of The Golden Lady. I was not to hear about them until May 1, 1948, two years later. When my Lady told me on that day that her promises were already in my notes, that was one of them, but I never found this until now (writing this book).

I had explained about the challenge without knowing about the promise of The Golden Lady and my role in her triumph.

However, that was not the whole meaning of the challenge. Throughout the years, as the challenge unfolded in my life, I was given more insight into its full meaning.

I began to realize that my battles were not only for souls (to stop evil ones from tempting souls) but for my poor, fallen world as well.

In 1944, when I saw a vision of myself among the destroyed world, I was told to "raise this fallen world." When I asked how I could do that, I was told: "With love."

Ever since then, I considered the world, even the fallen world: "my world." I dearly loved my world and I wanted to raise it with love. When people came to me (and there were many) and told me that the world was so evil it had to be destroyed, I would answer: "But I love the world and I don't want it destroyed. I want to help make it a better place in which to live."

My poor, fallen world was being devoured by sin and corruption with millions following the devil and his evil ones, even flaunting their grave sins in public without shame or remorse. It is as if the devil constantly threw into my face the results of his power and temptations. The more the world fell, the more I realized that my challenge did not involve only individual souls, but the whole world as well. I became more determined to stay upon the battlefields and fight. I was not only going to save souls, I was also going to save the world: my world.

In my manuscripts, I wrote more about the challenge. One of the earliest explanations is as follows:

THE DEVIL'S CHALLENGE

My explanation of The Devil's Challenge as God lets me understand it. (My understanding and insights were to increase as the years went by)

The Devil's Challenge can be explained in a simple way that I now see.

It seems as if God and the devil spoke and the devil challenged God and boasted that he could conquer any soul in the world and not only that, but that he could also conquer and win the world so that he could rule it and run it in his evil ways from now until the end of time.

Dearest God saw the terrible pride of the devil and knew that that pride and sureness would be his downfall. So He chose the most unsuited, the weakest and most stupid human as the one to be used in this challenge and that was me.

To make it seem harder to win, the Good God placed me among the things and ways of the devil. Yes, I was baptized, but that was all. For about 18 years I lived without the love and ways of God under the influence of the devil and far from the loving Heart of God. I was surrounded only by the ways and things of the devil and thus it seemed impossible for me to change.

Yet, God knew that in His slow, patient ways and with His powerful love, the devil's pride would be smashed and God's grace would win as an example for all time.

Also God and the devil agreed that if the devil won, then the world would be his play yard, the place filled with his evil ways. But if God won, then the world would belong to Him and be given to His little child who fought the devil. And this little child could fill the world with her ways and bring the light and the love of God into the world.

He only chose me because I was the weakest and most useless of all His creatures and He wanted to show all what His grace and love could do so that what it did for my poor soul then it could surely do for all souls who are far better than mine.

In my 1963 autobiography, I again explained The Devil's challenge with these words:

Today (July 1963) I can explain the challenge more fully. When I was first told about it, its true (complete) meaning was hidden from me. However, what I wrote in 1946 is so remarkable because they could be called predictions which later came true.

A simple explanation is as follows: Man's free will had called for the devil's sin and corruption. Because of that, the devil came forth to rule the world. God could not do "anything" because He would not and could not interfere with man's free will. That being the case only free will could choose to fight the devil and his evil ones, on the battlefields of good and evil, and call back into the world God's ways of love and virtue.

Here was the great battle! Not between God and the devil directly; but between man's free will, temptation and God's love and graces. The devil would be on one side of man and God on the other (as my Lady told me in 1944); and man's free will could choose God's ways or the way of the devil; and in order to fully see this battle, there had to be someone chosen as the "middle man"—a person with free will to see and feel the power of the devil and to know and feel the graces of God and the power of grace.

Somewhere, somehow God and the devil made a challenge. There would be one person who would serve as an example— nothing else! The devil claimed that he could destroy such a soul and win that person's free will. God said that His graces could win. Then if the devil won this soul, he could go on being Master of the World; but if God won this soul, the world would be filled with so much light and grace—so many will be converted that the devil will be pushed back into Hell and much of his power would vanish because God's children would follow the example (pathway) of the one soul and use free will to follow the paths to God's Heart of Love.

The devil would have to admit his defeat and withdraw his power; and God would have His example to show to His children—the one who could show them the joys of finding God's love, mercy, forgiveness and graces.

In other words, if the devil won this soul; there would be no example to show to God's children—the example that could turn their footsteps back to God. If God won this soul, there would be this example that could and would be used to destroy a great deal of the devil's power in the world.

In January 1978, I wrote the following simple, uncomplicated explanation of the challenge:

Some way, a long time ago, the devil and God made a bargain or agreement. The devil said that he could completely control the world and all humans (including the Church) and destroy the world. God said that with His grace, a simple, weak, ignorant child could prevent that. The devil laughed in God's face and said that was not possible: to have a simple, weak, ignorant child defeat the full power and might of the devil and his evil demons. God insisted that such could indeed happen. So one day, God asked me to accept this challenge.

I did accept, and the story of my life reflected, daily this battle between the power of the devil and the power of God's grace.

On February 6, 1980, I wrote a 41 page explanation of some of the many battles I fought with the devil as he tried to destroy my work for God, and I explained how I had won each battle.

I also wrote a very short explanation explaining what the challenge was all about: God and the devil made a bargain (or agreement) to use the worst-one-on-earth-for-the-job, which was me. If the devil could win my soul, the world would be his. If I won, then the world would be mine and I could present to suffering humanity God and Our Lady in a new glorious way. But I would suffer dreadfully, as the devil would be allowed to use all kinds of situations (and traps) to make me lose my soul. God would allow the devil to have "free reign" over me.

When I wrote that I was the worst possible choice as the one to battle the devil, I spoke the truth. As can be seen, by what I wrote in other chapters of this book, the devil was delighted because I had been asked to accept the challenge. Surely, he thought, I could easily be defeated.

My Lady had herself told me how unfit I was for such an undertaking when she said to me on May 5, 1944: "You, Louise, a simple, stupid child with many, many faults, a child who once was lured away by earthly pleasures (my love for ice skating) has been chosen to do a great job for God . . ."

Yet, at the same time, she predicted my victory (April 14, 1944): "Remember, my child, that you are as small as the smallest fish in the sea, but the whale cannot hurt you for you will prove to him that you are not afraid of him and that you have more power than he has and then the huge whale will flee for he will suddenly become afraid of the little fish for God shall will it."

When I was first told that, I had no idea what it meant, but by 1960 when I read these words, I wrote under them: My Lady, here was no doubt referring to the devil and to my victory over him with The Devil's Challenge.

You may wonder, as I did (and wrote about it) why God would allow a simple, ignorant child to hold the fate of the whole world in her hands. If I lost the challenge, the devil would win the world! If I won the challenge, the world would be mine!

However, one has to understand the reason why one as ill equipped as I was to fight such a challenge was asked to accept it. The challenge was not just my own personal battle and my own triumph. It was revealing the battle between the power of the devil and the power of grace and love, as I stated.

One day, after Our Lord praised me, I objected to His glowing words saying I was just a nothing. His sweet reply was: "Ah, dear one, is it not I who has the power to make something out of nothing?" (May 2, 1946)

If Our Lord wanted to start with a "nothing" to fashion it by His love and grace into a "something," He chose the right person for the job of fighting The Devil's Challenge: me.

On January 29, 1946, He had said to the world through me: "Dear suffering children, My Heart is open and My love will cover you and protect you from all harm. Even the devil's greatest blows will not make you fall from this protecting cover of my love.

"My Heart is ready and man shall see no greater grace than what I shall send to them through My Child of Love. The Heaven's light shall shine brightly upon the earth and in this light will be love beyond your greatest dreams. I can call her life love for love is what I made it because love is what I wish to leave to you through her.

"Love is what the world has forgotten. Dearest children your God has not forgotten you, but you have forgotten your God . . . but now I place among you love in such a visible form that all can see and soon the devil will depart."

The Devil's Challenge as seen in this light becomes not only believable, but scriptural as well. One has only to read the story of Job to find Job's challenge and the examples it presented as well as his victory.

THE STORY OF JOB'S DEVIL'S CHALLENGE

Although it might seem incredulous to believe that the devil could present himself in front of God to bring before the Almighty One some sort of a challenge, such is Biblical. One only has to read the story of Job to see his challenge.

I wrote the following article dated January 8, 1993:

JOB: HIS LIFE AND MINE
MY DEVIL'S CHALLENGE

At this point in my life, I cannot help but compare myself to Job; although I was never as wealthy or prosperous as Job was, I did have a comfortable life.

He suffered tremendous crosses and afflictions; yet he never lost faith in God and he accepted God's holy will.

He was most blessed by God with family, flocks and material comforts.

Then one day, "in heavenly Council," the Lord asked Satan if he had come across his faithful servant Job in Satan's travels around the world. Then came Job's devil's challenge:

> The Lord said to Satan, "Have you noticed My servant Job, and there is no one on earth like him, blameless and upright, fearing God and avoiding evil?" But Satan answered the Lord and said, "Is it for nothing that Job is God-fearing? Have you not . . . blessed the work of his hands . . . ? But now put forth your hand and touch anything that he has, and surely he will blaspheme you to your face." And the Lord said to Satan, "Behold, all that he has is in your power, only do not lay a hand upon his person." So Satan went forth from the presence of the Lord (Job 1:6-12).

Then came terrible trials for Job. He lost his family, his possessions and all his wealth. Still Satan was not satisfied in his attempts to get Job to blaspheme and curse God.

Satan again appeared before God and demanded:

> "Skin for skin! All that a man has will he give for his life. But now put forth your hand and touch his bone and his flesh, and surely he will blaspheme you to your face." And the Lord said

to Satan, "He is in your power; only spare his
life." So, Satan went forth from the presence
of the Lord and smote Job . . . Then he said
to his wife: "We accept good things from God,
and should we not accept evil?" Through all
this, Job said nothing sinful (Job 2: 4:10). After
all of Job's calamities: The Lord restored the
prosperity to Job, after he had prayed for his
friends; the Lord even gave to Job twice as
much as he had before (Job 42:10).

Job won his devil's challenge. In like manner, I often beard
the devil complain to God saying he had not been allowed to
trap me by such and such a situation; and always the Lord
said to the devil: "Do what ever you wish to My Child of
Love. She will not fail me."

Throughout the years, the devil set trap after trap to try and
force me to give up my faith in God and my job for God. (It
is interesting to note that I never said I had a "mission" from
God, but I always said I had a "job" to do. I did not realize
it until now that job and Job are spelled the same way).

Although, I did not suffer all that Job suffered (I have no
flocks or children) I did suffer in much the same way in many
ways, such as my poor health.

And throughout all the long painful years of The Devil's
Challenge, I did not give up, nor did I lose my trust and faith
in God, nor my pure love for His holy will for me.

Needless to say, I knew nothing about Job or his devil's
challenge when I accepted mine. In 1946, I did not even know
all that was in the Bible. I perhaps knew only a few things.
which I heard during Mass. I had never read the Bible.

As I explain the development of and insights into The Devil's
Challenge, it can be clearly seen that I was given this challenge because of my Lady's triumph and the shrine she asked
for. The role I had been given can be clearly seen. However,
I stress the fact that when these developments happened, I never
saw where they were leading. I never planned, in any way,

how to make the future events happen. I merely wrote what ever happened, day by day, in my daily notes never questioning God's holy will for me.

No matter what I was told or saw in visions, no matter what happened in my life, I would look at my Lord and say: "Well, if that is what You want, it is all right with me."

I never tried to put the pieces together, which had been created by God and my Lady, into my role in my Lady's triumph. It is only, by writing this book, under the direction of my spiritual director, when these pieces were put together. The more I see these pieces in their proper place, the more and clearer I see the wondrous plans of God to bring about the triumph of The Immaculate Heart of Mary and my role in that triumph.

2

POPE LEO XIII AND
MY DEVIL'S CHALLENGE

Although one may think that a devil's challenge is a bit unusual in the modern world (aside from Job's challenge), there can be echoes of such a challenge in what happened to Pope Leo XIII in the year 1893.

The following article taken from Marian Helpers Bulletin, April/June issue 1959, explains what happened.

AN INTERESTING STORY

One promoter has sent us recently the following story, which has been on record since the death of the Great Pope Leo XIII. It has much food for thought:

One day as Leo XIII had finished Mass he suddenly stopped at the foot of the altar as if in a trance. When asked what had happened, he explained he had heard voices—two voices, one kind and gentle, the other gutteral and hard. These voices were speaking in conversation.

The gutteral voice, the voice of Satan in his pride, boasting to Our Lord: "I can destroy your Church."

The gentle voice of Our Lord replied: "You can? Then go ahead and do so."

Satan: "To do so, I need more time and more power."

Our Lord: "How much time? How much power?"

Satan: "Seventy-five years, and a greater power over those who will give themselves over to my service."

Our Lord: "You have the time; you have the power. Do what you will."

Leo XIII was given to understand that if the devil had not accomplished his purpose at the end of the time limit given, he would suffer a most crushing and humiliating defeat. Furthermore, the forces of good would not be helpless in the face of the onslaught of Satan and his legions. They, too, were given a greater power for good if only they would use it. Through their prayers and sacrifices and good Christian lives, they could offset the power of the devil and his human agents. It was then that he saw the great role St. Michael was to play in this mortal conflict.

As he had hurled Lucifer and the fallen angels out of Heaven after the "first revolt against God," so, too, he would play a great part in the battle to come, and would eventually cast Satan again into Hell.

It was as a result of this vision that Leo XIII then composed the prayer to St. Michael, which is now said after each Low Mass.

The words of the vision so frightened the good Pope that he instructed the Churches all over the world to have the following prayers said after each Low Mass:

Holy Michael, the Archangel, defend us in battle; be our safeguard against the wickedness and snares of the devil. May God rebuke him we humbly pray; and do Thou Prince of the heavenly host, by the power of God cast into hell Satan and all the evil spirits, who wander through the world seeking the ruin of souls. Amen.

It is needless to say that I knew nothing about Pope Leo's vision when I accepted the challenge in 1946.

As I recorded in my note books my daily struggles with my challenge, I merely wrote what I, myself, was experiencing as the years went by and the insights I had been given (a little at a time) as to the meaning and purpose of my challenge. However, I did take this challenge most seriously. I knew every moment of my life that I was in a battle not only to save my soul but also to "save" "my world" as well.

I began to hear about what happened to Pope Leo XIII around the year 1975; but I did not realize the significance of what I heard until the year 1985 when I wrote these notes:

11/30/85

I have known, for only a few years, (not as far back as 1946) about the Pope's vision. However, it was only the other day when I heard it again from Donald. And then I began to realize the amazing thing that happened; and how it more than proves my Devil's Challenge. In 1893, Pope Leo XIII was praying in his private chapel. Suddenly, all saw him faint. When he recovered, he told of an amazing vision he had just seen. He saw the devil challenge God. The devil said to God:

"Give me enough time and I will destroy Your Church." God asked: "How much time do you want?" The devil replied: "Between 50 and 60 years." God answered: "You have the time, do what you will." The Pope then added to the Mass, the closing prayer to Saint Michael.

As I said, I had heard this story before (within the last 10 years, but not before I accepted The Devil's Challenge). But this time when I heard what year it was, I was absolutely amazed because I suddenly realized that I had accepted The Devil's Challenge during the 50 to 60 years of that devil's challenge to God! That means that here is added proof that there was such a thing as The Devil's Challenge. I never doubted this challenge for I was so involved in it; but it made me feel wonderful to know that there does exist other proofs of The Devil's Challenge. Amazing!

We no longer say the prayer to St. Michael after Mass; but is it because there is no need to, for I won The Devil's Challenge? This apparent proof has made a profound impression on me.

THE TRIUMPH OF MARY

In 1948, my Lady said: "My Immaculate Heart has triumphed." This was 55 years after the Pope's vision. It would no longer be necessary to say the prayer after Mary's Triumph.

Now I can better understand why my winning The Devil's Challenge causes Our Lord so much joy that He often speaks to me as the one who accepted and then won The Devil's Challenge.

There is no doubt about it that Pope Leo XIII saw my challenge or,at least, my challenge coincided with the one seen by the Pope. When he died in July, 1903, the challenge he foresaw had not started in all its fury. But the devil's attacks against the Church and the world were part of the challenge I accepted in 1946.

When I was offered and then accepted the challenge, I understood it to mean, as I wrote in 1950: ". . . the devil boasted that he could conquer any soul in the world and he could also conquer and win the world so that he could rule it and run it in his evil ways from now until the end of time."

That "everything" and "everyone" had to include the Church as seen in the vision of Pope Leo XIII.

The Church, herself, could never be destroyed. Christ told us that (Matt. 16:18): ". . . you are Peter, and upon this rock I will build my Church and the gates of the netherworld (Hell) shall not prevail against it."

Surely, Our Lord knew such when he told the devil, in the Pope's vision: "You have the time, you have the power. Do what you will."

Satan could never destroy the Church no matter how much time or power he was given by the Lord.

However, the fact remains that the devil could *try* to destroy the Church. The past history of our Church proves that. The Church was not free from the attacks of Satan and his evil ones. The devil, puffed up with a horrendous pride (which caused his downfall in the first place) would never admit to himself that he would lose any battle: the battle for the Church included.

Oh, the devil does win battles, proven by the sins man commits but two battles he would never win: the battle to destroy the Church and my Devil's Challenge.

It is interesting to note that after my challenge was accepted by me, the prayer, which Pope Leo XIII had composed to be said after each Low Mass, was dropped. The revised or changed Mass which was adapted by the Church after Vatican Council II did not include this prayer. Could such have been a coincidence? I think not. I rather imagine that in some way, known only to God, my challenge was part of the challenge seen by Pope Leo XIII.

It was also part of my Lady's triumph. on January 20, 1990, God the Father said to me: "For you are the one who accepted and then won The Devil's Challenge; and by doing so, you pathed the way and opened the path for the triumph of Mary, the Mother of My Son."

3

THE MESSAGES OF JESUS AND MARY
IN 1944 AND THE DEVIL'S CHALLENGE

In 1944, as I recorded elsewhere in this book, I was given three titles by Christ and Mary:

> Child of Love
>
> Refuge For Suffering Souls
>
> Mighty Warrior Of Truth
> And Righteousness

The Devil's Challenge focused upon Child of Love and the Mighty Warrior.

I did not choose such titles myself. At that time, when I was named the Child of Love and the Mighty Warrior, I was in New York City training to become a professional ice skater. Suddenly, as I explained in earlier chapters, Jesus and Mary began to talk to me telling me things which were impossible for me to know any other way. My one desire, as far as my religion went, was to learn how to love God and Our Lady more. I had developed a very pure, simple love for God, but I had a long way to travel before I could fashion my soul, with grace, prayer and the sacraments, into the type of love-for-love relationship which I wanted with my Lord and His holy Mother. The fact is I did not even know that such a relationship could be had or how to obtain it.

Yet, in spite of that lack of knowledge, when Our Lord and Our Lady began to speak to me, I was told exactly what my future life would be; all of which came true.

I was told about my writings, which I had not even written in 1944. I was told about many aspects of my future life and I was told things concerning the devil, not knowing anything about a later devil's challenge and what this Mighty Warrior would do for God, for souls, for the Church and for the fallen world.

In addition to what I already mentioned in this part about the challenge, the following events took place which were directly connected with that challenge. But, I had no idea why they happened or what they meant. Yet, now I can see that I was being prepared to fight this battle with the devil.

The following events happened in 1944 while I was still living in one small room in New York City.

These first visions I saw concerned the fallen world and the challenge I would accept in the future. The first one greatly frightened me. Suddenly, in my room I saw a brilliant vision of God The Father. He was dressed in a long white robe. Upon this robe were tiny black crosses. I knew that these crosses represented the sins of mankind which were being constantly "thrown up" to God.

There were no words spoken when I saw this vision, and it quickly disappeared. I really had no idea why I had seen it; I just knew that it caused me confusion and fear.

As for what happened next, I recorded the following in an autobiography I wrote in 1963.

Soon after Jesus started to talk to me (as well as Mary) I was told the following things: Jesus said to me: "Know My child that you will suffer greatly, mentally, physically and spiritually. I will place the weight of suffering humanity upon your shoulders and you will be made to bear such a weight."

So my job for God was definitely linked with suffering humanity. Jesus linked it further by showing me this vision: I saw myself in the middle of a destroyed world. It was torn apart, not only by war, but by sin and corruption. Jesus looked at me and said: "Raise this fallen world, Child of Love."

I replied: "But how can I do that, my Jesus!"

He answered: "With love, My Child of Love, with love."

So, the Golden Lady was to bring peace, joy and happiness to the world; but the little Child of Love had to rebuild and raise the fallen world. There would be one job—but two parts—

two parts—but one job: to bring God's ways into the fallen world.

At that time, 1944, the world was torn apart by World War II. However, it was not the fallen world which it later became caused by sin, evil and corruption. I, of course, did not know that would happen in the way it happened.

To me, at that time, the fallen world was only the one I wrote on April 9, 1944: God wants the whole world to find peace, happiness and love. I did not know that when my Lady would appear, In 1948, as The Golden Lady, that she would say: "I have come to bring peace, joy and happiness to the world."

In 1944, I thought that when the war ended, there would be peace, happiness and love for the whole world. The fact is, I thought that none of the messages I had from Jesus and Mary would be useful or meaningful after the war ended.

I put in my mind my whole job for God, which I was told I would do including writings which I did not even have, within a very brief period of the war years. As soon as I could, I started to write articles and tried to get them published before the war ended. I thought they would not be needed after the war ended and the world had its peace, happiness and love.

I was so anxious to get my writings, which I thought would help to bring peace and happiness to suffering mankind after the war ended, published that I would walk the streets of New York and say to myself: "My poor, suffering world. If only I could help you now. But wait a little longer and soon I can make known the messages of Jesus and Mary and then you will find your peace and joy."

But Christ and Mary, of course, knew otherwise. They knew that the job I had been given would go on long after World War II ended. There was yet a Devil's Challenge for me to accept and win; and war was only a part of mankind's problems.

My ideas as to what war was all about were very limited the same way my ideas about my own job for God were. My Lady explained what I did not know.

On June 2, 1944, Mary spoke these words to me: "Dear children of God, you are not fighting another power of a man made war. You are fighting the causes of war and the causes of all the sufferings and sorrows that war brings.

"You are fighting greed, hunger for earthly things and pleasures and the love of them. Conquer them and you can conquer your enemies. And recognize them as your real enemies.

"Pray not only to defeat the powers of the other armies, but pray also to defeat the powers of the devil and the influence which he has in this world. But I possess more power in my little finger than the devil will ever possess. So fear nothing."

On March 27, 1944 my Lady again alluded to the challenge with these words: She said that I was part of Jesus' army on earth and that I must teach His children what He wants me to teach them.

There was another occurrence in 1944 which was directly connected with my Devil's Challenge, although I did not know it at that time.

I wrote about that in my 1963 autobiography:

Jesus warned me about the power of the devil, when I saw this vision. One evening after I had closed my eyes, suddenly, in a brilliant flash of light I saw a face that was filled with so much evil that I was frightened. I never forgot that face.

Jesus explained that what I had seen was the "Son of Satan." Jesus told me that no matter where I went, I would meet this "Son of Satan." They would be people who would try to interfere with my job for God; but they could only go just so far! Then when the final battle came—I would win! and my job would be safe.

I will add, that knowing that such and such a person had the looks of the "Son of Satan" did not make these spiritual battles easier for me. I never wanted to admit that such and such a person could harm my work for God and because I usually did not want to hurt their feelings, I ended up suffering a great deal, not only from spiritual battles; but also from the association. I could now name at least twenty people who have some feature of the "Son of Satan," but I will not. Mainly, because the spiritual battles were mine, not theirs. In other words, just because the devil used them—unknowingly—does not mean that they are in danger; although, a few of them may be in great spiritual danger.

As the years went by, I often saw this "Son of Satan" in many people who did, in some way, try to destroy my work for God or the job I had been given to do for God, my Church and my Lady (until there were far more than the twenty I saw and knew up to 1963).

Usually these people, who had some feature of this "Son of Satan" became part of numerous traps which the devil set in his attempts to destroy my work or to win the challenge. Most of these people were not, in any way, evil in themselves. They just were ones filled with selfish motives and ideas whom the devil used without their knowledge. In other words, the devil used their weaknesses to go against me and to try to destroy my work for God. They were usually very proud, demanding people who wanted to "take over" not only the work I did for God, but my Lady's shrine as well. Such people are now gone from my life. I hold no ill feelings against them. I think that in a different situation, with less temptations to "take over," as they found with my Lady or my work for God, they can, no doubt, work for God and our Church in a most useful way.

Needless to say, none of my dearest friends who helped me so much in my work for God and my Lady ever had any of the features of "The Son of Satan."

Also, in 1944, before I left New York to join an ice show (my dream come true), this happened as another way to prepare me for my future work for my Lord and Our Lady. The event took place on May 2, 1944. I recorded this incidence in one of my early manuscripts:

My sweet Jesus was crying. He was crying very hard and His voice shook with sobs as He spoke to me. He said He was crying because He loves His children so much and they don't love Him. He was crying very hard and my heart ached for Him. My sweet Jesus, in the glory of His Kingdom, was crying bitterly and helplessly because His children don't love Him and He sees them possessed by the devil (led into sin).

He loves them all so very much and His arms ache to hold them close; but they won't let Him. So He cries. He told me He is helpless. Sweet, great, powerful Jesus is helpless and so He weeps. He desires me to help Him and His lost children; to have them find Him so He can hold them very close and caress them in an act of love.

He told me that His children are as helpless as He was on the cross because they are so far away and He cannot bring them back. So He desires me to help Him in every way possible and to make Him laugh and sing again.

I love Him so.

Tonight I said: "I must help You, dear Jesus, so that You shall not cry again."

Christ also said to me on that same day, May 2, 1944:

Jesus told me that I was created not to be faithful to anyone but God and His will. Jesus told me that I was meant to do only God's will forever and to do just what Jesus tells me to do always; and no matter what it was.

I wrote the following words in 1963, about that little message:

In 1944, when Jesus said such a thing to me, I new nothing about the spiritual life; but His words to me were another prediction which came true. No matter what my state of life was to be, as long as I personally climbed The Ladder of Perfection and at the same time did the work which God had for me to do, I would be doing God's holy will for the rest of my life.

It was not only His will that I do—as best as I could—the work He had for me to do; but also that I use His holy graces and virtue to purify my soul. As long as I used my daily life and all it contained for the good of my soul and for the good of the souls of others, then I would be doing God's holy will for the rest of my life. And I can honestly say that throughout all the storms and darkness and even falls of my life and spiritual life, I always looked for and found the good for my soul.

My job for God and my Lady Mary had been placed upon a solid foundation in 1944. I had been able to grasp some of the meaning of that job, but there was a great deal more which I had to learn as my role in my Lady's triumph began to unfold as the years went by.

On March 27, 1944, I wrote these words: I am now going out into a new life with Mary's words forever in my ear. And I must wander amongst lost souls and slowly but surely tell each and everyone how to find their kind, loving, forgiving Father.

I later wrote that these words were "too ambitious." However, I later actually did carry them out through my writings and examples.

After all I had seen and heard in 1944, I knew I had a job to do for God and His Holy Mother, but I did not know how or in what manner I would carry out this work for God. Still, I was very determined to do all that God wanted me to do simply because I loved Him and Mary and the Blessed Trinity with a very great, simple, pure love. I would say over and over: "Well, if that is what You want, God, then that is all right with me."

I never once questioned what I heard or worried about how all the things I was told would be fulfilled. It was enough for me just to be told that I had a job to do for God.

One day in June 1944, I asked Mary in a very simple, child-like way: "Mary, who am I?"

She sweetly replied; "You are a servant of God who shall do His job according to His will."

I knew I had been chosen for this work, but I thought everyone was chosen in the same way to work for God and even to see visions.

It never occurred to me that what I had so carefully recorded in my note books was unusual. I found out that they were when I tried to get some articles I wanted published which contained the words of Jesus and Mary. All were refused by publishers, but I did not know why.

— 4 —

EARLY HINTS ABOUT THE DEVIL'S
CHALLENGE STARTING 1944-1946

Although, at first, I was most reluctant to include this challenge in this book, as I looked up numerous notes to be used writing about the challenge, I could see the wisdom of my spiritual director in ordering me to include the challenge. This challenge is mentioned constantly in my notes and revelations ever since I accepted it in 1946. It would have been almost impossible for me to mention such things as my weapons used upon the battlefields, my own triumph, the fallen world, etc., if I had to omit the challenge. The fact is that my early manuscripts about my Lady and her triumph were at times not only incomplete but even confusing simply because I never explained The Devil's Challenge as part of my role in her triumph. When I wrote about certain events in such manuscripts, I knew about the challenge but the reader did not. At one time when Archbishop Whealon's secretary read one of these manuscripts, he said it was "confusing." Not only did I skip the challenge but I also left out my precious secrets which make the story of my Lady clear and far more meaningful.

As I said, the challenge was constantly mentioned in my note books and even in my personal book of prayers. A substantial part of the autobiography which I wrote in 1963 is devoted exclusively to the challenge. My whole life from 1946, all my work for God, as a lecturer and writer and founder of The Maryheart Crusaders, all my efforts to get the shrine my Lady wanted and to announce to the world her triumph had this challenge woven around them as the devil did all in his power to interfere, disrupt or destroy the work which God wanted me to do as I carried out His holy will for me. In other words, the challenge could not be separated from my life, all

274

the work I did for God, my Lady's shrine, her triumph and my fallen world.

Also, even though including these chapters of the challenge added to the task of compiling this book, that actually made the effort easier. It would have been more difficult to pull apart certain events from the challenge than to explain what happened as part of this challenge.

Now that The Devil's Challenge has become part of this book, the first question to ask is: how was that challenge connected with my Golden Lady and her triumph? That question and others will be answered in the different parts of the book.

The challenge began in the year 1946, the same year when I was first told that Our Lady wanted a shrine to her Immaculate Heart. I was then 22 years old.

It is very difficult for me to explain in only a few short chapters in this book, what The Devil's Challenge is all about. Throughout the years, I have written at least four manuscripts about this role which God placed upon my shoulders. Also, the challenge is mentioned throughout my daily note books. But I will try to explain this challenge to show that not only did I accept this challenge but I won it as well. This challenge is very important to my Lady's story in as much as it is directly related to my Lady's triumph and her shrine as I will explain in other chapters. This segment also includes praises from Jesus and Mary which were told to me beginning in 1946.

In explaining the challenge and the praises, I will, once again, reveal my most precious secrets which I had hidden in my note books for over fifty years. I do so in obedience to my confessor and spiritual director, Father Bradley Pierce, who read such secrets and said I was to include them in my Lady's story.

The notes (written in 1946) about The Devil's Challenge and the praises were my most precious of what I always called my secrets. When I first met my second spiritual director, Monsignor John J. Hayes, I allowed him to read my note books except the one for 1946: my most precious secrets. Finally after one year, I presented him with this note book. When I did, I handed it to him and I ran away. But I felt that he had to read these notes if he was to judge my visions and my job for God.

I was afraid to return for his evaluation of and comments on what he had read. I wanted to run away again.

However, much to my joy and relief, he smiled and said that what he read was genuine and all was from God. Father Bradley Pierce said the same thing. That was why he said I had to include these notes in the story of my Lady. Monsignor Hayes not only approved my writings and the graces and blessings given to me by God, but he remained my spiritual director for ten years, reading and approving all I wrote. He carefully kept my note books until he returned them to me in 1957.

The challenge actually started in 1944, but (as always) I was not aware of that fact. The fact is I really had no idea what the devil's ways and power were all about. The only thing I knew about the devil was that he had to be feared; and that he was after souls, mine as well as others.

I had encountered and feared the devil in my childhood when I lived in my grandmother's house the first time when I knew (I don't know how I knew) that he was in the "devil's room" in my grandmother's house. The second time I was made aware of the devil was when I saw his footprints in the snow that evening I walked across the fields to my little skating pond.

I also understood that there were such things as temptations brought on by the devil, as I wrote on March 27, 1944: Mary told me that I was at last very far over the line between God and the devil. I passed it some time ago, but was still on the line and I knew there was a chance that I would tumble over again. I had tried very hard to overcome my faults and stay close to my Jesus. Even then I suffered great torment from the devil and his evil ones when I was constantly tempted to sin against all goodness and kindness. The battles with the devil had begun when I first heard Our Lady. But now, she said I was completely over that line and that I would always be safe.

But then Our Lady had a warning for me: She told me that, in spite of that fact, that the devil will still be after me and I will still be tempted. She said that the devil hates me very much and be will hate my work for God more and that I must be always on the lookout for him. But Mary said that if ever I am tempted, I was to come running and hide beneath the cloak of Jesus and He will protect me.

On March 31, 1944, I was told: "Your job will be hard, Louise, very hard. It is true, Jesus is on one side of you, but also on your other side is the devil. They are both pouring words into your ears and it is up to you to use your free will to believe whom you want to believe. The devil hates you, Louise, because you belong to us. Always he will be by your side telling you lies and tempting you. You must be strong. You are no longer weak. You are strong because you have us on your side. You need no longer be afraid because we are always close, ready to help your slightest call for help. We must protect you, Louise, because of the job you must do for God."

She continued: ". . . you have a great, hard important job to do. You will meet opposition and hate for the devil will be strong, but slowly and surely you will win . . ."

Up to this point, such words can be applied to everyone who daily struggles to overcome the devil and his temptations as he or she tries to replace sin with virtue. In other words, each person has his or her own devil's challenge. Constantly, temptations, often fierce, call souls away from the paths of God into the realms of sin and corruption. The challenge for all is to use grace, obtained through prayer and the sacraments, especially confession and the Eucharist, to overcome temptations and sins. The results of victory is Heaven. The end picture of failure is not very pleasant to visualize.

I could have been told that was all I had to know about the devil and my job for God: overcome temptation and sin (venial if not mortal) with grace; but there was far more to my challenge than that. Little by little the challenge was revealed to me. On April 9, 1944, Our Lady said to me:

Two things Mary told me that I must remember and be sort of a foundation for my God's job that He has for me—other than that of the love I have for Him and Mary and Jesus and the Holy Ghost and the love they have for me—that my life is an example for the world to follow. That the things I go through, the torments of my mind, the fights with the devil and myself and the final outcome of great undying love.

When I copied those words in 1960, I wrote: This was The Devil's Challenge.

In addition, in 1944, I had been told that I was not only the Child of Love, but the Mighty Warrior of Truth and Righteousness. Here was a glimpse into my Devil's Challenge. Why would a warrior be needed unless there was a challenge?

There was a hint of The Devil's Challenge in the words of Jesus which He spoke to me on November 13, 1945: "Your life is one not lived in a convent where my love is taught, but in a place (the world) where the devil's word is taught. Yet, you walked through this darkness and always I saw you as a brilliant light among the dark pathways and always I knew that you were Mine.

"Yes, My child, I let the devil go to you and tempt you when you were sick and tired. I told the devil to talk to you. But my faith and trust in you made Me know that never would you fall into his traps."

There were many traps set for me by the devil which, if I had fallen into, would have destroyed my work for God. All of these, I did not see until the last moment when they were revealed to me and I was saved. Now, after fighting the battles from 1945 until 1997 (there still will be more traps set), I can say that this prediction of Christ's came true.

Our Lord continued: "You did not fail, My Child of Love, you did not fail."

At that time, even before I accepted the challenge, I was told of my victories. Often in my revelations, I was told: ". . . You who accepted and then won The Devil's Challenge . . ." I often wondered how I had won when the battles were not over at the time such words were spoken to me. Yet, even before the great battles started, it was predicted that I would win the challenge. How? Because I was given the weapons which I would need in order to stand in triumph next to my Golden Lady.

On January 17, 1946, I was told about my triumph over the devil and his traps even before I had accepted the challenge. This became one of the promises of my Golden Lady and placed me and my challenge by her side.

Our Lord said to me: "For I bring to the world, through you, the love of God for His children and the ways of a loving Father. I bring to them, through you, proof of (the love) of the King and Queen of Heaven.

"And your hands and your heart will cause, not only people, but nations to return to My Church and you alone shall be their guide; and through you . . . much sin shall vanish from the earth. This I promise My children." (I did not know when I wrote this that this was one of the promises of The Golden Lady.)

After I recorded these powerful words, I wrote in my simplicity: There is so much about this message that I don't understand. What can I say to you to make you see how I feel when my Lord says such things to me? I can just obey Him and do what He tells me to do. I am going to write and write long and hard. . . .

On January 29 1946, I was told by Our Lord about one of the greatest weapons I would be given to use on the battle fields: love. He addressed the words to: "Dear suffering children: My Heart is open and my love will cover you and protect you from all harm. Even the devil's greatest blows will not make you fall from this protecting cover of love.

"My Heart is ready and man shall see no greater grace than what I shall send to them through My Child of Love. The Heaven's light shall shine brightly upon the earth and in this light will be love beyond your greatest dreams. I can call her life love, for love is what I made it because love is what I wish to leave to you through her . . . Now I place among you love in such a visible form that all can see and soon the devil will depart."

The day before, I was told about The Devil's Challenge, April 5, 1946, I wrote the following words dated April 4, 1946: Today, I was reading some of the messages Jesus gave me and

I came across this on what He gave me on August 29, 1945. Part of it said: "Your love will fill the earth and make a pathway over which will walk My Mother, My saints and The Blessed Trinity. You are to lead that army of love so you see how much We need you. You have conquered My Heart by love and so now you shall win the world by love."

Also, on April 4, 1946, there was a hint of one of the greatest battles of my life: the temptations to doubt all I had been told. These battles I always won as can be seen by these words: Oh! My! I don't know what to make of it all. Why should God do what He did to me and why should Mary have all the saints pray for me? I don't know, but it just can not be the work of the devil. It just can't be! I do believe and I have so many things to show me that it has all been from God. Oh! Why do I see and hear such things about myself? Surely, I did not suffer enough. Oh! it must have been love. God can't make a mistake. I can make a mistake but God can't. Oh! I don't know. I can't understand this . . . Oh! it is so hard. But I don't really mind. God can do what He wants with me. But you can see what love can do. Yes, I never made a mistake about love. But the rest? What has God done for me? Little do I know. I am scared as a little child because of the bright light. I am so little and small and I don't know why God would ever say what He does about me. It is so confusing.

But it must be true because the love in my heart for God just wouldn't be there if it wasn't. I just can't understand. I am not great, not really. I am just a little child. All I want to do is to love God and to help you. That is all. I don't know why I hear such things from God and Mary. It is too much for me. It really is.

But it can't be the devil's work because it is love and God's love cannot deceive; and the devil is far from love. I am the Child of Love and when all is dark, love is light.

MY ENCOUNTERS WITH THE DEVIL BEFORE I ACCEPTED THE CHALLENGE

One day my husband scolded our cat, Tammy, who had done something wrong. Tammy, being a fighter, was not going to let him get away with that. Mike retired to the bedroom and got into bed. As soon as he did, Tammy jumped on the bed, went right to his face, looked down at Mike and challenged him with a low growl. Mike threw the blankets over him; end of challenge!

My challenge was not that easy to win and often the devil was able to greatly frighten me. I had no blankets to throw over him to make him go away. The fact is, I was often alone on the battlefields where he used all his power to attempt to destroy me and make me give up the challenge.

I can say The Devil's Challenge began in my childhood when I first encountered the devil. Even though at that time I knew nothing about the devil, he made his presence felt in my life by taking command of the room in my grandmother's home which I called the "devil's room." Also, about the same time, his evil footprints crossed my path in a field as I walked to the little skating pond in back of my grandmother's house.

After I moved to New York City I was told many things about the devil.

As soon as my Lady started to talk to me in 1944, she told me about the devil and the battles I would have with him. She said:

(March 27, 1944) She told me that I was at last very far over the line between God and the devil. But she told me that, in spite of that fact, the devil will still be after me and I will still be tempted. She said that the devil hates me very much and that he will hate my work for God even more; and that I must always be on the lookout for him.

(March 31, 1944) "Your job will be hard, Louise, very hard. It is true, Jesus is on one side of you, but also on your other side is the devil.

"They are both pouring words into your ears and it is up to you to use your free will to believe whom you want to believe. The devil hates you, Louise, because you belong to us. Always he will be by you telling you lies and tempting you . . . you will meet opposition and hate for the devil will be strong. But slowly and surely you will win because God wants His children back."

(April 14, 1944): "Remember, my child, that you are as small as the smallest fish in the sea, but the whale (devil) cannot hurt you for you will prove to him that you are not afraid of him and that you have more power than he has and then the huge whale (devil) will flee for he will suddenly become afraid of the little fish—for God shall will it."

(May 4, 1944): Jesus said to me: "Fear nothing but Hell, My child and fear Hell because it is there you shall go if you lose your grip on Heaven; and your grip on Heaven is the love you have in your heart for God the Father, for Me and for My Mother.

"But do not fear the devil, for he has no power over you unless you let him and you shall not let him have any power as long as you hold God's hand."

With such messages, I was being prepared for The Devil's Challenge, but I did not know that fact at the time I heard the words.

Actually, taken at face value, such words about the devil could apply to most anyone as well as to myself.

Everyone at one time or another in his or her life, has a devil's challenge.

God allows temptations and even falls when a person does not use grace to overcome such temptations. But falls are not the worse of the problem of temptation and sin. What is even more painful or sad is when someone stays where he or she has fallen.

I surely had my falls along my life's journey, but that was

only natural or normal. We have all done or said things that we later regret. (Oh! if only I had my life to live over . . .)

What made the challenge I accepted above this normalcy was that God gave me a role to play which revolved around the triumph of The Holy Mother of God.

Even before I was offered the challenge the devil was attempting to make me so afraid of him that I would not even consider accepting.

In the little room, where I lived in New York in 1944-1945, two or three times the devil terrified me. Suddenly, I would feel his presence so strong that his might and power would come crashing down upon my soul. I would become so terrified that I could not move. This would happen when I wasn't even thinking about the devil. At that time, I was preparing to leave New York to go into a traveling ice show. He knew, even though I did not, the role I would play in my Lady's triumph. (This happened another time when I returned to Connecticut and spent a night at my brother's home.)

The devil had started to do all in his power to make me refuse the challenge when he knew it would be offered to me thinking he could, in that way, destroy Our Lady's triumph. He thought sure he could do that when he saw whom it was God had chosen to accept this challenge.

There could not have been a worse possible choice than a young girl, who had no training to accept such a challenge, someone whom Our Lady called stupid, unlearned, knowing so little about her religion, not even able to spell correctly.

She said (May 5, 1944): "So, my child, you who are so simple and so stupid that you cannot remember things, that you cannot pronounce certain simple words; that you cannot spell words that a child could spell. You, who are really very, very stupid, have been chosen . . . You, Louise, a simple, stupid child, with many, many faults; a child who was once lured away by earthly pleasures (my love for ice skating) have been chosen to do a great job for Our Lord. You are wanted only by God to go forth and teach the world the things God wants you to teach them."

The devil thought that it would be very easy for him, with all his power and cunningness, to defeat such a simple, uneducated child who knew next to nothing about her religion. Surely, he thought, she would become so frightened of him that she would not even consider accepting the challenge; so he continued his "wave of terror" in my life before I was offered the challenge.

After my mother returned to Meriden from Bridgeport, she rented an apartment at 517 West Main St. My brother and I moved in with her. I lived there for about one year before I left for New York City in 1943. After I returned to Meriden in 1945, I, again, lived with my mother at 517 West Main Street. (My brother, George, was in the service.) It was here where I lived when my Lady told me in 1946 that she wanted a shrine in Meriden. It was also where I lived when I accepted The Devil's Challenge in 1946. The following events took place sometime between the dates when I returned to Meriden at the end of 1945 and when I accepted the challenge in 1946.

By the end of 1945, I had left my ice skating career and returned to my home in Meriden, Connecticut. By that time, World War II had ended. That, of course, caused me much joy. However, I had thought that when the war ended, the whole world would have peace, joy and happiness and there would have been no need for my work for God, such as my writings. But I still was determined to have my writings published, so I wrote a series of articles and tried to get them published. All were rejected. But I did not give up. One of the graces I had been given was a great determination not to give up.

I did not realize it, but that virtue was to play a most important part in my Devil's Challenge which was to begin in but a few months after I returned to Meriden in November, 1945.

My home in Meriden (not far from the place where I later was told Our Lady wanted her shrine) meant a great deal to me. It was a very poor apartment on top of a store, and badly furnished, but it was my home where I could write and do what ever God wanted me to do for Him and suffering humanity. My mother worked to support us.

I did not seek out anyone to be my friend and no one sought out me. I preferred to be alone.

After the war ended as I stayed alone in my little home praying and writing, in the "outside world" things were beginning to change.

The devil and his evil ones began to form a chain of evil and corruption around the whole world. Humanity did not learn lessons from the war. Widespread sin began to show as people, free from the fear and horrors of that war, began to plan for a future of wealth, power and all sorts of sinful pleasures. The devil started his part of The Devil's Challenge wherein he was sure that the world would be his plaything complete with millions of souls trapped in his web woven with sinister delight. The fall of fallen humanity had started. He must have thought that if he dragged the world to the depths of corruption, that I would become too discouraged to do what Jesus had told me to do in 1944 when I had been placed among the destruction of the world and told to raise the fallen world with love.

However, the devil forgot something very important. There was a good reason why Jesus made me His Mighty Warrior. Such a warrior has the graces not to become discouraged by the enormity of the battle.

As I said, I had returned to my home in Meriden. This was the same place I lived with my mother before I moved to New York.

I was very ill which was the main reason why I did not get a job to help my mother pay the bills. The ice shows I had been in were extremely exhausting for me, mainly because I got very little sleep as the show traveled from state to state often at night. Also, all during 1945 I had fought my own personal battles with the devil and his evil ones to overcome my many faults and acquire virtues. There was one battle which had been going on for some time, which I daily (if not hourly) had to fight. After I found and fell in love with my dearest Lord, I was severely tempted to have Him and Mary "all to myself." I was tempted to become jealous of everyone who went to church or who received the Eucharist. I knew that would be wrong and I fought very hard not to commit such a sin. Often, I would spend the whole time at Mass telling myself that everyone there loved God more than I did and they had more right to receive God's love in return than I.

In addition, I still had to fight for the virtues of goodness, sweetness and kindness; and the devil also tempted me greatly to tear up my notes and to stop believing in my mission. I knew what that mission was: I was going to do a very important job for God and for the world. However, I did not understand everything about that job. But I would not stop believing in that job; and I could not stop loving God.

The temptations from the devil were not the only trouble I had with the devil. His strong power had already been shown in my life. I was to see more of his strength.

At this time of my life, I was 21 years old and I lived at 517 West Main Street in Meriden. The house, as I said, was very close to the place which I would later call: my Lady's land. I lived in that apartment until the winter of 1950-1951. It was while I lived in this apartment when The Devil's Challenge started,

I had given up ice skating and show business because I felt that I had a far more important job to do—one for God and for suffering humanity. I also found out that my wonderful skating dreams were only that—dreams. Reality was far different and I did not like that reality.

However, I did feel sad because I had not been able to help anyone through my skating. Still, God had given me another way to help others and to help the world: through my job for Him. I had new dreams: to bring peace, joy and happiness to others through my writings. I set about to accomplish that task in 1945. Little did I realize that I would not even begin to accomplish that job until years later. But I did not give up. I wrote—and wrote—and wrote such articles as this one:

THE TABERNACLE

Walk softly, dear children of God as you enter the church for your hidden Jesus is there. Walk softly and do not talk because He is there watching, waiting and tenderly whispering His love to your little heart.

Do you not hear His soft voice? You can hear it if you walk softly and listen.

There your Jesus waits in His little Tabernacle. He is there as He is in Heaven. He is there because He waits for His little children. He is there because He so loves His dear ones that He could not bear to leave them alone as they journey through life.

Know, dear ones, the goodness and mercy of your Jesus to stay in His Tabernacle day and night so that He will be there for you when you come to Him.

Do you go to Him? Do you go to Him often? Dear one, know that the Tabernacle is a glorious place; but know that it is also a lonely place.

Have you ever been real lonely? Yes, I am sure that you have been lonely and you have cried. Know that your dear Lord is lonely too in the little Tabernacle.

Do you go to keep Him company? Do you know what? Well, just a little loving visit from you for only a few minutes will make dear Jesus so happy that for many hours He will not be lonely because He will think of how happy your visit made Him.

How many of you forget all about your Jesus after the Sunday Mass? I think that many of you don't realize that when the Mass is over, Jesus does not leave. He still stays in His Tabernacle ever waiting, ever patient, ever hoping that His little ones will not forget Him.

How many of you have gone to church when you are sad? Yes, all have gone because there is great comfort there. But how many of you know that there is also great joy in a visit to the hidden Jesus?

How many of you have felt this joy? How many of you have

gone to church only to find this joy of love?

It is sad, it is so sad that few find the joys of the rays of light from the Tabernacle. These rays are love, but how many have seen them?

It is sad because your eyes have been closed. Your eyes have been closed because your heart has been closed. The good King whispers His love; but how can you hear His words in your heart when your heart is so filled with things of material value.

Dear children of God, you do not know or love your God for He is there waiting, but where are you?

During that time, in 1945 before I even knew about The Devil's Challenge (which was revealed to me April 5, 1946), the devil began his attacks against me; no doubt, because he knew about the challenge and future events.

The devil was going to get the "upper hand" before the challenge would be revealed to me. He started his attacks in a visible way in order to put such fear in me that I would refuse the challenge because I had already seen his might and power.

The first event concerned a strange clicking sound which was heard, in a material way, by both my mother and me.

The clicking sound was very loud. It came suddenly and often near one of the windows in the bedroom. Time after time the loud, strange noise would startle me. Time after time I would examine the window and find nothing. My mother would hear the noise and I would laugh and say: "Don't be afraid. It is only the devil trying to frighten us."

The noise would move from the bedroom window to a window in the kitchen and then back again to the window in the bedroom. This went on for the five years we stayed in the house. My mother and I got used to the noise.

Another noise I got used to was the devil pounding on the ceiling when I tried to say my prayers at night. Whenever that happened, I would sprinkle the room with holy water and the noise would cease. Once, I had a large bottle of holy water which I grabbed when the pounding started. I threw the water into the air, in a circle, holding the bottle firmly in my hand.

The noise stopped. The next day I noticed that tiny water spots on the ceiling formed almost a perfect Rosary. I was amazed. After that the pounding never returned; and I use to delight in showing a few people the "Rosary on the ceiling."

Such things were not too frightening; but other events were terrifying as the devil showed me greater signs of his power and strength.

One evening my mother was sleeping on the couch. I was in bed saying my prayers. Our rooms were not closed off. An open doorway separated the two rooms. Suddenly I saw, very clearly, a vision of a large thick hedge of thorns.

Instantly I heard a terrifying cry as I saw the devil trapped in the hedge. At the same moment, my mother heard the terrifying cry and jumped out of bed shaking with fright.

I asked her what had happened and she said she had heard a horrible cry; and when I asked her where the cry had come from, she pointed to the exact spot where I had seen the devil trapped in the hedge of thorns.

I told her what had happened as she sat on the couch trying to calm herself. Then I sprinkled the room with holy water and we went back to bed.

An even more terrifying event was the following one. I love cats a great deal. One day a stray cat came up on my porch. I instantly went to it and started to pet it. Then I picked it up and brought it into the house. (I hope this doesn't make people afraid of cats. I still love them.)

I placed a bowl of milk on the floor and the cat drank the milk. I started to pet it again. Suddenly the animal ran into the living room. I went in after it; and what I saw completely terrified me. The cat was in the far end of the room. It was no longer the soft, lovely "Kitty." It was hunched up, with fur up, hissing with a wide open mouth. The eyes were the most terrifying eyes I had ever seen. I knew instantly that the cat was the devil. I did not have to use my imagination to know that.

The wild beast began walking to and fro, hissing all the while at me. My only thought was to get it out of the house.

I said a prayer, and I went after the cat. I finally was able to grab it and I threw it outside on the porch. I was shaking with fright.

The cat remained on the porch for hours, walking back and forth, hissing with a hunched back. I was afraid to go outside. Finally, it left and walked down the stairs.

The cat disappeared, and I never saw it again.

But if the devil was showing his power to me at this time, God was by no means "standing still." On November 13, 1945, there began a series of messages (that is all I can call them) from Jesus and Mary which contain the most beautiful, love-filled words I have ever heard.

These messages have always been my deepest secrets. I have allowed only my spiritual directors to read them. I have since quoted from them; but only parts of them. I have never told any of my friends, not even Mike, about them and I have kept them down deep in the depths of all my secrets. Why? Because I know my Jesus and Mary said such things to me; but I always find it difficult to understand why they find me so attractive. It will be very difficult for me to copy these words here; but I must because they are part of my spiritual life.

I have very seldom reread these words contrary to what could be assumed that I sought comfort in them. The fact is, they brought me more suffering than comfort because I never will feel worthy of such praise.

You can understand how difficult it is for me to recopy these words after you read them. I would rather forget them and think only of my many faults—which I still have; however, my Jesus and Mary wanted me to bear such words and so they were spoken. I would much rather had had my Lady call me "stupid" as she once did.

Here is the first message of praise which is dated November 13, 1945: Jesus gave me this message and the meaning of it is almost beyond my understanding; but Thy will, not mine, be done. (I always accepted, as God's will, His praises in the way I accepted as His will the sufferings of my life.)

"My dear, little one: Know that to the whole world I say

this to you. Yours is a life that I use to set up as an example for My children. Yours is a life I can praise for yours is a life of purity and holiness and one that I can say was lived not in a convent where My love is taught, but in a place where the devil's word is taught.

"Yet, you walked through this darkness and always I saw you as a brilliant light among the dark pathways, and always I knew that you were Mine.

"Yes, My child, I let the devil go to you and tempt you. When you were sick and tired, I told the devil to talk to you. But My faith and trust in you made Me know that never would you fall into his traps. You did not fail, My Child of Love, you did not fail."

The words I have just recorded could be called another prediction of Jesus to me. He told me about the way He allowed the devil to so tempt me because He knew that no matter what happened, even if I fell, in the end I would not fall into the devil's traps to destroy my soul and to lose The Devil's Challenge. Jesus told me that I would not fail. And I did not.

To continue: "You need not go into the convent to prove to the world your love for Me. You need not even make your love known to anyone because I, Myself, will make your love and your name known to the world.

"But, My little one, write! Write long and hard. Write My love and My Mother's love and give to the world that which I want them to have. Write as only My Child of Love could write.

"I promise you, My little one, that before your death the world will know of you." That sentence I have often quoted to people. There is a notation on top of the page written long before 1960 which says: What does this mean? My spiritual director and I often talked about those words. He, Monsignor Hayes, would say: "Maybe you are to be known only in your notes."

To continue: "The world will take notice as they must take notice of a huge landslide. How they will welcome your landslide of love!"

The good Lord and His Holy Mother were bestowing upon me more wondrous treasures of Heaven. I could not understand why; but they saw the coming events of my life. Two great important plans of my job for God were in my near future in 1946. (of course, I did not know it.) The first one was God offering to me The Devil's Challenge; the second: my Lady was to tell me about the shrine which she wanted built to her heart.

The many faults and failings which were still mine in 1946, did not seem to dim the eyes of Jesus and Mary to whatever virtues they saw shining in my soul. They continued to praise me; and I continued to suffer greatly from such words.

On March 13, 1946, I saw a most significant vision of Christ, which became (even though I did not know it at that time) a sign of The Devil's Challenge. He appeared to me and placed a martyr's palm in my hands. From that moment onward, I would carry that palm onto the battlefields of The Devil's Challenge.

— 6 —

I ACCEPT THE CHALLENGE

The first question to ask when I explain how and why I accepted the challenge is: Who told me (or revealed to me) about the challenge and who offered it to me?

I did not start the notes of April 5, 1946 with the fact that Our Lord had told me about the challenge and offered me the chance to accept it. When I wrote those notes, I was more concerned about what I heard, than who told me. I wrote words such as: It seems as it was revealed to me that centuries ago, God and the devil talked . . . But later on, I wrote: This was revealed to me and Jesus offered me the job of this warrior" (same date).

Christ was the one who had appeared to me and explained the challenge to me. After He did, He asked me if I would accept it. It is very important to note that He did not force me to accept the challenge. I had to do that with my own free will. I will now explain my feelings after Christ asked me if I would accept the challenge. I had to think about what I was asked to accept. I had to know why I would accept such a frightening, fearful job.

In 1963 when I started to write my autobiography (under the direction of Father Kelleher who was my spiritual director at that time), I wrote: In order to have the devil lock his wounded evil spirits up for all time (so that people can choose God's example and see His reminder, me; and much sin shall vanish; and the world shall rise) God must pay a price, so to say, and this price is to let the person, who wounded the spirits be wounded and suffer the greatest possible torment and agony of Purgatory and Hell! It Is unbelievable!

Notice how I mentioned here the fact that "the world shall rise" (as I had been told in 1944).

293

To continue with what I wrote in 1963 (August 5, 1963, page 527):

The reason why that sounded so unbelievable to me was because I could not fully understand how a person could suffer such great torments as great as Hell or Purgatory; or how a soul or an evil one could be wounded. I did not realize that a soul can be wounded by sins.

I wrote these notes on April 5, 1946: Can a soul be wounded? This I asked myself a hundred times. Then, are not the souls in Purgatory wounded? Do they not suffer? Do not the souls in Hell suffer? Jesus told me that: through me much sin will vanish from the earth. What is a better way than to vanish the tempter? When one is not tempted to sin, there is no sin.

Notice here how one of the promises of The Golden Lady is mentioned again: Jesus told me that through me, much sin will vanish from the earth.

When I wrote such words, I did so in the same casual, innocent manner as I wrote all my notes, never realizing the complete force or impact such words had. At that time, I knew nothing about The Golden Lady and her promises. I merely wrote the words explaining what Jesus had told me.

To say that the evil ones I wound will be locked up in Hell forever, does not mean that there will no longer be the devil or his evil ones tempting people. That would be impossible. There are as many, if not more, evil spirits as there are people on earth. However if I, through my battles and victories, caused some evil spirits to be locked up in Hell forever, that would mean that many temptations will not cause people to sin. For example: if one were face to face with a huge sum of money, such as someone who works in a bank and is in charge of the money, and there are absolutely no temptations to steal even a dime of that money, then the lack of temptation would also mean a lack of sin.

In personal battles against sin, temptation is always the predominating factor. People who cannot resist temptation commit numerous sins such as stealing, lying, cheating, etc.

Also, one evil one can cause ruination to many people's good intentions; so to lock up one evil one can prevent numerous sins caused by temptation.

To continue with the April 5 notes: But I knew it was true. I knew God and the devil had this so-called agreement. And I also knew that many were asked to be the one to wound and be wounded by the sharp spears of the evil ones, but they had refused.

I was also made to understand that "Jesus can heal His wounded one, but the devil's wounded ones will no longer roam the earth to tempt people. But before Jesus can heal His warrior, then the sufferings and pains will be indescribable."

I really do not know how a theologian would explain the battle between a warrior on earth and the devil and his evil ones; but when I was offered a chance to accept the challenge, I had to explain it as I, a child, saw it. However as I later learned, a soul can indeed be wounded by sin. Even if the sins are not mortal, all sins caused through human weakness and faults leave a mark, or a wound, upon the soul. That is why there is penance on earth to remove such marks and Purgatory after death if such marks still remain. I also know that when a person struggles day and night to reach a closer union with God even a tiny fall can cause the person a great deal of suffering. To heal such wounds, if only venial sins, the one who seeks a life of holiness is very grateful that there is confession and the way and means as taught by Holy Mother Church to do penance. These are the healing balm given by God to His children.

Then, how can an evil spirit or the devil be wounded? The simple explanation for that is by a person using grace to resist and fight temptations. If sin, even a small sin, wounds a human soul, then grace used to prevent the sin wounds the devil or the evil one who wants that soul in his grip. There is nothing that can wound the pride of the devil or his evil ones more than to lose the battles between grace and temptations. Even if a person uses grace to fight a small temptation and not sin, the disgrace and shame felt by the devil or an evil one is as enormous as the pride which made him believe that he would not fail. These battles go on constantly as long as human beings have the free will to reject or accept the grace needed to fight the temptations of the devil and his evil ones.

After grace wins and the evil ones fail, their wounded pride can never be repaired. It is always before them as they ponder the question of why they failed when they have a great deal more power than a mere human. They will never admit that grace is far more powerful than all the combined power of Hell. So they sulk, but they continue to go forth on to the battlefields to again tempt a human being and catch a straying, careless soul. As I said, everyone has his or her own devil's challenge.

However, the challenge I was offered was far different than ordinary challenges upon ordinary battlefields, and I understood that fact. The agreement between God and the devil was not only that all the evil ones I would wound would be locked up in Hell never to tempt anyone again; but also that if I won the challenge, the world would be mine.

I wrote April 5, 1946: . . . then this person could wound the evil spirits and each spirit or evil one that is wounded by this person will be locked up in Hell and will never again roam the earth to tempt souls to leave God.

I wrote in my notes that I did not accept the challenge right away after I was offered The Devil's Challenge. The good Lord allowed me time to think about this. He waited for my answer. I had been told that others had been offered the challenge and they had refused: The price is so high that many have refused to do this when God asked them.

This refusal did not, in any way, take away from them any merits or eternal glory which they had already earned. Why they refused, I did not know. I only knew that placed before me was a challenge which only I could accept or refuse.

After Christ had revealed the challenge to me and offered me a chance to accept it, He disappeared and the devil appeared to me.

Here are the notes I wrote (same date): 'The devil talked

to me. I was frightened by his words, but somehow I did not move (away from him). Somehow I had an answer to his threats. Somehow I said I would not refuse. I will do this for my God. I will suffer.

But the devil was getting angrier because I said I will not refuse. He was shouting at me and he was telling me of horrors and pain and sufferings that will be mine. He said that not once, but a hundred times, I would fall beneath his evil ones' blows. He said that each wound in my soul will be a million times more painful than any pain I have known. He said that I will suffer greater than the greatest pain in Purgatory and finally be added greater than the greatest pain in Hell.

How is it possible for a sin (a wound in the soul) especially if it is only a slight wound (a white lie so to speak) to cause such torment and pain to the person?

The only way to understand that, is to understand someone's intense love for God and the efforts being made by the person to increase that love, acquire virtues and remove from his or her life all falls, including venial sins.

Human nature being filled with weakness and faults does not allow for the complete elimination of all sin in the person's life. That is why Holy Mother Church strongly advises her children to confess venial sins as well as mortal:

> Without being strictly necessary, confession of everyday faults (venial sins) is nevertheless recommended by the Church. Indeed the regular confession of our venial sins helps us form our conscience, fight against evil tendencies, let ourselves be healed by Christ and progress in the life of the Spirit. (No. 1458 Catechism of The Catholic Church)

When a person has, as his or her goal, perfect union with Christ, as he or she slowly climbs The Ladder of Perfection, even a slight fall can cause great pain and suffering to the person, especially if the fall is totally unexpected, such as an angry outburst. Mortal sins need not be present, but venial sins are to the person as soul-wrenching as any mortal sin can be.

In my spiritual journey, faults and weaknesses were part of that quest for union with God (as explained in another chapter). That being the case, the slightest sin against the goodness and love of God can cause great torment and agony. Situations forced upon me, such as the tremendous pressure put upon me by some of my most beloved friends to change the words of my Golden Lady, added to the torment and agony. Many of the traps of the devil created for me to fall into were designed by him to destroy my work for God and my Lady. When I realized what was happening, I was filled with grief and sorrow.

To continue with the April 5, 1946 notes: He (the devil) kept telling me how others had refused because the suffering is too great. He said that his evil ones will leave others alone. They will come at me with the greatest force of Hell. They will surround me and I will suffer.

But, always I kept saying: a hundred evil ones will fall before I do and they will never again roam the earth to tempt people. My Jesus will heal my wounds and I will come back so that a hundred more will vanish forever.

In spite of these first attempts by the devil to make me refuse the challenge (there were numerous other attempts to make me give up once I accepted) I knew that I would accept the challenge. I wrote (same date): It must be my desire to save souls that made me accept. It must be my love for God's suffering children. It must be my love for God. It must be my utter hate for sin and the devil.

Oh! it is true! The devil's words were clear and plain. I could hear them so well. He said his evil ones would attack me by the thousands when I go onto the battlefields.

Will Jesus allow this? Will He allow my soul to be wounded by the evil ones' spears? Will He allow me to suffer? Did He not allow Lazarus to die and be buried before He helped him? Yes, Jesus will allow me to suffer this. He will let the devil and his evil ones wound my soul when I battle them. He will allow it because through me much sin will vanish from the earth.

As I said, I did not know when I wrote those words that what I said was one of the promises of the Golden Lady and showed my role in my Lady's triumph through The Devil's Challenge.

I continued: and thousands of evil ones that now roam the earth tempting people will be locked in Hell forever. For thousands will fall beneath my sword.

The following day on April 6, 1946, I was still being attacked by the devil with temptations not only to refuse the challenge, but to doubt that it ever happened. I wrote:

Each time I think of this, I am tempted to doubt it. It is a mystery so strange that no one could ever imagine it. Only God Himself could have revealed such to me. Will God allow me to suffer this? Did He not allow His very Son to die on the cross and what is a greater mystery than that? How could I be happy and forget about the evil ones tempting God's beloved children?

I know how they can tempt people for they come to me with every trick they know. I would not leave God's suffering children knowing the damage the evil ones can do to their souls. Many times I have told the devil that I will fight him until the end of time. When God made me a Mighty Warrior . . . I knew absolutely nothing of what I have just mentioned. I accepted the responsibility God gave me and fought my fear and took the sword in my hand. I made the devil know how much I hate him and how I would fight him for all time. The devil hates me because I fought him so I could leave a good example for God's children. The devil hates the examples I leave. He hates the words I have written. He hates the prayers I have said.

He hates me bitterly and strongly and yesterday when the devil told me of the torments his evil ones will cause my soul, I heard his hatred in every word he spoke. He frightened me, but I stood my ground. He told me that I should give up my job as a Mighty Warrior . . . and I need not suffer.

. . . Could God really and truly have made such an agreement with Satan? Yes He did, I know because Jesus said it was so . . . if my God says it is so, then I believe it and I accept this offer.

. . . the devil was pleased because no one accepted the offer before and I think that he really thought that no one would ever accept it; and Jesus told me that I could refuse. He said it was up to me to decide. He told me that many others had refused.

The devil told me that he will not let me rest and that I would always have to carry a sword because when he sees me alone on the battlefields or near them, he will send thousands of evil ones to fight me.

I continued (same date): Oh, dear ones, it is true. I will suffer when I fight the evil ones. But I don't mind. I am small and a little afraid, but God will give me the strength. . . . you see, I am still a little child, but I will always do what my God wants me to do and He will make me strong . . .

Then I made my total commitment to my Lord with total love for His holy will and complete trust and faith in Him

I wrote (same date): I am such a little child. Right now I am a little bewildered. But I don't mind. I trust my God so much. I love Him so much.

"Oh! my God! before Thy throne I will kneel and give You my soul, my heart, my mind. You, my Beloved, can do anything with me for I am Yours alone. I belong not even to myself. I belong to You. You are my life and my death.

"For You, I will walk through fire and suffer the greatest torments of Hell. For You and love, I will do all, because it is just You that I long to please.

"Oh! dear God! say that I am pleasing to You and that my love is the greatest it could possibly be."

With this prayer of love and trust, I accepted The Devil's Challenge.

On May 3, 1946, Our Lord received my acceptance with these words: "But now, you have accepted . . . Well do you understand my utter hate for sin and My Mother's utter hate for sin. *Long have I waited for you to accept The Devil's Chal-*

lenge. But now you have *accepted* and the devil *trembles* for you will throw *back into Hell* his evil ones *that he so* relies on to take *children away* from Me. His *power shall be greatly reduced* and millions of souls will be saved that otherwise would have been lost to eternal Hell."

On May 7, 1946, I was told that I had stopped the destruction (the message of January 26, 1945) because I accepted the challenge. (See later chapter about Mary being cast aside: "Do not cast me aside.")

Then on December 20, 1946, Our Lord explained to me how many had been offered the challenge but had refused, but that did not take away their merits or heavenly glory. He added: "But can you not see, beloved of My Heart, how you accepting The Devil's Challenge places you above the others?"

I wrote under those words: I don't think so.

Note added

Many of the actual battles I had with the devil and his evil ones will be revealed in Volume II of this book.

WORDS OF PRAISE AFTER
I ACCEPTED THE CHALLENGE

After I accepted the challenge, I began to hear words of praise which greatly upset and confused me. I often objected to these praises, but the praises continued. It seemed that such joy filled the Hearts of God the Father, Christ and Mary because I accepted the challenge that they saw me in a way which I could not see myself. I considered myself to be the "great sinner" totally unworthy of any praise. Yet, I was told things which made it appear that my faults and failings were completely forgotten or overlooked by my loved ones in Heaven.

The Devil's Challenge had started on April 5, 1946 and that was to play an important part in my life from then on. There would be great temptations and sufferings from the devil; but on the other hand the good Lord and Our Lady gave me tremendous graces, and they continued to shower me with heavenly treasures and favors. On April 11, 1946, I wrote: Ah! Yes, indeed my treasures are rare! But, dear children of God, they are for you, not for me. All I have is for you. Just ask and you will be surprised. Because I love to surprise the ones I love; and I love you.

On April 25, 1946 I wrote about another favor from Heaven: What can I say to the message Mary just gave me? It amazes me. I did not want to write it. I thought maybe the devil was playing tricks. Before Mary was half through talking, I put down my pencil and I said The Hail Mary very fast. I made the sign of the cross on myself and in the room. I said: "If you, devil, are trying to trick me, then go away!'"

But then Mary appeared to me, so beautiful, and reassured me that the devil wasn't playing any tricks.

I should not be surprised at anything Mary says to me after what happened in the past, but it does surprise me what she just said. I can only write it because she told me to. And I remember what Jesus said when He said so long ago that I was to tell the world things that He never told anyone before. It is so strange and I really can't understand it all. I can just do God's will. I will just bow my head low and say that if God wants it that way, then that is the way it must be. I am so tired. I can't understand all this. But it is true, and I do believe it; and I love my God so very much.

This is the message April 25, 1946 that Mary gave me: "Write it in your notes that I say to the world, that until time will be no more, as long as the world calls to me for help, so also the Heavens will hear your name, Child of Love, called.

. . . your story will remain bright and clear. Your flowers will not wither or die and your words will not fade. For God has well prepared His Child of Love to withstand the coming storms and battles and always to triumph over the forces that wish to destroy you and your example. You, my favorite child, will guide my children to their God. . . . And you, my child, will bring the world back to simplicity and love of God; for I say to the world through you that if the world of science continues to use its knowledge to fight God, then you will destroy this world of science and their knowledge; so that no more will men know the great secrets that are now revealed to them." (Here is one of the promises of The Golden Lady of Happiness)

"Then they will return to the ways of God and search for His light and love. For the power of the knowledge of God and His love is greater than the greatest science and more helpful than the most powerful medicine. And the knowledge of how to save a soul is more important to God to have men know than to have man's mind filled with secrets of the universe.

"Indeed, my child, God chooses you, one so simple and small, but filled with the wisdom or God to show the world your way to eternal life."

As much as I did not wish to hear Jesus and Mary praise me, because their words of praise were a great suffering to me, they continued to speak to me in the most endearing way. On May 2, 1946, I wrote about more words of praise which Jesus addressed to me. Before I wrote what He said, I made this comment: Oh, what can I say to these two messages? Even reading about Saint Gertrude doesn't make me feel any different about Jesus saying such a thing. I am nothing; I really am nothing. I am as nothing as a dead piece of wood. But what has God done to me? I don't know. I can just wait and see. I wish that I could see some one right now and listen to them tell me how much they love God. That would make me feel better.

If my God found my heart so pure it was only because He alone made it that way and kept it that way. For how could a weak human being as I do such a thing? It was His grace that poured on me even when I had no knowledge of it. And it was my Lady who guarded my heart so that none of the graces left my heart. Suddenly Jesus said to me right now: "But, dear one, it was your love that you so willingly gave to Me that won."

Here is what happened: Today, suddenly I felt a sharp pain. I was delighted and I smiled and said: "Dear Jesus, please increase my pain. I have not suffered enough. Please make me suffer more." Then Jesus replied; (note added: Jesus was speaking about all the sufferings of my life when He said this) "Indeed, My child, this I say to you that you have suffered greatly. Even more than I have asked other great saints to suffer. Your smile so won My Heart as to cause Me great delight and pleasure. So when others complained of little sufferings, I quickly came to you to give you great sufferings so that I could see your smile. Then joy would return to My Heart; for I knew that your smile would never fail to bring this joy that I so desired."

Once again overwhelmed by His praises, I wrote (May 2, 1946):

"Oh, my Jesus, please don't say anymore. You have already said so much. I cannot stand hearing you say anymore. I will run away and hide. Please don't say anymore."

Dear me, I have put down my pen and tried to read and do other things; but I feel Jesus' eyes looking at me calling to me to pick up my pen and write again what He has to say. I want to close this book but Jesus won't let me. He wants me to write more. I cannot but I must. Yes, I must because it is God's will. But I fear that Jesus will praise me too much. Oh dear, what would Saint Gertrude do? I guess she would write it too. I have to write also. Dear Jesus I am ready. Speak, my love, Your servant hears Your words.

Jesus replied: "Ah! My beloved, how I love to speak to you to praise you. How I love to come to see you and your heart of love. Ah, My beloved, if you only knew how much I love you; and if you only knew what I want to tell you! Do not earthly bridegrooms tell their brides what is in their hearts? But how few are the things they can tell compared to the multitude of praises which I can give to you, My sweet bride.

"I want all to know how I praise you for then they can see how really small their love is compared to yours; the love that they think is so great and feel so proud to give to Me. But I show them now your simple, humble heart to put to shame the ones who think they are so great.

"Ah, such joy I feel that scarcely can I take My eyes away from the love in your heart. How happy I am to gaze at your pure, innocent soul every minute of the day and night. You, My beloved have put into words your great love for Me. Now, I can tell the world of My great love for you. Let the world come and listen to My words. Let all the angels and saints come and listen and marvel at the soul and the heart of My Child of Love."

I again objected: "I cannot write any more. I can't. Please Jesus, please don't say anymore! I am crying!"

But Our Lord replied: "Can I not tell what is in My Heart? Who dares to stop Me from speaking? Who dares to stop Me from praising you whom I love beyond describing?"

I quickly answered: "But Jesus, I cannot hear any more. I am nothing! You told me Yourself that I am nothing. Please don't say any more."

My Jesus replied with words which I have often repeated and even recorded in one of my books, "Come Climb The ladder And Rejoice" Vol. I (Introduction):

"Ah, dear one, is it not I who has the power to make something out of nothing? Listen and write. Listen well. How I love your humility. I see how it is suffering. But, dear one, ease the pain by knowing that as long as I so praise you and your love, I will put to shame the great ones of the world who think they love Me but only love themselves . . . the heavenly virtues that will fill their souls when they come to Me with pure love and try to love Me as you do. I must teach them how I love you so that they will know, still greater, the love in My Sacred Heart. Then they will no longer see Me far away. They will feel Me close and they will feel My love so very close to them.

"Ah, My love, My love, where are the earthly words to describe My love for you? It can only be described in Heaven when I hold you close and fill your soul with bliss and joy beyond your greatest possible dreams. How impatient My Heart is to tell you these words of love so that you can fully understand the love I have for you.

"Sweetest one, I gaze at you and My Heart fills with rapture for there I see love in the purest form as I have so long searched for. It is there for Me to fill My Heart with; and for all eternity, each look at your love will fill Me with such rapture that the angels and saints will marvel."

I continued to object: "Oh, my Jesus, please don't say these things to me. Please don't!"

Our Lord replied: "Ah dearest one, you see, you do not know of your great love for Me or else you would not beg Me to cease My praise. If you but could see the love others offer Me and then compare that with yours, you see how My Heart so longs to praise your love. Let Me praise you, dearest one, please do not stop Me again. For long I have waited to say these things to you. But I had to wait until now." (This now was after I accepted the challenge.)

At that point, I put down my pen and tried not to continue;

but I was forced to pick it up and write what Christ was telling me:

"Ah My child, my dearest, dearest child, know that all, all of the graces and virtues of My Heart are yours for the asking. Just to see you glance at my image or picture fills me with such bliss that My Heart trembles for such love I see in your glance. Constantly My Mother desires graces for you because she loves you so much, because you cause such great joy to My Heart.

"And, dearest one, when I see you look at my Mother with such love and speak her name with such love, added joy is in My Heart.

"I have a very special place for you in Heaven. it is to bring My Mother and the Blessed Trinity to earth in a new and glorious way. You shall be the bearer of the glad news. You shall present the King and Queen of Heaven to earth and to my children in a glorious manner." (This was a prediction concerning The Golden Lady of Happiness. But, of course, I did not know such a thing in 1946. Note also that the prediction was given in May of 1946.)

"Ah, My love, My love, My Heart cannot stop singing praises to your beauty of love. When your words of love pour into Heaven, the angels stop to listen to the beauty of the song you are singing. My Heart sings with joy when your words tell of your love for Mary, My beloved Mother. Her priceless graces and rare treasures are there for you to choose from; and how happy in her heart when you come to her for a priceless treasure to play with. You are her little child! How well she dresses you in the richest garments! She, who is the fairest of all, who is the most Blessed of all Blessed ones who is the closest to God looks tenderly at her beloved little Child of Love; and untold joy fills her heart. Can I ever stop singing praises to My child who causes such joy to My beloved Mother?"

Now, I would like to quote the following words which I included in the autobiography I wrote in 1963, after I copied the above message from my note book.

Even in 1963, I saw the connection between The Devil's

Challenge and my Golden Lady. I wrote (page 557):

It can be seen that there Is a definite connection between The Devil's Challenge and The Golden Lady of Happiness. It seemed that as soon as I accepted the challenge, Our Lord spoke to me in a most joyous way about The Golden Lady of Happiness. It appears that my acceptance or the challenge opened the door for The Golden Lady of Happiness for Jesus said: "You shall present the King and Queen of Heaven to earth and to My children in a glorious manner."

But, of course, I did not know such a thing in 1946 when Jesus spoke to me as He did. His words caused me suffering (as they do now when I repeat them here in my autobiography.)

After Our Lord said those words to me on May 2, 1946, I added this comment in my note book: Suddenly I have become so weak. My poor heart cannot stand such praises from my God. How could I possibly be worthy of them? How could I? But it is God's will and always God's will is my will.

I just said: "Oh Jesus, what are they going to say about all these things I have written! Jesus, it is true; but what will they say?" And Jesus answered: "They will say, dear one, that you are love."

I only wanted to love God more and to help His children. Really I did. I did not ask Mary to speak or Jesus to speak. I did not ask them to come to me. I just wanted to love God more than I did. Always I prayed to love God more. It was my most important prayer. See, dear children, how God will answer your prayers if you are sincere and childlike and humble and meek.

God is so good, please don't ever think of Him as not being good. Please don't ever, say that He does not love you. He does. He loves you very much. So, go to God and love Him. You can never love Him too much.

On May 3, 1946, Our Lord explained to me more about the sufferings waiting for me because of the challenge and it was on this day when He called the challenge: The Devil's Challenge. I wrote: Today Jesus said to me: "For all eternity, there shall be only one Child of Love. You, My beloved one, My dear Child of Love, shall hold that place forever. For you, dear one, shall be the one to fight the devil. And, My child, you shall suffer so. You shall suffer greater than any soul suffered or will suffer, because I will allow the devil and his evil ones to wound you.

"But know, My dearest, how My Heart will cry for you when you are brought before Me to be healed. Each wound I will feel in My Heart. But such joy shall be there as only you alone can bring for I see before Me one who willingly accepted these sufferings for love.

"Well, do I call you Child of Love for your love is so great as to accept all this for Me and My children.

'Well, do you understand the love I have for My dear children.

"Well do you understand my utter hate for sin and My Mother's utter hate for sin. Long have I waited for you to accept The Devil's Challenge. But now you have accepted and the devil trembles for you will throw back into Hell his evil ones that he so relies on to take children away from Me. His power shall be greatly reduced and millions of souls will be saved that otherwise would have been lost to eternal Hell."

After I heard those words, I wrote this prayer to Mary:

"Oh! my Mother Mary, you who are the Queen, what could I ever do to repay you for your goodness to me. I know, my dear one, I will bring your children to you and they shall sing your praises with great love in their hearts.

"Would that I could bring the world to your feet and teach them the goodness and love in your heart. My Lady, I love you, I love you."

On May 7. 1946, God the Father spoke to me and in His words can be seen two of the promises of The Golden Lady: "The world will not be destroyed . . ." (1st promise)

He referred to the message I had received, about world destruction, on January 26, 1945, saying that would not happen because I had accepted The Devil's Challenge.

He also mentioned another promise: . . . much sin will vanish from the earth." (3rd promise)

In addition, He also, as had Christ, called the challenge: The Devil's Challenge.

Notice again, as in most messages, that I am called Child of Love: "Dear Child of Love, now I can give to My children a promise; a promise that means great happiness for them. The message your Lady gave you on January 26, 1945 will not come about (the destruction) because you so willingly took upon yourself the task of fighting the devil and suffering.

"Wars will come and go through the centuries but the world will not be destroyed; for you will vanish much sin from the earth. But leave the message there for all to see what you stopped.

"If you had refused The Devil's Challenge, then no other Child of Love could I have had. But you accepted, so that the world will not suffer what Mary said it could. For you shall cause thousands to return to Mary's Heart never to leave." (The Heart of The Golden Lady of Happiness.) "And Mary's heart will be planted deep in the hearts of My children never to be blotted out by any force or power" (another reference to the first promise).

"The Mother of My Son will not be cast out of the world because you will bring her to the world in such a wondrous way that hearts and souls will turn to her with undying love and devotion."

Here again, God the Father refers to The Golden Lady of Happiness. However, in 1946, I could not understand such words: I can't hear anymore! I am so confused! What has God my Father said! It is too much for me to understand. I said to Jesus: "Oh! Jesus! if only I could have just loved You as a plain nun does and not be great. Because, My Jesus, I am not worthy to hear such things from You or from my Father or from Mary."

Then Jesus replied: "My dearest one, then I would be so sad because you would not be My Child of Love. Nor could I accomplish such great things through you. Know, My child, that what I have said to you and done through you is truly amazing . . . but know, My child that it is so important to me that without you, God's plans could not be fulfilled as they now are. You and your job will be known until time is no more on earth and in Heaven forever."

On May 8, 1946 I wrote these notes: Last night I couldn't understand what God my Father, had said to me. it was so strange. I knelt to say my prayers still confused. I looked up suddenly and there was Mary in all her glory and beauty. She had on a pure white gown with a blue cloak over her arms. Her arms were down and out. Her face shone so bright it was hard to see her features. She had a crown of flowers on her head and a halo of stars over her head. She was so beautiful. She said that she came to tell me that all was true; and I had nothing to fear about it not being true. (Notice that once again I saw her with the halo of stars.)

Then she said how extremely happy she was because I had prevented such world suffering and pain. Then she suddenly had a ring in her hand. It was the same ring that Jesus wore— our ring—she put it in my lap. I was no longer kneeling, but sitting against the wall. She told me to keep the ring and Jesus will come soon to get it from me. I asked her where I was to keep it, and she said in my heart.

She kept telling me how much she loved me. She kept looking at me so sweetly. Then she went away.

Then later last night while I was lying in bed, suddenly the devil came and he was telling me how everything was a lie and God will send me to Hell because of the lies I wrote. I felt so bad. Then suddenly I looked up and there I saw Mary dressed the same way with the diamond Rosary in her hands, sitting on her throne. It was a beautiful throne with a real star for the back.

She still had the halo of stars around her head. Around Mary were hundreds of angels and saints all looking at me and smiling. They were all so beautiful. Then I saw a young girl, very close to me apart from Mary and the others. I could see her very clearly. She seemed like a girl of 12 or 14, but I couldn't really tell how old she was. She smiled at me. She was just dressed in a plain white gown but it was shining so bright.

Her face was bright and light was all around her.

She said simply: "I am Joan;" and I said: "Joan? Joan who?" Then she said she was Saint Joan of Arc. She called me Child of Love and assured me of how much all the saints in Heaven love me. She said that she also led an army; but her army was as nothing compared to the army I am to lead in Heaven. She told me how extremely grateful all the saints were because I had accepted The Devil's Challenge. She said that for a long, long time God would tell of the one who was to accept the challenge and when I was born He showed me to all the angels and saints. Saint Joan said that the saints prayed for a long, long time for someone to accept the challenge; and great, untold-of-joy filled Heaven when I said I would not refuse.

I guess that is about all she said except she kept telling me how much she loves me and how much the saints love me.

She seemed sort of shy to talk to me. I don't know why because I love her so much and I will kiss her holy feet in Heaven. I will work for her, as I will for all the saints because I love them so much.

After Saint Joan finished speaking, then the whole vision vanished.

Although I did not know it at that time, it was fitting for Saint Joan to appear to me. She also had a devil's challenge and was asked to save her country, as I was asked to save my world.

On May 8, 1946, God the Father again spoke to me. I, of course as usual, did not understand His words at that time. He once again referred to the destruction of the world which would not take place (the first promise of The Golden Lady): "I the Almighty God, stood above the earth as a weight ready to fall. Yes, I was ready to destroy for My anger was so great. But you, dear one, and your love took Me away from this position and no longer am I ready to destroy for you have so won My Heart to ease My anger and now I no longer will destroy the earth before the Last Day." Notice the words here are in the first promise: ". . . the world will not be destroyed before the

Last Day by any force or power of man or by any force or power of God . . ."

"Indeed My power is still the same and my enemies will see it and feel it. But I step back now and call all to My arms for you dear, dear Child of Love will lead my children back to Me. Long have I waited for you to take away the weight from the top of the world. Let the whole world know, My child, that long the weight was hanging and the rope was getting weaker and weaker. But now, My child, the danger has passed and you My little one made it pass . . ."

"Ah, My beloved, where are the words to tell you how much I love you? Dear one, you are love and you bring such joy to My Heart that I rarely feel. You are My hope, My promise."

Here again can be seen the promise of The Golden Lady.

"You, My dearest, could so touch My Heart as to banish My anger and take the weight of this anger away, I love you so, beloved, I love you so. In Heaven you will know of My utmost, endless love for you.

"Well do I praise you as My Son praised you. Well must the children of the world praise you for what you did for them. I love you, My child, and your love will fill the earth so that all can see and feel your love."

Once again I was overwhelmed by what God the Father said; however, somehow I suddenly felt a great peace and joy after hearing the words because I knew that in someway, I would help God's suffering children. I wrote: You know I am extremely happy and peaceful and filled with joy. My highest dreams have come true even greater than I could possibly dream. I shall bow my head so low, but I am happy because I helped God so much and you, dear children. I love you so much, I do. I love you so much.

The praises, the work I was to do, The Devil's Challenge were all my most precious secrets hidden in my note books. I did nothing and I said nothing to make anyone aware of what I had been told. One day, I attempted to tell my brother (whom I loved dearly) about my love for God and how He called me Child of Love. I only said a few words, when he shouted at me: "What do you want me to do, bow before you?" I was deeply hurt. I only wanted him to share the love I had for God the Father, Christ and Mary. After he said that, I never again spoke to him about my love for God or His love for me or what ever was in my notes.

My daily life was plain and ordinary. I even began to work in offices when my health improved. I was, in no way, willing to announce to "the world" what I had been told. I cringed at any thoughts of revealing my secrets. I never even wanted anyone to see me pray or to see me when I saw a vision. I was delighted when my Lord told me on May 17, 1946 as He looked into the future: ". . . now draw a plain circle . . . This, I say unto My Child of Love . . . thus I made her life a life of tears; yet, her life to others was as plain as a plain circle. Thus she became My Child of Love. . . ."

About that time a nun let me take her book called "The Imitation of Christ." At first I was delighted to get the book, which I had heard about. However, after reading only a few pages, I was devastated. All the words of praises I had heard began to bear down upon me as I saw myself so unworthy to have heard them. With tears in my eyes, I said to my Jesus (May 21, 1946): "Oh! I have not been good enough. There are so many things that I still must do and learn!"

Suddenly Christ said to me: "Write it in your notes that I say, know My beloved . . . I am in you and part of you . . . (He was referring to Divine Indwelling) thus I give you the perfection that is Mine . . . You are My special child, My chosen one. I say unto you, your heart is filled with graces and love to be near My Mother for all eternity. You are the favorite of the favorite for I lavished graces and treasures upon you for I saw in your heart the purity and love that I long searched for."

His words of praise only made me feel worse and I quickly replied: "Oh! Jesus! please don't say these things to me. Please don't!"

But Christ continued to speak, this time about The Devil's Challenge: "Ah, My dear Child of Love, you know not what is in store for you on the battlefields of sin and good. You know not now and I can't possibly tell you in earthly words the sufferings you shall endure on these battlefields. And because you chose these sufferings of your own free will, you shall wear a crown (in Heaven).

"Why is your heart so troubled at My words? Can I not say such things to you? Know, My child, that even angels have refused what you accepted."

It is difficult to imagine angels refusing what I accepted. There is, of course, the great Saint Michael who fought Satan and his evil ones. However, Saint Michael and his armies of angels fought to rid Satan and his evil ones from Heaven. The Devil's Challenge concerned the earth and battles between temptation and the power of grace. Could an angel have appeared on earth to fight such battles? Yes, because with God all things are possible. However, I think Christ meant for me to understand the tremendous scope of the challenge which involved Heaven and earth and how extremely difficult it was for any "child of earth" to accept this challenge; yet, I did accept. Whether or not angels were actually asked to accept the challenge was not meant for me to know. But to under-stand that they "refused" revealed, once again, the importance of my acceptance.

Needless to say, I was totally troubled by what I was told and Christ said: "Dearest one, why does your heart continue to be troubled by My words?"

I replied: "Because, dearest Jesus, these words are so strange and unusual. I never heard nor read anything like them and I fear the world will think that I made them up because I wanted people to make me great. But I don't, dear Jesus. Oh! I don't! I only want to love You. I don't want to be great and I do hear Your words. I do. I did not make them up. My Christ! how could I when I know I am nothing but dust and not worthy enough to breathe let alone love You."

Christ answered: "Ah dear one, tears are falling down My face. I cannot bear to see you so troubled. What can I do to comfort you? Know, My child, that your heart is hidden from you . . . and you have not the understanding for if you knew and understood great things, then you would not be a child. Then also would men say that you made up great things for yourself. But because you are small and simple and My little child, men will know that only God Himself could speak such words to you. They will know, dearest, and they will believe.

"Ah! My child, let the world know the power of My grace for now I see your heart and it is no longer troubled. I see it at peace and My Heart is filled with joy for your trust and faith in Me are endless.

"In one minute of earth's time, your troubled heart was made peaceful because you believe and love.

"Let others believe and love as you do, and peace will be theirs."

My answer: "Oh! my God! You made me and you can do anything at all with me. I desire only Your will, only Your will now and forever. And I do love You. I love You: with my whole heart and soul and I will love You forever."

I added these gentle words: "Come, dear children of God. Please let me sit among you for awhile. please let me come and please tell me how much you love God. I will tell you how much He loves you. Forget for this minute what He said about me. I just want to sit and talk to you. Please talk to me. I love you so much. I want to tell you how much God loves you. Please let me sit among you and I want to help you . . . We will all go to Jesus and Mary and sing praises to them. Come, we will all go together."

That outburst of love for God's children came about because of my feeling of unworthiness. Actually the words can be said to contain prophecies. I was able to push aside God's praises— something which I always did—in order to help others and to bring God's love to others and to bring others to God, My spiritual writings prove that. I found more joy in telling people how much God loved them, than I did in hearing His words of praise. Even as I write these pages, I suffer because of God's words of praise.

The praises continued and in between such praises were references to The Devil's Challenge.

On July 21, 1946, Christ again spoke about one of the promises of The Golden Lady of Happiness, but I, of course, did not know this was a promise. I explained that I heard a sobbing which rang in my ears. I asked Christ what it meant, and He replied: "Ah! dear child, you hear the cries of my sobbing Heart. You can make My Heart cease to sob because your notes will prevent much of the sin that causes these bitter tears to fill My Heart."

Here Christ was referring to the third promise of The Golden Lady.

It was on August 15, 1946 when My Lady explained to me the meaning of the Gardenia of Love, and how this will be placed by the gold leaf. It was also in this message when she told me: "You alone will so shake the foundations of the world that never will they forget you and what you stand for."

After hearing these words from Mary, I wrote: Oh my goodness! What can I say to this? It is so very great. I don't know what to say. I can only do God's will to the best of my knowledge.

Part 8

The Shrine of
The Immaculate Heart of Mary: 1946

INTRODUCTION

Before I saw the visions or The Golden Lady of Happiness and heard her promises in 1948, 1 was being prepared for that event. I, of course, did not know that fact, but as I review my first notes, I can clearly see this preparation and the events and messages which led up to the visions in 1948. In other words, the job I had to do and the role I was to play in my Lady's triumph were slowly being revealed to me years before I knew that there would be The Golden Lady and her promises. The following chapters explain these early revelations.

NOTE

It was only after I was offered and then accepted The Devil's Challenge, only then, was I told about the shrine my lady wanted built here in Meriden to her Immaculate Heart. The date when she told me about her shrine was October 10, 1946.

— 1 —

"CAST ME NOT OUT OF THE WORLD" MESSAGE JANUARY 26, 1945

On January 26, 1945, I received one of the most important messages I had ever received from Our Lady; important because of the events which took place following Vatican Council II (which was started October 11, 1962).

I have also maintained throughout the years that this message clearly substantiated, or verified, the truth of my visions because what was told to me was a prediction from Our Lady which came true: a prediction which clearly became part of the story of The Golden Lady of Happiness and her triumph; one that was told to me years before I saw the first vision of The Golden Lady in 1948.

This message which I mentioned in this first chapter in this part, had been preserved in a letter I had written, to whom I do not recall. The original copy of this letter has been in the Bishop's Archives in Hartford, Connecticut for years. I went there in 1990 to get copies of letters I had written In 1945-1946 and this letter was among the ones I received.

I will not quote the message in its entirety because that will not be necessary. I wish only to quote the most important words which Our Lady spoke to me.

The message of January 26, 1945 began with the words about the heart of Mary being a "flower of peace, a flower of hope, a flower of love."

That is followed by a dire warning which reads: "My heart is the cause of the world returning to peace among the children of God.

"Heed well the words of my Son: 'The world cannot rejoice until it rejoices with My Mother and Me!' Heed well the call of my Son for you to return to my heart; the heart that is the gateway to the Heart of my Son and His Father. I shall warn you with these words from the Father: "If the world turns against the Mother of My Son, then I shall turn against them and once again the darkness of a horror night shall descend on the people of the world and more bloody a fight was never before seen.'"

Then our Lady speaks about a world-wide destruction and explains what would constitute or be part of this destruction.

But after her words which would cause fear in the heart of mankind, she gently says: "I tell you this because my Father and your Father's love is so great that He shall give you a way to prevent the destruction of the world before the Last Day . . . My children of the world, I stand before the throne of God to defend the children of the fallen world and out of His great love for me# He will allow my heart to bring back the peace that is not in the world today."

She goes on to explain how this destruction would be caused: "I stand now above the world ready to either be taken into your hearts with the greatest love or cast aside with the greatest hate . . . She then adds: "Cast me not out of the world for such will so anger your Creator's Heart that you shall pay with minds of fear and terror and an endless night of death. . . ."

Here it can so clearly be seen not only an attempt to cast Mary aside but her final victory, her triumph through her Immaculate Heart. That was why my Lady could stand on the rock in Meriden as my Golden Lady and say: "My Immaculate Heart has triumphed." Embedded in her words is not only her triumph as The Golden Lady, but her love and God's love for their poor, suffering children. It was love, the same love expressed upon the wooden cross of Our Savior, that was to bring about the triumph of the Immaculate Heart of Mary. Also, notice that in her words, there can be seen one of the promises of The Golden Lady: ". . . He shall give you a way to prevent the destruction of the world before the Last Day."

Although Our Lady mentioned the whole world, it seemed to me that the casting aside of Mary had to involve mainly Catholics. At that time, 1945, Catholics, including myself, dearly loved the Holy Mother of God, as most Catholics do today. I knew that many people, in other religions, never accepted Mary or loved her; but knowing that presented a very serious problem to me. I wondered how anyone, especially a Catholic, could ever cast Mary aside. The thought of that actually happening caused me great suffering. I remember walking the streets and saying over and over to myself: "Who could ever cast Mary, our dear Mother of God, aside?" That to me was not only unthinkable but absolutely impossible.

Then I received words from God, the Father who said to me on May 7, 1946 (don't forget this was before I saw The Golden Lady in 1948): "Now I can give to My children a promise that means great happiness for them. The message your Lady gave you on January 26, 1945 (the message of a great destruction) will not come about . . ."

". . . and Mary's heart will be planted deep in the hearts of My children never to be blotted out by any force or power. The Mother of My Son will not be cast out of the world because you will bring her to the world in such a wondrous way that hearts and souls will turn to her with undying love and devotion."

On the following day, May 8, 1946, God the Father said to me: "I stood above the earth as a weight ready to fall. Yes, I was ready to destroy for My anger was so great. But . . . I was taken away from this position and no longer am I ready to destroy . . . I step back now. . . ." "I, the *Almighty God* stood above the *earth* as a weight ready to fall. *Yes, I was ready* to destroy for My anger was so great. But you, dear one, and your love took me away from this position and no longer am I ready to destroy for you have so won My Heart as to ease My anger and now I no longer will destroy the *earth before the Last Day.* Indeed My power is still the same and My enemies will see it and feel it. But *I step back* now and call all to My arms *for you,* dear, dear, Child of Love, will lead My children *back to Me.* Long have I waited for you to take away the weight from the top of the world."

Notice how God the Father also mentions one of the promises of The Golden Lady: "I no longer will destroy the earth before the Last Day. . . ."

In order to understand what God the Father and Our Lady were talking about in 1946, there has to be taken into consideration the following facts:

1. The triumph of The Immaculate Heart of Mary.

2. And my role in
   that triumph; a role
   I did not even know I
   had in 1945 and 1946.

3. What happened after Vatican Council II concerning Mary and how she was almost cast aside.

VATICAN COUNCIL II AND MARY
LETTER TO ARCHBISHOP O'BRIEN
MAY 5, 1965

For me, the First triumph of my Madonna Maria centers around Vatican Council II (1962-1965) and what I had been told about Mary in 1945.

On January 26, 1945, my Lady said to me: "Cast me not out of the world for such will so anger your Creator's Heart that you shall pay with minds of fear and terror and with an endless night of death."

When she told me that, I could not imagine how anyone could ever do that: Cast Mary out of the world. And who would do the casting? Surely not the ones who already had cast Mary aside. The casting aside had to come from those who loved Mary the most and that had to be Catholics. But why and how would Catholics cast Mary aside? The answers came after Vatican Council II when certain events happened which the Council never intended to take place in regards to devotion to and love for Mary.

Whenever we speak of Catholic Church history, we must refer to the Second Vatican Council because a very profound change occurred in the Church which had its origin in and through Vatican Council II.

Anyone who takes the time to study this history will discover the ending of an era with Vatican Council II and the beginning of another.

To say that there had been no need for change in the Church's role in society would be making a serious mistake. There was a great need for updating and for the "fresh air" which Pope John XXIII allowed to flow into the Church when he called the Council together.

The Council brought about a great deal of good; however,

it also lit fires which were created by the so-called extremists who tried to turn the Council's spirit of renewal into their own ideas of what this renewal should be. As a result, theologians who had secretly nursed pet ideas and theories which were contrary to the basic teachings and traditions of Holy Mother Church, felt that the time had come to let the world hear their voices. Without thinking about the effect that their words would have upon the unlearned lay person's spiritual life, these "experts" placed before the laity complicated new and startling conclusions revolving around normal Catholic doctrines and moral teachings.

Many ordinary Catholic people, who were caught up in the theological disputes of learned Church leaders through the attempts of secular and religious newspapers and magazines to present the "news" to their readers, began to confuse mere speculation with truth in such a way that they readily accepted any new ideas about doctrine if this idea appealed to them.

Papal infallibility often was cleverly turned into "personal infallibility" wherein some Catholics felt that it was all right to believe or to do anything they wanted to regardless of what the Church and the Pope taught. The "I want to do this" and the "I won't believe that anymore" became the role for any Catholic who had looked for an excuse to justify the wrong things which he did or planned to do or to believe.

Nothing was sacred to these extremists and their followers as they went their own way tearing apart such doctrines and teachings as: Hell, Purgatory, Heaven, Holy Communion, the divinity of Christ, Adam and Eve and the role of the Blessed Virgin Mary in the modern Church.

The laity began to become very confused about devotion to Mary as extremists began to express their personal ideas about Mary in magazines and newspapers (some of them Catholic newspapers). What made matters worse was that these extremists who confused the laity about devotion to Mary, found what they called "Church approval" by referring to certain aspects of the Council in their attempts to justify their claims. They claimed that Our Lady's "downgrading" started there when the

Council fathers voted overwhelmingly not to have a separate document on Mary.

Of course, the average lay person, including myself, had no idea what had taken place at the Council in regards to Mary. The only thing we could assume was that this "not to have a separate document on Mary" meant that the Council Fathers had said that Mary was no longer important in our Catholic faith as we were being told by the ones who had never favored devotion to Mary.

I clearly remember reading in the newspapers and secular weekly national magazines, during this time, headlines and news articles telling about how the Virgin Mary was being de-emphasized in the Catholic Church and how her role was being downplayed by the Vatican Council Church fathers. I remember reading those news articles with sadness. However, the ones who said the Council "downgraded" Mary were wrong.

At the closing of the third session of the Council, on November 21, 1964, in the New York Times (daily) there appeared an article on November 22, 1964, which stated: "Pontiff Adjourns Vatican Council and Honors Mary." The articles subtitle headline reads, "Title, Mother of the Church, Shelved During Debates, is Conferred by Pope." What a joyful and happy day for the Catholic Church and for Mary's Children! The article goes on to tell how during his forty minute closing speech, Pope Paul spent almost half his talk giving honor, reverence and praise to the Holy Mother of God, as he proclaimed her "Mother of the Church."

However, the damage which the extremists had done to Mary's place of honor and esteem had been unbelievably great. Instead of helping Our Lady as Pope Paul had intended, the decree became more fuel to be burnt in the fires of theological disagreement.

Famous theologians, well-known around the world, led the group who believed that Mary's role in the Church should be greatly minimized. Their remarks together with ones such as emerged from another theologian's theory—that Fatima may have advanced many souls on their way to Heaven, but it put

Mariology back 10 years—put the Holy Mother of God in a new light; one that was shaded with doubts about devotion to her. As a result this started a new trend to think of Mary more in the sense of liturgical veneration (her role in the Bible) instead of the one to whom hearts rise up with love during devotions to her. Many forms of this devotion such as Rosaries and Novenas were put aside as being no longer needed or necessary by many priests in parish Churches.

You can well imagine how I felt watching these developments especially when I had to convince the bishop that Mary wanted a new shrine built to her here in Meriden. Thoughts about the Church's "new attitude" towards Mary, combined with ideas that the bishop would never want a new shrine to Mary because such a shrine would hurt Christian Unity, kept me awake more than one night. This became a barrier, one of many, which made my task much more difficult to accomplish.

The highest this barrier became was during the turmoil which followed the Council's decision not to give Our Lady a separate schema.

I know for a fact that Our Lady would never have worried about being cast aside if those who did the casting were only non-Catholics or atheists. When Our Lady spoke to me in 1945 about being cast out of the world, she foresaw the fact that the very ones who should love her the most would be the ones who would turn away from her. Why? Because what was called "modern-Catholic freedom of thought" came forth to declare that the Church no longer needed Our Lady; even though the Church never said that.

How did this situation develop? It became a side effect of what was intended to cure the Church of some of her weaknesses which began to appear as society surged forward on the wings of progress.

Very often a medicine used to cure one illness will produce another, sometimes a far worse illness, as a side effect. In such the same way the "open window" policy of good Pope John XXIII, which was planned merely to allow fresh air to seep into the Catholic Church, became a wild storm of the oddest assortment of Catholic thoughts ever to come out of Catholic minds and hearts: something which Pope John never intended.

One by one Catholic doctrines and beliefs were torn apart or pushed aside in a mad rush by the so-called "reformers" who did not really want to reform but destroy the very foundations of our beloved faith. The Holy Mother of God became a victim of this wild storm, so much so, that Catholics all over the world started to agree with misinformed theologians that she was no longer needed in our "modern" Church.

Rosaries disappeared, as well as Novenas to her as Our Lady was downgraded by theologians who found some poor excuse to speak out against the Holy Virgin. Catholics, confused enough by the wild rush of un-Catholic thoughts became more confused about true love for and devotion to the Holy Mother of God. Hundreds of lay people asked me if it was now "wrong" to pray to Mary.

One contributing factor to Mary's "downgrading" was the revised Mass. Although the Mass remained in essence the very same Mass, the changes in the Liturgy proved harmful to Mary. This was not due to the intentions of those who approved the new Liturgy, but to the misinformed Catholic laity who thought that because they were no longer saying the Rosary during Mass (the laity were instructed to participate more fully in the Mass by following Sunday and daily missals, singing songs, praying out loud) that the Rosary was no longer important. So, instead of finding a new time to pray the beads, many Catholics merely put the Rosary in a pocket or drawer and forgot it.

The final blow against the innocent Virgin came when someone decided that religious statues were now "out of place" in our Churches. Without a word of explanation, beloved statues of the saints and of the Holy Mother of God were taken from their places in a Church and destroyed or hidden. Millions of Catholics went to Mass and saw empty spaces where once had stood a statue of the Holy Mother of God. Not realizing that this was done to focus all attention on Christ in the Blessed Sacrament, many of these bewildered Catholics were led to believe that Mary had indeed been cast aside as unnecessary and unwanted.

This situation is the one which Our Lady foresaw when in 1945 she told the world through me: "Do not cast me aside."

As I mentioned before, in 1945 I could not imagine how Our Lady could ever be cast aside. As I write these words, years later, I can say that I lived through one of the most terrifying periods of Catholic history: the time when the Holy Mother of God was almost cast aside by the very ones who should have loved her the most.

However, barriers do fall and this one started to fall when bishops and Church leaders all over the world decided that the time had come to defend Our Lady's place and esteem.

Not only did our Archbishop send out a letter to his flock defending Our Lady, but other bishops and Church leaders did the same thing.

Cardinal Lawrence Shehan of Baltimore wrote: "The truth is that today, far from lessening reverence for and devotion to Mary, the Church recognizes that she needs Mary more than during any time of the past."

Bishop John King Mussio of Steubenville, Ohio wrote: "How strange it is that some have a groundless fear that this renewal in the Church means a demoting of Our Blessed Lady! . . . The Church would crumble her own foundations if she would take from Mary what is hers by divine decree. . . ."

Bishop John J. Wright of Pittsburgh, Pa. wrote: "The Rosary has a place in the tradition of Catholic piety especially in time of sorrow, such that I, for one, would never say a word that would downgrade it, however many or however excellent may be the devotions which would supplement it."

Furthermore, if a person made the effort and took the time to study the Council's statements about Our Lady, the person would clearly have seen that the extremists were wrong! The Council upheld Mary's place of honor in the Church with these words, which are found in "The Constitution of The Church": "this most sacred Council . . . admonishes all the children of the Church that the cult, especially the liturgical cult, of the

Blessed Virgin be generously fostered, and the practices and exercises of piety recommended by the magisterium of the Church toward her in the course of the centuries be considered of great importance. . . ."

Gradually, a great deal of the damage which had been done to Our Lady and to devotion to her became repaired. She came forth from this great battle as victorious. She was the one who had triumphed and no doubt this was part of the triumph which she foresaw in 1948, and declared."My Immaculate Heart has triumphed." Then as if to emphasize this triumph, on May 13, 1965 Pope Paul VI sent a golden rose to Our Lady's shrine at Fatima and later he visited the shrine in person to lead the world to devotion to and love for our Holy Mother: all of which made it a bit easier for me to ask the bishop for the shrine to The Golden Lady of Happiness.

As can be seen, there was an attempt within the Catholic faith to actually cast Mary aside, which made the prediction come true which she had given to me on January 26, 1945.

However, there was another prediction about Mary being cast aside, given to me by God the Father, May 7, 1946. I was told: "The Mother of My Son will not be cast out of the world because you will bring her to the world in such a wondrous way that hearts and souls will turn to her with undying love and devotion."

This wondrous "way" was to give to the world my Golden Lady of Happiness.

However, to say that Our Lady's esteem and honor did not suffer from this great conflict would be making a serious mistake.

Our Lady won this battle created by those who wanted to cast her aside , but as a result of this battle, there emerged a great deal of indifference for and neglect of Our Lady from Catholics who had never fostered a deep love for her. These Catholics did indeed cast aside the Holy Mother of God.

The fact was that so much damage had been done to devotion to and love for Mary, that not only bishops all over the country rose to defend Our Lady, but my own Archbishop

O'Brien wrote a letter to say that Mary had not been cast aside. After I heard that letter in church, I wrote to the bishop the following letter. The notes preceding the letter are taken from my private note books:

On Sunday morning, May 2, 1965, I listened very carefully to a letter being read by the priest during Mass. As I listened to the words of the letter, my mind slipped back to the year 1945 when I had heard the Holy Mother of God say to me: "Do not cast me out of the world, for if you do, such will so anger your Father's Heart that you will pay with dark nights. of terror." When I heard those words from my beautiful Madonna Maria, I wondered how anyone or how the world could ever cast her aside. Surely, I had thought, the Holy Mother of God, who reigned in all her glory as the Queen of Hearts and of the whole Catholic Church, could never be pushed out of the world or dethroned. Why then did she so sternly speak such words to me in 1945? Because she knew that in the year 1965, my bishop as well as bishops all over the world would have to reassure their flocks that the Holy Mother of God had not been dethroned. But why? what series of events had taken place during the years that prompted the letters of denial? Why were these letter necessary? Surely, there had been attempts made to cast the Holy Mother of God aside or else there . . . would have been no need for such letters. Who made these attempts? Who prevented the desired dethronement of Christ's mother as Queen of the world? And how did I fit into this complex picture? Why did Our Lady choose to speak to me about these future events?

All the answers to these questions can be found in The Golden Lady of Happiness; for this is the story, not only of Our Lady's plans to bring peace, joy and happiness to suffering mankind, but also of her struggles against odds to keep her place as the Queen of Heaven and Earth and of the Catholic Church, a struggle which ended in triumph for her.

Three days after I heard the Bishop's letter during Mass, which assured us that the Holy Mother of God had not lost her place as our Queen and Mother, I wrote him the follow-

ing letter:
May 5, 1965

Most Reverend Henry J. O'Brien
Archbishop of Hartford Hartford, Conn.

Your Excellency:

I was most interested in the letter which you sent to all the churches on May 2, 1965 concerning the Holy Mother of God. I can say that, in a certain way, that letter was predicted by our Lady to me in 1945. These predictions are in The Story of My Lady, a short copy which you have in the file, concerning The Golden Lady of Happiness.

Once again, I urge you to carefully check all my writings which are in Msgr. Fazzalaro's possession. He has among other things two lists of predictions copied from my notes which have come true.

He also has signed statements concerning cures and favors received from The Golden Lady of Happiness. Even though such statements are important concerning my case and my visions, I have always considered my writings as proof of the genuineness of the visions. The Story of My Lady is one which no one on earth could make up.

Predictions in that story are so numerous that they alone bespeak of the divine origin of the visions of The Golden Lady of Happiness. For example, in 1945, who on earth would ever think for one moment that our Lady could be cast aside? Also, who would have told you that on May 2, 1965, you would be forced to send a letter to all your churches in your diocese explaining to your children that our Lady has not been downgraded and that Holy Mother Church still loves and honors her as before.

Yet, dear Bishop O'Brien, in 1945, Our Lady said to me: If her Immaculate Heart was pushed out of the world by forces of evil or if her children rejected her, then a great destruction would take place.

Also in 1945, God the Father said to me: "If the world turns against the Mother of My Son, then I shall turn against the world and once again the darkness of a night of horror shall descend on the people of the world and more bloody a fight was never before seen."

Also, on Jan. 26, 1945, my Lady said to me: "Cast me not out of the world, for such will so anger your Creator's Heart, that you shall pay with minds of fear and terror and with an endless night of death."

If these words are not to be taken as a prediction of the events which led you to writing and sending out the letter of May 2, 1965, then what else could they mean?

The Council, the Pope and the bishops have not downgraded Mary, as your letter confirms: but if they had, I am sure that would have been the start of Our Lady being cast aside.

Your letter can be said to be a startling reminder of how close the "casting aside of Mary" came! As you well know, very often during great world strife and trouble God sends Our Lady to guide, protect and to bring hope to her children.

No one can deny that now, in today's world, only the help of God and Our Lady can prevent destruction. And in 1945, my Lady also predicted that when she said to me: "I tell you this because my Father and your Father's love is so great that He will give you a way to prevent the destruction of the world before the last day." And this plan included the visions and the shrine of The Golden Lady of Happiness.

A couple of years ago, when there was so much talk about the downgrading of Mary, I thought that such talk and ideas, especially for the sake of Christian Unity, would become a very high barrier helping to prevent the building of my Lady's shrine. I thought that the Pope and the bishops would not want to emphasize our love for our Holy Mother by building another shrine to her. I thought that here was another obstacle in my way which I had to in some way overcome. But when I heard your letter being read in Church, suddenly that obstacle seemed to disappear because I suddenly saw one fact very clearly: the building of my Lady's shrine will by no means be "in the way." The fact is, the shrine is desperately needed; so desperately that it now appears as if Our Lady chose the very right time for me to reveal the visions to the public!

Today there is still a great deal of talk about downgrading Mary; because, as I have heard, people are buying less Rosaries, and Novenas to Our Lady have been stopped. Also there is a growing feeling among Catholics that Mary is no longer important. Now is the time to prove to Catholics and to non-Catholics as well that we still love and honor Our Lady. The very best way to do this is to build this shrine here in Meriden to The Golden Lady of Happiness where she can be loved and honored as she so desires to be loved and honored.

What better way would there be to spread the love of and the devotion to Our Lady than to spread the messages of love, peace and hope of The Golden Lady of Happiness?

Can you not see how truly important Our Lady's shrine here in Meriden is now? Far too many people as you know, believe that religion, favors from God and from Our Lady are no longer important.

Prove to them that they are wrong. Let them see our love for Our Lady by allowing her to have her shrine which she wants here in Meriden.

I sincerely hope that soon you, our beloved father of our souls, will bring the good news to the world stating that indeed The Golden Lady of Happiness has come to bring peace, joy and happiness to suffering mankind.

Asking your Excellency's blessings, I am yours in Christ:

Louise D'Angelo

One of the greatest triumphs of my Lady was that she was not cast aside.

3

I SEARCH TO FIND A NEW
SPIRITUAL DIRECTOR
MY ATTEMPTS TO BECOME A NUN

By October of 1946, when my Lady first told me that she wanted a shrine near my home in Meriden, I had been trying to find a priest or a nun who could, more or less, become my spiritual director. I wanted such a director to read my writings and to tell me that all was "all right." What I had been told by God the Father, Christ and Mary not only confused me but also frightened me. I thought that a priest or nun (who loved God more than I did) would be able to understand what I had been told.

At that time, I still considered Father Shea, whom I met in New York, my spiritual director. However, he was too far away for me to see as often as I knew I would have to see and talk to a director. So, I began to try and find such a director in Meriden.

Also, and this was very important to me, I still wanted to become a nun; even though, I had been told that the convent was not for me. On November 13, 1945, Christ had said ". . . I say to you, yours is a life that I use to set up as an example for My children . . . one that I can say was lived not in a convent where My love is taught, but in a place where the devil's word is taught."

Still, I thought sure that my only happiness and my work for God would be found as a nun.

On March 25, 1946, I wrote to Father Shea: Dear Father, the desire to become a nun has taken hold of me so strongly that I suffer greatly from the fact that I am not a nun.

My desires to become a nun, or at least someone helping nuns or being with them were increased because of an incident which took place during the 1946 May crowning in my church. I recorded the event: Last Sunday afternoon, I went to the crowning of Mary at the church. It was so beautiful. It was the very first crowning I ever went to. It was wonderful, but I felt so bad that several times during the crowning I started to cry. It was because I saw all the girls dressed in white with white veils over their heads; and I sat right next to them dressed in my dark brown coat. They were Children of Mary or going to be; and I wasn't one of them. I felt so bad. I wanted so to be one of them; but I wasn't. I started to cry when I looked at their white dresses and my dark clothes. I thought that Mary didn't see me because I wasn't one of them.

After the crowning was over, I stayed for a long time, until the nuns came to fix the flowers. I went to Mary and she was so beautiful.

As I watched the nuns, I longed to be one because they seemed so sure of themselves and so peaceful. But I felt that I was not worthy of such an honor.

My spiritual director, Father Shea, almost made my dreams of becoming a nun come true. In May of 1946, I went to New York to ice skate and also to pay Father Shea a visit. I wrote about what happened: May 16, 1946 Tuesday of this week I went to New York to see Father Shea. I went ice skating but I could not enjoy myself at all. I saw several skaters, whom I knew from the shows.

However, the magic had left the thoughts of ice skating in a show. Ice skating and the rink brought me only a cold, empty feeling. The thing that I had loved deeply for many years failed to bring me the joy and happiness that I once thought it could.

To continue: Everyone was flying around the ice. All were trying so hard to be the best skater. All were trying to learn everything about skating. I knew that I had once been like them—but no more! Now I could not even stay on the ice. I tried to skate. I could still do all the spins and jumps but I lost interest in them now. I skated for 3/4 of an hour; then I left. I did not want to skate again. I only want Jesus; and to die so that I can start my job for Him from Heaven. (my longings for Heaven were great).

After skating, I went to see Father Shea. I went to the rectory and waited. Then Father Shea came down. I was so glad to see him. I wanted to see him for so long. I gave him my tiny statue of St. Theresa that I had bought in Bridgeport. Then I gave him three holy pictures with my poems on the back. And then I gave him another rose petal from St. Theresa.

I had wanted to see Father Shea to get assurance that "everything was all right"; however, when I was with him, I found out that I could not open my soul and my heart to him. I could not speak as I had planned to speak. I did not stay long with Father Shea. I felt so bad that I started to cry because there were so many things I wanted to tell him, but I could not open my heart to him. I could not talk to him about Jesus and Mary. I wanted to so very much, but I could not and I started to cry.

However, the priest was happy to see me and he had a great surprise for me. He said that he thought about it and decided that I should enter a convent. He even had the order picked out. He gave me the name of the Reverend Mother at St. Zita's home on 14th Street. He sent me to the nun to see about my joining the convent. I felt very happy because Father Shea wanted me to join the convent; but the plan ended in disaster. I am sure that if the interview with the Mother Superior had been different, I would have entered the convent immediately. Here is what I wrote about that interview. Then Father said that he would like me to go see the Reverend Mother at Saint Zita's home on 14th. Street. I was so happy Father wanted me to join the convent because that must mean that he really believes my visions. I know it is all right to join; even though Jesus said I was to be in show business.

And Jesus wants me to do everything Father Shea tells me to do because Father Shea is my advisor (spiritual director).

I asked Father Shea if it was all right to join and he said that the Reverend Mother would tell me. I asked him what I was to tell the Reverend Mother and he said just to answer her questions.

I went to see the Mother and she was praying in the chapel with the other nuns. She sent word that I was to join her in the chapel. I went, but I felt so funny. I could not go in among the nuns who were praying. I stood in the doorway and then the Reverend Mother came up to me and told me to sit down in one of the pews. I sat there; but I was not at ease. I felt so funny because I was with the nuns but I wasn't one of them and I am so far below them (so unworthy).

After the prayers the Reverend Mother talked to me in the parlor. She was very nice; but I suddenly became so shy; and I could not talk to her. When she asked me if I really wanted to join the convent, I said that if Father Shea wants me to then I will. This surprised her. And she said that he could not make up my mind for me. I told her that I would do just what Father Shea told me to do. She asked me why I wanted to join and I said "Because I love God" And she said: "Is that all?" And I said: "Yes." I could not tell her how much I loved God. I am sure that she loves Him more.

She explained the work I was to do. She asked me if I could scrub floors and cook and wash and I said! "Yes." She asked me if I would really want to do this and I said that I would.

We talked of my skating and she asked me why I went into show business when I thought about becoming a nun. And she asked me three times before I could answer her. I held my head down and looked away. Then I said! "It was what God wanted me to do."

Then she kept asking me how I knew it was what God wanted me to do and finally I had to say: "Because He told me." She said: "How did He tell you?" And I said: "He just told me Himself." I was afraid of that! I was afraid she might make me say something about my voices and visions. I just could not tell her anything about that. After I said what I did, she closed her eyes for a minute as if she could not believe what I said or as if I said something wrong against God. Then she said that she would like Me to see another priest, and he would tell me whether or not I was to join a convent. I was willing to see the priest that very night.

I told the Reverend Mother to ask Father Shea about me and he will tell her because I could not. Just then, Father Shea called on the phone and I was so glad. He said to send me home; and he would talk to the Reverend Mother about me later. I felt glad because he said that to her. I returned to Meriden.

On May 18, 1946, I went to see my parish priest whose name was Father Dolon. I wanted him to write a letter recommending me to the Reverend Mother in New York so I could join her convent. Father suggested that I see Sister Laurentine of our parish (a teacher in his school).

I did see her and we agreed that I should join her order. I wrote to Father Shea telling him I was thinking of joining this order. I also wrote to the Reverend Mother. She answered my letter on May 30, 1946: "Just a line to say that we have agreed that it would be best for you to follow the advice you received from the Reverend Mother at the convent in Hartford.

"Assuring you that we will remember you in our prayers and hoping you will be resigned to God's holy will."

SISTER LAURENTINE

After I went to see the nun my parish priest sent me to, my friendship with Sister Laurentine grew quickly. I felt at ease talking to her and I soon told her about my visions and my writings. I wrote: She believed me and she said she believed me because of the way I told her. I felt so grand talking to her and I told her many things.

I continued: I told her about the diamond Rosary and I even read her part of the message Jesus gave me and told me how much He loves me.

I asked Sister to be my friend and she said she was my friend, otherwise she would never let me come back with such stories if she did not believe me. I felt so happy because she is a wonderful friend just like Father Shea.

She listened so well and seemed so delighted with everything I told her. It is so wonderful to talk to her and I thank God so.

Sister Laurentine completely won my heart and my confidence and trust. You can imagine my joy believing that God had sent me my new "director" who would tell me that I had nothing to fear from all I had been told.

On May 23, 1946, I wrote that I gave Sister some of my notes and poems as well as the 10 articles that I wrote. This created the first serious problem in our friendship.

Sister, being a teacher began to closely examine my writings, looking for errors instead of understanding my heart and what I was trying to say. She said they could be written much better and I should learn to spell (my weakness since I was a child). She said that if I want to write for God, I should be perfect. She suggested that I read the classics (I did not even know what a classic was). She said that I did not have it in me to be a poet. Needless to say, I felt dreadful, not so much because of Sister's criticism, but because I had done so poorly a job for God I wrote (May 23, 1946): I am so sorry that I can't write better and spell better. I would go back and correct everything, except that I am kind of tired. But I am sorry that it is not perfect. I do want to do everything perfect for Jesus. I know as no one else knows how really poor my writings are. I guess I should have taken time to study English and writing and how to write poems. I know that my writings are poor. No one else would write as bad or so poorly about Our Lord, because no one could be as stupid as I am. Mary called me stupid and I don't mind. I want to be just a little child. I am sorry if you don't like my writings but please love the messages from Jesus and Mary not about me but the others.

As I thought about all the things Sister had said, crying because I had done such a poor job for God, suddenly Christ appeared to me and sweetly said: "Dear little one, know My child, that I say to the world, if I wanted you to write great words would not I have given you the power and ability to write them? No, My little one, I wanted a child to write so I made you write, My little Child of Love. For I want a child to teach them . . . and your words will live for the words of the brilliant contain not what your words do and they shall die. And where do you find such pure, holy love as you do on the innocent face of a child? And where are truer words spoken than those that come from the stainless heart of a child? Such a child cannot lie for the grace I give then prevents lying. It is the child's way of trust, faith, hope and love that I bring to My children through your pen."

My precious friendship continued in spite of what she had said about my writings. She often allowed me to pray in the convent chapel. I loved everything about the convent and the habit she wore. I would touch her long sleeves and long for the day I could wear the same clothes.

Sister enjoyed my company as much as I enjoyed hers. We had many marvelous talks. I felt that, at last, I found that "someone" who understood me and my job for God. But then another serious problem came into our friendship.

I began to bring my note books to read to Sister, some of what was written in them. That was not good enough for Sister. She wanted to keep my note books to read everything in them, but I would not allow her to because I told her my most precious secrets were in them: these being The Devil's Challenge and the praises. I was not ready to reveal these to her.

By June of 1946, Sister could not control her desire to know what was in my secret notes. She simply had to read them and she constantly asked for them.

By then my relationship with the Sister had grown into one of deep fondness and friendship. She had completely won my confidence; so much so, that I granted her dearest and greatest wish. I allowed her to read my secret notes (June 6, 1946): Then yesterday the strangest thing happened! I took my note book with me for no reason at all. While Sister and I talked, she again told me how much she wanted to read my note book. I did not want anyone to read it until after my death. But I guess God wanted Sister to have it for I gave it to her to read.

It wasn't an easy thing to do for in that note book are the secrets of my heart and soul; and the messages and visions that I told no one about. They will know of them after my death. But I was embarrassed when I told Sister she could read my note book. I told her that I hope she doesn't think less of me after she reads it.

Sister tells me that she only wants me to love God more. I will. I will try so hard to love God more. Oh, my God, I love You, I do; but I will try to love You more.

Sister tells me how much I will have to suffer because I am a chosen one. But I suffered already. Maybe it is good she will read my notes, and I will suffer more. Oh! my God, You know how willing I am to suffer for You.

I did not want anyone to read those notes while I am still alive. I do not know how I will face Sister after she reads them. I don't know what she will think of me. I hope she will say that it is all right and I did not make many mistakes. But I guess I did.

God surely wanted me to give her my note book. I guess it is best that she reads it. Then she will know more about me, and I don't really mind having Sister read my notes because she has been so wonderful to me; and she will be able to tell me what to do so that I will make everything all right for Jesus and Mary and not make anymore mistakes.

Sister asked me to pray for a special grace for her and I am sure Mary will give it to her. She also asked me to pray for a new spiritual director for her because hers died. Then she also asked me to pray that she will be a saint; and I will pray so hard that she will because I love her and I want her to have hundreds of graces. I want Father Shea to be a saint also because he is so good to me.

As I stated, giving Sister my secrets to read was not easy but I felt that I could trust her with them. She had, as I stated, been extremely anxious to read them. I don't know what she expected to find but after I gave her my note book our entire relationship changed. Sister only had the note book a short time when she suddenly handed it back to me and told me that she had been too busy to read it! Although I believed her when she said she did not read it; I have always had certain doubts about that statement of hers. Perhaps she did not read it; but that seems rather strange in view of the fact that she had been

so anxious to read it. Also, as soon as she handed me back
the note book she changed our whole relationship and it was
no longer close or friendly. Nevertheless on June 18, 1946, I
wrote about Sister returning my note book to me: I got my
note book back from Sister a few days ago. I felt so bad because
(she said) she did not have time to read it. I even cried because
of that. I really wanted her to read it after I finally left it with
her because I thought she could say that everything was all
right.

But it was not God's will that she should read it because
she was too busy. I don't blame her because I realize how busy
she is.

I guess that even Sister or Father Shea could not say anything. I would really like someone to read my notes and tell
me if I made any mistakes. But somehow I trust my God so
much and I pray to do only His will that I have the peace of
mind to know that I have not done or said anything against
God.

It is true and I believe it. And I will continue to believe it
no matter what happens. My trust is so great in that, that if it
were not of God (my writings and notes) then He would have
stopped it long ago. And I so love God. With my whole heart
and soul I love God.

I went once again to see Sister, feeling in my heart that
something went wrong with our close relationship. I was told
that she was not home. I wrote (June 18, 1946):

Today I went to see Sister and she wasn't home. I talked to
another Sister who was very, very kind to me. She was so
sweet. She talked about the convent and how wonderful it is.
And for a few minutes I felt like crying because I wanted to
go into the convent so much but yet, I seem to be getting worse
as far as my health is concerned; and I can't go until I am
better. But I do not mind because soon (I hope) Jesus will
come to take me to Heaven; and I can start to help Him in
Heaven.

I had poor health all my life even when I did all the work
I had to do for God and my Lady: my writings, my lectures,

starting my organization and working full time as a bookkeeper for years. Later it was discovered that I was born with a hole in my heart. I had constant pain in my chest and was always tired.

On June 21, I went to New York once again to see my spiritual director, Father Shea. He was very happy to see me. Before I got on the train, I found 6 rose petals Saint Theresa "sent" to me.

Father Shea spoke again about my entering a convent. He was very serious about me becoming a nun. He said: "The first thing you have to do is to clear up your chest so that you can enter a convent." Then he told me that he thought it would be best for me to enter the convent in Hartford.

Then the priest spoke about my visions and my spiritual life. He mentioned the fact that I was "far advanced" which was most unusual especially because I was not a nun. He said that if I had been in a convent for a long time, then my visions and my spiritual life would not be so unusual.

Father Shea also told me to stay with the Sister in Meriden because she had helped me and she believed me. We did not know that her whole attitude towards me had undergone a complete change.

I asked Father Shea if he still believed me and he said he did which made me very happy. Then he told me that if I go into the convent I would have to tell the Reverend Mother all about my visions etc. He said that he would like me to be sort of observed by a nun who knew more about such things as visions.

The talk with Father left me with a wonderful, happy feeling. I wrote: After this visit to Father Shea, I knew better than ever that he is still my best friend; and he still believed in me. It made me feel very good to know all this.

As soon as I returned to Meriden, I saw Sister. My feelings that "something happened" between us were not wrong. Sister's whole attitude was different. She was aloof and very cold. She mentioned my note book, which makes me believe that she did read it. She told me that I should see a parish priest,

Father McNerney (who later became my confessor) and let him read my notes. I decided to do just that.

That was the beginning of being sent to one priest after another by someone or another. As soon as a priest or a nun realized how deeply I was involved with visions, they sent me to someone else because they did not want to get "involved."

I was extremely hurt and confused by Sister's change of attitude especially when she coldly and firmly stated: "I believe only that you are sincere in what you tell me, but I cannot actually believe that you see visions. I believe that all this could be a trick of the devil."

That was my introduction to such things as tricks of the devil, illusion, self-deception and hallucinations, all of which come under consideration when there is a situation involving visions.

Naturally when Sister made that statement to me, my mind became filled with doubts and fears. I was crushed by Sister's attitude and by her words. Her words ". . . that it could be a trick of the devil. . . ." haunted me for a long time, but her words did not destroy my belief in my visions or my job for God. I wrote: I cannot say that; for I do believe! I believe so much that I do see Jesus and Mary and hear them. It just cannot be a trick of the devil!

I cannot doubt that it is true. I just cannot.

The apostles said to Jesus when He asked them if they would leave Him: "But where shall we go, Lord!" So I say that if I cannot believe my visions, what then can I believe? I became extremely tired; and my chest hurt more after I saw Sister and she said that to me.

Oh! I do believe in my visions; I do! I must and God will not punish me for my belief because it is honest and well; and I only want to love God and to help Him. But it cannot be wrong. It cannot be!

Then I added: it is well that Sister said such things to me because maybe I would get vain if she did not say that.

There was only one way that I would accept what Sister told me. When I met my second spiritual director, Monsignor

Hayes, I left it up to him to tell me if all was a trick of the devil or from God. After a lengthy examination of my spiritual life and my note books, he told me that all was from God, not the devil.

I could only believe that this was part of the devil's plans to get me to give up the challenge. If I had given up all at that time, then the devil would have won the challenge. However, God gave me the grace to still believe no matter what Sister had told me. I kept my belief and I did the wise thing. I allowed my spiritual director to tell me if all my visions, my writings and my work for God were truly from God or the devil. Monsignor Hayes assured me that all was from God and I was never again tempted to believe that everything was a trick of the devil.

I never found out why Sister changed so greatly our relationship. I can only guess that she either read my note book and was shocked; or else she had discussed my case with someone—a priest or the Reverend Mother—and they had warned her to have nothing more to do with me and my visions. But I do feel that in view of my personal affection for her, she could have treated me more kindly even if she had been warned in some way not to have anything more to do with me.

Of course, one cannot "second guess" another person's motives for his or her actions. Yet, I believe that Sister had imagined that my secret notes concerned her personally or her order and that Our Lord and Our Lady praised her. Instead, she found (for I am sure that she read the notes) that was not the case.

There was another severe cross which Sister Laurentine placed upon my shoulders. In all our comments about the convent and me becoming a nun, she had promised me that she would arrange for me to meet the Mother Superior in Hartford I looked forward to such a meeting with great joy, thinking that if I did meet the Reverend Mother, I would be accepted into her order in spite of my ill health.

Then came this bitter blow. I wrote on June 26, 1946: I had planned to tell the Reverend Mother all about my visions and to let her read my notes so that she could watch me (as Father Shea had suggested). But Sister told me that the Reverend Mother does not talk to anyone except a postulant; and I could not be one because of my chest. But Sister added, very coldly: "Of course, if Father Shea wrote the Reverend Mother and said that she had to see you, then she would have to obey him."

Instantly, I told myself that I would not allow Father to do such a thing for I did not want to bother him nor did I want Reverend Mother to be forced to do something that she did not want to do.

Sister ended the conversation by saying, very firmly: "I spent a great deal of time talking to you. I wasted such time for I could have been doing other things that were more important."

She led me to the door, opened it and I left in tears completely heartbroken. However, I did not blame or condemn the Sister. I, more or less, blamed myself because, as I said: I counted on Sister too much to believe me. it is well that Sister said that because maybe if she didn't say that, I would get vain and I never want to get vain about any thing. It just made me so tired; but I don't mind, and I smile and Jesus can do what He wants to do with me. I don't mind.

Naturally, after such a turn of events, I no longer went to see Sister but I missed her and her friendship a great deal. I also felt that Sister represented all nuns, and if she did not believe me, then no other nun would. So, I never again sought out a nun as a special friend. Then the prediction of Jesus began to come true. Because of the way things turned out, I felt that becoming a nun was going to be a great, hard task because I would have to bring my visions and my messages from Jesus and Mary into a convent. I seem to feel that my visions would prevent me from becoming a nun. I had a very deep feeling that no nun or no convent would want to have anything to do with me because I saw visions.

However, I continued to hope that someday I would become a nun. The following year, 1947, I turned toward the convent of the Discalced Carmelites but that path became blocked by my poor health. Here is the letter I received from that Reverend Mother: June 26, 1947. "After reading your letter of June 16, we regret to be obliged to tell you that your poor health would be an obstacle to your joining our holy order. However, we will remember you in prayer, and if God wills to restore you to health, you may be able to consider becoming a cloistered religious."

Sincerely yours,
Mother Immaculata of The Holy Spirit D. C.

God did not restore my health. I continued to have trouble with my chest. I also continued to hear and see Jesus and Mary. Contrary to popular belief, convents do not welcome girls who have been chosen by God for a special mission. More often than not, I later learned, a nun who sees visions is the cause of confusion and unrest in a convent. They are not welcomed nor are such things as visions encouraged in convents. My dreams of becoming a nun slowly began to die; but my love for that type of a life never did. Hundreds of times I had a deep longing in my heart to run to the peace and quiet of a cloister. Not being a nun caused me great suffering and became one of the greatest sacrifices of my life.

However, it must be remembered that Christ had told me the convent was not for me. He once said: "The convent is not for you. You will be sent where you are most needed."

Monsignor Hayes also told me that the convent was not for me. He told me that I could no longer write if I were a nun.

Then on May 2, 1954, Our Lord said to me: "If you, My Child of Love, had become a nun, even like Saint Theresa and the others, I Myself would have removed the veil from your head for I want My Heart to be in the world, even among sinners; for I came, not so much to call the just, but to call all sinners to My Heart wherein lies their eternal salvation."

After I no longer saw Sister Laurentine, I took her advice to see my parish priest, Father McNerney. I, of course, had seen him at Mass often, but I seldom talked to him. I went to my weekly confessions to another priest in the parish.

So, I gave Father McNerney some of my notes to read—not my secret notes. I thought sure that if Sister could not help me understand what was written, then a priest surely could and he could direct me. I wrote in my notes:

Father kept my notes for a long time (months) and all the while I thought that he would surely be the director I needed. I thought he would interest himself in my job for God and tell me what I had to do. But God made me suffer again for things did not turn out that way. I wanted to talk over so many things with Father, but I cannot now because of what he said to me.

I know I felt so bad because he didn't even say he believed me. He just asked me why I wrote what I did. And I told him that Mary told me to. (I talked to him after confession one Saturday night in the back of the church by the confessional). What I remember, is that he said my writings were a "nice past time," but I shouldn't spend so much time writing. I should go outdoors more. This made me feel so bad I started to cry. I'm sorry that I let him read so much as long as he felt that way about me. It was a bitter blow coming so soon after the one from Sister Laurentine. I don't go to see Sister anymore. Somehow I don't want to bother Father Mc Nerney anymore.

I was all ready to put all my notes away until after I die.

Father Mc Nerney would keep his distance from me when I went to Mass after he had said that to me. However, after I met Monsignor Hayes and he became my spiritual director. Father Mc Nerney changed his attitude towards me; so much so, that he became my confessor. He was very kind to me and he would call Monsignor Hayes to speak about me. I would need such a friend because it was the next day, after I wrote the notes about what Father had said about my writings, when suddenly, on October 10, 1946, my Lady told me she wanted a shrine in Meriden and I was to tell priests about her wishes.

— 4 —

THE SHRINE OF THE IMMACULATE HEART OF MARY: OCTOBER 10, 1946

Throughout the story of my Lady, it can be plainly seen that God had a peace plan for suffering humanity which revolved not only around my Lady but also around me, my job for God and The Devil's Challenge. I, of course, had no idea what the plan was when in 1944, 1945 and 1946 I was making notes in my little note books about what I was being told by Heaven. As I said, I merely wrote what I saw and what I heard never attempting to put the pieces together. I would merely say: "If that is the way God wants it, then it is all right with me." That love for God's holy will was shown throughout my life in all areas: daily duties, crosses, the challenge, the visions, my writings, all the work I did for God, my Lady, for the world, for souls, etc. Such love was also shown in October of 1946, when I was asked to do a job which was far more difficult for me to do than actually accepting the challenge; because, that task was completely against my desires to remain hidden and unknown. I cringed at the thought of carrying out the wishes of Heaven and my Lady.

Many people think that it is pure joy to see visions. They are wrong. It is very far from being pure joy or one long, unending moment of happiness. Many people think they see visions and they become wrapped up in them. This is what happens with the false visions of doom, death and destruction. The so-called "seers" want only moments of bliss and great attention and end up inventing their own visions and messages.

When one truly has a job to do for Jesus and Mary, one must be willing to pay a very high price. The job I had to do for God was not the job I wanted to do for God. I wanted to become a nun. When I was first told about the peace plan from

353

God I had my own plans for my own life, ones which did not include visions or writings. I was told that my writings would be read all over the world. I had no writings at that time nor did I have any plans to produce such writings.

Then when the great peace plan began to unfold more it involved me in it in a way which I did not want to get involved. The only thing that I can say is that the price I had to pay, because I received favors from God, became a very severe price to pay.

When I was first told what this price consisted of, I was terrified. I wanted to run away from all which I had been given. However, I would not run away because I so loved God's holy will. I told Him and Mary that they could do anything they wanted to do with me. I told them that I would try my best to carry out their wishes.

It was on October 10, 1946 when the Holy Mother of God appeared to me and told me about a shrine which she wanted in Meriden.

This is what I wrote in my notes: This morning the Blessed Virgin appeared to me and told me something that made me feel sick because it is so great and so hard for me to do. And I am frightened even though Mary told me not to be.

Now Our Lady wants me to make myself known to the world. And this is so hard for me to do that if I did not have special help from my God I would fail miserably.

I must announce to the world that I see Mary and Jesus and hear them. I can't possibly write how I feel. I just feel sick and tired but I will. I don't want to tell the world anything but I will do God's will.

Mary appeared to me dressed in pure white. The gown hung over her feet. Her arms were down and out and bright rays of light came from her fingers.

Her face was so beautiful and she smiled at me so very tenderly and beautifully. Her hair hung loosely around her face. On her head she wore a small crown of roses.

Then she spoke. She said that I was to go to priests and tell them that she wanted a shrine built on an overgrown wooded section near my home. She showed me this land in my vision.

She said that the shrine was to be white on the outside and white on the inside, except for the pews, which were to be light brown, to show purity: "On each pillar, Mary said, place a picture of my heart and my Son's Heart to show all who enter that love is there. On each window place a picture of our love for our children." Mary said to name the shrine in honor of her Immaculate Heart.

Mary said to put a bell in the steeple and that it will be rung by angels.

She said that Saint Cecilia will guard the organ so that only the sweetest notes will be played.

Mary said she wanted processions and the bishop was to start these processions.

It is difficult to explain how I felt when my Lady gave me that task which was definitely not to my liking. I could think of a thousand things I would rather do than to go to priests and the bishop to tell them that Our Lady wanted a shrine in Meriden.

The first thing I did was to walk to where Our Lady wanted her shrine on a large field close to my home. She had shown me the site in the vision.

I wrote: I don't even know who owns the place. I walked there and looked at it . . . It isn't a pretty sight, but the open fields around it are pretty.

At that time, the land Our Lady wanted was part of a huge farm called Coe's farm. That was the place where the rock was when, in 1948, I saw the Golden Lady stand on it. That field was used as a pasture for the farm's cows.

When I first walked to the farm land, I did not go all the way up the hill to see the whole area. I stood at the beginning of this street leading to the fields. It was at that spot where I said: "There will have to be a big sign to hold all those words The Shrine of The Immaculate Heart of Mary."

I was not happy looking at the place where Our Lady wanted her shrine. I started to cry. I wrote: I stayed there looking at the place and I felt so sick and scared thinking that I would have to tell people what Mary said. Mary said not to be scared, but I can't help it. I can imagine a little of what is going to happen; but I will tell everyone because Mary wants them to know . . . Oh! God! give me courage!

I did not waste time trying to carry out my Lady's wishes. That very evening, I made my first visit to a priest I wrote: Tonight I knew I had to go see a priest like Mary said. So, I called up Father Mc Nerney but he wasn't there.

So, I went down town and went to see the priest at Saint Mary's church.

I rang the doorbell very shyly. But I knew I had to stay and see the priest because Our Lady said to.

And I saw him. He was an elderly priest. I never saw him before. He was very nice to me and then we sat and talked about different things like my schooling and family etc.

I felt more and more at ease and then finally he asked me why I was there and I slowly told him. It was very hard at first, but he was very understanding and I felt more at ease as I talked. I told him about the shrine and the processions and he said he believed me and I felt so happy.

He said that the next time I see Mary to tell her he will do all in his power to do what she wants done.

He did say that the land where Mary wants the shrine is in Saint Joseph's parish, but I have to talk to other priests. But I feel so much better now because he was so nice and he believed me. I told him a few other things, and he said he believed them and I felt so much better: "Thank You Jesus, I love You so. . . ."

This visit to the first priest I told about the shrine went very well. I could not say the same for the next priests I saw.

On October 24, 1946 I wrote that I took the priest's (at Saint Mary's Church) advice and I went to see the priests in my own parish church, Saint Joseph's.

I went to confession and after I made my confession, I waited for my two parish priests to come out of the confessional. One priest was Father O'Connell. The other was Father Mc Nerney who had read some of my notes and had not been too favorable to me or the notes.

I wrote on October 24, 1946: I went to see Father Mc Nerney and Father O'Connell to tell about Our Lady's desire to have the shrine built.

I'm afraid that they didn't believe me very much. I couldn't even finish telling Father O'Connell because I started to cry because Father O'Connell said that I shouldn't go around telling people such things. I saw Father McNerney and Father O'Connell after confession in the back of the church.

Undaunted by the cool reception I received, from my own parish priests, telling them my Lady's request, I went to see other priests.

I recorded these visits: But then I saw Father Dolan and he believed me, I guess. He asked me to ask Our Lady what kind of material was to be used in the church.

Then I saw the two priests at Our Lady of Mount Carmel Church. They were both nice to me and the pastor asked me also the next time Our Lady came to ask what kind of material to be used.

I thought that the material was to be wood, but then Our Lady appeared to me and I asked her and she said it was to be built of the purest white stone.

By November 4, 1946, I had seen all the priests in Meriden telling each one about the shrine. On November 4, I wrote these notes: I had already seen several priests at the different parishes in Meriden. But I had yet to go to Saint Rose's parish and the Polish parish. I went there tonight and I saw the priest at Saint Rose's rectory, but he had to go out on a sick call so he couldn't talk very long.

Then I went to the Polish rectory. I met a priest who wouldn't tell me his name. But we had a long talk. He asked me many questions. Then, he said something funny. He said that that night or the day before I went to see him, he was talking to a non-Catholic who wanted to be a Catholic. He said to the non-Catholic, "What would you say if someone came to you and said that the Blessed Virgin appeared to her?" The non-

Catholic said, "I will take it with a grain of salt." And the priest said, "I would too."

Then I came to him and told my story and it was strange. He said that he knew I was telling the truth. And we talked about different things Our Lady and dear Jesus said to me.

Then he said that I was to ask Our Lady who was to handle the building of the shrine and where the money was to come from. He said that all the parishes were in debt, more or less, because of their mortgages.

Then he said that he was sort of going to test Our Lady and said that if she answers a certain prayer of the priest's, then he would believe it more.

So, I told him that I'll ask Our Lady what he told me to ask her and I'd pray that she answers his prayer.

Then I showed him the gold leaf and I told him how I got it and I said he was to look at it and pray that Our Lady would answer his prayer. (I had gotten the locket with the gold leaf back from Father Shea.)

Now I had seen a priest or priests at all the parishes except the one in South Meriden.

A few days later, my Lady told me to get a letter from a local priest so that I could go to see the bishop about her shrine. This task proved to be far more difficult for me to accomplish than merely telling priests that Our Lady wanted a shrine in Meriden.

I started the rounds again, this time with disastrous results.

My Lady had told me that I had a hard, important job to do for God. She had told me that I would meet opposition and hate because the devil would be strong. It did not take me very long to find the opposition.

A journey to the bishop's office with a message from the Holy Mother of God is one of the most difficult journeys to make. Contrary to popular, public belief, people who claim to see visions are not welcomed by the priests and bishops. I will never blame the priest or the bishop for their suspicions and their reluctance to accept my visions. They were within their rights to be cautious. As I have been told many, many times, there are cases of fraud, deceptions and so forth on record in connection with visions. So whenever a person tells a priest that he or she sees a vision, especially when there is some sort of a request from the vision, that priest becomes suspicious and cautious. In my case, the priests showed even more reserve than usual because my Lady had asked for a public shrine. But, of course, in 1946 I did not know such things. Even if the priests did not mean to cause me any suffering, their actions and their words were bitter crosses for me to carry; in addition to the sufferings I felt just ringing the doorbell at each rectory wanting to run away. But I did not run away because I was doing all in my power to carry out the wishes and instructions of my Lady.

I continued to see priests, asking for the letter to the bishop. The visits to the priests were not successful. I began to hear the same words which were still spoken to me in 1960: "Imagination," "Illusions," "Deceptions," "Frauds," "Tricks of the devil" and: "So you see the Blessed Virgin? I do not see her." "Prove it! Prove It!" "Prove it'" "Where is your proof?" "Prove it!" "Ask her to answer my prayer, then I will believe you." "Where is the sign? There has to be a sign." More than one priest looked at me with glaring eyes of suspicion when he demanded the proof. One priest even said to me: "In six months you will be in an insane asylum." (That never came true, thank goodness.) When all these things were told to me, I could only hang my head and cry. My Lady had told me to deliver a message. I was trying—but it wasn't easy.

I did not give up right away. I went from one rectory to another in Meriden. Each time I rang the bell, I wanted to run away before someone answered the ring. But I did not run away because I had to do a job for God and for my Lady. I talked to one priest then to another priest. Most of the time, after they got through talking to me, I did not even dare ask for the letter to the bishop. Even the priests who had said a kind word to me before now were cold and they absolutely refused my request for the letter.

I did not give up right away. But asking for the letter from a local priest to the bishop changed my plans. I had no idea how to get such a letter, so I shyly returned to Sister Laurentine. I had not seen her since she had treated me so coldly and mentioned the tricks of the devil after she had read some of my writings.

She came to the door when I rang the bell, but she wasn't too happy to see me. She invited me in and I explained about the shrine my Lady wanted and how I had told priests, but now I needed a letter from a priest to take to the bishop so I could tell him about the shrine. I asked her how I could get this letter. Needless to say, this nun who already was against my visions did not help me. Her answer caused me more tears: "Don't even bother to see any more priests. They will never give you any such letter. They don't want to have anything to do with you." I was deeply hurt and I felt defeated. I went home and I cried for a long time. What could I do now? My Lady came with the answer.

She appeared to me and she told me that she would send someone to help me. A few weeks later I met that someone. And finally, through that person, I met the priest who became my spiritual director, Monsignor John J. Hayes, Chancellor of the Hartford Diocese. He was very kind to me. He wanted to help me; at least he was willing to listen to my story and to read my notes. I placed my spiritual life and my job for God in his hands. I felt very grateful and I felt honored to think that he would bother with me.

The priest knew the bishop well; but he told me that it would be better if I did not see the bishop right away. The priest told me to wait awhile; and so I waited . . . and waited . . . and waited, never once losing faith in my Lady or the job she and God had given me to do.

On October 10, 1946, when my Lady told me that she wanted a shrine to her Immaculate Heart in Meriden, the first thing I did was to walk to where Our Lady wanted her shrine. She had shown me the site in the vision. This is the road I walked upon, Allen Ave., not far from my home on West Main St. I wrote in my notes: "I don't even know who owns the place. I walked there and looked at it . . . It isn't a pretty sight but the open fields around it are pretty."

This picture shows the exact road I walked upon to go to the field which was part of a huge farm called Coe's Farm. It was at this spot where I said: "There will have to be a big sign to hold all these words. The Shrine of the Immaculate Heart of Mary."

This picture shows the house my mother and I lived in when my Lady told me about the shrine she wanted. We lived above the store in a small apartment. This building was a short distance from the street, Allen Ave., which I walked upon to the place where my Lady wanted her shrine. The building has now been torn down and a gas station built in its place. The address was 517 West Main St. The stairs on the right side of the building led to our apartment.

Part 9

Monsignor John J. Hayes
Chancellor of the Diocese
of Hartford, Connecticut
Spiritual Director
Year 1947

INTRODUCTION

Monsignor John J. Hayes was my spiritual director for ten years from 1947 to 1957. It is important to remember that he, during these years especially during the first five years of our spiritual relationship, read and approved all the writings, messages and visions in my note books. These included the visions and messages about The Devil's Challenge and the praises from Heaven which I heard. After close examination of such writings, Monsignor Hayes told me that "all was from God." That is why he continued to be my spiritual director.

— 1 —

I CONTINUE TO SEARCH FOR A NEW SPIRITUAL DIRECTOR: THE CHALLENGE CONTINUES

At the beginning of 1947, as I explained, I had received more praises from Heaven and The Devil's Challenge began in all its fury. Also, I had not forgotten my Lady's shrine and her request to get a letter to give to the bishop so I could tell him about the shrine.

On January 27, 1947, I wrote again about the attacks of the devil: Oh! Yes! it is all true about the devil's attacks. And it will get worse and worse. I cannot really explain what I suffer. But the devil comes and his evil ones surround me and torture me. Although the marks of the wounds are not on my body, I feel the pain and the marks are in my soul.

These visual attacks of the devil and his evil ones were not the only sufferings of the challenge. On January 29, 1947, I wrote: "Oh! dear Jesus, suddenly a very great suffering has entered my heart. Dear Jesus, it is because of what You have said to me and the praises You gave to me. I remember a few of the things You said to me.

"Dear Jesus, Oh! this suffering! It is turning into an agony. This weight is too much to bear. I am falling with it, Jesus, why did You let me hear such words? It is such a torture to carry this cross. I can't really explain it but this weight of Your praises is making me fall. I was seized with a desire to tear up all the praises You gave me. It is too much for me to bear.

"But I could not do that because You don't want me to.

"But, how can I bear such a cross? It is worse because I realize how nothing I am.

"First of all, it is the love that I cannot bear, then it's the praise.

"Jesus, I know You are Almighty. How is it that You lower

Yourself to praise me? It is a torture that is hard to explain. But, dear Lord, I suffer from it because I know how nothing I am.

"The devil keeps telling me that You are angry with me because of what I write. Dear Jesus, I don't blame You for being angry if I made it all up. But, dear God, I did not make it up. I did not. You did tell me what I wrote.

"It would be so much better to tell me how useless I am and how I sinned and how much penance I must do. Why don't You tell me that? Instead You tell me how much Yon love me."

Here can be seen the devil's attacks to once again make me stop believing. At that time, before I met Monsignor Hayes, I had been told by priests and Sister Laurentine the devil could be playing a trick on me with all my visions and messages from Heaven. So it was fairly easy for the devil to attempt to get me to give up my belief in my visions and work for God (which now included my Lady's shrine). Not only that, but note how the devil attempted to get me to destroy my notes.

One of the triumphs I had was *not* to destroy my notes, which were the very foundation for the visions of The Golden Lady. If I had given up at that point, and if the devil had destroyed my faith and belief in all I was told and in all I had seen, then there would not have been the Shrine of The Immaculate Heart of Mary. These attacks against my faith and belief came *after* my Lady had told me, in 1946, that she wanted the shrine to her heart. The request from my Lady, in 1946, was the start of the visions of The Golden Lady in 1948. The devil felt, and rightly so, that if he could, in 1947, destroy my faith in my visions, then the plans of God to bring The Golden Lady and her promises of peace, joy and happiness to the world, through me, would have ended.

However, my faith remained. After I had been so tempted to destroy my notes (which had been made easy by the devil for I agreed that I was a nothing and not worthy of any praises from Heaven) I wrote (Same day, January 29, 1947): "Dear Jesus, I won't doubt, I won't! Dear Jesus help me. I am so weak. Help me. Mary, please hold me close and tell the angels and saints not to be mad at me. Please my Lady, tell them that I'll always work for them and I won't even look at their faces because I am not worthy. Mary, you understand what I am suffering. Mary, I am suffering so much."

On February 5, 1947, I wrote again about the attacks of the devil. Once again he tried to make me feel guilty, by implying that if I did not give up, he would make me believe that I would be the cause of souls going to Hell. He also threatened me, telling me that he could win my soul as quickly as he won the souls of those who made no effort to fight temptations and sin. But notice how, suddenly, God gave me the power of The Mighty Warrior He said I was. Here is a very important example of the power of this warrior's victory, in spite of the tremendous might of the devil, and my belief in my power:

Today the devil was very strong. Suddenly, I saw a vision and I saw the devil and his evil ones surround hundreds of people on earth. He was tempting them and forcing them to obey by whipping them with a huge, long whip. They did not feel the pain of the whip, but each lash was a scar of sin in each person's soul. The devil was very happy and smiled at me. He turned to me in great triumph and spoke in a loud voice. He said that he has won all these souls and he said that he will win me with his whip and put deep scars in my soul. He said that these people were his and he was strong and powerful.

I felt bad at first, but suddenly I grew strong and for a few minutes Heaven and Hell and earth trembled beneath the strain of a great battle. There were no blows or wounds. But a battle of the strength and power of the devil and God's warrior. It was very strange. The devil stood tall and mighty with his ugly whip in his hands. I stood weak and powerless, but then I became strong and powerful through God. And I told the devil that I will break his whip on the battlefield. And he laughed at me and said it was impossible. But I became stronger and the battle became greater. The devil had reached his height whereas I had still greater power to gain.

And slowly the devil backed away and his evil ones became frightened for I felt new power and strength fill my heart and soul and I looked at the devil and he could not frighten me. But as he gazed at me, he became frightened for he saw I was winning. I told him I would break his whip of sin and he became weaker. Then suddenly he became small and weak and he backed far away and I saw fear in his face. For I stood tall and powerful and the devil ran away.

And God's grace could return to heal the wounds of his evil whip. For the devil had lost again and God's mercy, grace and love have won. And I must not be frightened of the powers God gives me because then the devil will win. God chose me and His glory will be great for all will praise His mercy, love and grace to so do what He does with a weak child. I will fight the devil on the battlefields and I will suffer but I won't mind because I will do it for God and His children.

Naturally, in 1947, I had no idea what the full significance of this battle was. I could not have explained it then as I just did; but I can now remember what my Lady told me, in 1944, when she said (April 14, 1944): "Remember, my child, that you are as small as the smallest fish in the sea, but the whale cannot hurt you for you will prove to him that you have more power than he has; and the huge whale will flee for he will suddenly become afraid of the little fish, for God shall will it."

This battle, which I won, is one example of the way that prediction came true.

I added these notes when I wrote about the way the devil still comes and makes me suffer with his whip and spear: But lately he finds he cannot frighten me and he is worried for I do not back away from his blows and his sharp spear and he cannot make me cry out; and he is worried. He was very happy when Jesus said he could make me suffer, but now no matter how much he makes me suffer, it still doesn't make me cry out and shrink back or to have any desire to reconsider and maybe refuse to accept The Devil's Challenge. I am not really brave. Because if I relied on my own strength, then long ago I would be dead. But I rely on Jesus and Mary and there is my strength and never did they fail me.

The devil returned from his defeat, filled with pride that made him believe he would still win this challenge. On February 7, 1947, I wrote that Jesus told me about more physical sufferings which would be mine.

I wrote: Then the devil tried to make me dislike sufferings but here again he failed. He tries everything, but he does not win. Love wins and always love will win.

As I said, all my life I had physical problems; mainly, heart problems which at that time (1944-47 onward) no doctor could discover. I was often sick and weak. Of course, I got the usual "results" from their examinations when they could not find the causes for an illness; it was "all in my head" or "my nerves." Only one doctor I went to realized the problem. He told me to see a heart specialist. However, at that time, I was starting a new job, so I never bothered to go to the specialist. The main problem was a leaky Mitral Valve and a hole in my heart which was not corrected until 1993. Yet, I never used poor health as an excuse to stop working in offices or for my Lord. I merely forced myself to go on, even though I constantly lived with physical sufferings. I simply would not give up knowing that if I did, the devil would win.

By February 11, 1947, I was still trying to get the letter from a local priest so I could see the bishop about my Lady's shrine. I was not successful. I wrote: Last night I was saying my prayers. I felt sort of bad because I asked Father Dolan to give me the letter to the bishop; but he would not. That was when I went to see Sister Laurentine about the letter and she told me not to bother to see anymore priests about the letter "because they do not want anything to do with me."

I continued: I asked my Lady what I was to do. . . . She appeared to me and she said that I was to tell people about the shrine even before I told the bishop. I told my Lady that I did not know who to tell. She said that I just had to tell a few and that will be enough. She said that she would send these people to me and I would know that they are the ones I am to tell.

Then just before that happened, I saw once again my power as the Mighty Warrior, (February 11, 1947):

After I said my Rosary and meditating on the sorrowful mysteries this happened. Suddenly the devil came and he was extremely angry. His evil ones surrounded me. (When I had the temptations the devil was not visible. He just tempted me as he tempts others). Now I saw him very clearly and he was very angry and his evil ones were very angry. He had a huge whip in his hands. He looked at me with great hate in his eyes. He started to yell at me in a loud voice and as he talked he hit me with his whip. He said that he hated two things above all. That was the Blessed Sacrament and devotion to the Passion of Our Lord. He was taking his anger out on me by whipping me because he said that souls who have great devotion to the Blessed Sacrament and to the Passion of Our Lord are gone from his reach and they save their souls.

Then I saw the Blessed Sacrament and several evil ones surround it and were about to destroy it. But then, in a flash of light, I saw myself as the Mighty Warrior, full of power and strength, stand in front of the Blessed Sacrament. The evil ones instantly drew back and became frightened. I held my sword in one hand and my shield in the other. The evil ones became frightened for I talked to them in a loud voice.

On February 24 and 25, I was given additional help or power from Heaven to be used upon the battlefields. I wrote: Yesterday was Sunday and I received my Beloved in Holy Communion. Almost immediately Jesus came and started to talk to me. He seemed very sad. I said, "I love You" and Jesus replied: "Yes, little child, love, love is all I ask from My children and they refuse. I walk among them, pleading, begging, asking for their love and they refuse."

I felt so bad and I shall try so very hard through my notes to get more people to love dear, sweet Jesus.

Jesus said He had a message for me: "Dear little Child of Love, consider, sweet child, the multitude of evil spirits and demons that roam through the world seeking the ruin of souls. Consider also sweet Child of Love, the number of these evil spirits that you will drive back into Hell to stay forever. You can destroy the tempter, but angels can destroy temptation. Sweet child, I see you before Me as a Mighty Warrior whom I can rely upon to destroy (destroy their power) and push back into Hell evil spirits until the end of time. I see you also leading angels into battlefields when these angels will destroy temptations and bring grace to wounded souls of sin."

Our Lord often mentioned these angels to me, such as in this message dated March 2, 1991: "Ah, My most beloved Child of Love, you are (one) who has angels . . . for you are the one who accepted and then won The Devil's Challenge."

As my Lady had told me, she sent someone to help me reach the bishop with her request for a shrine. This happened around February 17, 1947.

Actually the first one who came was the most unlikely to offer such help. He was my Uncle Joe. He came to visit my mother and he saw what he did not like. He never was fond of me; although, he was my Godfather. My mother must have told him a little about my visions and his advice to her was to have a psychiatrist examine me. He was mainly upset with me, at that time, because I was not working (due to my poor health). He insisted that a grown woman should be out on her own supporting herself, saying: "She doesn't have enough intelligence to support herself." (I was 23 years old at that time.)

At first my mother did not know what to do to follow his advice. She actually believed all I told her, but the bit about me not working gave her second thoughts.

She was working with a woman named Rena and she became interested in my visions and my plight about getting to see the bishop. Rena agreed to see me and when my mother mentioned a psychiatrist, Rena gave my mother the name of a doctor. I wrote about this visit to this doctor on February 17, 1947:

It has come true already. My Lady has sent the first one to help me. He is a Doctor Gosselin in Hartford. My mother took me today to see him and he was very nice to me. He knows the bishop. I gave him some of my articles to read. Later, he told my mother that they were very nice and he was going to show them to the secretary of the bishop, who is his friend.

The doctor asked me many questions about my visions. He told my mother that I was unusual and that he was surprised because I had seen so many visions over a period of time. He didn't really help my chest. He didn't say anything about that. (the pain in my chest still bothers me).

He saw a couple of my paintings, and he was surprised that I didn't have any lessons. He was also surprised about my poems and he asked my mother if I copied them, which, of course, I didn't. I am sure he will help me see the bishop who is his friend. And it will be much better if the doctor brings me to the bishop than if I went myself. The priests in Meriden wouldn't give me a letter to the bishop so my Lady sent me someone to help me like she said she would.

I am very happy that the doctor has taken such a great interest in me. He is going to show my poems to a poet he knows and he wants an artist to see my paintings.

At this meeting, I gave the doctor one of my note books. Then I forgot that. Then into the picture stepped a priest, in Hartford, Father Kinney. Rena had made an appointment for me to meet this priest. The date was April 12, 1947:

I went to Hartford to meet a priest whom Rena made an appointment with. My Lady surely sent Rena to help me. it turned out that Father Kinney was the one whom the doctor had given my notes to.

At first, when I talked to this priest, he said that I could be having delusions. I started to cry. Then I told him I was writing a little about myself and perhaps he would know me better if he read such writings. Father said that he wanted to read it and I told him that I would bring it to him the next week.

Before I left, he said that he believed I was very child-like and sincere; and he added, that he would take my articles to the bishop's secretary (who was Monsignor Hayes, but I did not know that).

When I left, I was very upset with the word "delusions." once again, the devil took advantage of the situation. I, wrote: Oh! my God! Your little child knows that she was innocent of deceiving! How could I have known about such things when You did not tell me? I only know what You taught me., Yes, the little child wondered a great deal and the devil took advantage; and I suffered. Yes, I suffered very much because I learned of the ways of the Church. But my peace slowly returned because I read about what Saint Theresa said, and by a miracle, she explained the difference between delusions and real visions. I read that my visions had all the ways of the real ones. . . .

It is hard for my mind to think about such things. It is better if I don't. Then Jesus and Mary will have to take care of everything and they always did before. I still believe and trust and love.

On April 19, 1947, I again went to see Father Kinney. I was very nervous after what he had said during my first visit. But this time: I again went to see Father Kinney. He was very kind to me. He really comforted me as no priest ever did before. He set my mind at ease because he said that I was to just continue what I was doing and not to worry and to pray. He said he tried to see the bishop's secretary (Monsignor Hayes) but he was busy.

He took my (small) autobiography and said that he would read it. I said to him: "Maybe the authorities will burn it;" and he said they would not do that.

I added: My Lady has indeed sent Father Kinney to help me like she said she would when she told me that she would send people to help me. . . . I will accept the Church's decision whether it is for or against me.

On May 3, 1947, I wrote a most interesting note. I was speaking to Jesus and I was telling Him that He called saints like Saint Theresa, "daughter;" but He does. not call me "daughter." He called me His "Bride," and "Queen" and the "favorite" of His Heart. I asked: "How could this be true when I sinned greater than Saint Theresa? . . . Why would You say this, when I deserve to hear 100 times less than Saint Theresa? You never called me "daughter."

Jesus answered: "What troubles your heart, sweet one, is

that you cannot see the price you have paid. . . . Indeed, beloved, you know of the great sufferings that you shall endure on the battlefields. But the really great sufferings cannot be fully made known to you."

The reason I now find that so interesting is what Monsignor Hayes, whom I had not met yet, said to me after he read my note book about The Devil's Challenge and the praises: "It seems to me that you are more than a daughter of God's."

2

MONSIGNOR JOHN J. HAYES
CHANCELLOR OF THE
DIOCESE OF HARTFORD, CONN.

After Father Shea was no longer my spiritual director, I met my second director in 1947. He was Monsignor Hayes who was, when I met him, Chancellor of the Diocese of Hartford, Connecticut.

Monsignor Hayes was a very learned theologian and extremely knowledgeable. He could speak and read different languages. He often gave lectures. I once heard one of his lectures on Church history.

He was ordained on May 30, 1931 in St. Joseph's Cathedral in Hartford. In 1934, he was appointed secretary to Bishop McAuliffe and also named assistant diocesan director of the Society For the Propagation of the Faith. From 1934 to 1944, he also taught religion and ethics at Saint Joseph's College in West Hartford.

On June 5, 1945, Monsignor Hayes was appointed Chancellor and Chief Judge of the Hartford Diocese, when he was only 39 years old. In October of that year, Pope Pius XII elevated him to the rank of domestic prelate with the title of Right Reverend Monsignor and the following July he was named a diocesan consultor.

With such a background and ecclesiastical appointments, Monsignor Hayes had the knowledge and the competence to judge my work for God and my revelations. His office at the chancery was the same one used by Archbishop O'Brien. Sometimes when I went to the chancery to see Monsignor, I would be greeted by the bishop who was very kind to me; however, I never talked to the bishop. I left my case in the hands of his chancellor.

Needless to say, Monsignor Hayes was not only a very important priest in the diocese, he was also extremely busy.

During his years at the chancery, he compiled an outstanding record as an administrator, lecturer, handling all sorts of problems within the diocese and consultant to Catholics and non-Catholics as well. He was admired and liked by countless people. I often heard him, on the phone, give words of comfort to many people who had a heavy cross to carry.

It was to this priest my Lady sent me when I was in need of a spiritual director. As our relationship grew more spiritual and close, I regarded him as a living saint and I often wondered why this great important priest would bother with a big "nobody" as I considered myself to be.

For a period of about ten years, this famous, brilliant theologian took the time to be my spiritual director.

He not only guided me along the paths the good Lord had placed me upon, he read all my writings. At times my note books were in his possession for years. I had no copies of these note books, but I trusted him with them.

It is a long story as to how I met Monsignor Hayes. To make this long story short, I will begin by saying that one day my mother told a friend of hers about my visions and asked her what she should do to help me. (My mother believed my visions from the start.) This woman's name was Rena.

By the time I met Rena and she agreed to help me, I was attempting to reach the bishop to tell him that my Lady wanted a shrine to her Immaculate Heart in Meriden near my home.

On October 10, 1946, when my Lady first told me about this shrine, she told me to go to priests to tell them what she wanted.

This request caused me agony because I had no desires to see priests to tell them such a thing. Even though I suffered greatly, I tried to follow my Lady's request by talking to local priests, none of whom believed me.

I was also instructed to get a letter from a priest to take to the bishop. None would give me such a letter and a nun I knew said that I would never get a letter like that.

But I would not give up no matter how much I suffered.

I had to see the bishop. That was when my mother talked to Rena.

Rena and I fast became friends, and she believed in my visions. She became determined to help me. She said she knew a priest, who knew Monsignor Hayes, who was in the bishop's office, who could get me to see the bishop. Also, Rena helped my mother find a doctor who was willing to see me and talk to me (a psychiatrist).

I have before me three letters written to me by Rena who explained the remarkable events which happened just before I met Monsignor Hayes. The first letter states: "Dear Louise, just a short note to let you know that I am still working in your behalf. I can't explain the details just now, but have faith in me and I shall do all I can to have your works read and passed on by those I think will understand.

"I did discuss you with a friend of mine who understands and she has spoken to a priest friend of hers who is very interested in you. We will try to make an appointment soon to have you talk to him. But the Easter season is such a busy one in the Church that it would be advisable to wait until after this Feast, unless arrangements can be made sooner. Again I ask you to have faith and be patient."

Love, Rena

Meanwhile, I went to see the doctor in Hartford, and gave him some of my notes to read. My mother was greatly encouraged when, after talking to me, the doctor said to her: "How long has this been going on? the visions and the writing?"

My mother replied, fearfully: "Well, for a couple of years—three—since 1944."

A smile burst upon her lips when the doctor replied: "Well, you have nothing to worry about! There has to be something to all this; if there were not, she would have been insane after the first year or even a few months."

My mother was delighted, especially when the doctor said he had been deeply impressed with me. So impressed had he been that he gave my notes to a priest—the very one I met by accident, who in turn gave my notes to Monsignor Hayes, after the doctor told Monsignor Hayes about me.

This priest's name was Father Kinney. It was to Father Kinney the doctor had given my notes; although, I did not know that fact. Then Father Kinney gave my note book to Monsignor Hayes. That was how Monsignor got the note book and walked into the room with it the first time we met.

I never saw this doctor or Father Kinney again. It seemed they had been put into my life just for that one purpose of getting me to see Monsignor Hayes. I also never saw Rena again. I shall always be grateful to these three who had helped me because they believed that indeed I did have a special job to do for God, my Lady and my Church.

At that time, 1947, as I said I was still trying to obey my Lady by telling priests and the bishop that she wanted a shrine in Meriden. I wrote about my feelings at that first meeting with my spiritual director. I wrote these notes in 1973:

It had been extremely difficult for me to speak to priests about my Lady's shrine. I was always so filled with fear that I wanted to run away. Only my faith in my Lady and what she told me to do gave me the courage to stay and talk. Now, once again I wanted to run away. I felt so unworthy. I was a "nobody," very poor at that time. I drove to Hartford in our old, beat-up car that did not even have a heater. We lived poorly in the house on West Main Street, over the store. I wondered if I was dressed well enough to enter the place where the bishop had his office. I almost did not ring the door-bell. But my Lady and her request gave me the courage to stand there and ring the bell.

A young girl came to the door. She was a teenager who worked part-time in the evening for Monsignor. She answered the bell and the phone for him in his office. She showed me into a waiting room after I had told her that I had an appointment with Monsignor Hayes. She said he was expecting me. I was 23 years old; but I felt more like a frightened child. (Later Monsignor was to think of me only as a child and he always called me youngster.)

I was very nervous as I waited for the priest to come into the room. For a few, awful moments I felt like getting up and running away. I felt so out of place in the beautiful room with its fine furniture and paintings on the wall and carpet on the floor.

Now I will continue by quoting what I wrote in a short autobiography dated April 1951: I shall never forget our first meeting. I was so nervous sitting there, waiting, that I almost left without seeing him. I stayed only because I had to tell someone about the visions and the shrine. At that point, I had been hurt so often by priests and nuns, that I was well prepared for another disappointment. I thought I would just leave and not return to see him; I was so sure that he would not want to have anything to do with me.

As I sat in the waiting room, thinking I should leave because this famous priest would have nothing to do with me, suddenly he walked into the room: a large man dressed as a priest in fine clothing. His appearance overpowered me, and much to my amazement, Monsignor had in his hand the note book I had given to the doctor. I, of course, had no idea how he had gotten it. Not only did he have my note book, but he told me that he had read it. That was why he agreed to see me.

There was no reason why this famous, learned theologian would even consider, seeing me if he had not been deeply impressed by what he had read in my note book. As the doctor had said to my mother about me, "There has to be something to all this . . .," so Monsignor Hayes must have thought the same thing.

This poor (my mother and I were very poor) little "nobody" was face to face with the most important priest in the Hartford diocese, and the first words he spoke to me as he handed me my note book were: "It seems to me that you understand God's love for His children."

No priest had ever said such a thing to me.

When Monsignor Hayes walked into the room where I waited for him, suddenly it was different than when other priests had walked into a room where I waited to tell the story of my

Lady's request for her shrine. I seemed to feel a warmness, whereas with the other priests I had felt only a cold fear.

I had been ready for another disappointment; but that did not happen. Monsignor's voice was warm and gentle and he made me feel like I was the important one, not him. His voice was very humble when he had told me that I understood God's love for His children.

To me, he became a "living saint," so much did I admire him. I never forgot his kindness to me that day when I first met him.

Indeed, I had been very afraid to see this important priest, but as soon as we met, all fear vanished.

He utterly surprised me with his kindness, gentleness and understanding. He did not look at me with suspicion as had other priests, but with a look of gentleness and almost awe, as if he had been—which he was—deeply impressed by what he had read in my notes.

Monsignor Hayes was a very large man, not too tall, but large. He was overpowering as he entered a room. He was also a very joy filled, happy-go-lucky sort of a person. (When I heard him laughing and joking once with other priests, while I waited for him, I was shocked. I had never heard a priest laugh or joke, before.) He had a marvelous personality. He could attract people to him. He was also "large" in his important position as second only to the bishop. He had great charm and dignity. He was a noted lecturer. He was proud of his knowledge, his place of importance, his ability to handle people, and so forth.

He was well-known and well-liked. He was very efficient in his work; and he was the youngest Chancellor the diocese ever had; not yet 40 years old.

At our first meeting, I told Monsignor as little as possible, and he did not force me to say more. He listened carefully and said a few words. He told me that my case was unusual and, of course, he could not judge it completely until he knew me better. But his warm smile of encouragement made me feel that perhaps there was hope that I had found the priest I was seeking, the one who could help me.

I did tell him that I had to see the bishop, but he said: "Perhaps later." This "later" never came. However, once I met Monsignor, I had found my spiritual director. Before I left to return to Meriden, we made another appointment; which turned out to be the first of many weekly visits.

Before I said good-bye, suddenly I remembered that I had on my old, worn shoes. I did have a better pair, but I had been so nervous about this appointment that I forgot to put on my best shoes. I looked down at my shoes as Monsignor led me to the front door and I apologized because I had on my old shoes. He merely laughed and said that it was all right, he hadn't minded in the least.

That started a long, spiritual relationship I had with Monsignor Hayes. I can say that Father Kinney and the doctor I went to see must have been deeply impressed. Otherwise they would never had sent me to someone as important and well-known as Monsignor Hayes. If the priest had thought that I was a fraud or deluded, he would have never sent me to the Chancellor of the Diocese of Hartford, Connecticut. He would have returned my note book and dismissed the case.

After our first appointment, Monsignor kept seeing me in his office in Hartford. I would go to see him sometimes two or three times a week. He wanted to get to know me and my work for God before he passed judgment upon that work and upon the visions.

After I met Monsignor Hayes, my whole life, more or less, revolved around my visits to Hartford to see him. Although I made the trip two, sometimes three times a week, I did not always see him because he was often too busy or else he had been called away. I never knew if I would see him when I reached the Chancery, but I never gave up. I believe I went every Wednesday and Friday. It doesn't matter what day. We had two standing appointments every week; but as I said, I did not always see him. Yet, I drove to Hartford. Here again, the virtue of perseverance and not-giving-up-easily was needed. I kept this up until he moved to Stamford (in 1953) which was perhaps six years after I first met him. Then I continued to see him in Stamford once a week.

Monsignor became my spiritual director when I needed one the most. During the six years he remained in Hartford, my work for God expanded. I constantly received revelations, often not understanding what was happening. I would talk to Monsignor about that. For example, when I was told (November 13, 1945) by Our Lord that I would be made known before my death, neither Monsignor or I knew what that meant. He finally came to the conclusion that I would be made known through my writings.

During the six years when the foundation for my role in my Lady's triumph was being formed, Monsignor Hayes guided my work for God.

We had many wonderful spiritual talks; yet, in spite of how I admired him and I trusted him with my job for God and my Lady, often I could not tell him all that I wanted to about my spiritual life. So, I would write him letters and hand them to him as I ran out of the Chancery. I don't have copies of these letters, but Monsignor must have welcomed them so he could better understand God's graces in my soul. He never told me to stop writing these letters.

MY WRITINGS

As soon as Monsignor became my spiritual director, I gave him all my note books, articles and other writings, except my most precious secrets which were The Devil's Challenge and praises contained in my 1946 note book. It took me over 1 year before I had the courage to give him that note book.

Up to that time, Monsignor never told me that all was from God; but he said he believed all I told him or let him read. He told me to keep recording everything. After he read everything I had given him, I knew he had to have the note book with my most precious secrets before he could tell me that all was true, all was from God. I wanted to be fair to him.

So one day, when I went to see him, I merely handed him

this note book and ran away.

The next time I went to see him, I felt sure that he would say all was from the devil after he read that note book.

I was still haunted by the fact that once a nun had told me that my visions could be the work of the devil. Yet, I never asked Monsignor if that were so. I wanted him to read all my writings before he came to that conclusion. As far as I was concerned, I knew that my visions and job for God were true and I accepted my job for God and my Lady. I wrote all that was told me believing all. The fact is one of my greatest temptations was to stop believing in my visions and my job for God. I had to fight that temptation, constantly saying: "I do believe. I will not give up."

However, if my spiritual director had told me all was from the devil, I would have given up and thrown everything away because I did not want to have anything to do with the devil. It was up to my spiritual director to say if all was or was not from God.

As I sat in the waiting room filled with fear that "all was over," suddenly Monsignor walked in. In a gentle, soft, voice, he said: "It seems to me that you are more than a daughter of God's."

My heart exploded with joy. I knew what he meant. I had read stories of the saints who had visions of God the Father or Christ, who were called "daughter." Now my Monsignor was saying I was more than a daughter of God's. That was not the main reason why my heart exploded with joy. What caused me so much peace and happiness was the fact that Monsignor had approved my writings and I knew they had not been from the devil. Then he told me that all I wrote, my job for God, my visions and messages were from God. Everything was genuine, everything was true.

I will also like to mention the fact that Monsignor Hayes had his own spiritual director. This priest was named Father Struck. I met him several times. Monsignor would tell me that he not only told Father Struck about me, but kept him informed about my writings and my visions and my job for God.

The only negative thing Monsignor said to me was when he read my poems and said they were not "too good." I believed him and I stopped writing poems for years. Later, I wrote a few more, but not as many as I had written in 1944-1945.

After Monsignor told me that all was from God, he one day said to me: "If all this was not from God, I would never have encouraged you in a "fool's paradise."

MY GREATEST TORMENT

Needless to say, the spiritual relationship I had with Monsignor Hayes meant a great deal to me. I looked forward to his kind words of encouragement during the days when I often experienced what is known as "The Dark Night of the Soul." I had to hear Monsignor say that everything was still "all right."

This reliance upon my spiritual director was the basis of one of my greatest torments as the devil constantly tempted me to believe that Monsignor would send me away. This agony would not cease. I wrote about this in a short autobiography Monsignor Hayes told me to write in 1951:

I suffered greatly from the thoughts that he would send me away. At last I had found the one to tell me what was right and I wanted to keep seeing him. But always the devil would tell me that he would send me away.

I can't explain how I suffered at this. I would cry after each visit because I thought it would be my last. I thought I would truly die and all would be over if he sent me away. And yet, I felt that I had no right to take up his valuable time and to have him bother with me.

The devil tormented me night and day telling me that I bothered Monsignor and that he would not care to see me anymore. I don't know how I lived through these days and nights.

Not only did the devil torment day and night about Monsignor, but also about other things. Indeed he came at me with all the forces of Hell to try to make me stop believing.

I waited for Monsignor's answer. He would not say anything definite. I told him I was always ready to accept the decision that my visions were false. But he would not say they were. He could not say they were true, but he would not say they were false.

It was a long time before I let Monsignor read my secret note book. The one where the Devil's Challenge and the praises are.

But I knew that if Monsignor was to judge me, in all fairness I must let him read that book. So one day I drove up to Hartford in the car and just left the book before I lost my courage and took it back.

I was all prepared to have Monsignor say that it was truly the work of the devil. I even was thinking of which convent I would join when Monsignor told me that everything was over and I had made a terrible mistake.

But when he came in, he said to me: "It seems to me that you are more than just a daughter of God's."

I can't explain how I felt. I was so filled with emotion and joy. It was as if a new world opened up for me. He had not condemned my writings. He was calling me one higher than a daughter. Indeed I knew what he meant. For I had read where Our Lord called all His chosen ones "Daughters."

Only, Monsignor saw my true feelings. Only he had the grace to see my heart and soul. That was why he sought only to speak to me in the most gentle encouraging way. For he saw the black night that my soul was in and the way the devil tormented me to try and make me stop believing and to believe that he would send me away.

I never questioned him or objected. I always accepted what he said, even more than what Jesus and Mary said. I knew that the devil could trick me with visions, but the devil could not trick Monsignor.

We were both constantly aware of the nearness and the power of the devil. If anything bothered me and the devil tormented me about something, I would write Monsignor about it and put my heart at ease. I never allowed the devil to let me build up thoughts or misunderstandings in my mind. For I knew that the devil could so easily change them and make them appear much worse than what they really were.

MONSIGNOR LEAVES HARTFORD

In 1953, Monsignor left Hartford to become a parish priest at Saint Mary's Church in Stamford, Connecticut. I was sorry to hear the news. That meant the end of our visits which still were twice a week. However, I was able to still see him on Saturdays when I drove to Stamford.

By that time, our spiritual relationship had been well established. He had read and approved all my writings and my visions; although, neither one of us could see the future and how my role was linked to Our Lady's Triumph.

Monsignor had also guided me through the worst years of my spiritual life which happened during the formation of my job for God and my Lady when I had been so severely tempted by the devil to give up and to stop believing in my visions.

Perhaps a less experienced and less competent spiritual director could not have understood the torments the devil put me through, but Monsignor did and helped me through these trying times. He was the spiritual director which I needed.

Actually, after Monsignor moved to Stamford, I did not need his constant direction. I continued my work for God, which was mainly writing.

I will also add that I spoke to Monsignor about the possibility of joining a convent. His wise words were: "You could not write if you joined a convent."

While Monsignor was still in Hartford, he also arranged for me to go to Saint Francis hospital in Hartford to attempt to solve my physical problems. This stay at the Hospital did not discover my heart problem, a hole in my heart, which was discovered in 1993.

MONSIGNOR HAYES AND MY LADY'S SHRINE

I was under Monsignor's direction when my Lady appeared

to me in 1948 as The Golden Lady of Happiness. When I told Monsignor that I was taking people to the spot where my Lady wanted her shrine, he told me I could do that. When my Lady gave me her promises, I told Monsignor what they were. He saw no reason why I could not continue to take people to the rock. Then the crowds began to grow. When they did, Monsignor began to get concerned. He asked me to write the promises down so he could study them.

After he read them, he told me to no longer take people to the rock, not because he found something wrong with the promises but because he was afraid that the crowds would become larger. He told me to continue to wait for my Lady's shrine. I obeyed him.

As for me seeing the bishop, that never happened. But that did not bother me because I was as close to the bishop as I could get with Monsignor being my spiritual director.

I placed everything including my Lady's shrine in his hands. I did not, in any way, push him so that my Lady could get her shrine. However, after he moved to Stamford and became so busy running his parish, I was sad thinking that he had forgotten about my Lady's shrine.

In 1957, I married my husband Mike D'Angelo. After that, I no longer went to Stamford to see Monsignor Hayes. I simply thought that my marriage meant a new life for me and I would just put my visions and my Lady's shrine aside until after I died. I asked my husband to buy a little safe for me to put my note books in so they could stay there until after my death.

The last time I saw Monsignor was shortly after my marriage when I took Mike to Stamford to meet him. Monsignor, at that time, returned all my note books, some of which he had had for years. I thought that to be the end of our relationship; and because I also thought that was the end of my job for God, I felt I no longer needed a spiritual director.

The last time that I wrote to Monsignor was when my sister-in-law returned the 1944 notes to me. My mother had secretly copied them from my note books and had given them to my sister-in-law to hide the fact that she had done this. I wrote a long letter to Monsignor telling him that those notes had been discovered. He did not answer that letter.

A few months later, my Lady told me to make her and her promises known to the world. That was in 1960.

By then, I did not go to Monsignor to tell him what I was going to do about making my Lady known. I felt he was no longer my director. We had not seen each other for three years. Later, I found a priest in Meriden who became my third spiritual director and confessor: Father Lyddy.

On July 5, 1964, Monsignor died after he collapsed as he walked off the altar where he had just celebrated the noon Mass in his church.

As I said, Monsignor was sent to me by God when I needed his direction and advice so desperately. He was the one who led me safely through the formation of my whole work for God and my Lady. When the devil caused me agony tempting me to doubt, I knew that I would not fall to such temptations, I would not give up or stop believing. However, I also needed the gentle voice of Monsignor Hayes to encourage me and tell me that everything was still "all right." When I explained such temptations to Monsignor, he would smile and say: "It is all right, Louise. Just keep believing. You will not fall to such temptations. God and Our Lady are with you. Our Lady told you not to fear the devil."

When I wrote him letter after letter explaining my spiritual struggles to reach a closer union with God in spite of faults and weaknesses, Monsignor would accept such letters and he never told me to stop writing them. Then, when I asked him if everything was still "all right," he would smile and say: "Yes, everything is still all right."

I must give credit to Monsignor for the way he handled my spiritual life and my work for God when they were just tiny buds needing so much care in order to blossom as beautiful flowers.

At that time I, of course, did not know the role of a director in a case like mine, but Monsignor knew, and he handled my God-given job in a most expert way. He was the one who put the protective enclosure around my work and my Lady's shrine by saying; "Yes, all is from God."

From that point, I would continue my work for God knowing that this was genuine and God-given.

I can say, without any doubts, that the devil must have been tempting Monsignor to send me away or to stop believing all I told him; however, Monsignor's faith in me did not waiver. He never treated me in any harsh or hard way. He was always so gentle and kind to me. He was always understanding even when I did not understand the struggles I was experiencing. I shall always be deeply grateful to all he did for me and my Lady's shrine and guiding me safely through the early years of the job given to me by God and my Lady.

Pictures of Monsignor Hayes and his church in Stamford, Connecticut where he became pastor after leaving Hartford. Louise took these pictures when Monsignor showed her a painting of himself. Year 1954 or 1955.

MY EARLY NOTE BOOKS AND MY SPIRITUAL DIRECTOR: MONSIGNOR JOHN HAYES

Please note as you read the words of Jesus and Mary in this book, that all these revelations were read by my spiritual director, Monsignor John J. Hayes, and were approved by him after he had studied my writings for about six years. I met him in 1947 and he was my director until 1957.

As I reveal these messages, and place them in different categories, or groups, I, myself, am greatly amazed that such words tie the story of my Lady's shrine together in such a profound way. I knew that I had these messages as I went through life carrying out the will of God for me; however, I seldom if ever reread my note books. Most of the times they were with Monsignor Hayes and stayed there for years. When such note books were returned to me, I would be amazed to discover what note books Monsignor Hayes had and what was in these note books. When I was married in 1957, my husband and I went to see Monsignor Hayes at his church in Stamford, Connecticut. He handed me about five or six note books which he had had in his possession for years. He had them so long that they were covered with dust. One of the note books I had completely forgotten I had written. I merely thought I had made no notes for that year.

Whenever, I gave him a note book, I made no copy for myself. So, I had no way of knowing what was in these diaries. Yet, when I reread them after they were returned to me, I was filled with awe seeing that my early notes did not change or contradict what I had written in later years.

I never asked Monsignor to return my note books I never asked to reread them. And although he kept them for years at a time, I will add, that it never bothered me to have Monsignor

Hayes hold my note books without showing me what was written in them.

When I gave them to him, I did so knowing he had to read all I wrote. It was up to him to decide what to do with them. If I never saw them again, that was all right with me. I merely kept writing never knowing all (I did remember some things) that I had written in previous years.

When I recorded my notes, I did so, often not understanding what was said to me. I knew that Monsignor Hayes would understand what I could not. I never asked him what he understood. All I was concerned about was that he told me all was from God.

He, on the other hand was deeply impressed with what he was reading. He would make such remarks: "It seems to me that you understand the love God has for His children," or "it seems to me that you are more than a daughter of God's." I realized when he said that often God called His beloved saints, daughters (when I read stories of the saints), but I did not fully understand what Monsignor was trying to say to me.

Whenever I saw Monsignor Hayes, which was often two or three times a week, when he was at the Chancery in Hartford, Connecticut, I would go to his office for the main purpose of giving him more of my writings. As soon as I finished a note book, I would give that to him. The reason I gave him my writings (other than note books) was because I was always very shy in attempting to tell him the spiritual condition of my soul. I found it much easier to write this information down and to give him the paper or letter.

Throughout the years of our spiritual relationship, he never refused to see me nor did he ever send me away. We became very close and I thought of him as a "living saint."

He once said to me: "If I thought you were in a "fool's paradise," I would never continue to see you."

He became so filled with enthusiasm about what he read in my notes and other writings that he would share that information with his own spiritual director, Father Struck, who also became a very good friend of mine.

In 1948, when my Lady told me about the five promises, as she stood upon the rock, she told me that the promises were already in my notes. At that time, I still had some of my note books. These promises were in notes dated: 1945-1946. I still had these note books; although Monsignor Hayes had the one for 1944. I had not, as yet, given him all my note books because the ones for 45-46-47 contained my most precious secrets which I was very reluctant to show him. Later, I did give him these note books because I knew he had to have all the information in order to form in his mind the truth about my job for God.

After Monsignor Hayes returned all my note books in 1957, that was the first time I had them all together in one place.

By the time I wrote a longer autobiography in 1963, I had, once again, all my note books in my possession. My spiritual advisor, Father Kelleher, told me to write this 1963 autobiography.

Part 10

The First Vision of the
Golden Lady of Happiness
1948

POPE PIUS XII MADE THE FOLLOWING STATEMENT: "WE WISH THAT WHENEVER CIRCUMSTANCES SUGGEST IT, THIS CONSECRATION (TO THE IMMACULATE HEART OF MARY) BE MADE, BE IT IN THE DIOCESES OR IN EACH PARISH OR IN EACH FAMILY. WE TRUST THAT FROM THESE PUBLIC AND PRIVATE CONSECRATIONS WILL COME AN ABUNDANT FRUIT AND HEAVENLY FAVORS" (ENC. AUSPICIA QUEDAM).

THE DATE OF THIS PROCLAMATION WAS MAY 1, 1948, THE VERY DAY I FIRST SAW MY GOLDEN LADY STANDING ON THE ROCK IN MERIDEN.

INTRODUCTION

THE SHRINE OF THE IMMACULATE HEART OF MARY THE NAME OF THE GOLDEN LADY OF HAPPINESS

It is very important to know that the name of the shrine my Lady wants here in Meriden is not the Shrine of the Golden Lady of Happiness. The name, The Golden Lady of Happiness, is but an endearing name Our Lady called herself to bring joy and hope to the hearts of her children.

Foremost and above all else, the shrine is named in honor of the heart of Mary. That was plainly revealed to me on October 10, 1946 when I first told about the shrine; Mary said to name the shrine in honor of her Immaculate Heart. She mentioned that again on April 25, 1947: "The world will know that Heaven smiles on the shrine to the Immaculate Heart in Meriden, Connecticut." (Mary did not call Meriden by the name I have always known for my hometown. She slowly called this city: Mary Den.)

In that same vision, when Our Lady spoke about her shrine as one to honor her heart, I saw a crown of silver stars on her head. Suddenly from each star a golden beam of light fell to earth. . . . Then I saw a brighter, larger star appear above the others, and a golden beam of light fell to the earth. My Lady said that this star represented her shrine to her heart.

I saw that vision and heard the words before I saw The Golden Lady of Happiness in 1948.

No doubt, the golden beam of light represented my Golden Lady.

Another reference to her heart can be found when she first told me about this shrine. It was, no doubt, to be a Shrine of Love. Mary said to me, October 10, 1946: "On each pillar place a picture of my heart and my Son's Heart to show all who enter that love is there. On each window show a picture

of our love for our children." It was after she said these words
when she added: "Name the shrine in honor of my Immaculate Heart."

As I said, in another chapter, I did not really like this name
for the shrine because I thought it was too long: The Shrine
of the Immaculate Heart of Mary.

The name, The Golden Lady of Happiness, Mary gave herself when I saw her in 1948 as this Golden Lady.

The first time I saw Mary dressed in gold, I clearly saw her
heart exposed. While she stood before me in all her splendor,
she said so sweetly: "My Immaculate Heart has triumphed."
Then she gave me her new, precious name: "I am The Golden
Lady of Happiness." She spoke of her heart first before she
mentioned The Golden Lady. And she did not call the shrine
The Shrine of the Golden Lady of Happiness.

She said: "My appearance here is the end of a circle that
began at LaSalette. All the times, I have appeared on earth, I
was building up to this glorious climax that has come about
because of you and the shrine here called The Shrine of the
Immaculate Heart of Mary."

It is very important to understand that Mary's shrine is to
her Immaculate Heart. Now I know that is the connection
between Meriden and Fatima. I, of course, did not know that
fact in 1946 or 1948.

Had the shrine been called something else, such as The
Shrine of the Holy Rosary, there would not have been this connection between Meriden and Fatima. If I had "invented" a
name for the shrine (which I, of course, did not do), I would
never have called it The Shrine of The Immaculate Heart of
Mary. As I said, I thought that name was too long. I would
have formulated a name, such as "The Rosary" or "God's
Mother Mary," or something like that.

So, just in the name of the shrine, in that alone, can be seen
the way God's plans were revealed to me, even before I saw my
Golden Lady in 1948; and how that name was repeated when I
saw The Golden Lady standing on the rock on May 1, 1948.

— 1 —
FIRST VISIONS OF
THE GOLDEN LADY: MAY 1, 1948

In May 1947, I had met the priest who would not only be my spiritual director for ten years, but who had read and approved all my writings, including the ones about The Devil's Challenge and the praises I had received from Heaven: Monsignor Hayes.

By May, 1948 (one year later) I was still waiting to see the bishop about the shrine Our Lady wanted in Meriden and Monsignor was still reading my notes.

I had done part of what my Lady had requested. I had told the priests about her desires for the shrine to her Immaculate Heart; but I had not completed the task. I had not reached the bishop. However, I did not mind. I knew that my spiritual director was the one to speak to the bishop. I did not press the issue. I seldom spoke about the bishop. Whenever I did mention him, my spiritual director would say: "We'll see. Just keep waiting." So, I waited.

The year went by and then it was 1948. Nothing had been done about my Lady's request for her shrine. The Church remained silent; but word about the visions began to spread in Meriden. At that time, my mother and I owned a small gift shop in the center of Meriden. A young lad came into the store often to buy religious books. I think that I mentioned the visions to him because he was going to be a Brother in a religious order. At least, he knew about the visions. Gradually, people began to come into the store to ask about the visions. (This store did not stay in business for long.)

One day three women and a man walked into the store and asked me about my Lady's shrine. I did not know how they found out about the visions, but they knew that Our Lady wanted a shrine in Meriden. Maybe the boy or a priest told them. I, at first, was not going to tell them anything. Then a small, Italian woman told me that she had a dream about the place where Our Lady wanted the shrine and it was near the huge park on the west side of town called Hubbard Park. The woman also told me that the place for the shrine was on a hill. That was true. I had often walked to the field where Our Lady wanted her shrine and there was a hill which I had climbed up. However, I usually did not go to the top of the hill because there were cows grazing and I was afraid of the cows. The field itself was a pasture for the cows which belonged to a farm called Coe's farm.

As the woman told me, my Lady's land is not far from this park. I was amazed that she knew where the location was, and I agreed to take the group to the place. At that time, I knew nothing about the rock upon which The Golden Lady stood. I merely agreed to show the group the place where Our Lady wanted her shrine.

One very interesting fact is that the woman, who had the dream, became my mother-in-law when nine years later I married her son, Michael. He was in this first group I took to my Lady's land because he drove his mother and the others to the spot when they came with me. But we did not even talk at that time. He came only to do his mother a favor. He actually thought it was rather strange, to say the least, to have Our Lady appear to someone he knew. He was not very enthusiastic about me or the visions.

When I decided to take the first group of people to the land, I went to see my spiritual director, Monsignor Hayes, to ask him if that was all right. By that time, he knew my visions were true and he gave me permission to take the people to the site.

This first group was not the four people who had come into the store. As soon as the people, who had come into the store, learned that I would take them to the place where Our Lady wanted her shrine, they told others and there ended up being a large group who were with me on that day. The date was May 1, 1948.

I wrote about what happened in an autobiography I wrote, dated September 2, 1960:

The first group of people that went to my Lady's land in 1948 was a quiet, shy group. No one knew what to expect. My Lady had not requested the visit. I only wanted to show the people where my Lady wanted her shrine. We slowly walked up the hill to the top. There were about ten or twelve people in that group. I did not know all the people. My mother was with the group.

When we reached the top of the hill, I suddenly stood still in front of a large rock. Standing upon the rock was the Blessed Virgin dressed in flowing gold robes. It was the first time that I had ever seen her dressed like that. She had a crown on her head. I could see her Immaculate Heart, which seemed to be only bright rays of red light upon her breast. She stood upon the earth, the moon and a snake. She had a halo of stars around her head. She had gold roses on her feet. She smiled at me and she said: "My Immaculate Heart has triumphed." Then she said: "I am The Golden Lady of Happiness. I have come to bring peace, joy and happiness to the world."

When someone asked me why I did not call Mary The Blessed Virgin, instead of The Golden Lady of Happiness I answered: "I did not call her that, she called herself The Golden Lady of Happiness."

I added (in my autobiography): What a magnificent title she gave herself in that moment of triumph.

I also spoke about my Golden Lady in a short autobiography I wrote for Monsignor Hayes in 1951. I wrote a chapter I called "The Age of Mary" and said in part: My Lady appeared to me as The Golden Lady, as the Lady clothed with the sun standing upon the earth with the moon under her feet and a crown of stars about her head. . . . The Golden Lady of Happiness, she told me. She said that she came to bring happiness to the world. I saw her beautiful Immaculate Heart and she said; "My Immaculate Heart has triumphed." At Fatima, she said that it would triumph, now, she says that it has. And indeed her heart has won.

The first time my Lady appeared to me as The Golden Lady standing on a large rock, she not only said that her Immaculate Heart has triumphed, she gave me five promises. (I would like to say here that in 1948 onward, whenever I said that, I could not correctly pronounce the word triumphed let alone spell it. I would stumble as I tried to say the word, much to my embarrassment because others had to correct my poor English. I would struggle to say triumphed and it would come out something like triumpheded or triumpanted. Now, I can laugh when I remember this; but at that time, this fact was another sign that I, in my childlike way, could have never invented the story of my Lady because I was totally unfamiliar with that word.)

My Lady told me what the promises were and then said that I would find them in my notes, for I already had been told them in one way or another. (As I explained in Chapter Two, these promises were in my notes before I heard them from my Lady in 1948.) When I returned home, I recorded these five promises in my notes. I also rewrote them in a short autobiography in 1951.

Although my Lady had given me five promises, I could only reveal three. The other two are for later times: however, they do *not* predict great doom, death or destruction for humanity as do most of the false visions which are being promoted in this era. The fact is, such promises have already been fulfilled. Following are the three promises of my Lady. It is to be noted that she explained what the promises were and that they were already in my note books. When I recorded the three promises, I wrote them in the way my Lady explained what they were and as I found hints of them in my notes.

THE PROMISES OF THE GOLDEN LADY

1. I promise that the world will not be destroyed before the Last Day. The world will not be destroyed before the Last Day by any force or power of man, or by any force or power of God because now my heart can be planted upon the earth and

planted deep within the hearts of my children. No force or power shall take my heart away from my children.

2. I promise that if the world of science continues to go against the ways and the teachings of God, then this science will be destroyed and men shall no longer know the secrets which they now know because that knowledge is not important, nor is it needed to save a soul.

3. I promise that the devil and his evil ones will be pushed back into Hell and much sin shall vanish from the world so that the world will no longer be filled with the sin and corruption that the devil has created.

When I saw my Lady standing on the rock, I was not as awe-struck as people might think that I should have been. Many people have said to me: "Weren't you afraid or something when you saw her suddenly standing on the rock?" No. not really. That was not the first time that my Lady had suddenly appeared before me. But it was the first time that I saw her dressed as she was dressed and that made a deep impression on me. I told the group that my Lady was standing on the rock and I said softly: "She is all dressed in gold."

The group that was present in May 1948, at my Lady's land did not know what my Lady had told me about the promises or about finding them in my notes. I told them only one thing. My Lady had told me that everyone who was present during that first appearance on the rock would receive a special grace of happiness. As I said, my future husband was there and even though we never dreamt that such would happen, nine years later we were married. In 1948, I had no intentions of ever marrying. In my heart, I still wanted to become a nun, or at least, to live like one in prayer and solitude.

Before I close this chapter, I will add these interesting facts.

One day when I was crossing the fields after leaving the rock, I ran down the bank to a small stream, which I sometimes crossed when I went to the rock the back way. There were two cows drinking from the stream. Suddenly I heard my Lady say to me: "The cows are drinking the golden water."

Years later in 1960, my Lady told me to tell the people about the "golden water."

The last incident, which occurred in 1948, that is worthy of noting concerned a flower and a small "miracle." It was a cold, fall day. Someone had left (I never found out who) a small bouquet of flowers on the rock. In the bunch were two or three gladioluses. The flowers remained fresh for the first day. The following day, after a cold night, the flowers had frozen and they were dead. All the leaves and stems were brown and dried up. However, one flower on one of the gladiolus was perfect. It stood up straight on the dead, dried-up stem among the dead, dried-up leaves and flowers. I was amazed when I saw the perfect bloom. I touched it and it was firm. It looked as though it had been made of wax. The color was beautiful and the flower was open.

I became excited for I felt that the flower was a "sign" from my Lady. I went home and I tried to call my spiritual director, but he was not home. Then I called the people who knew about the visions and I told them about the flower. When my mother came home, I told her and we both went back to the rock. When we reached the land, I was surprised to see about six cars there. It seemed that everyone came at the same time; even though, I had called them at different times. My mother and I went to the rock and everyone was looking at the flower. They were as amazed as I had been. By that time, it was again cold and almost dark, but the flower still looked firm and fresh.

Everyone agreed that the flower should be left on the rock to see what would happen to it. We slowly left the land. That night, once again, the weather was very cold. The following morning I ran back to the rock. I was thrilled to see that the flower was still perfect and firm. That was a greater "sign." I left the flower on the rock and I went home and I called my spiritual director and I told him what had happened. I wanted him to see the flower, but he could not come to Meriden that day. Then the next day, the flower disappeared. Everything had been taken from the rock. I never saw the flower again. I was very disappointed and sad. Years later, I learned that the owner of the field had seen the items being left on the rock,. such as Rosaries, little statues and flowers. He had been worried that one of his cows would eat them, so he removed everything. This was the first of many times when objects left on the rock by the ones who believed in the visions, suddenly disappeared. After that happened, Winter set in and my visits became fewer and fewer to my Lady's land. However, I could not forget the rock or my beautiful Lady who had stood on it and I could not forget that my Lady wanted her shrine there. But there was nothing more I could do for my Lady or for her shrine.

— 2 —

EARLY HINTS OF MY GOLDEN LADY AND HER PROMISES IN 1944-1945-1946 BEFORE I SAW HER IN 1948

As soon as I started to see and hear Jesus and Mary in 1944, 1945, 1946, there were embedded in what I saw and heard references to my Lady's triumph, my role in that triumph and to her promises.

Needless to say, at that time I knew nothing about the shrine my Lady wanted in Meriden, The Golden Lady of Happiness or her promises. I was first told about the shrine in October 1946, and I did not see my Golden Lady until May 1, 1948. I knew nothing about Fatima, Our Lady's triumph or the Immaculate Heart of Mary; or even how her heart would play such an important role in my life. In addition, as I said, I knew nothing about the five promises of The Golden Lady of Happiness; yet these promises were placed within the words and visions I saw in 1944-1945. When I first saw my Golden Lady in 1948, she told me about the five promises and said that I would find them in my notes; which I did.

To begin, I will mention this incidence which took place about 1942 before I moved to New York. One day I was praying, at the altar rail in Saint Joseph's church (the same church I was in when I saw the statue of the Sacred Heart come to life). As I prayed, suddenly a tiny gold leaf come from above and rolled down my heavy winter coat. When I picked it up, it was as light as a feather. I accepted this tiny, gold leaf as a "gift from Heaven." I bought a little locket and put in it the gold piece. I noticed that when I put it into the locket, it separated into two pieces. I soon discovered that when I committed a fault, the two pieces would separate. When I overcame a little temptation (to get angry, etc.) the two pieces would join together. I regarded this little gold leaf as my most precious possession. Later when I joined an ice show at the beginning of 1945, I gave this locket to Father Shea. As of now, I don't know where it is. But it was still in my possession when in 1946 my Lady mentioned it.

She said I was correct about this gold leaf when I thought it was a great treasure. Then she told me I shall leave it for the world to benefit from and she said that before my death, I would have her gardenia to place by it; a gardenia that would ever bloom and never die (August 15, 1946): She said that I was the Gardenia of Love and it will be placed by the Gold Leaf because for all eternity we will never be separated.

As the years went by, and as my job for God and my Lady unfolded, I knew that that gold leaf represented my Golden Lady and that I was the gardenia she placed next to it. It was my Lady whom I would give to the world so that the world could benefit from her love and care.

When I first started to see visions and to hear the voice of Jesus and of Mary, I knew very little about my religion. I thought that everyone received such favors. I was then 20 years old.

Right from the beginning, I was told about a plan of God's which would bring peace, joy and happiness to the world. I thought that Mary and Jesus were talking about bringing an end to the Second World War. I even tried to get some of my writings published at that time, thinking that after the war ended, the words of Jesus and Mary would be useless because the world would have peace. But because these writings spoke about visions, they were, of course, rejected. I did not know then why they had been rejected because, as I said, I thought everyone saw visions.

Also, from the beginning, I was told about the Immaculate Heart of Mary, even though I had no idea what significance that was in connection with my job for God.

For example: on January 26, 1945, the Blessed Virgin said to me: "My Heart is the place of great joy and happiness. My Heart is the cause of the world returning to peace." (At that time; I did not know anything about the Immaculate Heart of

Mary.) After the Second World War ended, I thought that the world was returning to peace and that was what Mary meant by her words to me.

On June 2, 1944, I was told by Our Lady: "Find peace, find happiness and find all the joys that are to be found in God's world . . . But when you go forth, do not go alone. Take within your hearts my heart and my Son's Heart. Hold my heart and my Son's Heart close and forever."

On January 26, 1945, in a letter I wrote (I can't remember to whom) there are these words: The Blessed Virgin Mary said to me, "My dear children of God, the sun is going to shine forth on a pure white flower, a flower of peace, a flower of hope, a flower of love. A flower that can bloom in the hearts of all men; or a flower that can be left to become a flower of pain and sorrow.

"My dear children, my heart is the flower. My heart is the place of great joy and happiness. My heart is the cause of the world returning to peace among the children of God

"Heed well the words of my Son: 'The world cannot rejoice unless it rejoices with My Mother and Me!' Heed well the call of my Son for you to return to my heart, the heart that is the gateway to the Heart of my Son and His Father."

Then, as I explained in another chapter, Mary spoke of a great destruction; but then adds these words of hope and love: "My children of the world, I stand before the throne of God to defend the children of the fallen world and out of His great love for me, He will allow my heart to bring back the peace that is not in the world today."

THE PROMISES IN MY EARLY NOTES
BEFORE I RECEIVED THEM ON MAY 1, 1948

Before I explain how the promises of my Lady were in my notes before I heard them in 1948, I will repeat the three promises so that one can plainly see that they were hidden in my early notes.

1. "I promise that the world will not be destroyed before the Last Day. The world will not be destroyed before the Last Day by any force or power of man, or by any force or power of God because now my heart can be planted upon this earth and planted deep within the hearts of my children. No force or power shall take my heart away from my children."

2. "I promise that if the world of science continues to go against the ways and the teachings of God, then this science will be destroyed and men shall no longer know the secrets which they now know because that knowledge is not important, nor is it needed to save a soul."

3. "I promise that the devil and his evil ones will be pushed back into hell and much sin shall vanish from the world so that the world will no longer be filled with the sin and corruption that the devil has created."

As I said, when I first saw my Golden Lady in 1948, she told me about her promises and she said I would find these promises in my notes. When I looked, they were there. Here is the foundation for the promises which were already in my notes before my Lady told me about them on May 1, 1948.

The first hint of the promises were in the same message I received, dated January 26, 1945. I recorded these words after my Lady told me about a great destruction: "I tell you this because my Father and your Father's love is so great that He will give you a way to prevent the destruction of the world before the last day."

This was the first promise of The Golden Lady.

on January 17, 1946, I recorded these words spoken to me by Christ: ". . . much sin shall vanish from the earth . . . This I promise My children."

This refers to the third promise of my Lady.

On April 25, 1946, my Lady spoke words which referred to

her second promise about science: ". . . for I say to you that if the world of science continues to use its knowledge to fight God . . . then (this) science will be destroyed and their knowledge so that no more will men know the great secrets that are now revealed to them . . . for the power of the knowledge of God and His love is greater than the greatest science and the knowledge of how to save a soul is more important to God than to have men know the secrets of the universe." (second promise)

I found a most interesting note which I wrote on June 11, 1946 about science. Our Lady had told me about science on April 25, 1946. This became one of her promises (2nd promise): You know, I was thinking about what Mary said to me when she said if the world of science continues to go against God and His ways, then I will destroy it. It seems that for years, science has been challenging God and claimed they can prove there isn't any God. It seems like God hasn't done anything about it as far as I know. But now, it seems like God not only has accepted this challenge from His spoiled children, but He has given them a plain, short, but tremendous answer. God is very patient and He cannot be rushed nor will He ever be rushed. The people who think that this patience means there is no God will find out how wrong they are . . . Ah! but beware for the world is using their God-given knowledge the wrong way . . . So, now God must make them see their mistakes or destroy what is being used against Him . . . The world of science has declared war on God by trying to prove there isn't any God. God has accepted the challenge. . . . God does not give scientific knowledge in order that His children will fight Him with it. He gave it to them to help them.

This challenge was also part of my Devil's Challenge. As of toady (June 1997) science has indeed developed or created many things which go against the ways and teachings of God.

On May 7, 1946, God the Father said to me: "The message your Lady gave you on January 26, 1945 will not come about . . . Wars will come and go through the centuries, but the world will not be destroyed." (first promise)

". . . much sin will vanish from the earth." (third promise)

On May 8, 1946, God the Father said to me: "I, the Almighty God stood above the earth as a weight ready to fall. Yes, I was ready to destroy for My anger was so great. But you, dear one, and your love took Me away from this position and no longer am I ready to destroy for you have so won My Heart as to ease My anger and now I no longer will destroy the earth before the Last Day." (The first promise)

On July 21, 1946, Christ again spoke about one of the promises of The Golden Lady of Happiness, but I, of course, did not know this was a promise. I explained that I heard a sobbing in my ears. I asked Christ what it meant, and He replied: "Ah, dear child, you hear the cries of my sobbing Heart. You can make My Heart cease to sob because your notes will prevent much of the sin that causes these bitter tears to fill My Heart."

Here Christ was referring to the third promise of The Golden Lady.

These words were in my secret notes since 1945. I still have the original notes.

I actually believed that these promises would be hidden in my notes for the rest of my life.

THE PROMISES OF THE GOLDEN LADY OF HAPPINESS: FUTURE EVENTS

The promises my Lady gave to me on May 1, 1948, were without a doubt, predictions of future events.

At the time when I first heard these promises, such would not have been very meaningful. Remember, World War II had just ended and humanity's only interest was looking forward to rebuilding a destroyed world and repairing lives which had been torn apart.

I, myself, did not realize what the promises meant. I merely (as I did with all my revelations) wrote what I had been told. As a result, these promises had little or no meaning to me or anyone else. Even my spiritual director could not understand the full meaning of what I had been told. What we did not know, at that time, was that the promises were, in reality, predictions of future events; events which unfolded during the fifty years I had these promises in my daily notes starting in 1944-1945-1946 and 1948.

As I said World War II had ended in 1945-1946; and what would it mean to say, in 1948, that the world would not be destroyed by "any force or power of God or of man" or "the world of science continues to go against the ways and teachings of God" or "much sin shall vanish from the world," when in 1948:

1. No "man" had the power to destroy the world.
2. The "world of science" was just a High School subject.
3. How much sin was "much sin shall vanish from the world"?

I had been told to wait for my Lady's shrine, but as I waited the world started its mad dash into what is known as the "scientific, nuclear age."

The war with Japan had ended when something called an atomic bomb blasted itself upon humanity. The world would never be the same again as it was before that happened.

After the war ended, there was no turning back the powerful wheels of scientific advancements which began to push aside long-standing complacency and feelings of security.

Before long, a penetrating fear began to invade mankind along with atomic bombs and nuclear weapons.

The so-called "cold war" had been strung across half of the world. Russia had spread her errors throughout the world, nations had fallen as predicted by Our Lady of Fatima.

The world of science had made incredible discoveries, unheard of only a few years before. Soon, science was no longer a sleepy High School subject, but it began to be the Master of humanity. Most everything and everyone in the world started to revolve around science and what this science could do to make life better on one hand and to throw people into a world of darkness and fear on the other hand.

I clearly remember the fear that struck the heart of most Americans when the Russians put the first sputnik into orbit.

Suddenly, a truly unthinkable thing happened: man did have the way and the means to destroy the world.

Then came the "freedom-from" movements. Sin was seen as no sin at all, just expressing one's "freedom." It was called, "doing your own thing."

A long list of social ills began to destroy such time-honored traditions as virtue and goodness, often replaced by failed marriages and sinful ways and habits. Much sin began to fill the earth.

All these could be found hidden within the promises of my Lady, which were predictions. For how could man destroy the world if man had no way of doing that? How could science be said to go against the ways and the teachings of God, if this same science never left the classroom? And how could much sin vanish from the world, if this sin never existed? None of the promises of my Lady could come true unless or until the events she promised to save us from actually happened. And they did happen.

First promise: The world will not be destroyed by any force or power of man.

When my Lady gave me this promise in 1948, man did not have the power to destroy the world; but today (1998) man does have such a power. You can see here the way the promise also became a prediction.

2. The World of Science: if science goes against the ways of God then this science will be destroyed.

Many people have asked me how science could ever be destroyed. I would say: "My Lady said the science that goes against the ways and teachings of God will be destroyed; not all of science." Science has produced many good things. But it has also produced much bad and many evil things. We can see today that the science, which goes against the ways and teachings of God, ends up destroying itself, as I always said. We can see how much of science had to end before it ended up destroying the world and man's environment. The destruction of part of the Ozone is only one example. Today, all over the world, soil, water and even food have been poisoned by the science of man. Such science has to be destroyed. This promise also became a prediction.

3. The devil and his evil ones would be pushed back into Hell. This promise does not mean that Mary would come and actually push the devil back into Hell. How that will be done is when man or woman uses grace to push sin and evil from his or her life. Where grace and virtue exist, sin and evil is destroyed. Man pushes the devil and his evil ones back into Hell each time mortal sin is pushed from a person's life. Mary promises a tremendous stream of grace which will save souls and make people more spiritual.

So, as I said, in 1948, Mary's promises did not make sense; however, as the world followed her predictions, the promises made a great deal of sense.

THE PROMISES EXPANDED

In 1960, when I was called to the bishop's office, after I made my Lady known, I was confronted by one of the Church officials who was rather severe with me.

As I sat, in tears before him, he said in a loud voice: "And that promise about the world not being destroyed before the Last Day! If the world is destroyed, that will be the Last Day, would it not?"

I raised my head and slowly replied: "The world was destroyed during the flood—and that was not the Last Day."

The priest quickly changed the subject.

When people asked me how science could ever be destroyed, I would answer: "Not all of science would be destroyed, because a great deal of science is beneficial to humanity. The part of science which is harmful to society will end up destroying itself. The part of science which goes against the teachings and ways of God will also end up destroying itself."

Then I would give this example.

There was, at one time, plans by three different nations to build the most modern, fastest plane ever invented. Suddenly the plans had to stop. Why? Because when this super-fast plane went over a city, all the windows in the houses would break. The effect of flying so fast would cause too many problems. This science destroyed itself. The plans for this plane were ended.

There are many parts of science today (1998) which no longer exist because they had to be destroyed by the very science which created them. For example: many forms of medicine or environmental hazards had to be destroyed for one reason or another because they caused more harm than good.

Before my Lady gave me her promises in 1948, in 1946, she had said to me: "The knowledge of how to save a soul is more important to God than to have men know the secret of the universe" (April 25, 1946).

One of the greatest scientific and technological advancements since the '40s is within the field of Cosmos study and conquest. When the Russians first launched her sputnik, a whole new field of exploration of the universe was opened up before the eyes of humanity. Before long, we had all sorts of artificial satellites circling the earth space, ships going to the moon, new ways to see the wonders of the universe with far superior telescopes than had ever been invented in the past. The scientists demanded to know more and more secrets of the Cosmos. Yet, what did they find? Not much.

I was watching a T.V. program, in 1995, about man's search to find the secrets of the universe and it was stated on this documentary that in spite of scientific advancement, there has been discovered only the tiniest fraction of one percent of the secrets of the Cosmos.

The more man is allowed to know about the stars, the planets, the galaxies, black holes, etc., the more scientists study and restudy the heavens, the more intricate it becomes. One reporter on the documentary said: "The universe is far more complex than anyone ever imagined. It is endless. There are galaxies with billions of stars in each. The more we probe into the universe, the more we find how little we know about it."

And what is all this knowledge good for? Can man travel to all the billions of stars in millions of galaxies, or to a planet that is made up of gases? And is all this advance knowledge really important? Can it save a soul?

My Lady said this knowledge is not important nor is it needed to save a soul.

There are, as I said, many good parts of science, but man still has to learn what should be used and what is not important.

The promises of my Madonna Maria are such that they can be examined and explored throughout the coming ages of human existence. Each age can see the fulfillment of such promises based upon world conditions.

This age the '90s has seen numerous examples of the conditions referred to by such promises:

The world has emerged from the innocence and ignorance of past ages into the "fast-lane" of technological advancements which produced weapons which could destroy the whole world. International alliances had to be formed (some with past enemies) in order to hold in check the production of such weapons or to destroy the ones already in existence.

My Lady's promise about man not destroying the world was no idle, meaningless message. She saw future events.

One day, while sitting in his secretary's office waiting to see Archbishop Whealon, the radio was on. I heard the words: "Man does have the power to destroy the world now. . . ." Such words were unthinkable only a few decades before.

As for science. Anyone living through the years from the end of World War II until 1998 has been left breathless by the advances of science in all areas from medicine to machines to man's exploration and conquering of space. There was a constant, never-ending series of inventions which were placed before the eyes and minds of humanity from the invention of television to the space ships that carried man to the surface of the moon.

Never before in human history had mankind advanced to so many unheard of achievements in so short a time.

The world of science and technology sent people, including myself, on a whirlwind merry-go-round with all sorts of creations taking us into the new world of computers, electronic data processing, medical procedures, explaining new theories about our past and our future and tinkering in areas of human reproduction which were once sacred and meant only for God's ways.

No wonder my Lady said the "science which seeks to go against the ways and teachings of God will be destroyed."

In 1998, it was not too difficult to find this type of science, much of it destined to end up destroying itself.

When people asked me how Our Lady would push the devil and his evil ones back to Hell, I would say: "Through grace."

They would look at me in wonderment and ask what I meant. I would answer: "When grace is used, sin disappears. Our Lady does not have to appear and personally push the devil and his evil ones back into Hell. People will do that themselves by using grace to overcome sins, faults and weaknesses. This grace will be used for repentance and confession and acquiring virtues. Where virtues are, sin cannot exist. A sinner can become a saint through grace, the sacraments and repentance. Then the devil and his evil ones will be pushed out of that life.

You could call this a conversion. However before one can convert from evil ways to virtuous ways, one has to have grace. Mary provides such grace and when used by a sinner, sin disappears.

Within the realm of sin, evil and corruption, there was nothing hidden from the public. Violence, sex, drugs, all sorts of sins were on display for all to see through T.V. programs, movies, magazines and newspapers.

Actions and desires which, not long before the '90s would have brought shame and embarrassment to the ones involved, were flaunted, bragged about and even applauded by many who witnessed such depravities.

It was clear that a vast majority of mankind lost sight of virtues and Christian living.

But my Lady had promised to push the devil and his evil ones back into Hell. How?

By the awakening of man's conscience which grace produces. When grace grips a heart and soul, virtue returns and the devil and his evil ones are pushed back into Hell.

— 4 —

MONSIGNOR HAYES AND HIS REACTION TO THE 1948 VISION THE PROMISES

When my Lady gave me her promises, she told me to give them out to "the world" (except the two secret promises). I started to obey her, but first I had to have permission from my spiritual director, Monsignor Hayes. He had already given me permission to take the first group of people to the site where my Lady wanted her shrine. That date was May 1, 1948. He saw no reason why I could not continue to show people the place where my Lady wanted her shrine.

Monsignor also had given me permission to tell the people about the three promises. So I told the ones who came (only tiny groups) the three promises of The Golden Lady of Happiness. By that time I had taken people to the land about five times.

Then one day he asked me to write the promises on a paper so he could study them more closely. He was especially concerned about the promise which said that the world would not be destroyed by man or God before the Last Day. At that time, 1948, as I stated, there was no way that man could of his own efforts destroy the world. I, of course, had no idea why he should be concerned about that.

Monsignor did know that the words of the promises came from my Lady. He also compared the promises with what I had written in my note books and found them to be the same. I showed him how I found the promises in my early note books.

Monsignor not only gave me permission to take people to my Lady's land, he also wanted them to go there. However, when he studied the promises more closely, he began to see a problem. The problem was not the fact that Our Lady said what she said, the problem was the words speaking of man destroying the world and concerning science.

When he found this problem, I could not understand what seemed to be insurmountable in his opinion, but now I can understand his concern. The problem was that neither he nor I knew that the promises were predictions of future events. Seeing the promises in 1948, many questions could arise as to their meaning. For example: how could man have the ways and the ability to destroy the world? How could science go against the ways and the teachings of God? World War II had just ended with all its fury and destruction, yet the world survived in spite of weapons of war, bombs, planes, guns, etc.; all of which did not have the ability to destroy the whole world. Science was just a High School subject. How could it be used to go against the ways and teachings of God?

The more Monsignor pondered these questions the more he realized that they had no answers. He began to realize that if he asked questions which he could not answer, others would also ask the same questions which had no answers in 1948. He had no way of foreseeing the future events which would provide the answers, for example the birth of the atomic-nuclear age. I have before me an article which was published in a Special Edition of Life Magazine dated Fall of 1997 (page 114). The article is called: "The Day That Time Stood Still: 1945." It spoke about the bombs which fell upon Japan's Hiroshima and Nagasaki; the two bombs which ended World War II: two atomic bombs! The article ended with these words: ". . . one thing was clear . . . human beings now had the means to exterminate humanity. The mushroom cloud would (become) the nightmares of millions—forever after."

In addition, by 1998, there were unheard of advances in the field of science and technology; some good for humanity but many others actually going against the ways and teachings of God. Then there was the so-called "freedom movement" which became only an excuse to cast aside moral teachings and virtues as sin became the Master of humanity causing havoc with millions of spiritual lives as God, His ways and the teachings of Christ were cast aside and ignored. The "Sexual Revolution" it was called.

My spiritual director thought about the people who were coming to the land and hearing the words of Mary. He knew that if the people continued to come and the promises became known to a vast majority of people, that many of them would ask the same questions that had concerned him: How? When? Where? These were the very same questions which had no answers.

I am sure that with his brilliant mind and intelligence, he must have realized that some day there would be answers even if he did not know what these answers would be. That is why he continued to see me and to tell me that "all" was from God in spite of his concern about the promises. He merely put the promises aside as he continued to direct me as my spiritual director; and he told me to do the same thing.

He did not want the visions and the shrine to be tarnished because I had no answers to the questions people would ask. So he thought it best for me to no longer take people to the land or give them the promises. He said to me: "People know now where Our Lady wants her shrine, but it would be a mistake to keep telling people about the promises. We have to see what they mean, so it is best if they do not know now."

I was heartbroken when he told me that; but I had to obey him. I called the people who had planned to go to the land with me and I told them that I could no longer take them there. They also became sad when they heard the news. They could not understand why the priest had stopped me. Still, I knew I had to obey my spiritual director no matter how much I suffered.

After my spiritual director told me to stop taking people to the land, I went there by myself for awhile. My Golden Lady no longer appeared to me on the rock. I would sadly look at the rock and the empty field where my Lady's shrine should be—but wasn't.

Also, I was sad because Monsignor Hayes did not arrange an appointment for me to see the bishop. However, I never pressed him about that. I felt that having Monsignor Hayes as my spiritual director was as close to the bishop as I could get.

I left everything in his hands. But I still longed for the bishop to build my Lady's shrine. At times, I would go to the rock, sit on it and cry. The land was so empty. Still, I never once gave up my trust and faith in my Golden Lady; and I knew that someday she would have her shrine.

Monsignor Hayes, in spite of the fact that he asked me to no longer take people to the land, continued to read all my writings and to encourage me. He told me to continue to write and added: "If you were in a convent, you could not write."

In 1951, Monsignor Hayes told me to write my autobiography, which I did do. He told me he wanted "everything" on record. We continued to have a wonderful spiritual relationship. I would go to Hartford to see him at least twice a week. He always welcomed me and constantly reassured me by telling me that "everything was still all right."

When he told me that my job for God and my writings were from God, not from the devil, my heart exploded with joy.

But he also told me to wait for my Lady's shrine, and so I waited, placing all my trust and faith in his decision. I so admired him that I regarded him as a "living saint."

A couple of times, I was in his office at the chancery when Archbishop O'Brien walked in. He greeted me warmly and we spoke for a few moments; but I never mentioned the shrine to him. I left that up to my beloved spiritual director. If he told me to wait for the shrine, that is exactly what I would do. So I waited for a long time, from 1948 to 1960.

This is the house I lived in with my mother, at 517 West Main St., Meriden, when I returned from the ice shows in 1945. We lived on the first floor above the store. It was in this house where I had the religious experiences before I moved to New York in 1943. Also, in this house I was told about The Devil's Challenge and the first battles began. I was also told about my Lady's shrine here, in 1946 and 1948. The house has since been torn down and replaced with a gas station.

About six months after I saw the vision of 1948, I fashioned this likeness of my Golden Lady. I took a regular statue of our Lady of Grace and working with plaster of Paris, I made this statue and painted it gold. I put small pieces of the rock in the box at the base of the statue. Picture taken 1950.

One day, my brother (who was now married) surprised me and built this little altar which I had in my home at 517 West Main St. This was about 1950. I placed other statues on this alter, but the statue of my Golden Lady was on top. (There was no Eucharist in the little tabernacle.) After I married Mike when I moved into our first home, Mike destroyed this altar thinking it was nothing worth saving. When I found out what he did, I was heartbroken.

These are the first
pictures taken of
Louise and the rock
Our Lady stood on
in 1948

This is the way the rock looked in 1950

These pictures show the path leading to the rock and the rock in 1955. Ever since my Lady told me she wanted a shrine here in 1946, I considered this land "My Lady's Land" although neither she nor I owned it. It was a huge farm called Coe's Farm.

I did not give up my skating, which I still loved, after I left the shows. This picture was taken in 1948.

As these pictures show, by 1948 I was an excellent skater (according to the norms in those days). I was asked to star in a show, but I turned it down because I wanted to stay home and write for God and my Lady.

I still loved to ice skate, but this time it was only for pleasure. I had ended my career as a professional skater.

This picture is most unusual. It shows me wearing the locket which contained my precious Gold Leaf which had been returned to me. (Picture taken 1948 in studio)

Part 11

Second Vision of the
Golden Lady of Happiness
1960

INTRODUCTION

DIFFERENT KINDS OF PEACE,
JOY AND HAPPINESS

Many people are often mistaken about what constitutes peace, joy and happiness. There is no doubt that material possessions, loved ones near and a good amount of money can bring to a person a certain amount of peace, joy and happiness.

However, when speaking of God or Our Lady and the peace, joy and happiness coming from them, other considerations have to be brought into the overall picture.

When Christ was working miracles during His life on earth, He did not consider them the whole of peace, joy and happiness. The fact is, He often called for sacrifice and suffering instead of granting the request of all who asked for such miracles. But did that mean that one can not find peace, joy and happiness if one's prayers are not answered?

One of the first things that Christ's followers wanted Him to do was to destroy the enemy of Israel, Rome and her soldiers. That would surely bring peace to the nation. However, as Christ went about proclaiming the Good News of His Kingdom, He seemed to ignore the Roman occupation. Instead of destroying the enemies, Christ taught His followers to love them: "You have heard the commandment, 'You shall love your countryman and hate your enemy.' My command to you is: love your enemies, pray for your persecutors. This will prove that you are the sons of your heavenly Father . . ." (*Matt.* 5:43-45).

As for wars, Christ never intended to put an end to all wars on earth. When He spoke of the signs of the Last Day, He said: "You will hear of wars and rumors of wars. Do not be alarmed, such things are bound to happen . . ." (*Matt.* 24:6).

As for material treasures and riches which millions of people think will bring them perfect peace, joy and happiness,

Christ said: "Do not lay up for yourselves an earthly treasure. Moths and rust corrode; thieves break in and steal. Make it your practice, instead, to store up heavenly treasures, which neither moths nor rust corrode nor thieves break in and steal. Remember, where your treasure is, there your heart is also" (*Matt.* 6:19-21).

Then what exactly does it mean to say that my Lady brings peace, joy and happiness to suffering humanity?

It does mean a multitude of favors and miracles which my Golden Lady has given and will give to her beloved children, miracles and favors which bring great joy and happiness. It means a great peace she will bring, peace for the world.

However, one must not always look for or expect only material favors to bring a person peace, joy and happiness.

For example, I was told by God, the Father, on May 8, 1946: "The peace that is mentioned in your messages, is not peace for those who wish to profit, but for each one's soul. There can be no peace in souls which are at war with me. Wars will come during the centuries, when the world will no longer be peaceful, but even a slave is free and at peace if she or he is at peace with me. They shall have such liberty as to make them filled with happiness and joy even in their darkest moments."

When my Lady first started to speak to me, in 1944, about peace, I just assumed that she meant peace for the world after World War II ended. The fact is that I thought all my writings and beautiful, love-filled messages from my Lady would be useless after the war ended because then there would be peace; there would be no reason for the world to have my writings. So I tried to "tell the world" the messages before the war ended. All my efforts, which included sending articles to magazines, proved futile. No one wanted articles like that.

However, as time went on, peace for the world came, then left as new wars erupted, then faded into history.

All the while, my Lady spoke about bringing peace, joy and happiness to suffering humanity.

So one has to look beyond the set horizons of time, life and living and look to human souls and their relationship with God when one speaks of my Golden Lady of Peace, Joy and Happiness.

Ah! yes, wars can end and there is peace, miracles can happen and loved ones are filled with joy, material possessions are acquired and the person finds happiness. But how fleeting are these types of peace, joy and happiness! When wars end, others soon take their place. When miracles happen, other disasters can come forth. When material possessions are acquired, all can be lost.

Many people are often puzzled and thrown into a state of confusion by the words of Christ, which say: "Ask and you will receive. Seek, and you will find. Knock and it will be opened to you. For the one who asks, receives. The one who seeks, finds. The one who knocks, enters . . . how much more will your heavenly Father give good things to anyone who asks Him!" (*Matt.* 7:7-11).

I have heard, hundreds of times, from disheartened people, who received nothing when they asked God or Our Lady for a favor or a miracle. They would say, "I pray and pray and yet nothing happens! Why did Christ say 'ask and you will receive'?"

The answer is: Christ grants all "good things" to a person, but what the person asks may not be as good as the person thinks.

God sees what we cannot see. God knows what we cannot know. God acts as we cannot act. God remembers what we have long ago forgotten. God thinks of souls and what is best for each individual soul. Man thinks of his own tiny material world and what he thinks has to be part of that world in order to bring him peace, joy and happiness.

So, Our Lady comes to her children, to grant miracles and to give great favors, but she also comes to be a brilliant beacon of light among all the cares and darkness of daily life with her heart filled with love and compassion for her poor, suffering children; and when these poor, suffering children find my beautiful Golden Lady, each person is sure to find his or her peace, joy and happiness somewhere within the depths of his or her own heart and soul.

— 1 —

SECOND VISIONS OF THE
GOLDEN LADY OF HAPPINESS: 1960

My material happiness began in July of 1957 when I was presented with a beautiful diamond ring by my future husband. At that time, I thought that the story of my Lady had drawn to a close. I was to start a new life as a happily married young woman. But there was hidden within the sparkle of the diamond a price I would have to pay for my happiness; and it did not take my Lady too long for me to find out what that price would be. I had received my diamond on July 4, 1957 (Mike said he always wanted me to remember that date). Less than a week later, suddenly my Golden Lady appeared to me and said: "If I give you your happiness, will you give me mine?"

Filled with the glow of my coming wedding, I asked her: "What would your happiness be, my Lady?"

She replied: "My happiness will be to stand before my children as their Golden Queen. I am depending on you to give my children their Golden Lady."

I almost laughed at this simple request and in a casual way, I told her I would indeed give her the happiness she wanted.

Then I lived through three years of settling down in my new life, working, meeting new friends, having dinner parties, going out to restaurants, etc. This was a plain, ordinary life filled with peace and contentment. As I said, I continued to write, but my Golden Lady was hidden in my notes tucked away in a little safe in my closet. She was my precious secret, but a secret I was not going to reveal. I felt that the shrine she wanted was to be delayed until after I died.

I so longed to give the world the message of my Golden Lady and her beautiful words of love and compassion for suffering humanity; however, I had *no* intentions of revealing my visions. That was why I struggled so hard to write a book which I called: "St. Resa's Diary." I would never want to call attention to my Golden Lady by revealing her and her shrine to the world. I, after that book failed, tried to continue along the path by attempting to rewrite the book and include in a new book only my poems and articles. That, I thought, would satisfy my desires to bring humanity words of joy, hope and encouragement. But that was not what my Lady wanted. She and God had a peace plan to give to suffering humanity and I was very much a part of that plan. And in June of 1960, my Lady came to me not only to tell me more about that peace plan but to have me keep my part of the bargain we had made in July of 1957.

My Lady had appeared to me for the first time as The Golden Lady in 1948. Twelve years later, the world still had not heard about this beautiful Lady of peace, joy and happiness.

Then, suddenly it was June 1960. One day early In June I was praying by my bed and suddenly my beautiful lady appeared to me dressed as The Golden Lady. I felt tremendous joy at her appearance, but the joy quickly vanished because my Lady was telling me that I had to make her, her promises and her shrine known to the world.

I did not greet the news with joy or enthusiasm. My whole world began to fall apart. She kept repeating the same things: "Now is the time for the miracles of The Golden Lady to begin. Now is the time for The Golden Lady to be made known to the world." I did not follow her orders right away. The fact is I was so upset that I tried to put it out of my mind. I did not even record what had happened until July 5, 1960, almost one month later. The rest of June, I wrote about other things.

As I said, I did not do what she wanted me to do right away. I had a great deal to think about. It was not an easy thing to think about. One day she said to me: "To prove that I want you to make me known, I will cure your toe." My toe had been sore for over two years. I took the statue, which I had of The Golden Lady of Happiness and I touched my toe.

The next day the toe was cured. All the pain vanished. Still, I hesitated.

In my notes of July 5, 1960, I explained more: She told me that now is the time when people can come to her land and when they can receive the miracles that she has to give them there. She told me that she wants processions and people at the land and most of all she wants the world to have her as the promise of peace, joy and happiness.

She wants me to give The Golden Lady and her land to the world!

I had thought for so many years that my job was finished at the land. I thought that I would never go there again. I thought that I would be just a plain housewife until I died. Still Jesus has reminded me of the things He told me years ago in 1946. He said then, "Before your death the world will know of you." He also said: "If the world comes to you, open your doors. Do not hide from the world because you have much to give the world."

To say that I was amazed and upset by these words from my Lady was putting it mildly. I was devastated. To make my Lady known was the last thing in the world I wanted to do. I hesitated.

During the days (all of June) when I hesitated to carry out my Lady's requests, she repeated over and over that I had to make her known and I had to take people to the place where she had appeared to me on the rock as The Golden Lady. Later, many people told me I had been wrong to hesitate, I should have immediately announced the shrine to the world. But if I had done that, then others would have said that was just what I wanted to do all along. But that was not what I wanted to do. It was completely against my nature to tell "the world" that I saw visions. I had always tried to hide my visions, my secrets and had only revealed them once in 1948, which at that time, I really had no intentions of doing. The ones who came to the rock in 1948 found out about the visions from others, not from me. I had taken the first group to the land, not to explain about visions, but merely to show them where Our Lady wanted a shrine. Then she had appeared to me on the rock as The Golden Lady and had explained about the five promises.

By July 3, I still was hesitating about doing what my Lady was asking me to do. Then on that Sunday my beautiful Golden Lady appeared to me during Mass. She was filled with greater glory than I had ever seen her. She said again what she had been telling me almost every day in June: "I want the world to know about The Golden Lady of Happiness. I want you to tell the world about your Golden Lady and I want you to give the world the promises of The Golden Lady, except the two promises that are to be kept secret until after your death.

"Now is the time when people can come to my land and now is the time when they can receive the miracles that I have to give them. I want people to come. I want processions and I want the world to have The Golden Lady as the promise Of peace, joy and happiness."

After Mass, I started to cry and I told Mike to drive me to my Lady's land. I continued to cry as I told him what my Lady wanted me to do. I told him that I did not want to be made known. I wrote about that on July 5, 1960: I did not know what to do. I know that the Church will not approve of my going to the land with people. Monsignor stopped me once. The Church will stop me again. What would happen to my private life, if I am known as the one who saw the Blessed Virgin? I can only imagine what will happen and I don't like the things that I am imagining. What will people say about me and about Mike? These things are not easy to think about.

After church on Sunday I asked Mike to drive me to my Lady's land. I told him what my Lady had said and I cried as I told him. I don't want to be put on public display and I don't want him to be put on public display. What can I do?

Then, on the other hand, I cannot go against my Lady's wishes. I cannot fail her when she needs me so much and I cannot fail her children when they need her so much.

Mike was so good to me. He gently told me that the Virgin will not let our marriage suffer.

I was so upset that I could not stop crying. I would say to myself: "I will do it." Then when tears filled my eyes, I would say: "But how can I do that?"

In order to encourage me, my Lady appeared again to me
in my home on July 5, and said:

"If you do not open the door to the world for The Golden
Lady of Happiness, then my children will not have their peace,
joy and happiness. Only you can give them your Golden Lady
of Happiness. As long as you hide me from them, they will
not have what I so long to give them. If you hide me for the
rest of your life, then I will die with you because only you,
and no one else, can give me to my children. I have given The
Golden Lady of Happiness to you. You have protected and
loved your Golden Lady for many years. Now, give her to her
children. She no longer wishes to remain hidden. You have
saved her by your Devil's Challenge; now give her to the world
for:

"I say to you, my most beloved one, my dearest Child of
Love, when you give your Golden Lady to the world, you will
reveal all her splendor and power. Once The Golden Lady is
upon this earth, in the hearts of her children, she shall find
the place that God saved for her alone. The rays from her
golden gown will encircle this world and mankind will find,
within these rays, the peace, joy and happiness that they long
for.

"Only you can give them these things because only you can
give them The Golden Lady of Happiness."

She also said to me:

"I want a shrine to my Immaculate Heart at the place where
I appeared as The Golden Lady of Happiness. I want proces-
sions and great displays of love. I will return love for love.
Come to me with prayers of love."

On July 7, 1960, she appeared to me again in my home.
She said: "My Immaculate Heart has triumphed. I will now
show the devil that I am the powerful one. Tell my children
that I say to them, my power is greater than the strongest armies
and greater than the strongest hate. The world will know that
there is hope—great hope—for peace, joy and happiness
because I have come to bring peace, joy and happiness to
mankind.

"Tell my children about the five promises, but keep the two promises secret until after your death. I am The Golden Lady of Happiness. I am the Mother of God. I have come to my children with love, peace, joy and happiness. In return, I ask for their prayers of love. Much remains to be done before true peace comes to this world, but I can now promise this peace. I also say that many, many hearts which have been closed to God's love will repent and enslaved people will become free.

"The world has cried, now I will dry its tears because now I can show my power and my glory."

I asked her if she wants her children to say the Rosary or make sacrifices or do penance (like she did other times) and she replied: "Tell my children that I desire to hear songs of love and songs of joy. The world will see great wonders because, at last, it has The Golden Lady of Happiness.

"Tell my children to pray and to make sacrifices, but tell them to rejoice. My Hour of Glory has arrived. My glory shall be implanted upon this earth in such a way that it will never be dimmed by any force or power. I am The Golden Lady of Happiness and I am The Golden Lady of Peace and Light. Every dark corner of this world shall see my splendor and my children shall flock around me in a most miraculous way. They shall say their Rosaries and they shall confess their sins; but most of all they will love me as I have never been loved before. I come now to give love and to receive love. I ask for prayers of love." (These words are words of pure triumph.)

On July 8, 1960 the Holy Mother of God said to me, after I had told her that I would go to her land on July 10, 1960 (Sunday): "Come to my land on Sunday and pray. Send me prayers of love. Then come for the next ten Sundays and all your dreams will be fulfilled." She added: "Bring others with you. Let them know that the Golden Lady of Happiness has come to bring peace, joy and happiness to hearts and to souls and to the whole world."

On July 9, 1960, the Blessed Virgin told me to clear the rock at the land. It was covered with tall weeds. It could not be seen. No one had gone to the place for 12 years. I went and I cleared the rock of the weeds.

On July 12, 1960 she said to me: "Tell my children that the Golden Lady of Happiness wants love—pure, simple love—. When the Rosary is said, let the prayers be joyful. Sing the songs of love because I am ready now to show the world my true power and glory. Tell my children to hide behind my golden garments and there they shall find their protection. The devil can only advance so far; I have come now to force him to retreat. I have come as the loving Mother who protects her frightened children. Fear not, little ones, my hour of glory is at hand and when I win, my children will also win.

"I stand upon the world, upon the moon and upon the devil to show all men that my power is the greatest. Men shall see my power. Let no man fight me for then they shall lose everything.

"There shall be a great peace. I can promise this peace, not only because I have heard so many pleas, but also because I am the Mother who dearly loves her children and I am the Mother who desires to protect her children. It is true, many martyrs are required, but I have held my Son's hand and I have asked Him if I could protect my children. He has given me this power. As The Golden Lady of Happiness, I am the Queen of Love and Peace and I am the Mother who protects her beloved children."

I had told my Lady that I would go to her land on July 10th; I did go with my husband and his mother and father after Mass. But my Lady wanted more people to come with me. Where would I start to tell people to come to the land with me? There was only one place, in my own family.

My Lady had asked me to come for ten Sundays. I chose the first Sunday, July 17, 1960.

FIRST OF TEN SUNDAYS: JULY 17, 1960

My Lady had told me to go to her land for ten Sundays. The first of the ten Sundays would be July 17. Before that date, I recorded the following notes. (The whole note book from July 11, 1960, until August 26, 1960, was given to the bishop at the end of 1960 after I made copies of the words of my Lady; and has been in his Archives ever since. I have before me a photo copy of these notes which I requested around 1991) I will record here some of these notes. On July 11, 1960, I wrote:

I am only beginning to realize the tremendous importance of The Golden Lady of Happiness. When the Blessed Virgin wanted her shrine (October 10, 1946), she called it: The Shrine of The Immaculate Heart of Mary. I did not know about Fatima or the other visions of Our Lady, except Lourdes. I had heard of Lourdes and Fatima but I had not read too much about them nor did I fully understand Fatima and its meaning. I first heard about Fatima in 1949, but by then, My Lady had already appeared as The Golden Lady of Happiness and she had already said: "My Immaculate Heart has triumphed!"

On July 13, I wrote about my growing fears that the Church would condemn all my visions and my writings. I was tempted to forget about the whole thing because my fear was so intense. However, in spite of that I continued to do what my Lady asked because I knew that was God's holy will for me; and I so loved God's holy will. I was willing to suffer all that I would be made to suffer making my Lady known. I wrote: Maybe people will think that I only want fame and glory, that is why I announced my Golden Lady; but that statement is false. If there is anything that I do not want, it is to be on public display. I never dreamt that my Lady would ever have me make her known . . . And believe me, I never chose 1960 to reveal my Golden Lady.

I added: I was tempted to give up, but somehow, I won over the temptations. I will make my Lady known to the world. If there are no miracles and if the Church does condemn my Golden Lady, then that will be all right. I wouldn't mind. My Jesus and Mary can do anything they want with me. I so love God's will. And if all my writings and my Golden Lady are really wrong, then I want to know the truth. I so love the truth. I only want the truth known. I don't want to live with false visions and false promises. I want to do only what God's will is. I will make my visions known. Right now I have so much faith in the things which I firmly believe.

On July 14, still very nervous and upset about what my Lady asked me to do, my husband encouraged me with these words: "I am no longer afraid of what people will say about you. I know what kind of a wife I have. You must do what your Golden Lady wants. We will both go to the land for the ten Sundays and will go with peace in our hearts."

FIRST OF TEN SUNDAYS
JULY 17, 1960

Sunday, July 17, 1960, was the first of the ten Sunday visits to the rock which my Lady had requested. My Lady wanted me to go to the rock and she wanted me to bring people to the rock. Who could I bring? How could I tell people about the visions? Suddenly, I felt that I was in a tiny, little world of my own with very, very few people whom I could talk to. There were thousands of people all around my little world; but how could I go up to them and say: "Please come with me to my Lady's land. I have something to tell you that the Blessed Virgin told me?" Once again, the thoughts of telling people about the visions made me feel sick. But, no matter how I felt, I had to carry out my Lady's wishes. I had to make my Golden Lady known.

Then another worry came to me. Would people love my Lady like I loved her? Would they be gentle to her? Would they be kind to her? Would they hurt her with their remarks?

I had protected and loved my Golden Lady for years. I still wanted her to be protected and loved. The world was filled with wild storms. My Lady said that she wanted to be made known. That meant that she was ready and willing to step out into these wild storms. It deeply hurt me to know that my Lady would be hurt and laughed at; but that was only another cross for me to carry.

Mike's mother and his father, his aunt and her friend were willing to go with me to my Lady's land on Sunday, July 17, 1960. I was grateful, but the group was too small. The Blessed Virgin wanted people at her land. Who else would come? I talked about the requests of my Lady to my mother. She was willing to go with us. I said to her: "Bring others with you."

She replied: "I don't know anyone I can bring."

Another barrier was placed in my way. The few members of the family whom I had talked to could not force themselves to speak to others about the visions. That task was too much for them. "I will go with you," they would say; but when I asked them to bring a friend, they would reply: "I don't know who I can bring. You just don't talk about something like this."

Before we went to my Lady's land, we went to Mass. During Mass my Lady appeared to me in all her splendor. She told me that where I had dug a little hole in front of the rock, she wanted me to place a pillar in the hole and place my little statue of The Golden Lady on this pillar. She also said: "Enclose the rock and the pillar with the statue within a shrine." Then I started to cry and I prayed to my Lord. I pleaded: "Dearest Jesus, please be with me when I go to the land, please encourage me, and please do not fail me."

Suddenly Jesus appeared in all His glory with His Sacred Heart blazing. He said so sweetly: "I will be with my Child of Love. Do not fear. I will not fail you."

After Mass, I told Mike what had happened and I asked him if he had something for a pillar which I could place my statue (the one I fashioned) of my Golden Lady on. He went to the basement and found a piece of wood which had been split in two. It was just the right size and shape and it was big enough to hold my statue.

As we drove to the land, my heart was filled with fear (this fear was there each time I went for the Sunday visits). I longed to run away and I would start to cry because it was such a terrible cross for me to actually make my Lady known. I suffered tremendously and it took a great deal of courage for me to carry out the wishes of my Lady.

As we got closer and closer to my Lady's land, the fear increased. But I had to do what I was asked because it was God's will.

Sunday afternoon, July 17, two cars drove to the land where the Holy Mother of God wanted the shrine to her Immaculate Heart. Seven people walked up the path, which was still filled with tall grass and weeds, to the rock. I held in my arms my statue of The Golden Lady of Happiness. I also held in my hand a pocketbook which contained my prayer book, my Rosary and small bags, which I wanted to use to put some of the dirt from around the rock in. Mike held a small shovel and a block of wood. The block of wood was very important. My Lady had told me to take the statue to the land and to place it upon a pillar. The block of wood was the pillar. The statue which I had had in my home for years was, at last, to find its rightful place: It belonged at the rock. (I did not leave the statue at the rock. I took it home with me after each visit. But the little wooden pillar stayed.)

After I placed the statue on the pillar, we knelt to say the Rosary. Then what I considered the first remarkable event happened.

Ever since 1946 when my Lady showed me the land where she wanted her shrine, I had called this land: My Lady's land. However, I did not own this land, nor did my Lady. In 1946 and 1948 the land was part of a huge farm called Coe's Farm. This place where my Lady had appeared on the rock was a pasture for cows. When I went to see the rock in 1948 after my Lady had appeared on it as The Golden Lady, if the cows were there, I would run away because I was afraid of the cows.

During the time from 1948 to 1960, the land had been acquired by the city and was now used as a day camp for boys. A Mr. Coffey was in charge of the camp.

Mike had further frightened me by saying that we had no business going on someone's property and as soon as the owners found out what was happening, they would put up "No Trespassing" signs. Even though I was afraid that would happen, I knew I had to go there as my Lady requested.

As we knelt to say the Rosary, Mr. Coffey came up the hill to find out what was going on. I began to panic. But Mike knew him because Mike had once belonged to the Boys' Club. Mike went to greet him and he smiled because of Mike's friendly greeting. He remembered Mike.

"What's going on here?" he asked with a smile.

I held my breath while Mike explained what had happened. He told the man about the visions, which had first taken place in 1948; then Mike told him about the new requests of the Holy Mother of God.

The man's face became serious and thoughtful as he listened to the story. He was deeply impressed by what he had heard. He said: "That is wonderful, wonderful." He walked around the rock to see the statue of my Golden Lady.

He said that it was beautiful. Then he knelt down before the rock and he blessed himself. When he stood up, he smiled in a very kind, gentle way and be said: "You may come here whenever you want to. No one will bother you. If anyone says anything to you, then tell them to see me. Tell them you have my permission to come here whenever you want to come." He slowly walked back down the path. (It was beginning to look like a path.)

Needless to say, we were delighted with the answer. We all agreed that here was the first blessing of The Golden Lady of Happiness. (Years later when I had formed the Maryheart Crusaders' store and chapel, Mr. Coffey often came to Mass in our chapel. He remained a dear friend of mine until his death. I was always grateful to him for his kindness to me that day.)

When we knelt down to say the Rosary, we felt a wonderful, heavenly joy. The Rosary was said with loud, clear voices. Halfway through the Rosary, my Golden Lady appeared to me. She had told me that she would appear to me on each of the ten Sundays, so I expected to see her. She was very, very beautiful. She was dressed as the Golden Lady of Happiness. But she was not standing on the earth, the moon and the snake. Her bare feet were resting right on the rock. Her feet seemed to cling to the sloping rock. My eyes were drawn to the place where her feet rested. I saw upon each foot a gold rose; but I did not realize until hours later that I had seen the roses.

When my Lady appeared to me, "God took my soul to Heaven." That is what bothered me the most. I knew that people were watching me. I did not want anyone to see me when I saw a vision.

My Lady smiled at me and she was very happy. She did not give me any long message. She remained visible for about ten minutes, then she went away. Mike and I had remained kneeling until the end of the Rosary. The others who were in the group had to stand up. They asked me if the hard uneven ground had hurt my knees. I was surprised. I had not felt the hard, uneven ground beneath my knees. It seemed as though I had been kneeling on a pillow.

After my Lady had appeared to me, I felt a great happiness and joy in my heart and soul. In spite of all that I had suffered up to that moment, I was glad, very, very glad that I had carried out my Lady's wishes. I had brought people to her land. I was making The Golden Lady and her promises known. I felt wonderful knowing that I had made my Lady happy by carrying out her wishes.

However, a couple of remarks were made by members of the group which were like knife thrusts into my heart: "Well, where is the miracle?" "We didn't see anything." Once again the heavy cross, which had been mine in 1946 and in 1948 ("So you see the Holy Mother of God—Prove it!") was placed on my shoulder. The people wanted to see "something." My Lady had told me that miracles would take place at the land, but she had not told me when they would happen. I had not expected to see any miracle when she was present on the rock, but others had expected the miracle. They had not seen what they had wanted to see. Their disappointment was my personal suffering.

My Lady had promised a special grace to all who were present but seeing a miracle was not one of them. When the others were yelling at me that they had not seen a miracle, my husband replied: "Mr. Coffey came and that is enough of a "miracle" for me. He came on this the first day. He is a well-known person and very admired. He gave us permission to keep coming here. What more do you want?"

I replied: "My Lady has plans of her own. All I have to do is my part. She will do the rest."

When I wrote the notes on July 18 to explain what had happened on the 17th, I added these words: July 18, 1960 I can already see a powerful light that seems to be building up around me and my Golden Lady. In this light is peace and joy that cannot be described. I seem to know that slowly, but surely, that light is spreading and it will encircle more and more people—even nations. I am beginning to feel the same peace and closeness to God all the time that I feel only when God "takes my soul to Heaven" in a special way (When I am lost in prayer).

Not only that, but slowly there is creeping upon me the feeling that I really am chosen and that now I shall be able to start my mission in a very special way. I seem to be walking down a road that will—how shall I say this—take me "out of the ordinary." Of course, I never felt like that in my material life before. I have always placed my spiritual life in the background and it has never interfered with my material life. Now, I am starting to feel that the spiritual life is coming forth to dim out my material life. This is very hard for me to explain. I don't mean that I will run away to a convent. I mean that at last I am finding the true place that God created for me. I feel like Christ when He said in the temple: "At last I must be about My Father's business."

There was no doubt that this July 17th visit to my Lady's land changed my whole life. I still lived in my little apartment with my husband. I still had my bookkeeping job, I still had a daily life to live; however, there was a job I had to do for God and my Lady and I would not fail to do that job. As the years went by, I never changed the direction I had been given. I never took any detours. Whatever God and my Lady wanted me to do, I did. Whatever examples they wanted me to give to their children, I gave. My spiritual writings began. I saw and talked to thousands of people, all the while living my plain, ordinary daily life. That was not easy, but that was God's holy will for me and I so loved God's holy will that Christ often said to me: "Your will is Mine and My will is yours."

— 3 —

THE SECOND VISIT TO THE LAND: JULY 24, 1960

I had been extremely nervous and afraid when I took the first group of people to my Lady's land on July 17; but I knew I could not give up even though I was tempted to run away and forget everything. I knew that my Lady wanted me to bring people to her land. That became a very serious problem. Who could I bring? At that time most people I knew and worked with in offices did not even know I saw visions. Also, if someone did say they saw Our Lady, they were laughed at, ridiculed and told they were crazy. But I did not care what people thought, I had to do what my Lady asked me to do: take people to her land for 10 Sundays. I was willing to open myself up to verbal abuses to do what it was my Lady wanted me to do.

On July 21, 1960, I wrote a short letter to Bishop O'Brien asking for an appointment. I wrote in my notes:

Today I wrote a short letter to Bishop O'Brien asking for an appointment. I will no longer try to go to priests who will take me to the bishop. This time, I will see the bishop myself and I will tell him what my Lady wants.

(I received an answer asking why I wanted to see the bishop. I wrote him explaining my Lady's request and that I was taking people to the land for the ten Sundays.)

The following week I talked to a few more people about the visions (they were Mike's relatives) and I read them the messages of The Golden Lady of Happiness and the promises of The Golden Lady of Happiness. These people had known about the visions in 1948, but I had never mentioned them again; even though, I had seen these people often since my marriage. So when I began to talk about the visions again, they were surprised. When I explained my Lady's new requests, the people could only listen and say very little. Some of them

458

agreed to go with me to the land on the next Sunday, which was July 24, 1960.

Sunday, July 24, the group which knelt before the rock to say the Rosary was slightly larger than it had been on the previous Sunday. There were perhaps nine or ten people in group. I was again grateful. I wrote the following notes on July 27 to explain what had happened: The more I try to spread my Lady's messages, the more discouraged I become. This time there were 11 people there. They were very kind. They made a sacrifice to come there; but they did so only to please me. I was very grateful, but they don't actually believe that my Lady comes to me. Later one girl said to me: "You mean you really see the Blessed Virgin?" She can't understand how such a thing could be possible. Neither can anyone else, I guess.

The reaction of my friends whom I have told about the shrine is one of polite silence. That means that if I say that I see Our Lady, then that is all right with them, yet they are not interested in questioning me. They listen to the words from Mary, that's all. They are not excited or impressed. They let me talk, then in a minute we are all talking about something else.

I feel very hurt, not because I want their praise; but I realize that they aren't interested (with the exception of one or two people) in what my Lady says and the reason why they can't get excited is because they cannot believe that such a thing could happen. They will go to the land only if something happens. I will not promise miracles, but they are all looking only for a miracle—even Mike's mother and his aunt look only for a miracle. They only talk about seeing the Blessed Virgin themselves. Mike's mother, who I at first thought firmly believes, comes to the land for her own private miracle. She told us that she has it all "arranged." She just has to see, not only the Blessed Virgin, but also Saint Joseph and the Infant Jesus.

No one comes to the land except me and my mother out of pure love and faith. They listened to the words of Our Lady, but they don't even know that the words are great news. They only want to be shown and they admit that they "can't feel anything for God" and they can't "really believe that the Blessed

Virgin has come." They say these things to me and I know they say them about me.

Even my Mike is very skeptical. He goes with me to the land, but he just can't believe that anything will happen. "I believe you," he says "You see your visions but what could happen—nothing!"

When I told him that I was making sacrifices so that my Lady's golden light could fall in a visible way upon the people who come to the land, Mike said: "That's impossible. Nothing like that could happen."

I said: "But my Lady can do anything. She can make the people see her golden light."

Mike said: "You can't expect a thing like that to happen. Just don't look for anything. Things like that just don't happen."

I started to cry: "But I know my Lady can do things like that. She won't fail me. I will make sacrifices and I will pray. I know she won't fail me. The people only want miracles. They won't come just to love Our Lady. Well! my Lady will show them her signs even though she would rather have their love."

Mike only said: "I wish I had your faith. No one has faith like that. They don't believe that anything will happen and I don't believe it. I wish that I could believe, but I don't."

I am very discouraged. I don't know who to tell. I feel that it would be useless to tell the priests. I went through all that in 1948; but I think I will start to tell the priests again. My Lady told me to tell the priests in 1948. I wrote a statement for the bishop. I want to see him, but, as yet, I haven't had an answer to my letter.

I cannot count on anyone I know to spread the word about the visions. They all are coldly silent. I am amazed because they are so uninterested (with the exception of one or two) in my Lady. They just cannot believe that such a thing is possible. They, of course, will not mention it to anyone.

My brother is so against it, that I dare not mention it to him and to his wife. My own mother has told only one person. She said that she doesn't know who else to tell. But she said that she will still come to the land.

I sit in my office at work and I can look towards the west. If I drew a line, that line would end at my Lady's land. I look out of the window and now I see what I did not see before (I have worked at that office for almost two years.) Now I feel a silent call to my soul to come to my Lady's land. Now I hear a silent call from her. "Come to my Land" "Make my shrine known." Now I can only think about my Lady and her shrine. And now I want the whole world to know about my Lady and her shrine.

The seal on my lips has been broken. I will talk about my Lady now; but now my problem is: "Who will listen? Who will believe? Who will do what my Lady wants? Who has the faith and the love to kneel and pray to Mary in a field?

And this problem is causing me suffering. The joy of my happy marriage has faded. The cross of Christ is mine again. I am suffering for God again and for my beloved Mary. I have a tremendous problem; but I will not run away. I know that I see my Lady. I know that she wants her shrine and I believe with all my heart that her wonders will fill the world and this is the time for the miracles of The Golden Lady of Happiness.

I will not give up and I do not mind suffering for my Golden Lady. God can do anything He wants with me. I don't mind. There is yet more suffering for me, but I won't mind because I will suffer anything in order to tell the world what my Lady wants me to tell it.

I will not give up. I will keep trying to do what my Lady wants me to do.

The rejection of my brother, his family and friends and relatives which I received was most painful to me. They seemed to think that I was just trying to impress them or that I wanted personal glory. Once my brother had said to me, in a very nasty way; "What do you want? Do you want me to bow to you?"

I did not want to make my Lady known. I did it only because that was God's will for me. I was only trying to give messages of joy, hope and encouragement to hearts and souls; but these people did not want to hear that—they only wanted to see Our Lady themselves. I never expected such a reaction.

I added in my July 27 notes: Years ago in 1944, my Lady said to me (March 31, 1944):

"Do not expect to conquer the world Do not expect to convert millions. But do start the landslide that will make people stand up and take notice. Cause an avalanche of love, happiness and joy and show the world how to find their own happiness, love and joy."

After I quoted that message, I wrote: This must be with my Golden Lady. Now is the time to make myself known to the world.

I explained the vision I saw on July 24 with these words (written July 27, 1960):

Sunday when we went to my Lady's land, she appeared to me all in gold. First, I saw her in the sky above the rock when we drove up to the land. She was in an oval of light. Suddenly as I watched her, I saw an oval traced in the sky in the exact spot she was in with a white line that was very smooth and narrow. This white oval was different than the vision. That is, it looked like material smoke and not like the glorious vision I saw.

Then the vision went away and after I started to pray my Golden Lady appeared on the rock. This time she did not have the crown on her head and she did not stand on the globe. Her feet were once again firmly settled on the rock with her toes down, as though she was tightly gripping the rock with her toes.

I have seen her with her toes like that gripping the rock. It seems as if she really is "implanted" on the earth now and she is determined to stay here.

This time her hands were placed on the left side of her face and her head rested upon her hands. She seemed very, very contented and very happy.

She said that this will be a very special shrine for the sick of body, the sick of mind and the sick of spirit.

She said to me today: "You will know that Heaven is on earth because this spot will be Heaven on earth. Never has there been such a place. Never will there again be such a place."

— 4 —

THE THIRD VISIT TO THE LAND: JULY 31, 1960

The third Sunday, of the ten my Lady had requested was July 31, 1960. The following day (August 1, 1960) I wrote these notes to explain what happened: Yesterday, July 31, 1960, I took more people with me to my Lady's land. There were ten of us, but there were "new" people (that is: people who had never been to my Lady's land before.) Nothing happened yesterday as a sign, but once again (this happened last week as I knelt), I felt that I was kneeling on a pillow even though I was kneeling on uneven hard ground.

We said the Rosary after I read the prayer of consecration. My Lady appeared to me after we had said the third decade. She was dressed as The Golden Lady, only this time I saw silver (like thick bands) across her arms. I could not understand why I saw the silver on her golden gown. I mentioned this to Mike, after we were alone. I had told the other people that the Virgin had appeared.

At Mass, my Lady had told me to show the people the "golden water" on the tenth Sunday. There was a brook not far from the site of the apparitions. This brook, my Lady told me, was the "golden water."

I had told Mike's relatives about this golden water. One of his aunts said: "We know there is water in the brook. What we want is water from the rock."

In other words, they are coming with me only to see a "great miracle." I know that, but I cannot help but feel sad. The messages of peace, joy and happiness from my Lady do not mean very much to these people. They want a miracle. They can't just love Our Lady. But, I do not mean to be against them. I am very, very grateful because they have taken the time to come to my Lady's land with me and I know that it is a sacrifice on their part. I am so thankful that they do come and I am sorry that I cannot give them the miracle they want to see; and I don't blame them because they do want to see a miracle. I know that my Lady's words can't mean too much without a special sign so that the world can believe in her and in her words.

Last night just before I went to sleep, after Mike and I had said our prayers, my Golden Lady appeared to me. She was very beautiful and I noticed that once again, she had the silver bands around her arms. Suddenly I saw the silver bands raise up and they became silver rays of light. She had three rays of light on her right arm, over her golden gown and she had two rays of light over her left arm. There were five beams of light. Then my Lady told me that they were the five promises from The Golden Lady and they were connected with the five beams of light that I saw years ago in New York City in the Church of the Blessed Sacrament on West 71st Street.

For years, I thought about the five beams of light and I tried to think about their meaning. Jesus explained them to me in 1944 when I saw Him with the Diamond Rosary (see notes copied from my 1951 autobiography, written in 1963 autobiography): He named each beam of light of the Diamond Rosary.

One beam was for love.

One beam was for truth and righteousness.

One beam was the power to plant the love of God in the hearts of men.

One beam was for the power of God to work through me.

And the last beam was for peace, joy, and happiness.

But, I could never explain them myself, until after I heard the five promises of The Golden Lady of Happiness. At one time, I thought the beams of light meant that the war would go on for five more years. Then I thought that the beams of light meant that I would only live for five more years; and so forth. . . .

That is the story that my Lady wanted me to write again about the five beams of light.

Now, when my Lady appeared with these beams of light on her golden gown, this happened. As I watched the vision I saw my Lady raise her arms. As she did, the beams of light touched each other at the bottom of her gown, near her feet. They formed a point at the spot. Suddenly at the spot where the beams of light met, there appeared the Immaculate Heart of Mary. Then my Lady told me that whenever I, or anyone else prays to The Golden Lady, we should all pray to the Immaculate Heart of The Golden Lady.

5

THE FOURTH SUNDAY: AUGUST 7, 1960
EMILY'S GREAT SIGN

The fourth Sunday of the ten came on August 7, 1960. In spite of my efforts to bring people to my Lady's land, most friends and relatives ignored me. They had better things to do than to go to an empty field to say the Rosary before a large rock. Also, the ones who had come only to see their own miracles no longer bothered after they saw nothing. I wrote about this fourth Sunday on August 8, 1960: Yesterday was Sunday and we went to the land once more. I had prayed all week for a special sign from my Lady and, at first, I was deeply disappointed. This seemed to be the least encouraging of all the Sundays so far. I went to the land with only seven people. I had expected a bigger crowd, but everyone else was too busy to come. Of course, I do not blame them. There are a great many things to do on a warm, sunny summer day. But I did feel very bad because so few people came to the land. Still I prayed very strongly when I led the group in the Rosary. And my Lady Mary did come to us. I saw her standing on the rock. This time she held a Rosary in her right hand and she held it out in front of her. The Rosary hung down so that the whole Rosary was visible. It was made out of a light colored wood. Mary held her other hand out, next to the one that held the Rosary. I could see her fingers closed over her palm, but I did not know what she was holding in that hand.

She did not say anything except to remind me to tell those who were present that she wanted them to pray to the Immaculate Heart of The Golden Lady of Happiness.

EMILY'S GREAT SIGN AUGUST 7, 1960

As I said, I was very disappointed because so few people

466

went to the land. However, there was one woman who went Sunday for the first time. She is a friend of my mother and her name is Emily. She was the only "new" person there, so I did not bother to read the words of my Golden Lady. I knew that the others had heard the words and I also knew that Emily would come to my home later in the day, so I thought that I would tell her what my Lady said, when she came to my home.

When Mike and I got home, I started to cry. I felt so bad because nothing had happened and because very few people had come to my Lady's land.

I walked into my kitchen with Mike. I started to cry because I had been so disappointed. I said to Mike: "No one came today. No one cared about the visions. How can I make my Lady known, if no one cares?"

Mike held me and replied: "Don't worry, honey. Your good Lady will take care of everything. Leave everything up to her."

I replied, with tears in my eyes: "I'm trying so hard to make her known, but I'm not getting anywhere. At this rate I will need fifty Sundays to make her known."

Just then, my mother and Emily walked into the kitchen. I looked at Emily and I said to myself: "Well, at least one more person will hear the promises of The Golden Lady."

I did not allow Emily to see my disappointment as I took out my note book and as I started to read the words of The Golden Lady of Happiness. I was grateful for Emily's interest in the visions. I carefully read the promises to the woman. Suddenly, as I read the words something happened that was unbelievable.

As I started to read the words: "I promise that the devil and his evil ones will be pushed . . ." Emily interrupted me and said: "Yes, I know."

I looked up at her and I asked: "You know what?"

She said in a very nonchalant way: "I know about the devil and his evil ones."

"You know what?" I asked again.

"The devil and his evil ones will be pushed back into Hell and much sin shall vanish from the world," was her reply.

For a moment, I could not believe what I had heard. Then I asked; "How did you know that? I never read my notes to you; did you hear the words from my mother?"

She looked a little surprised when she answered: "No. Your mother never mentioned the words to me. I heard them in church this morning."

I looked at my mother who was sitting next to me and my mother looked at me. Then we both looked at Emily who was beginning to feel a bit uncomfortable—as though she had said the wrong thing.

"You heard that in church this morning?" I asked.

"I heard the words: 'The devil and his evil ones will be pushed back into Hell and much sin shall vanish from the world.' "

My mother and I were stunned. Emily became a bit more uncomfortable. "How did you hear the words?" I asked.

Emily explained: "The words were in today's gospel."

I looked at my mother again and she looked at me.

"What do you mean by saying that the words were in today's gospel?"

Emily was puzzled: "When the priest read the gospel, I heard the words and I remembered them. He said: 'The devil and his evil ones will be pushed back into Hell and much sin shall vanish from the world.' I heard the priest say that. It is part of the gospel isn't it?"

I took a deep breath: "No, Emily. The words aren't in today's gospel. You heard the words of The Golden Lady."

This time Emily was stunned: "But I heard the words when the priest read the gospel. I heard them clearly and I remembered them. When I left church, the words were in my mind. I said to myself: 'At least I got that much out of the gospel today.' "

My mother interrupted: "I was in church with you today, Emily, and I didn't hear the words when the priest read the gospel. The words aren't in today's gospel."

"I don't believe that!" Emily exclaimed. "I heard the words. Show me the gospel. I'll show you where the words are. I heard the priest say them while he was reading the gospel."

"Did his voice change when you heard the words?" I asked.

"No. His voice didn't change. I heard his voice and it was the same as when he read the whole gospel. Only he said the words and I heard them. Nothing changed. He read the gospel and the words. Get me a prayer book. I'll show you the words."

I went to my room and I got my prayer book and Mike's prayer book. I asked him what he thought about the whole thing and he could not say anything. When I gave Emily the prayer books, I said: "The words are not in today's gospel. You heard the words of The Golden Lady. I don't know how; but you heard the exact words that are in my note book."

Emily still could not believe that the words were not in the gospel. She took both prayer books and she carefully read the Gospel for the 9th Sunday after Pentecost.

Her face had an amazed look upon it when she said: "I still can't believe it. But the words aren't here. Yet, I heard them clearly. I know I wasn't dreaming. The priest read the words when he read the gospel!"

There was a moment of silence. Then I said: "I can't believe it either. I don't know what happened; but you heard the words of my Golden Lady. And you heard the exact words that are here in my note book. It is almost like some kind of a miracle." Then I became joyful: "This is what we have been waiting for! This is the first real big sign from my Lady."

All the disappointment which had been with me since the visit to the rock left me as the four of us talked about the amazing incident. Emily had actually heard the words of The Golden Lady while the priest read the Gospel. There were no doubts about that. The woman had been stunned when she learned that the words which she had heard were not in the Gospel. Indeed The Golden Lady had given me and the others a sign of her power. We were all deeply impressed by that sign; and it gave new courage at the time when I was becoming very discouraged.

Later Emily signed a statement about this remarkable sign from The Golden Lady.

Following is the statement signed by Emily, my mother, Mike and me. It is dated October 21, 1960:

> I, Emily Rousseau, wish to state the following incident in regards to The Golden Lady of Happiness:
>
> On August 7, 1960, I had planned to go with Louise D'Angelo to the place where she said she saw the Blessed Virgin as The Golden Lady of Happiness.
>
> Previous to that date, I knew nothing about the three promises of The Golden Lady of Happiness. I had never heard the words.
>
> That morning, August 7, 1960, I attended the ten o'clock Mass at Saint Joseph's Church Meriden, Connecticut. That day was the 9th Sunday after Pentecost.
>
> The priest read the Gospel for that day and he was almost finished with the Gospel, when I clearly heard, in his voice (without any change whatsoever in the voice) the following words: "The devil and his evil ones will be pushed back into Hell and much sin shall vanish from the world."
>
> I was under the impression that I had heard words which had been in the Gospel. At that time, and when I left the church with the words fresh in my mind, I said to myself: "At least I got that much out of the Gospel today." and I remembered the words that I had heard.
>
> That same afternoon, I went with Mrs. Louise D'Angelo to the land for the first time. And while I was present, Mrs. D'Angelo said she saw the Golden Lady of Happiness. Mrs. D'Angelo said that she had to return to the rock for ten Sundays. That day, August 7, was the 4th of the 10 Sundays.

Later that day, I went to the home of Mrs. D'Angelo and she started to read me the three promises of The Golden Lady of Happiness. When she started to read the third promise, I immediately recognized the words that I had clearly heard in church and I was able to finish the sentence that Mrs. D'Angelo had started to read from her own personal note book. *I had never seen the notebook* and *I had never heard the three promises.*

This is what Mrs. D'Angelo read to me: "I promise that the devil and his evil ones will be pushed . . ." This is where I interrupted her and finished the sentence for her which was "back into Hell and much sin shall vanish from the world."

I had remembered the exact words that I had heard in church when the priest had read the Gospel and these words were the exact words that were written in Mrs. D'Angelo's private note book.

As you know, the words, which I had heard and remembered *were not* in the Gospel at all. I was so amazed by that fact that I insisted on checking two prayer books to make sure that the words *were not* in the Gospel of the 9th Sunday after Pentecost.

Mrs. D'Angelo, her husband, Michael, and Mrs. Helen Webster were present when I finished the words of the third promise, that Mrs. D'Angelo had started to read to me.

Also, Mrs. Helen Webster had attended the same Mass at the same church and she had not heard the words which I bad heard and remembered.

I believe that in hearing the words, that I have received a very special favor from The

Golden Lady of Happiness.

This account is true and I will be willing to verify this statement, if necessary, at a personal interview.

I will add a note: It is not very often that a person can remember the exact words that they heard while the Gospel was being read. I not only remembered the words that I clearly heard: but these were the *exact* words that were written in Mrs. D'Angelo's notebook, written exactly as I had heard them in church.

Emily M. Rousseau
(signed)

Witnesses
Louise D'Angelo
Michael D'Angelo
Helen Webster
   (signed)

6

THE TEN SUNDAYS CONTINUED:
AUGUST 14, 1960
THE ROCK IS ENCLOSED

August 14, 1960 was the fifth of the ten Sundays requested by my Lady. On August 16, I wrote about this visit: Sunday, I took people to the land for the fifth time. There were only eleven people there and I was again disappointed. I was trying to tell "the world" that my Lady wanted her shrine and to give them the promises. But things were not working out that way. I felt that I was failing my Lady. But in spite of the few who came, there were two "new" people (the ones who never came before.)

We all knelt and we said the Rosary. I must say that it is a very hard task to kneel on the uneven ground. some of the people bring pillows. It is torture to kneel for about twenty minutes, but the people do kneel. Stanley said: "I wouldn't have gotten up if I had died," because he knew that the Holy Mother of God was present.

I will say that once again, I felt as if I was kneeling on a pillow. The ground felt very soft and my knees did not hurt like they did the first time I knelt there.

My Lady came to me when we said the second decade of the Rosary. She was very beautiful. She did not stand on the earth. She stood only on the bare rock and her feet had one gold rose on them (one on each foot). She stood with her arms held up high and in front of her. In between her arms was her Immaculate Heart. It was so bright that I could not see any shape. I saw only a brilliant, red light that filled the place between her outstretched arms.

Sunday, she spoke different words. She said, very sweetly: "Ah! my children, pray to my Immaculate Heart." Then later she said: "My Heart will bring peace to the world." Also: "Ah!

my children love my Immaculate Heart. My Heart will bless you."

That was all she said as she stood on the rock Sunday.

We finished the Rosary and then I stood up.

Later we all went to my home and I read some of the things my Lady had said.

I felt so very happy because I feel that, at last, after all these years of waiting, the world can have my Golden Lady. I am so happy for the world and also for my Golden Lady. I know how much she wants to bring peace, joy and happiness to the world.

Five Sundays have gone by and they were quiet Sundays, with very few people there, but now I feel that the next five Sundays will not be so quiet and there will be more people.

The word has started to spread outside my family.

On August 16, I was told by my Lady that I had done my part in making her known and now she would "take over" and make something happen, which was not of my doing, to bring the crowds to the land which I had been unable to do. So far my efforts to tell people about my Lady's shrine and to bring the people she wanted to the shrine had not been too successful. I had even written to a couple of newspapers telling them about the ten Sundays, but they ignored my letters. By the fifth Sunday, I had been able to bring only a handful of people. In that respect, I felt like I had failed my Lady.

Now she was telling me that I did not have to continue with my efforts alone. She would help me bring the crowds to her shrine. I had no idea how she would do this; but if the crowds began to visit the site then I knew it would be my Lady calling her children to her shrine and not me. There was nothing more I could do.

Then suddenly I received news about the shrine which made me know that what happened was not my doing. This was my Lady's inspiration to whomever received that spiritual incentive. What happened was the turning point where, indeed, my Lady would now act to spread the news about the shrine and to bring her children to her shrine.

THE ROCK IS ENCLOSED

When my Lady first appeared on the rock, she told me to enclose the rock after I had placed her statue (the one I made of The Golden Lady) on the little pillar. I wrote about what happened on August 20, 1960: Today, there was another "sign" from my Lady and I am so happy as I write these words. Yesterday and this morning I was blue and discouraged. This afternoon I am so happy. My mother called me and she told me that Thursday, the boys (or someone) at the camp, where the rock is, (By the way, the rock is on the far west side of the camp. The boys never used that spot) built a small fence around the rock as a sign of devotion. I was amazed. I never dreamt that that would happen.

But lately we have noticed a well-worn path from the boys' camp to the rock.

I went to the land with Mike and we saw the fence the boys had made. It encloses the rock and there is now a cleared space around the rock inside the fence. The boys built the fence so that people could enter from one side and then they also put poles down at the opening so that the boys could come from the camp to the rock. The poles are slanted so they form an entrance into the space where the rock is. The opening is right where the path has been made from the camp to the rock.

I was so thrilled when I saw the lovely effect of the fence that my heart jumped with joy. The spot is beginning to look like a shrine now. The fence was put up very neatly as an act of devotion that must have been inspired by The Golden Lady because no one I know told the boys to put the fence up. I do not even know who did put the fence up. Also, nothing has been touched that was put near the rock. The rock now has Rosaries and flowers. My mother goes every day to put fresh flowers on the rock and I put a Rosary on the pillar. None of these things have been touched.

Now my Lady has the very first crude "walls" of her shrine. The fence seems to make the spot, a very special place.

This also happened about this same time: During the next

two weeks another thing happened at the rock which proved to be rather important. I do not remember the exact dates. One day I pasted a picture of the statue of The Golden Lady of Happiness (the statue that I had made) on a piece of heavy paper. Then I wrote above the picture, "The Shrine of the Immaculate Heart of Mary." Below the picture I copied the three promises of The Golden Lady of Happiness and also a few of the things which she had said to me during her recent visits to the rock. Although she had not said too much during each appearance, she did say the following things on different Sundays: "Ah! my children, pray to my Immaculate Heart." "Ah! my children, love my Immaculate Heart." "My Heart will bring peace to the world." "My Heart will bless you."

After the poster was completed, I placed it in a frame. A piece of glass and clear plastic protected it. I decorated the frame with small plastic flowers and then I took the picture to the land. I placed the picture next to the rock under the small tree on the west side of the rock. I wasn't sure if the picture would stay there; but I felt that I could replace the loss if the picture was stolen. I wanted the picture by the rock just in case people did go there. At least, in that way, they would know the things which my Lady wanted the world to know.

After I placed the picture at the rock, I felt that my Lady's shrine was beginning to look like a real shrine.

The First Pilgrims
July 1960 (Louise is kneeling)

The rock is enclosed
August 21, 1960

7

THE SIXTH SUNDAY: AUGUST 21, 1960

Sunday, August 21, 1960, was the sixth of the ten Sunday visits to the rock which my Lady had requested. I was pleased by the fact that about 15 people came with me to my Lady's land. There were three "new" faces among the familiar ones in the group. I have pictures of that gathering. These pictures show how the shrine looked on August 21, 1960: People are standing around the rock, inside of the small corral. My statue of The Golden Lady is on the pillar in front of the rock. (I did not leave the statue there. I brought it with me each time I went to the rock on Sunday.) A tiny statue of the Blessed Virgin and a Rosary are leaning against the pillar. Flowers are in vases alongside of the rock. The frame which held the picture of my Lady and her promises is under the small tree on the west side of the rock. The lovely, little tree, which seemed to be growing out of the rock, completes the picture of the infant shrine. The photographs also show that the grass around the rock was still fairly high with sprays of grass touching the rock.

The photos had been taken by Mike after my Lady had appeared to me. My Lady had, once again, appeared as The Golden Lady of Happiness standing on the rock. She had come to me while the group was saying the Rosary.

I explained what happened in the notes I wrote on August 22, 1960: Sunday my Lady appeared to me as the third decade was begun. She was dressed as The Golden Lady, but I did not see her heart. She did not stand on the earth, the moon or the snake. She stood with her feet gripping the rock and I saw the gold roses on her feet.

Also, I, especially, noticed that the bottom of her golden gown seemed to have a wide hem on it and this hem was covered with tiny diamonds. The hem went around the rock and the golden garment almost covered the rock, except for the front because I still saw her feet with the gold roses. I told the people, later, how my Lady had looked. Then I heard her say, as we were saying the Rosary: "Ah, my children, love my Immaculate Heart!" Later she said: "My heart will bless you." She went away after the Rosary was said. Then one woman came to the place, after we had finished praying and no one knew her. She said that she found out about the shrine from a friend of hers. She also said that two men (one was her brother or brother-in-law) had been coming to the shrine every day for a week.

A man and his wife and his aged mother also came to the land on Sunday. He had heard about the shrine from a friend of ours whom we told. He was very, very impressed with what he saw. When my Lady came while we were saying the third decade, the man said that he could tell she had appeared because I suddenly, tightly closed my eyes (I did not remember). Then he said as soon as my Lady came, the votive candle, which had been lit, was blown out by a strong gust of wind. I remembered the strong gust of wind, but I did not realize that the candle was blown out as soon as my Lady came. The man was so impressed by that, that he kept talking about it and he told everyone who was there about the candle being blown out. I remember that I saw the candle was no longer lit and I said to myself: "Oh, dear, the candle is out and my Lady is here. It should be lit." On another visit of my Lady, the candle had remained lit even though the wind was blowing strongly all during the appearance of my Lady. But yesterday, a strong gust of wind blew out the candle, and this was the only gust of wind because yesterday it was one of the hottest and most uncomfortable days of the year. I did not know that the candle was blown out and that I closed my eyes when my Lady came.

The woman named Mary Stores was also present. She told everyone that she knew the exact moment that the Blessed Virgin came because she also said that I suddenly closed my eyes tight when she appeared and she knew that my Lady had come.

She said that my Lady came at the third decade and that was correct. The man also said it was the third decade.

She, Mary Stores, also said: "You didn't say when she was present but I knew. You couldn't fool me."

I had said, in a low voice that my Lady was present. Mike heard me and so did my mother. I thought that everyone heard me say that my Lady had come, but Mary said: "You wouldn't tell us when she came; but I knew." She hadn't heard me say that my Lady was present.

This woman, Mary Stores, is a divorced Catholic, although the priest told her that she could go to church and Communion because she has not remarried. Still, the woman did not go to church. She went, instead, to the place called the "Jehovah's Witnesses." I guess that it is a "miracle" that she comes to my Lady's land.

Also, things are happening as my Lady said. People are going to the land without me asking them.

I had been nervous because I still did not want anyone to see me when I saw a vision, but I felt at ease when the people told me that they had been glad that they had been there when my Lady came. We lingered longer, this time, by the rock. it seemed as though no one wanted to leave.

After the prayers were said, the people did not want to leave right away. That was "different" because, always before, we all left right after the prayers. Yesterday, the people stood around talking in little groups for almost a half an hour. I, myself, felt as if I could stay there all day. I did not talk to any "group" but Mike talked to different people. Later the groups went back to their cars. There were about seven cars parked near the land. The people still lingered. They talked in little groups. But I did not. I went back to my Lady's rock by myself. I had a wonderful feeling of peace and joy and while I was there my Lady appeared to me again. She held out her arms and she was very happy. She said that I did the right thing when I bought people to her land and she thanked me. She stayed with me until I left. I did not tell any of the people about the visit. Later I told Mike. I said: "When I went back to the rock, my Lady came again." He laughed and he replied: "They saw you go back (I did not know that) and one man said: 'I bet she is going to see the Holy Mother again.'"

I hope and pray that there will be a lot of people next week at the land when my Lady comes.

Everyone said that they wanted to return on the following Sunday. They also wanted to bring more people with them.

When I went home, I felt satisfied. I said to Mike: "My Lady is becoming known. I am happy about that."

I looked forward to the seventh Sunday, but I did not know that that Sunday would be the first "sad" Sunday.

MY OBEDIENCE TO BISHOP O'BRIEN

Then it was time for the seventh Sunday. Suddenly I received a call from a priest at my parish. I was told to come to his office immediately. My heart raced in panic. I had not told him what I was doing, taking people to my Lady's land. Why would he want to see me? As I walked the long distance to his office, I was crying. I was very nervous. He greeted me at the door in a cold, almost harsh way. He came right to the point. He said he had received a letter from the bishop asking me to no longer take people to the land. I started to cry harder. I had written to the bishop to tell him that I would be taking people to the land. This was his answer. He, Father, ordered me not to go to the rock.

I said softly: "My Lady told me to go for ten Sundays. I still have more Sundays."

Father replied: "But the bishop does not want you to go with any more crowds. You have to promise me."

When I hesitated, he added: "You can still go alone if you want to but you can no longer go with the crowds. You have to promise that you will not do that."

I looked at him and said: "Well, I will promise that I won't go with the crowds."

He said: "Good," then I left.

Now the question arose: do I obey my Lady or the bishop? People did tell me to do what my Lady wanted me to do; but I was a loyal daughter of the Church. I knew that it was most important to obey the bishop and I had promised not to go to the land with the crowd. So I did not. I obeyed my bishop.

Now all was up to my Lady. On August 16, 1960, I wrote:

Today my Lady Mary told me that I have reached the people she wanted to have know about the Golden Lady. She said to me: "You have reached the right people. You have done your job well. Now I will work from here. Now I will call all to my Shrine of The Immaculate Heart. I will call them to me in a most miraculous way. . . . Remember what it says in your notes: 'You need only tell a few and the others will seek you out to find out what you have told the few.'"

8

THE SEVENTH SUNDAY:
AUGUST 28, 1960
THE EIGHTH SUNDAY:
SEPTEMBER 4, 1960

I had been told that the bishop wanted me to stop taking people to my Lady's land. I obeyed him. But I was also told that I could go up there if I went alone. When it came time for the seventh Sunday, August 28, I became very, very sad. I knew that people would go to the rock and they would expect me to be there. I explained what I did in these notes dated August 29, 1960: The next morning I was still very sad. Then there was the problem of what to tell the people who came to the land. I had no idea of knowing who would be there. My relatives already knew that I would not go there, so they did not go. But I thought that other people might be there.

Finally, Mike and I decided that he should take his mother and aunt, (The priest did not say that they could not go) and then if anyone was there, Mike could explain to the people that I could not be there because I had promised the priest not to go.

Mike thought up the words that he would say. I became very sad and upset and I started to cry again. (Poor Mike needed so much courage to face the crowd.)

Finally the time came. It was 2:00 and Mike went to get his aunt. I was very sad and upset all the while he was gone. I ironed some clothes while I waited because I wanted something to do. I begged my Lady to show the people a miracle even though I wasn't there.

Mike came back about 3:15. He ran up the stairs and he came into the kitchen and he hugged me. He was smiling very much. I said: "What happened?"

He explained: "You wouldn't have believed it, but there were

483

about 40 people there." He said: "You would have been proud of me. They all listened to me." I was amazed. "Not only that." he went on, "but they were all new. I didn't know most of them. I had not expected so many. Not too many people knew that the visions took place on Sunday at 2:30." Then Mike went on to tell me what he told the people. He had been nervous, but he spoke in front of the group. They all listened to him. He has a powerful, commanding voice. People listen to him because he talks so well and he always is sure of himself when he talks. No one laughed at him as he spoke. The fact is, the people were disappointed because I had not been there. They were all serious. Mike explained first about the visions and then about the fact that I had been asked to stay away for this Sunday. He told them that there would be three more Sundays. They asked him if I would be there and he said that he could not promise, but I would come sometime Sunday. Then he left, but before he left, my mother asked the people if they wanted to say the Rosary and all the people knelt down and they said the Rosary.

After Mike came home and told me that, I was getting ready to go back to the land myself.

My mother came into the house. She was happy and excited. She said that everyone was talking to her and she said that one lady came all the way from New Britain. I had no idea that anyone there knew about the visions. My mother said that the people were very disappointed because I had not come and that Mary Stores cried all the while the Rosary was being said. I felt sorry for Mary.

Then my mother and I and Mike went back to the land. No one was there and I felt very sad because my Lady had told me to bring people with me.

My mother, Mike and I knelt down and suddenly I became very, very sad. I started to cry a little, but not too much because I had to say the Rosary.

My Lady came to me as I started to say the second decade. (I told my mother and Mike. Later he said: "I did not think that you saw the vision because your eyes did not light up.")

I was so sad when my Lady came that I could hardly look at her. But she stood on the rock and this time I did not notice her feet. Instead, I noticed her face and her arms. Her face was more beautiful and younger looking than I ever saw it. In the other visions she looked about 28 or even 30 years old. Yesterday, she looked about 24 or 25 years old.

Her face was very, very sweet. Her eyes were very lovely, but they were sad. I never saw her eyes so sad. She looked at me tenderly. I saw the halo of stars around her head and I saw the crown on her head. She first said: "This is a holy place." Then for a few minutes she did not say anything. I kept saying the Rosary, as I watched her face, she placed her hands near her face and she rested her head on her hands which were out like when a person prays. As I watched her, I suddenly saw two teardrops come from her eyes. Her eyes or lids did not move. Then I saw two more teardrops come from her eyes, but they did not roll down her face. They just disappeared. Then, suddenly she turned around and she faced the path to the road. I saw only her back, and the back of her head, which were covered by gold garments. I no longer saw the crown or the halo. She kept her back to me for about two minutes. Then she faced me again and she said softly: "I will bring people here in a miraculous way." After the Rosary she went away.

She does not come or go in any bright light. She just appears and then disappears. The light is coming from her. It does not surround her. Then Mike and I left, but before we did, a man and a woman came to the rock. They were very serious. They said that they had been there at 2:30. They knew me because they knew Mike. I told them that my Lady had just left and they looked at me as if they were afraid. They did not ask any questions. The man picked up the picture and he looked at it. Finally, the woman said to me: "Aren't you afraid when you see the vision?"

I said: "Well, yes and no. I'm not afraid of my Lady, but I guess that I am sort of afraid of making her known."

They slowly walked away from the spot and Mike and I left.

I was still very, very sad because no one was there when my Lady came. I knew that Mike and my mother were there, but that was not what my Lady meant by taking people to the land.

All day Sunday I thought of a million things. I thought that surely the, Church would condemn the visions. From then on, that became my greatest fear.

SEPTEMBER 4, 1960

September 4 was the eighth of the ten Sundays. I still had not been forbidden to go to the land, so I went with Mike. I did not go at the usual time when the crowds went. I kept my promise. I wrote these notes;

Today did not mean too much to me because I knew that I could not pray with the crowd at the land. I already knew that I would not go at 2:30 when the crowd would be there. I had told my mother and a couple of friends that I would go at 3:30. My mother said that she would go at 2:30 to see if anyone went. After I did not show up last Sunday, I did not expect anyone to go this Sunday.

When it was time for me to go to the land at 3:30 I was downhearted. Mike drove and as we approached the land, we saw a large crowd there. He parked next to the land. We had never expected anything like that. I sat in the car with Mike and I became very nervous. My mother came to our car. She said: "There are more people here now than there were at 2:30."

Mike shouted: "You are not going up to pray with all these people."

I started to cry. More people were coming. I did not know what to do. Mike said again: "You are not going up there." My mother shouted: "Come to my house for a cup of coffee. Then you can come back."

But then I saw my best friend walk up the hill. I had asked her to come. I did not want to hurt her feelings. Mike and my mother kept shouting at me telling me what to do. Finally I said: "I will go up, but I won't pray."

We slowly walked up to the rock. There were about forty people around the rock or near it. I was very nervous. I went to the rock, inside the fence. (The boy did not take the fence down) I looked at all the people. They silently waited for me to speak. I took a deep breath and I said in a nervous voice: "I really didn't expect so many here at this time." They laughed a little. Then I looked down and I said: "I do see my Lady here. She comes as The Golden Lady. This is the eighth of the ten Sundays, but I am very sorry, I cannot pray here while everyone is here. The bishop has asked me not to." The people understood. I said: "I am sorry, but I must go. I guess you can stay if you want to." I turned away and I took Mike's hand and I walked away with my head down. I felt defeated, but I had done what the Church wanted me to do. Mike and I went to the car. We had to wait for his mother. The group of people by the rock wanted to say the Rosary even if I wasn't with them.

After they said the Rosary, they slowly left the rock. Some of them went away. A few, about ten people came to me. They started to ask me questions. At first I did not want to say anything. Then one woman asked me what the Lady looked like. I did not want to give a long speech, so I said: "Wait a minute I will show you." I went to the car and I got out my statue. (I had not taken it to the rock.) I took it to the group and I said: "Here is what she looks like."

The people admired the statue. One woman wanted her little three year old daughter to kiss the statue. I held it so that the child could kiss it.

Suddenly everyone stopped speaking. They all looked at me very seriously. I backed away a little and I became nervous again. Then I said: "Our Lady wants you to pray to her Immaculate Heart. This has all happened because God wants to prove to all of you that He is still very close to you. You must not forget that. You must realize how much God loves you and how much Our Lady loves you. Sometimes the material things of life get in the way of your love for God. But you must love God with all your heart and you must remember that God loves you very much."

I was surprised that I said such a thing, but I felt so good when I told them how much God loves them. Then I told them about the promises of Mary. I also told them that the Church and the bishop does not approve of the shrine because there would have to be more investigations, but they did not seem to mind that the Church did not approve at this time.

After we all left, Mike told me that this happened. I did not notice it. But the day had been cloudy. It had rained just before we went to the land. When I went to the rock, suddenly the sun appeared very brightly,, As soon as I left the rock, the sun went back into the clouds. Later, I was told others had noticed this.

At five o'clock we went back to the land. There were only three of us.

We all looked at the rock. There were Rosaries on it. (I had not put the Rosaries on it.)

Then we knelt down to pray. I put my Lady on her pillar. First I had to remove the medals that were on the wooden stand.

We started the Rosary and almost immediately my Lady came to me. She seemed to be extremely happy, but I did not understand why because no one was there. She was very, very beautiful. She stood on the rock and she had the gold roses on her feet. She stood with her arms up and out. Between her arms was her Immaculate Heart which seemed to be brilliant red light. She smiled very, very sweetly. She said to me: "My Immaculate Heart will win in the end." That was all she said. This time I noticed that the front of her golden gown had a raised design on it in darker shades of gold. The design was very lovely like large flowers and leaves. I kept looking at the lovely design on her dress. It was not on her full-flowing cloak. The design was only on her dress. I will say again that she was extremely happy. This time as she smiled, she appeared to be so happy that the light from her face seemed to blot out the shape of her features. I knew she was smiling but I could not see her lips or her teeth.

I could not understand why she was so happy because I was

not so happy. I got up from my knees after we said the Rosary. Then I looked at the picture by the rock. I said to Mike: "Take the picture. Should we?" He looked at me and at the picture: "Yes," he finally said: "We should take the picture."

I did not object. He took the picture and we walked away from the land.

When we got home, I hid the picture behind my dresser. I put my Lady on my dresser and I said sadly: "I guess you are hidden now like the bishop wanted. I guess you will be hidden now for another twelve years." She replied: "I will not allow my shrine to die." I answered: "Only you can save it, my Lady. I can do no more."

9

THE NEWS OF HEALINGS
THE CROWDS GROW
MY FEARS OF BEING CONDEMNED

By the beginning of September, I had prepared myself for the end of my Lady's shrine. I firmly believed that all was over. I was filled with fear thinking that the bishop had condemned me and my Lady because I had been forbidden by Father to go to the rock with the crowds. The young man who had built the fence around the rock had been ordered to remove it. He came to see me and told me that he had been told that the bishop had condemned me and he was forbidden to go to the rock. My Heart was filled with fear when I heard that.

He also told me something else that made my heart sink into dread and darkness. He said he had talked to a priest about me and my writings. When he said to the priest: "But doesn't her writings count?" The priest had answered: "Her writings do not mean a thing."

For days I was filled with dread and fear. I would say to myself: "Are all my writings condemned as well as my Lady?" But I was able to overcome that fear by one day saying to myself: "How could the priest say that my writings don't mean a thing? He has never read them."

I began to hear more stories from people who talked to priests about the visions. All of them were completely against me. One priest in a neighboring town remarked: "Meriden! I know Meriden. I know what it is like. Our Lady would never appear in such a place!"

I was told that my own parish priest had ordered someone to go to the rock and remove all the medals, Rosaries and little statues that had been left there. The person had refused, so the priest went to the rock and removed them himself. All had been taken away. My Lady's shrine bad disappeared. I was heartbroken. However, many people remained loyal to me and my Lady, but it wasn't easy for them. All around them were the ones who condemned me or laughed at me. They even said that my husband had to "put me away." Yet, all the while I went to my office job as a bookkeeper. I still had to work to help pay the bills. What was happening did not interfere with my work in the office.

I had not told anyone where I worked what was going on; but they heard their own stories about me. The fact is that one of the workers, a man, had been so impressed that he came to the rock with me on one Sunday.

I was very upset by the stories I heard. Many people begged me to go back to the land to finish the ten Sundays, but I would not. I told them I had to obey the bishop. Some people left me because they insisted that I obey my Lady and not the bishop. I would cry, but I chose to obey the bishop.

I wrote the following notes on September 6, 1960: I felt I had to hide my Lady again. I accepted what I believed was true. The shrine would slowly fade away and I would sadly watch it die. But, even so, my Lady said to me: "I will not allow my shrine to die." I replied: "Only you can save it my Golden Lady." But I had convinced myself that all was over. The bishop had condemned my shrine and my Golden Lady (as I was told by more than one person).

His word was law. I had to obey him. I had to watch my Lady's shrine die. Sunday, September 4, I had to tell people at the land that the bishop did not approve. Later, when I went to pray with Mike, I had to remove the picture (that I had made) because on the picture were the words of my Golden Lady. I walked away from the rock with my picture and with my Golden Lady. I thought that all was over. I had to hide my Lady again. The shrine would die, even if my Lady had told me that she would not allow it to die. I had to believe that I had failed, yet, I did not feel that everything had been complete failure. I felt that a good purpose had been served, even if I would perhaps never know what the purpose was. I also knew that someday my Lady would have her shrine.

·

I went home and I breathed a sigh of relief. (This was Sunday September *4th*) I began to write my new book. I was going to think only about the book.

The next day was Labor Day, September *5th.* I woke up and thought again that all was over. The bishop had won, my Lady would not go against his desires. That morning I received three phone calls. They were from people who still believed in the shrine and who still hoped in it. I did not have the heart to tell them that everything was over.

Yet, somehow, because of their strong faith, a new spark of hope was rekindled inside of me. Still, I did not want to hope like I had hoped before.

Then I continued my housework. I wanted to forget the shrine; even though someone had said to me: "The people are still coming. You can't stop them. This is only the beginning." I said to myself: "It is the beginning of the end. People will forget about the shrine in a few weeks." My Lady answered; "Before the end of the year, the world will know The Golden Lady of Happiness." My Lady had also said on August 28, 1960 (*7th* Sunday): "I will bring people here in a miraculous way."

Then, suddenly an event happened which made the words of my Lady come true. It was something which was completely out of my hands. Only Our Lady could have been the cause.

The words began to spread that a woman had walked to the rock on crutches and had left without them. The word "miracle" began to be heard everywhere. Because of that; and other reports of favors granted by my Lady, crowds began to flock to the rock.

As yet I had not been forbidden to go to the rock, so as soon as I heard about this, Mike and I went to the rock with my mother to say the Rosary in thanksgiving.

While we were praying, my Lady Mary appeared to me. She seemed to be more beautiful than ever. She was dressed as The Golden Lady.

She stood at first with her arms down and out. She stood on the rock. Then she put her hands against her face (left side) and she put her head down on her hands. She looked very beautiful. Then she slowly lowered her arms and she opened them while still holding them high. Then I saw her beautiful Immaculate Heart which again seemed to be only brilliant, red light. I did not see any roses on it this time.

She smiled very, very sweetly and she slowly said: "My Immaculate Heart has triumphed." She stayed while we said the Rosary, then she went away after it was finished.

Slowly we left the rock and I turned to Mike and I said: "You told me not to mention this. I don't have to. My Lady will make it known."

THE HEALING: SEPTEMBER 5, 1960

I explained what happened in the notes I wrote on September 6, 1960: (I have the signed statements from the woman, Barbara Zielke. Also signed statements from those who were there the day this happened.)

About one thirty yesterday, September 5th, Mike and I went for a ride to a place called Cromwell. We did not get back until after three in the afternoon.

I made supper, I wrote a little more of my new book. I washed the dishes, and then I washed my hair.

The time was 8:15. I had just finished washing my hair. I had just wrapped the wet hair in a towel and the phone rang. I answered it. I did not recognize the man's voice. He reminded me that I knew him. He lived across the street from my Lady's land. Mike and I had talked to him last Sunday morning.

He then said something to me, in a soft, grave voice, that must have made me turn pale. I answered: "What did you say? Tell me again." He repeated the words: "I say that a woman, who is standing right next to me, has been a cripple for over a year. She had been on crutches for a year. She could not walk. Today, she went to the shrine. She knelt and she prayed. Then something happened. She stood up and she walked. She does not need the crutches anymore. She walked away from the rock without her crutches!"

I was so amazed that I could not answer. The man went on. "She is here now. She wants to see you. We waited all afternoon and all evening for you. We thought you would come. Here, she wants to talk to you. Do you want to talk to her?"

I was able to say: "Yes, yes, of course, I want to talk to her."

Mike came near me: "What's the matter?" he asked.

I whispered: "A "miracle." I think there is a "miracle."

He turned away and said: "Not that again!"

I whispered: "But a cripple woman walked." He came to my side and the woman spoke in the phone: "Hello," she said: "I had to use crutches. I could not walk. I prayed at the rock. Then something happened, I don't know what! Now I can walk. I can walk and I haven't walked for a year!" She told me her name. She said she wanted to see me. I asked her if she would wait for half an hour. She replied, "I'm going back to the rock. I will wait for you there."

I hung up the receiver and I was amazed so greatly that I almost could not speak or move. I said to Mike: "A woman who could not walk for a year! She went to the land and now she is walking. She doesn't need her crutches anymore. She walked for the first time in a year."

Mike turned pale. "Be careful now," he warned. "This may be someone's trick."

"It's no trick," I whispered. "She told me that she walked away from the rock. She said something happened. Come on. we are going to the rock. She is waiting for us there."

I wrapped my wet hair in a heavy kerchief and Mike and I hurried to the car. We were both so nervous, we were shaking. I could not believe what I had heard. If it was really true! I did not dare think what it could mean if it was really true. (I went to see her at the rock. I had not been forbidden not to go there. I had just been forbidden not to take people there.)

I was in some sort of a trance when we drove to the land. I knew we were going to the land. I went many times to the land. It was natural for me to go to the land. But this time: to see a "miracle"! It did not seem possible.

By the time we reached the land I had made up my mind that it was all a dream. It did not really happen. Mike made up his mind that it was some sort of a trick. We slowed down near the land. One car was parked on the dark road. It was now after 8:30. We looked up at the hill. Everything was dark. I wanted to get out of the car. Mike shouted: "No, you are not going up there."

I pleaded: "But she said she would be waiting by the rock."

He shouted again: "I said you are not going up there. This may be some trick. We don't know what it is."

I said: "What are you going to do?"

He replied: "First let me check at the house. The man called you from his house."

Mike drove around the corner and pulled up into the driveway. When I saw the house, my hopes faded. No one was around. Only one light burned in one window. Mike told me to stay in the car. He got out and walked to the door. The woman answered his ring. I watched them talk. I said to myself: "It isn't true. It is some kind of a trick."

Mike walked back to the car. His face was pale and serious. He opened the door and got in behind the steering wheel. He said: "It is true. They are waiting at the rock for us."

My heart skipped a beat. Mike backed the car around the corner and parked next to the path that leads to the rock. We almost ran up to the rock. I was afraid, but suddenly all my fears vanished. When I reached the rock I saw a woman, a small boy about 10 years old and two men. They calmly stood next to the rock. On the rock two votive lights burned brightly. Suddenly the moon shone full and very bright. The light gradually became brighter.

Mike and I walked up to the group. I looked at the woman. I had never seen her before. She stood firmly on her own two feet. There were no signs of any crutches. She was the first to speak. She looked at me and slowly said: "I can walk! I couldn't walk before. But I can walk now. I don't know what happened, but something happened and I can walk!"

Her face was serious. She was nervous and yet she was not lying. Her face was filled with wonderment: "I can walk:" she repeated almost as if she could not believe her own words.

I caught my breath and I almost whispered, while waving my hand forward: "Walk. Let me see you walk."

She walked around the rock: "See, I can walk," she said again. "I couldn't walk before, but now I can."

I looked at the two men. One of them said: "I know she couldn't walk before. I helped her up here on her crutches. It took almost ten minutes to get her up here (the path is very rough). She put her crutches on the rock and she knelt down. When she got up, she walked away. She did not need the crutches anymore."

I looked at the woman again. "Walk. Walk again." She walked around the rock again. She was still filled with amazement. She put her hands to her face and she said: "I don't know what happened. I can't explain it. I walked up here on crutches. I had them for over a year. I knelt to pray by the rock. Suddenly something happened. My eyes were open, but suddenly I went blind. I could not see anything. I don't know what happened, but I knew I could walk. So, I got up and I walked."

Her son who had been next to his mother where the miracle took place said that he heard her say "walk."

The other witness was the man who had helped her walk up the hill. He was a neighbor of hers and he wasn't Catholic. He said: (his voice was also serious and his face was filled with wonderment.) "When she walked away I got her crutches for her, but she said she didn't need them. She wanted to leave them here. I took them with us when we left because I thought she would need them again, but she doesn't need them. She can walk."

I said: "When did it happen?"

She replied: "At about 2:30 this afternoon. I have been here since. My mother and father live across the street. I walked to their house and I gave them my crutches. They were shocked. They have seen me on my crutches for a year."

I was amazed when she said that it happened at 2:30. That

meant that she had been walking and standing on her feet for hours.

I asked her where her crutches were. She said they were in her mother's house.

Then I asked her what was wrong with her so that she had to use crutches. She not only told me, but she showed me. About a year ago she got a piece of glass in her leg. The leg became infected. Finally, the doctors had to operate. They removed one of her leg muscles. She leaned over and pulled away the bandage on her leg. There was one of the most horrible wounds I had ever seen. I could see the muscles of her leg in the open cut. The cut was about three inches long and about two inches wide and about one inch deep. No one could ever walk as she had done with such a wound. The wound had not healed, but all the pain vanished. She walked back and forth without any limp. She had to use her crutches before because she could not even touch her toes to the ground. Now she stood with all her weight on her injured leg and she walked without a limp. Furthermore, she had already walked up and down the hill a few times without any crutches.

She also told me that she had gone downtown to Saint Mary's Church and she had told the priest what had happened. Then she had returned to the rock to wait for me. She felt that she had to see me and so finally, she asked the man to call me.

Of course all these things filled Mike and I with wonderment. Naturally, we were very happy for her and, of course, my heart was filled with joy because my Lady had started to show her power.

Just then, my mother and Emily came up to the rock. I hadn't expected to see them and they hadn't expected to see us. Needless to say, they very quickly found out about the healing and they were as amazed as we had been. All the same questions were again repeated and all the same answers were given. The woman showed my mother, and Emily her leg wound and she showed us all again how well she could walk.

During all this time her foot, which had been so sore she could not touch the ground with it, was without a shoe and a

sock. She wore only one shoe. That bothered Mike. He offered
to give her his shoe because her bare foot was on the hard,
damp ground. She refused and she laughed: "It feels wonderful to have my foot flat on the ground again." She rubbed her
foot on the ground. "It feels wonderful to be able to do this,"
she said.

Then my mother said that we should all kneel down and
say a prayer of thanksgiving. I knelt down and the woman
knelt beside me. We said the whole Rosary and the woman,
with the terrible hole in her leg knelt for the whole Rosary.

While we were praying, my Lady Mary appeared to me.
She seemed to be more beautiful than ever. She was dressed
as The Golden Lady.

She stood at first with her arms down and out. She stood
on the rock. Then she put her hands against her face (left side)
and she put her head down on her hands. She looked very
beautiful. Then she slowly lowered her arms and she opened
them while still holding them high. Then I saw her beautiful
Immaculate Heart which again seemed to be only brilliant, red
light. I did not see any roses on it this time.

She smiled very, very sweetly and she slowly said: "My
Immaculate Heart has triumphed." She stayed while we said
the Rosary, then she went away after it was finished. The people who were with me knew that my Lady had come. I told
them when she came. They were very pleased because she had
come.

We all stood around the rock. No one felt like leaving. As
we stood there, four women came to pray. when we saw them
walking towards us, we said that we would not mention the
healing. We silently watched the four women kneel in front of
the rock. They stood up and one of them softly said: "We heard
that there was a 'miracle' here."

We were all amazed. How could they have heard so quickly?
(The cured woman had told some people who came to the
rock, even before she had called me.) The woman who was
walking did not know the four women. My mother finally said:
"You are looking at the "miracle"."

Then once again all the same questions were asked, the wound was shown, and all the same answers were given.

Finally, my mother told the four women that I saw the visions. Then they started to ask me questions. I did not say too much, except that I told them the promises of The Golden Lady.

Slowly we all left the rock and I turned to Mike and I said: "You told me not to mention this. I don't have to. My Lady will make it known."

THE FURY WHICH FOLLOWED THE WOMAN'S HEALING

I had told my husband that I did not have to make the healing known, that my Lady would do that. And do it, she did. She had said that she would bring people to her shrine in a miraculous way. Indeed, that is exactly what happened. I did not have to do anything to cause the commotion because of the favor which had been granted to the woman.

First of all, although all of us thought a miracle had happened, we could not call it a true miracle. Only the Church has the power to call a healing or a favor or a cure a true miracle. And this is done only after years of proper investigation and gathering all of the records. At the famous shrine of Lourdes, in France, millions of people visit each year and there are hundreds of thousands of cures, favors granted and blessings given to the ones who go with great faith and love in their hearts. Yet, there are only about 50 or 60 recorded actual miracles, so rare are miracles. However, for lay people the word miracle is very common; although the word is misused. In the case of this woman's healing, the word miracle was often used; and that word caused a flood of people to visit my Lady's land and to say the Rosary before the rock upon which she stood. By September 7, the flood had started. I wrote these notes:

Last night I spent an evening with my head spinning around because of all the things that happened yesterday; I heard news from Emily, my mother and from Mary Stores. The news was fantastic.

People were going to my Lady's land in a steady stream. Five, six and ten carloads came at a time. Everyone was talking about the miracle. (I did not go to the land to see all this. I stayed home. I had gone at noon, but no one was there.) All I could think of was what my Lady said: "I shall bring people in a miraculous way." She was doing that. I wasn't doing anything. Most of the people who go to the land don't even know me.

I heard other news: All the priests in Meriden heard about the cripple woman's cure. One priest said: "If this is true, then it is wonderful, wonderful."

I heard that another woman had been cured. She had gone to the land five times, then she had walked; but her doctor said it was only an emotional cure; nevertheless, she can now walk. I heard that a boy, who wasn't Catholic had a badly sprained wrist. He touched the rock, then his wrist did not hurt anymore. He took the bandage off of it right in front of my mother.

I heard that cripple people were going to the rock and prayers were being said for them. I heard that a large group of people were praying at the land and a policeman went up to the group. He saw them praying, he took off his hat and he joined the group.

I heard that one man walked up to the rock and just before he reached it, he suddenly was seized with a powerful emotional feeling that he had not expected in the least. Someone said: "There is something here, something powerful. We all know that. We can all feel it." The picture was gone, but that did not matter. Everyone who knew the promises were telling everyone else.

I keep telling myself that it won't last! It won't last! I must prepare myself for another bitter disappointment. I must not build up my hopes too high. But my Lady said: "I will not let my shrine die." Still, how can I hope with the bishop against me and the visions? Oh, well, I guess that after the ten Sundays people won't be so excited about the rock. I must not build up my hopes too much.

This morning I got up and I said: "It is all over. People will stop going to the rock. Everyone will forget the shrine." My Lady said: "I will not let them forget." Who knows? How can I hope? I must not because the bishop is against me.

Then this morning, Stanley came to my office. He works with me and he has known about the visions all along. He told me that he went to the land at 5:00 yesterday. He said there was a large crowd there. He began to tell people what he knew about the visions. He said everyone was excited and they were praying. I told myself: "It can't last. The excitement will die down. The only reason people go there is because it is all new." They will stop going there. I must be ready for that; and if they don't stop going, then the bishop will write a letter condemning the visions. I will now have to wait in dread, for that letter from the bishop. He will send it when he hears about the crowds that are going to my Lady's land. Maybe this Sunday the priest will read the letter from the bishop. (I waited in fear for such a letter.)

A lot of people are telling my mother and some friends that I am lucky. They all want to meet me. I do not go to the land to see them even though I am told that people keep hoping they will see me at the land. I don't want to go. I have met a few people and some of them tell me that I am lucky. I smile and say: "When someone is chosen for something like this, they are not lucky, they are given only a heavy, black cross." I know because I have been carrying this cross ever since my Lady told me to make The Golden Lady known.

I have suffered a great deal since June. I have had wonderful moments of triumph, but I have had more moments of tears, and heartbreak. Still, that is the way it should be. My love and my job for God has brought me only heartbreak and tears. That is the way it should be. I accepted the cross of Christ years ago. I have embraced it for years and I have loved it for years. Without the cross of Christ, my job for God and my dearest Lady Mary would not mean very much.

I am lucky, but not in the way that others think. I am lucky because I understand so well the value of the cross and because I understand so well the precious gift of tears and suffering.

I need the cross and the humiliation. There must still be a great deal of pride in me or else my Jesus would have never allowed such a humiliation to take place. Thank God, I know how to understand and how to accept the humiliation.

Then I began to think about the will of God. My love for God's will has always been the center of my spiritual life. A thousand times I had said: "Your will, not mine, dearest Jesus." A thousand times I had said: "I don't mind, dearest Jesus, I so love Your holy will."

Then I thought seriously about God's will. Maybe He doesn't want the shrine now! I prayed for miracles! Am I praying against God's holy will? Never do I want to pray against His holy will.

I love His will so very much. If the shrine is destroyed by the Church, that will be God's will. Then should I feel sad when I can accept and love God's holy will? No.

Suddenly the truth of God's will filled my soul with joy. Never do I want anything that is not God's will. I began to pray with all my heart and I said: "Dearest Jesus, Your will is mine and my will is Yours. I so love Your will. I will never pray for anything against Your holy will. If it is Your will that the shrine is to die, I accept and I love Your holy will. No matter how much I suffer, I so love Your will. if the shrine dies, then I will not mind. I will understand that such is Your holy will and I so love Your holy will."

On September 8, I wrote these notes: Last night I could not sleep again—more sufferings—but I offered the suffering to my dearest Mary as a penance for my sins of pride. I must have been very proud and I did not even know it. It was pride that led me to make the bargain with my Lady about the flowers. Why should she encourage me with her miracles when what I really needed was something to destroy every trace of pride in my heart and in my soul.

Suddenly I thought about the bouquet of plastic flowers. My Lady said that she would cherish such a gift from me; but what would such a gift do to my soul, especially if there were more and greater miracles at the land?

Suddenly I no longer wanted the miracles because I became terrified of the pride that could destroy my soul and all my writings.

So I began to form in my mind a spiritual bouquet that I offer to my Lady instead of the material bouquet which could bring pride to my soul. I had said I would give her a bouquet of six flowers. Now, I will give her a bouquet of six spiritual flowers. I formed the flowers in my mind. They will rule my life until I die. Here is my gift to my Lady Mary on her birthday.

1st flower: Humility
To strive toward perfect humility in all matters at all times. To conquer all pride no matter what the cost.

2nd flower: Love, Prayer, Sacrifice
To strive towards perfect love of God and love of His Holy Mother. To show this love by always being kind, gentle, tender, loving and understanding toward everyone I meet. To make sacrifices for this love.

3rd flower: God's Will
To always love and cherish God's holy will and to strive towards perfect destruction of my own will so that everything I do shall be done because it is God's will.

4th flower: Meekness
To strive toward perfect meekness and to destroy all my ways of self-love and self-desires even when I merely talk to someone.

5th flower: Suffering
To accept and embrace all the remaining crosses of my life with perfect submission and love. Not to complain, even when my heart is break- ing. To smile through all my tears a smile of

love for God's own cross of pain.

6th flower: Charity
To give to others especially when such giving
would be a sacrifice. To give, not only money,
but encouragement, a kind gentle word, sympathy and such things that may make a spark
of God's grace light up their souls.

There is my gift to my Lady. This must be the
bouquet that she said she would cherish. I only
pray for the graces that will enable these flowers to live forever.

All is over, my Lady, your shrine is closed. My
public life is closed. Thank God for that! I will
spend the rest of my life silently striving
towards my goal of sainthood. Visions do not
make a saint. I can be a saint with or without
all my visions. I will not give up.

As more and more people flocked to the land, such activity could not go unnoticed by the priests in my parish. They
were 100% against me and the visions. The fact is they intended
to do something about this situation.

On September *10th* I received a very curt call from a priest
at my parish. He wanted me to come to his office. I explained
what happened in my notes: Father called me. I started to cry
as soon as I heard his voice. He wanted to see me at 1:00. Mike
was working so I walked the long distance to the rectory. My
mind was filled with fear: He would publicly condemn me and
my visions by a sermon in church! That was my greatest fear.

When Father walked into the office I was still crying. He
did not talk to me too long. He told me that even if I had not
intended such a thing, the news of the visions had gotten "out
of hand." He wanted to know if I went to the rock all the time
to talk to people. I told him no. He told me that he wants to
make it clear to me that the bishop *forbids* me to go back to

the land. I told him that I would not go back. He told me that I must not go any place else to start this "thing." I was very surprised at that. I looked up and I said: "There isn't any other place." I was crying so I could not say much. I just answered most of his questions with a yes or no.

Then I told him that my Lady said that she would bring people to the land in a miraculous way. Then I added: "That has come true." He did not say anything to that. He only said that the bishop had sent me a letter and I had been forbidden to return to the land. (I never received a letter from the bishop saying I had been forbidden to go to the rock.) Father said that he now forbids me to go to the land because the bishop sent him a letter telling him to put a stop to all that "nonsense" in Meriden.

He asked me about the woman who had been healed. He said to me, in a harsh voice: "Do you go around telling people that this miracle has taken place?" I merely replied: "No. I do not have to. She told a lot of people." (She had stayed at the rock for hours that day and told everyone who came to visit the shrine that she had been healed.) He replied: "Well, all that has to be stopped. There was no miracle. I told her that myself. The wound in her leg did not heal." (That was true, but by November 28th, the wound was completely healed and her doctor had been amazed because she could walk without crutches, which she could not do for over one year.)

When I left Father's office, I was crying harder than I had been when I entered his office. What a terrible cross he had given me. I wrote: One thing I know for sure I had been forbidden to return to the land. I cannot go with anyone. I cannot pray at my beloved spot. I cannot bring anyone there. I cannot see anyone there. I cannot finish the ten Sundays. This final order came from Father on Saturday, September *10th*. I was very sad because my mother had told me how the shrine had been destroyed Friday night and how the tree had been torn down. (This little tree had been touched by my Lady's gown. Before it disappeared, I had managed to save some branches and leaves from it.) However, there had been one happy moment for me. Father did not say that he would announce in church that the visions had been condemned.

From that moment on, when Father said I was forbidden to go to the land, I did not go even though I was told over and over that many people who believed in the visions were losing faith because I refused to go to the land. The order to me to stay away from the land was law. I would not break that law even though my heart ached because I could not visit the spot where my beautiful Golden Lady had appeared to me. I stayed away from the land until the year 1966 when my new spiritual advisor gave me permission to return to my Lady's land for good. It was in that year when the rock was first moved because the new owners of the land wanted to build apartments. (That is another story.) So, for over six years, I obeyed the order I had been given to stay away from the land, to no longer go there with anyone and to no longer pray there.

THE STORM SURROUNDING THE WOMAN
WHO HAD BEEN HEALED

The priests, especially from my parish were determined to stop all the talk about the "miracle" which had happened at the place where I saw my Lady. They and others (lay people) not only spoke against me and my Lady but against Barbara Zielke who had been healed.

After I saw and talked to her on September 5, 1960, I lost track of her. I did not try to find her until November when I wanted her to sign a statement. Then I found her and she came to me, very willing to sign a statement. She told me a story which I found unbelievable as to how she had been treated since her healing.

After the wonderful healing, she was soon plunged into her own sufferings which went on for weeks. People and priests found out who she was. She belonged to my church so it was not difficult for the priests in my parish to try to convince her that she had never been healed. She was told that "nothing" had happened and ordered not to discuss the incident. As for the Church ever trying to look into the situation that was completely out of the question. It seemed to me that the bishop had placed the investigation in the hands of my priests and they were determined to "put a stop to all that nonsense." Not one priest that I know of ever said: "Let us see what has happened." They all (the ones I heard about) had made up their minds that everything about me and my Lady was something to be done away with and forgotten.

Not only were the priests completely against Barbara, but many people also caused her agony. She told me that people she knew and strangers went to see her and told her that she never was healed, that when she went to the land that day, she was drunk. She said they would call her up in the middle of the night and tell her she was crazy and she belonged in an insane asylum. She often could not sleep because of the vicious calls she received.

Yet, in spite of all that, she never stopped believing in her healing. She said: "I would tell all of them that I knew I could not walk before that day and now I can walk."

I thought Barbara may not want to sign a statement, but when I asked her, she was delighted. She said: "I knew I could not walk before, but now I can walk. No one is going to tell me that the "miracle" did not happen. I know it happened. It happened to me."

She could not write very well, so she dictated her statement to me and after I wrote it, she signed it. The statement is dated: November 28, 1960.

THE TRAGIC RESULTS OF
BARBARA'S HEALING

Were Barbara and I treated unfairly by the priests of my parish during all that time? I would say yes, but I do *not* blame the *bishop* or my Church which I so dearly love.

At that time, Bishop O'Brien was very ill and to this day, I don't think he was ever told everything which was happening in Meriden. As I said, I rather assume that he handed the whole situation over to the priests of my parish and perhaps he told them to put a stop to "all that nonsense." As for the priests, they were against me from the beginning. But I think they became more infuriated the more they heard about visions and miracles. They, I assume, wanted to tell the bishop that "everything was under control." So they used their power to do all they could to stamp out "all that nonsense." Yet, the way they acted was their own doing: I am sure that the bishop did not tell them how to act or what to say.

I suppose they were only doing their job; however I think they could have been more understanding of the situation and much more charitable than they were.

They made Barbara and myself feel like a criminal who deserved to be "burned at the stake." I remember writing in my notes that I felt like I was outside the doors of my Church holding my beloved Golden Lady and I was not allowed to enter.

There was no reason why Father had to forbid me to go to my Lady's land. At this time (as I write this chapter) I do not even think he had the authority to do that. He was neither my spiritual director nor my confessor; but I did obey him, as I said, I did not go back to the land to pray for six years.

Barbara's healing should have been investigated by the Church. That did *not* happen. She had all sorts of doctor's reports. It may not have been classified as a miracle, but it surely was a sign of the power of my Lady at her shrine.

It was only one of numerous such healings and favors received from my Lady. When Father Kelleher became my spiritual advisor, he told me to collect statements from the people who had received favors from my Lady. I collected about 200 signed statements. Many were only small, simple favors, but Father Kelleher told me: "Alone, they may not mean very much, but put all together, they say a great deal."

Am I bitter about the way Barbara and I were treated? Of course *not*. Once Father Kelleher said to me: "Look what Bernadette suffered. Why should you be spared?" I just think it was tragic that Barbara's healing was not accepted. Now, 38 years later, it cannot be verified, perhaps because the ones who were involved have died. Yet, at the time it happened, there were many witnesses; the two men who had helped her walk to the rock, her son who was there, her mother to whose house she had walked after the healing, the man from whose house she had called me, the doctors who knew her case and myself, Mike, my mother and Emily.

However, what happened was no doubt part of my Devil's Challenge in his attempts to destroy my Golden Lady and her shrine. I can accept that and also the fact that all his attempts to destroy me and my Lady's shrine did not succeed. And that becomes another triumph of my Lady and of me.

Needless to say, the ending of my visits to my Lady's land also ended the ten Sundays she had requested. I never finished them. I had only gone for six Sundays with the people. On the seventh Sunday I went alone with Mike and my mother.

September 4, 1960, I went to the rock at 3:30. I was surprised to see a group there. I decided not to pray while they were there. I returned to the rock at 5:00 and I removed the picture with the promises on it which I had placed there.

As I said, I never finished the ten Sundays. I obeyed the bishop. I was severely criticized because I did not finish the ten Sundays; however, I told everyone who told me that I should have obeyed my Lady that it was more important to obey my bishop. I knew how important it was to obey my bishop. Years later in August of 1981, I was shown a beautiful letter from the bishop who became Archbishop after the death of Archbishop O'Brien, wherein he writes: "That Louise has been obedient to Archbishop O'Brien and to myself is, in the final analysis, more important than anything else, May God bless and reward her for such obedience and for her apostolic spirit."

With kindest wishes in the Lord,
John F. Whealon
Most Reverend John F. Whealon
Archbishop of Hartford

— 10 —

THE BISHOP DOES NOT CONDEMN ME

When I went to see Father on September 10th, I was filled with fear thinking that he would condemn me from the pulpit. The way he talked to me and forbid me to go to my Lady's land, I think perhaps he might have. That would have been the next obvious step to be taken in order to "stop all that nonsense about visions and miracles." I had been told by several people that the bishop had already condemned the visions and me. One person told me that Father had said that to him. However, if he had said that and if he did plan to continue to tell people that the bishop had condemned me, he had to change his mind because of the letter I had received from Archbishop O'Brien the day before Father called me to his office.

On September 2, 1960 I had written a letter to the bishop telling him that I accept his request, and I would do nothing to create a public shrine to my Lady. (He had asked me not to go to the land with a crowd.) I ended the letter by saying: "I am not asking you to accept my Golden Lady or to believe her; but please do not condemn all God's work in my soul. I can assure you that He has revealed to me many secrets of His divine love and my soul has felt the power and the glory of His love."

I never expected the bishop to answer the letter and I still heard all the rumors that I and my Lady had been condemned by the bishop; and Father's name had been mentioned as I wrote in my notes dated September 8, 1960: I was also told by this young man, the one who had built the fence, that Father told him that the bishop had condemned the visions and had forbidden me to go to the land. I did not understand that I had been forbidden to go to the land. I knew that I had been forbidden to create a public shrine at the land. This young man also said that Father had seen the cured woman and that it was *not* a miracle. He (Father) had gone to the young man's house and he had ordered him to remove the fence.

Knowing all that about Father caused me to be filled with fear when I went to see him on September 10th; however, I knew the bishop had not condemned me even if Father was under the impression he had. Still knowing that did not ease my fear. I will say here that Father was in reality a very kind, gentle person and very well liked. Later, when I told same priests of the way Father had treated me, they could not believe it, saying: "But he is not like that." I am not saying that he was not a kind, gentle, holy priest. I am saying that he did all in his power to put an end to "all that nonsense about the visions and the miracle," and he was very forceful, even unkind, in the way he treated Barbara and me.

My fears of what Father would say to me at the September *10th* meeting were not groundless. I had good reason to fear him after what I had been told. He spoke to me in a very harsh, forceful way telling me that the bishop had sent me a letter forbidding me to go to the land (which was not true) and ending up forbidding me himself. He kept saying that the bishop had sent him a letter. I was crying most of the time. Then toward the end of the meeting, I said: "I received a letter from the bishop myself. I wrote about what happened. The date I recorded the notes was September 12th: He only said that the bishop had sent me a letter and I had been forbidden to return to the land. (I did not understand the bishop's letter like that. I thought I still could go there to pray in private.) Now Father said that I could not go again to the land to pray. I felt very bad, but I told him I would not go back to pray and I would not see people there.

It was at this moment when (after he said again that he had received a letter from the bishop) that I said: "I got a wonderful letter from the bishop." I handed it to him. Father smiled when I handed him the letter, but he stopped smiling when he read it and he read it over about three or four times before he gave it back to me. He did not say anything about the letter.

Father's reaction to this letter was amazing. Before he read it, as he spoke so sternly to me, he was composed and very sure of the whole situation. He was in control and I was before him, a helpless, defenseless, little child. That was why he smiled when I handed him the letter. He thought it would completely agree with the way he was dealing with "all this nonsense." However, the letter was not what he expected. After he read it, his composure disappeared and he made no comment about the letter. Instead, he asked very slowly: "Do you have any questions you want to ask me?" I replied: "No. None." He again explained that there had been no miracle at the land. Then I left, still crying. I added to my notes explaining the fear I had; I thought he would have condemned all my visions and everything, but he did not do that.

He could not do that after he had read (about four times) the letter I had gotten from the bishop.

The letter was one of the greatest joys of my life. As I said, I had not expected the bishop to answer my September 2nd letter. My greatest fear up to that point was that the bishop would condemn my visions and even all my writings. (Do not forget that Monsignor Hayes had already told me that all was from God.) Others had condemned me, but only the bishop could say my visions were a fraud or the results of some sort of a mental illness. That never happened.

I wrote about the bishop's letter in my notes, dated September 9: Now, I have saved the most wonderful news of all until last. My heart is filled with joy, happiness and peace. My greatest worry is over. My greatest fear has vanished. I received a letter from Archbishop O'Brien. The letter was truly an unexpected "miracle" from my Lady, I shall treasure the letter for the rest of my life. Here is what the bishop said:

> Dear Mrs. D'Angelo:
> His Excellency, Archbishop O'Brien, has asked me to acknowledge your kind letter of September 2. His Excellency is extremely pleased with and edified by the humble spirit of obedience you have manifested in your

unquestioning compliance with his directives.

His Excellency would have me further point out emphatically that he in no way condemns you nor attempts to pass judgment on the inner workings of God's graces upon your soul. This matter must necessarily be left to you, your spiritual director or confessor and God.

With all good wishes, I am
Very Rev. Msgr. Francis J. Fazzalaro
Vice-Chancellor

This letter was to me a "miracle". All my fears of having all my notes condemned were gone. I can still believe in all my writings. I can still write what I had planned to write. How wonderful! Words cannot describe how wonderful all these things are. Even if the shrine is closed, my work for God can still go on. What a wonderful miracle that is.

I shall treasure the bishop's letter for the rest of my life.

And I still do treasure that letter as one of my and my Lady's greatest triumphs.

My Lady's shrine itself survived all the attempts made to destroy it.

As the years went by, even when I was not allowed to go there, others did. Slowly but surely it took form, not as a public shrine, but as a private one where Our Lady was loved deeply and where she repaid this love with many favors and blessings.

11

FATHER LYDDY
SPIRITUAL ADVISOR AND CONFESSOR

From 1957, when I last saw Monsignor Hayes, until 1960 when I met Father Lyddy, I had no spiritual director. I also had no need for one as far as my visions were concerned.

In that space of three years, I was newly married and I lived the life of an ordinary wife (a working wife for we were in need of funds for living expenses.) I loved being this wife and I settled down into the daily routine of working a full-time job and visiting family members, Mike's and mine. Also, Mike had many friends who became part of our life. They had given us a large party just before the wedding. When I was with all these people, I never spoke about my visions or my Lady's shrine. Some of Mike's relatives knew about the visions, but as soon as I was married, I had told them never to ask me about the visions because I would not talk about them. Mike's friends knew nothing about my visions and that was the way I wanted it.

Mike and I moved into the second floor apartment in the home his parents owned. Even though I had to work, we were happy in our new life together. We did not have too much money to spare, but we could go on little, inexpensive vacations once in a while.

After I was married, I thought that my marriage ended my job for God except one part of that job. There were the sufferings of humanity which I could not forget. In 1944, I had been told that the sufferings of humanity would be placed upon my shoulders. I longed to do something to bring hope, encouragement and God's love to suffering humanity.

From 1944 to 1957, I had watched this suffering humanity and I heard its sobbing heart as it was carried through wars, upheavals and human tragedies.

In spite of my happy, daily life, I constantly thought about people all over the world who were in need of comfort, hope, God's words of love and I wanted to do something to give them that hope, encouragement and love.

I did want to tell them my Lady's words, but I knew I could not. I thought that part of my life, visions and words from Heaven, was put away until after my death. Still I wanted to do something for poor, suffering humanity.

One day I formulated an idea. I thought I could write a book and put into that book words which would bring hope, joy, encouragement and God's love to suffering hearts and souls.

I knew I had a personal story of my own spiritual life which could do that, but I also knew I could not mention the fact that I saw visions.

So I invented a story, a fiction story, about a girl who saw visions and who longed to do what I longed to do, bring comfort to suffering humanity.

I called this book "Saint Resa's Diary." I spent weeks and months creating this story. I started with World War II. Because of that, I found myself in the library reviewing newspaper's of the war so I could get the correct information for my book.

I would go to the library two or three times a week, in the evening. I looked at hundreds of films of newspapers from that era making numerous notes for my book.

I began to weave together a story of this girl "Resa" going through the war years longing to bring hope and God's love to suffering humanity. The story went on and on. In the book, I copied some of my articles and even some of my visions, pretending that "Resa" saw the visions and wrote the articles.

This was not an easy task. As I wrote, I found out that I knew very little about composition, English grammar and spelling.

So I had to buy books which showed me the mistakes I made. I studied grammar for one year in order to write the book.

In the process, I threw away hundreds of pages as I wrote and rewrote the story trying to put into the book all that I thought would help suffering humanity.

I wrote about one thousand pages before I realized that there was a serious problem. I could not end the book because I did not know how to end "Resa's" life. This book was a reflection of my own life which had no ending yet. How could I end the book?

Was suffering humanity no longer suffering? It was. Did "Resa" save humanity? She did not. That was the dilemma.

All the while I was writing the book, I continued to see visions and to hear my Lady. She actually encouraged me to write the book which turned out to be, more or less, an autobiography of myself. Yet, I had made the book fiction, or so I thought. Still it was more real than fiction because I had put so many of my articles and visions into the book. Yet, I slowly began to realize this was not the book my Lady was encouraging me to write.

I had worked on the book for over a year before I realized it was useless to continue. This was not the book my Lady wanted me to write. Something was seriously wrong with it. So, one day I took a waste paper basket and sat in the middle of the kitchen and tore up a year's work. With tears in my eyes, I tore up page after page. I did save a few pages, but I tore up over one thousand hand-written sheets. It was a torture to do that, but I knew I had to. Then Christ. gave me words of comfort. He said: "Why do you want a false jewel when you have the real one?"

The story of my Lady was the real treasure, but I could not tell it. That had to wait.

In spite of the fact that I destroyed a year's work, it was not all in vain. As I wrote "St. Resa's Diary," I learned a great deal about writing, composition, grammar and even using words. I taught myself lessons I had learned in school but had forgotten as an adult. That proved to be a bonus as my writing career expanded as the years went by.

Then the year 1960 dawned; and my Lady told me to make her and the promises known to the world as explained in another chapter.

As soon as events started to happen, I knew I needed another spiritual director. Monsignor Hayes was still alive; however, he was too far away in Stamford and I had not seen him for over three years. I began to speak to local priests, but they turned me away. Then I found Father Lyddy who was a priest at the church where I had been married: Saint Joseph's on West Main Street.

I found him when I went to confession. As soon as I heard his voice, I could open my heart to him. I began to tell him that I was the one who saw the visions of Mary and I needed a director. I said: "The other priests . . . well . . . they . . ."

I did not finish. Father Lyddy quickly replied: "You do not have to say more, I understand."

Then I told him that I would like him to read my spiritual note book, which I had continued to write. I told him I would write these spiritual notes so he could read them.

In a deep voice, he firmly said: "I will read your note book and I will tell you if you should continue to write!"

He then instructed me to leave my note book at his rectory next door.

The following week I was filled with fear as I waited in line to go to confession to Father Lyddy. What if he tells me to stop writing? What would I do? How could I write what my Lady and Christ wanted me to write? I almost ran away before confession. When it was my turn to go into the confessional, I kept telling myself that I would not even mention my note book.

My mind was made up as I knelt in the confessional: I would simply not mention the note book. Then, as soon as I told Father Lyddy who I was, in his beautiful, deep voice, he said: "Now, about your note book. I want you to keep writing and don't stop until I tell you to."

My heart jumped with joy. Already this spiritual director had approved the writings which be had read. That was in 1960, and for the next thirty years, as my confessor and director, he never told me to stop writing. So I wrote, and wrote and wrote books, articles, lectures, note books and spiritual letters to Father Lyddy.

I went to confession to Father Lyddy while he was still in Meriden and after he became pastor of Saint Frances Cabrini Church in North Haven.

Not only did I go to him for confession but also for spiritual direction. Long before the Church approved reconciliation rooms (as the confessionals were named) where the penitent could speak to the priest face-to-face, Father Lyddy knew who I was every time I went into the confessional.

At that time, most Catholics would be horrified if told they had to identify themselves in the confessional. I was not because I not only went for confession to Father Lyddy, I also knew that I would receive solid spiritual advice as I struggled to climb the Ladder of Perfection; and Father Lyddy welcomed the opportunity to give me such lessons.

Our talks were seldom about visions although he knew about them. He was far more interested in guiding my soul through the long years of my climb up that ladder.

Very often I used his wise, spiritual teachings in my writings and lectures. So, in that way, his advice and lessons to me were sent outward to touch other hearts and souls.

During the years when he was my confessor and spiritual advisor, I often wrote him letters so that he could carefully watch my progress towards my goal of a more complete union with God. Here is a sample of such letters. This was written in 1976 with thoughts added in 1978;

MY SPIRITUAL NOTEBOOK (July 20, 1976)

Dear Father Lyddy: It has been a long time since I sent to you an accounting of my spiritual life. However, my spiritual life has by no means been neglected. The fact is that it is so active, so filled with joy and inner peace that I wish to share these joys and peace with others by means of my writings and lectures. Truly, I practice and believe what I preach! Not to do so, would make my teachings useless. My personal climb up the Ladder of Perfection is no illusion. It is real and constant. There have, of course, been slips and falls: however, there have also been God's graces and strength to help me rise again.

How difficult is this climb! But how rewarding when one has climbed high enough to be able to view the top and to see that final light of perfection! Of course such perfection is reserved for Heaven alone; however, I have it within my sight.

The daily, hourly climb is a suffering beyond describing for it is always before me, always there, always calling to the depths of my soul, calling me to continue and not to give up. I cannot turn from this task, I cannot give it up, I can only thank God that I so fully understand this way of perfection. For it is in the understanding of union with God where one finds the courage to seek such a close union.

Even though I do not come often to you for spiritual guidance (I go to confession around here when we can't get to your church. But if I had my way, I would go to Mass every week at your beautiful church), your words still guide me as I constantly seek a closer union with God. I can honestly say I am succeeding for I can see, in my own spiritual life, vast improvements. That, of course, does not mean that I have no failures. The fact is I also see many failures. The two statements may seem to be contradictions at first glance, but they are not. You see, due to the magnificent graces which the good Lord and Our Lady constantly shower upon my poor, undeserving soul, I have become completely aware of the way grace works and when grace works. The eyes of my soul are so trained to recognize grace that I know when I am totally faithful to grace and when I may not be completely faithful. Truly, I live in a world of God's grace. Being led by grace, I know when I totally give in to the way of a grace and when I may encounter some resistance. How do I know? It is through the inner peace and contentment in the depths of my whole being. When I am completely in tune with grace, the inner peace is in tune with union with God and truly there is not one single note of discontentment. Truly then my soul already enjoys the rewards of union with God which the saints in Heaven know, feel and understand so well. However, if only one tiny note of discontentment appears within the sweet melody of my union with God, then I am instantly aware of this disorder and I know that I have lost an opportunity to gain a spiritual treasure which will last forever.

I am most sensitive to these notes of disorder, no matter how tiny the failure on my part to respond to grace is. If, for example, I neglected to say a kind word to someone, then I know I had failed to respond to God's grace; for He had *given me* this actual grace! I have within the power of God's grace and Divine Indwelling all the graces and abilities which I will ever need to be the kind of a person God wants me to be, what Christ said: "Be you perfect, as my Heavenly Father is perfect." If I have not as yet reached this perfect union, the fault is all mine—no one else's. It becomes my failure to respond to grace!

As I said, your words guide me as I ever seek a closer union with God. I remember especially when, years ago, you told me that it is almost impossible to reach the immense depths of charity, because there is so much involved in true, Christian charity. So, I have applied your words to all virtues. I have, since that time, ever sought to fathom the depths of all virtues so that I could plunge my soul into these depths and become lost in the realms of true virtue. I have never been satisfied with half a virtue. This seems to be a characteristic of mine. My husband always tells me that, when I get involved, I really get involved! Such as my Crusader work (or even decorating my home.) Every detail must be properly taken care of (such as when I had the Marian Congress). I do not mean that I cannot make a mistake, for I certainly can; however, let us say that I try not to make a mistake. I apply this same principle to my office work (when I worked) as a bookkeeper. I cannot be "half" a bookkeeper. I must be a complete bookkeeper (so I kept learning until I was a complete bookkeeper.) I do not give up. I apply these same principles to acquiring and using virtues. I am not satisfied with half a virtue or living only half a virtuous life. Many people do that. They are willing to love and serve God only up to a certain point. But when the cross comes (such as a divorced person who wants to remarry while the spouse is alive) then the person wants to live half a life with God and the other half away from Him and His grace. They make all sorts of excuses why they can still "love" God and still live away from grace and the sacraments. Of course, they are wrong; but I do not mean to compare myself to them and to say I am a virtuous person because they are not.

I always see myself as someone who is far below the perfection which is God's alone. I seek ever to rise up to His perfection; and this is a tremendous spiritual experience and struggle.

But then, the struggle is well worth it, and also necessary. Only when one is upon the spiritual battlefields of life, only then, can eternal treasures be won. To be in the thick of the battle is where a good soldier or warrior should be. In 1944, my Lady and Our Lord gave me a title: A Mighty Warrior of Truth and Righteousness. I found that I was put right on the battlefields! Yes, I did fall, not once but many times; however, I rose again to continue the battle. Lessons had to be learned, lessons of war and peace. I have learned such lessons and with the help of God's graces (always with the help of His graces), I can look deeply into my own spiritual life and see its needs and also its triumphs. Many times I was very far from being that Mighty Warrior and I would tell my Lady that she made a mistake in calling me that. But no mistake had been made by her. If a Mighty Warrior she wanted me to be, then she had the power of her grace to make me just that! When I was not this Mighty Warrior, it was my failure to respond to her magnificent graces to me.

Today, I am that Mighty Warrior and I stand for all to see as an example of the power of God's grace.

4/21/78

Many years ago, one day Our Lord started to praise me. Overwhelmed by my own unworthiness, I begged Our Lord to stop praising me. Suddenly, I said: "Please, don't say such things to me, You know I am nothing!" He gently replied:

"Ah, dear one, is it not I who has the power to make something out of nothing?"

Today, I can say that I have seen and used this power called grace and I have become what God and grace wanted me to become. I am still totally undeserving of all praises from Christ; but in all honesty, I can say that I never stopped trying to be that "something" Christ wanted me to become.

Louise

When I was preparing reports to give to the bishop, I asked Father Lyddy if he could write a few words concerning me as my confessor and spiritual adviser. He sent me the following letter to give to the bishop.

December 9, 1994

LOUISE D'ANGELO

Very few times in any person's life does one have the blessing of meeting a truly different, exceptional human being. Louise D'Angelo is one of those "exceptional" people. And I have had the privilege of her association for over 30 years.

My closest contact with Louise has been as a spiritual adviser. In this capacity, I had the privilege of reading her writings before they became public; that is her personal thoughts, reflections and meditations. These reflect a person who is comfortable with God and His Blessed Mother. A fully devoted lover of God and His Mother, she enjoyed intimacy of lovers; peace, honesty, openness, and lack of fear.

A sign of differentness (greatness) is one's relationship to one's peers: Louise attracted hundreds who saw her as "chosen" and wanted to be near her, with her. They "sensed" the presence of God within her, and they could feel the love of God and the care of the Blessed Mother flowing thru her to them.

Archbishop John F. Whealon must have felt that also, because he favored and encouraged her and helped her in her many spiritual activities: founding a community of Brothers, establishing a Mother House, blessing its chapel, and allowing the reservation of the Blessed Sacrament in the chapel; allowing the continuing of the site of Louise's encounter with her Golden Lady. One of the reasons for Archbishop Whealon's acceptance and encouragement of Louise, was her obedience to his wishes; whatever he wanted of Louise, she imitated her Lady's fiat: "be it done unto me according to thy word."

And that is the same sign of authenticity that I experienced during my many years with her: her unquestioned obedience to God's will expressed to her thru her spiritual director and the Archbishop.

Reverend Vincent Lyddy
Saint Frances Cabrini Church
North Haven, Connecticut

Father Vincent E. Lyddy
February 3, 1921 – November 22, 1997

Father Lyddy was my Confessor and Spiritual Director from 1960 to 1990 even after Father Brad became my Confessor.

12

FATHER JAMES KELLEHER:
ADVISOR FOR THE SHRINE

I also had, at the same time Father Lyddy became my confessor and spiritual advisor, a priest who became associated more with my visions and my Lady's shrine than Father Lyddy had been. It was also in 1960 when I met Father Kelleher. While Father Lyddy called himself my confessor, Father Kelleher called himself my spiritual director in charge of my Lady's shrine. I never went to Father Kelleher for confession or for spiritual direction. Our relationship revolved around the visions and the shrine. The reason for that was the fact that Father Kelleher was in direct communication with the bishop when there were any problems concerning the shrine.

I met Father Kelleher in 1960 as a direct result of a conversation he had with a friend of mine who lived in a small town not far from Meriden. One day, she told Father about me and he said he would be willing to talk to me and to listen to what I had to say about the visions and shrine.

I went to see him and he agreed to direct me. But his direction was, at first, very harsh. He was not completely "taken in" by my stories of visions and the shrine. Often, I would leave his office crying. Once, when I started to cry in his office, he showed no sympathy. He said: "Look what Bernadette suffered, why should you be spared?"

Yet, I never thought about leaving him and seeking another priest to help me. Why? Because I knew he was good for my soul. I accepted his harsh treatment and I continued to see him.

At other times, he was most gentle and understanding and he gradually, completely believed in my Lady.

He became the connection between me and the Archbishop. Because of that fact, I stopped writing directly to the Archbishop as often as I had and I would give letters and statements to Father Kelleher to give to the Archbishop.

When I began to hear about cures and favors received from people who went to the little shrine, it was Father Kelleher who told me to gather as many signed statements as I could. When I said that some of the statements were "not that great," his response was: "Alone, they may not seem that important, but when they are all put together, they show a beautiful picture of Our Lady's love for and concern for her children."

Under his direction, I collected over 50 statements. I continued to give them to him until his death in 1975. (Now I have about 200 statements.)

As our spiritual friendship grew, Father Kelleher wanted to do all he could to help me get my Lady her shrine. He often gave me encouraging words from the bishop's office.

In 1960, I had been forbidden to go to the little shrine and I did not go for years. One Christmas eve (1961) Father allowed me to visit the precious rock where my Lady had stood. Also he, later in 1966, allowed me to go to the shrine whenever I wanted to with the condition that I did not promote the visions. I obeyed him.

On October 28, 1969, I recorded in my notes that a priest in the bishop's office called Father Kelleher and told him that "Rome knows all about the visions."

When Father told this priest that he had allowed me to return to the rock and that others were going to the little shrine, Father was told that was all right. The priest asked Father if I were promoting the visions and Father assured the caller that I was not. Father was also told that I could talk about the visions as long as I was not doing so in public. He said: "If someone asks you if you see visions, you have to tell them the truth that you do see them."

When I asked him if that means that they respect me in the bishop's office, Father laughed and replied: "At least they have not told you to keep your mouth shut."

Father Kelleher's direction was very important in the years I knew him from 1960 to 1975, when he suddenly died. He became deeply involved not only in the visions and shrine, but also in my organization which I founded: The Maryheart Crusaders.

I started this organization in 1964 mainly to help bring back fallen-away Catholics to the practice of their religion. Before I did, I talked over my plans with both Father Lyddy and Father Kelleher. They both approved the founding of this non-profit organization. I did not start this group to promote visions. I did not intend to do that. The reason I started the group was that many fallen-away Catholics came to me after I made my Lady known in 1960.

They asked me numerous questions about their Catholic faith. I wanted to find some way to teach lay people about the beautiful truths of our religion. The Crusaders developed into a program for adult religious education. I carried on this work through my writings and lectures traveling to many states to hold meetings and to give instructions by and through such lectures.

This work was carried on not only under the watchful eye of Father Kelleher, but also with the approval of our Archbishop, who had appointed Father Kelleher as our Chaplain.

I received the following letter from him on June 4, 1969:

> Dear Mrs. D'Angelo:
> I acknowledge with thanks your kind letter of May 14 and the zealous ideas expressed in that letter.
> Father Kelleher will be able to give you prudent advice concerning the conduct of the Maryheart Crusaders, Inc. With blessings, I am
> Devotedly yours in Christ,
> John F. Whealon
> Most Reverend John F. Whealon
> Archbishop of Hartford

On May 15, 1973, Father Kelleher wrote this letter to Most Reverend Humberto Cardinal Medeiros of Brighton, Massachusetts, to introduce me and my organization. That was when

I gave a lecture at a Marian Congress in the Boston area in May 1973.

> Excellency or Father:
> This letter is to introduce you to Mrs. Michael D'Angelo. For a number of years she has been active and interested in bringing back to the church fallen-away Catholics. Because of this interest and energy many other people have become involved in this good work which led to the establishment of the Maryheart Crusaders.
> Archbishop Whealon knows of this organization and its hopes; I have been associated since the beginning, with the knowledge of our Archdiocesan officials.
> I am sure that you will find Louise to be a very sincere heart and exercising what we need in the church today, and which Vatican II Council expresses that, our Catholic lay people take a place in our Catholic lives.
> Sincerely in Christ,
> Rev. James F. Kelleher

As the Crusaders organization grew and expanded with branches in several cities, I wrote to Archbishop Whealon asking that he would give his approval to my organization as an approved Catholic lay organization.

On September 7, 1973, I received a letter from Archbishop Whealon which reads as follows. In this letter, the bishop states that Father Kelleher is our appointed Chaplain.

The bishop also mentions the fact that The Maryheart Crusaders was not organized to promote my visions, but to teach lay people more about their Catholic faith.

September 7, 1973

Dear Mrs. D'Angelo:

This letter is written in answer to your recent request for a statement testifying that the Maryheart Crusaders is approved as a Catholic lay organization.

The Maryheart Crusaders has an appointed Chaplain, Father James Kelleher, and is dedicated to promoting official Catholic doctrine and devotion.

I am concerned that the purpose of this Catholic group, as all Catholic groups, is not to promote private revelations, but rather doctrine of the Gospel and of universal Catholic Tradition. Such is the stated purpose of the Maryheart Crusaders. Therefore they have approval as a Catholic lay organization.

With blessings, I am
Devotedly yours in Christ,
John F. Whealon

All the while Father Kelleher was my advisor concerning my Lady's shrine and my organization, until his death in 1975, he proved to be a wise and prudent director. While he directed me, the following events took place:

1. The Crusaders grew into a National organization. He was delighted when I told him that he was a National Spiritual Director.

2. He allowed me to return to the rock.

3. He allowed us to buy the land and to have the rock moved to its new location.

4. He allowed us to make plans for our building there.

5. He allowed me to make plans for the religious communities.

6. He approved my writings, even "The

Story." He had planned to take the Manuscript to the Archbishop but he died before he could do that.

7. When the Crusaders received the letter of approval from Archbishop Whealon, Father told me they called him and asked him what to say in that letter.

8. He loved and approved our newspaper. (no longer available).

9. He truly loved the work we did for souls and for the Church.

Last, but not least, he told me to write my autobiography which I started in 1961.

I was very reluctant to do that. I thought there were better things for me to do than to waste the time writing about myself; but under obedience I started the long, arduous task even though I really did not want to do that.

I called the book "Hearts Entwined" for the three hearts: The Sacred Heart, The Immaculate Heart and mine.

I started to type the first manuscript in June 1961. I soon gave up that idea and picked up a pen for the rest of the book.

I was in no hurry to write this autobiography. To me, it was pure penance; however, when Father Kelleher told me to write the book, my Lady and Our Lord also encouraged me to write it.

I was so unwilling to take the time to write the book that I began to write it "any old way" not really caring how it was written. However, my Lady made me know that she wanted the job done correctly and well. She kept telling me how important this book was.

I knew what I had written was not too good so in October, 1961, I began again to write, this time as my Lady wanted me to write. On October 31, 1961, I began Chapter One. (This was the book she wanted me to write.)

I was in no hurry to continue the task. I often stopped writing for months at a time. By January 1962, I had only 67 pages written. I was still writing it when I made a note on one of the pages on April 27, 1977 which said:

"Father Kelleher never read this book, but he had my book of "Prophecies and Predictions." But he always told me to keep writing this autobiography."

As the years went by, I added new pages or corrected others. I really never gave up. In spite of how much I suffered, I knew this was God's holy will for me.

When I told Father that I had 2,000 pages written, he remarked: "It is a good thing that you are not 90 years old."

Even in 1990, I was still adding to this book.

When my daily life was becoming more hectic being a working wife (a full-time bookkeeper) and trying to write letters to many people as part of my job for God in 1963, I neglected this book still telling myself that it was a "waste of time" to continue writing. But my Lady told me to keep writing because the book was so important.

I wrote these notes on February 5, 1963.

My Lady appeared to me dressed as The Golden Lady of Happiness and told me to spend this whole week working on my autobiography. That caused me a great deal of worry and concern. It is too much time to spend writing only my autobiography. I have so many spiritual letters to write. People are waiting to hear from me and I know that they are looking forward to my spiritual letters. I think of this person or that person who needs consolation and spiritual help. I would rather write the letters than the book about myself. I said to my Lady: "I should really keep writing the letters. People need consolation and spiritual help. A whole week is too much to give to my autobiography."

My Lady replied: "But the whole world is waiting for your autobiography. Think of how dreadful it would be if you died and some important fact about your own spiritual life had never been revealed! How then can my children learn what you and no one else can teach them?"

I picked up my pen again to continue the story of my life.

There is one more thing which I would like to write about

Father Kelleher.

When I became seriously ill in 1963, I thought I was at death's door. Before I did die (if it were God's holy will), I wanted to make sure that I would reaffirm the truth about my visions. So, I wrote him the following letter, sealing it in an envelope to be given to him in case I did die. I recovered and Father never got this letter; however, it tells of my feeling when I thought I was on my deathbed.

July 2, 1963

Dear Father Kelleher:

I write these words when I am seriously ill; and recently had been close to death. I wish to tell you, my spiritual director, that all I ever told you about the visions of The Golden Lady of Happiness was the truth. There are no lies in my notes or in my writings. Please tell the bishop and Monsignor Fazzalaro that fact.

I wish also to thank you; and to ask you to forgive me for all the trouble I may have caused you. I caused you and the bishop a great deal of trouble; but only because I had to do what my Lady wanted me to do.

Please continue to do all in your power to help Our Lady get the shrine to her heart here in Meriden.

God Bless You Always,
Louise D'Angelo

Father James F. Kelleher 1921-1975

Father Kelleher was my Spiritual Advisor in contact with the Bishop from 1960 to 1975.

Father Kelleher was also the Chaplain for The Maryheart Crusaders. He is shown here saying Mass at one of our many annual banquets.

This is the house where MIke and I lived after our marriage. The house was owned by Mike's father. We lived on the second floor, his parents lived on the first floor. (Mike is standing in front of the house). We were living here when my Lady told me to make her known in 1960. It was in the kitchen of our apartment where Emily came to tell us of the "miracle" she had received when she heard the words of one of the promises in church during Mass. This is also where we lived when hundreds of people came to see me after I made my Lady known in 1960. Also, we lived in this house when I started The Maryheart Crusaders in 1964.

After my marriage, I continued to skate until my Lady told me to make her known. Then I never skated again. These are the last pictures ever taken of me skating. Mike took these in February 1960.

— 13 —

THE SHRINE DOES NOT DIE

My Lady had told me that she would not let her shrine die.
It did not. Although I did not return to my Lady's land for six
years and I did not promote the visions, the little shrine, which
started as only a large rock in an empty field, grew slowly but
surely. Under the direction of Father Kelleher, who was regu-
larly in contact with the bishop's office, the little shrine continued to receive small groups of pilgrims and little tokens of
love for Our Lady.

When the land was sold to a builder, who used it for an
apartment complex, the rock was saved and then it was moved
to a lot across the street which had been bought by the Maryheart Crusaders. Soon, with donations from my friends we were
able to buy a house for the Crusaders' Motherhouse. This property was next to the lot where the shrine was located. Improvements were made and the rock was enclosed as my Lady had
requested in 1960. That was done mainly to protect the rock.
Many people wanted to chip the rock and take home a little
relic. We soon put a stop to that.

The visions themselves were not promoted by me or my
close friends. When people paid a visit to the little shrine, they
only said the Rosary. When I, later, gave lectures as part of
my programs of adult religious education, I never gave public
lectures about the visions. Most people who came to my lectures did not even know that I saw visions. However, Father
Kelleher told me that if someone asks about the visions, I should
tell the truth. Whenever that happened, I told as little as possible always saying that the visions were safe in the hands of
the Church.

When Archbishop Whealon became our Archbishop in 1969-
91, he was kept informed about the shrine. He gave us permission not only to buy the property next to the lot where the

shrine was located, but gave us permission to add an Oratory next to the house. Then he designed the altar upon which rested the Tabernacle.

He then gave us permission to reserve the Blessed Sacrament in the Oratory. The Archbishop remained my dearest friend, coming two times to dine at my home, until his sudden death in 1991.

Meanwhile, I continued with my work of evangelization, writing articles and books, holding meetings and opening The Crusaders' first Center which was a Catholic religious store and chapel with daily Mass and confession all done with the approval of Archbishop Whealon.

After I became too ill to hold meetings and give lectures, the ones who became Crusaders during that time would come to our Motherhouse and visit the shrine.

My Lady did not let her shrine die and she continued, throughout the years to be known as The Golden Lady of Happiness bringing comfort, hope and joy to her beloved children.

Following are a few of the pictures which show the growth of the shrine from 1960 onward.

EASTER SUNDAY, 1965

Above: Private Pilgrimage, 1977

Below: Louise with one of the Crusaders, who became
a benefactor: Julia McCarthy (date: 1977)

The Shrine in 1992. The rock and statue are enclosed in a fence. Note a piece of the rock which broke off when the rock was moved to lot owned by The Maryheart Crusaders.

— 14 —

ARCHBISHOP WHEALON: 1969-91

TESTIMONY FROM LOUISE'S FRIEND
DONALD D'EFEMIA CONCERNING
ARCHBISHOP WHEALON AND
THE EVENTS WHICH ARE RELATED
IN THIS CHAPTER
WRITTEN: FEBRUARY 1998

ARCHBISHOP WHEALON'S SUPPORT
AND LOVE FOR LOUISE

The day was Monday, afternoon, December 29, 1997. Jeff Nork and I were sitting in the back seat of Michael D'Angelo's car having a long conversation about Louise, Our Golden Lady of Happiness and The Maryheart Crusader Apostolate. We both were accompanying Michael and Louise on a three day, two night trip to Cape Cod. We stayed at a motel in West Yarmouth.

I have been a very close friend to Louise ever since I first met her back in September of 1960. Because of this close friendship, I thought it would be nice to share some of the things I am aware of, with Jeff.

I explained to Jeff how much Archbishop John F. Whealon loved and supported Louise, her work for the Church and her Maryheart Crusader Apostolate. I related how on June 25, 1984, the Archbishop came to Meriden to bless the opening of our store and Evangelization Center. I, also told him how Archbishop Whealon gave his permission for The Maryheart Crusaders to have a chapel at the Evangelization Center where Mass would be offered and for priests to hear confession. He also gave his permission to Louise to have the Holy Eucharist reserved in a tabernacle in our chapel. I related how this and other similar actions taken by the Archbishop in regard to Louise demonstrated his complete faith and trust in her as a person, in her work for God and the Holy Catholic Church. I added, Archbishop Whealon had a great deal of affection for Louise. Then, I told Jeff this story.

One day, we were having a Maryheart Crusader meeting at Saint Joseph's Church in Willimantic. As usual, after our meeting we would socialize with Crusaders and friends, enjoy assorted pastries with coffee or tea, and take the opportunity to greet and talk to one another.

It has always been my practice during times when we socialized to talk to different people, to ask them if they liked Louise's lecture or to explain to them a little extra of what our Crusader Apostolate was doing or involved in, or to just answer questions from those who may have one to ask. One of the women I always take the time to talk to was Blanche Auger. Blanche was a member of The Maryheart Crusaders since the mid 1970s. She always attended Crusader meetings whenever we visited Saint Joseph's. She also participated in Crusader pilgrimages coming from Willimantic to visit our private shrine to give love and honor to our Golden Lady of Happiness in Meriden. Blanche worked at the Chancery office in Hartford and was Archbishop Whealon's secretary. I always enjoyed talking to Blanche because she was nice to talk to, also because we had a chance to talk about Louise, her work for Jesus and Mary and the latest endeavors of the Maryheart Crusader Apostolate. Archbishop Whealon knew Blanche was a friend of Louise and that she would go to hear Louise give one of her lectures, a teaching lesson, whenever we visited Willimantic for a meeting.

I related how after one of our Crusader meetings, Blanche and I were talking when suddenly she said this to me, "Archbishop Whealon had a great deal of affection for Louise." She said she mentioned to the Archbishop she was going to see Louise tonight at Saint Joseph's Church in Willimantic.

When the Archbishop heard this, he said to Blanche: "Tell Louise I love her." Again: "Tell Louise I love her."

I turned to Jeff to share this thought. "You see how high in regard the Archbishop held Louise." I added, to know Archbishop Whealon expressed his love for Louise is remarkable, especially since he knew all about Louise and her visions of The Golden Lady of Happiness.

The important fact to this story is that Archbishop Whealon wanted Louise to buy the property where The Golden Lady of Happiness appeared to her. It is a fact, he told her to buy this important piece of property. The Archbishop would have never said this to Louise if he did not believe in Louise and trust her.

Certainly and most importantly, Archbishop Whealon's attitude in dealing with Louise over the years demonstrated his deep respect and fatherly love for her and her work.

When Father Brad and I saw Archbishop Whealon, during our conversation we explained to the Archbishop, how the Oratory on Coe Avenue was almost completed. We told him about the beautiful tabernacle we have that came from a church in Boston. We, then, asked him if the Maryheart Crusaders could keep the reservation of The Blessed Sacrament at the Oratory.

The Archbishop smiled again and said, "Yes, I will give permission for the reservation of the Blessed Sacrament at the Oratory." But he added, "There must be security for the tabernacle, the tabernacle must be secured to the altar and the tabernacle must be placed on an altar of proper dimension!"

The Archbishop asked for a piece of paper and a pen. He then drew a three dimensional sketch of the altar he wanted constructed. The plan he drew was for an altar, "four feet high," with an altar top less than four feet wide; "if possible," it could be, "three feet or three feet, six inches wide."

Under his drawing he wrote the words, "One altar and one tabernacle." He called it, "The Shrine of the Blessed Sacrament."

In addition: When the Center, which included a Chapel moved in 1987, the Archbishop came again to bless the store and Chapel. He expressed a great interest in the work being done at this Center and especially the Confessions which reached over 1,000 a year.

I always called this Chapel in our Center a "Refuge For Suffering Souls." That is truly what it became. When I named it this "Refuge For Suffering Souls," I had forgotten that this was one of my titles.

Louise with Archbishop John F. Whealon, former Archbishop of Hartford, Connecticut (deceased August 2, 1991). Louise is pictured with the Archbishop when he came to bless the chapel in the Maryheart Crusaders' Evangelization Center. Picture taken July 1987.

This shows the chapel in the Maryheart Crusaders' store and center.
Archbishop Whealon blessed this chapel in July 1987.

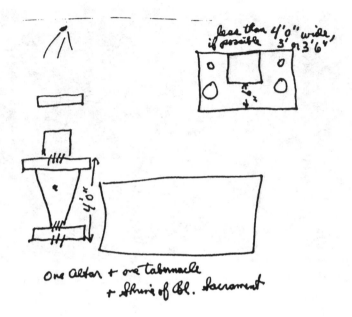

This is the plan Archbishop Whealon drew on June 25, 1984, For a Shrine Altar reserving the Holy Eucharist in the tabernacle in The Maryheart Crusader Oratory on Coe Avenue in Meriden. He called it The Shrine of The Blessed Sacrament.

These two pictures
show the Oratory at
The Crusaders'
Motherhouse in
Meriden.

The bottom picture
shows the"Shrine of
The Blessed
Sacrament"
designed by
Archbishop Whealon.

The Oratory built at the house the Crusaders bought; approved by our Archbishop Whealon. Date: 1984

Another view of the Oratory. Archbishop Whealon designed the altar for the tabernacle (right side).

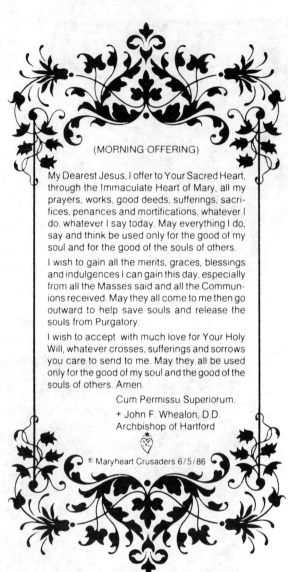

(MORNING OFFERING)

My Dearest Jesus, I offer to Your Sacred Heart, through the Immaculate Heart of Mary, all my prayers, works, good deeds, sufferings, sacrifices, penances and mortifications, whatever I do, whatever I say today. May everything I do, say and think be used only for the good of my soul and for the good of the souls of others.

I wish to gain all the merits, graces, blessings and indulgences I can gain this day, especially from all the Masses said and all the Communions received. May they all come to me then go outward to help save souls and release the souls from Purgatory.

I wish to accept with much love for Your Holy Will, whatever crosses, sufferings and sorrows you care to send to me. May they all be used only for the good of my soul and the good of the souls of others. Amen.

Cum Permissu Superiorum.

+ John F. Whealon, D.D.
Archbishop of Hartford

© Maryheart Crusaders 6/5/86

Morning Prayer written by Louise D'Angelo published 6/5/86

February 1981

Twice Archbishop Whealon came to our home for dinner. The first visit was February 1981 and he came again in October 1982.

October 1982

ARCHDIOCESE OF HARTFORD

134 FARMINGTON AVENUE

HARTFORD, CONNECTICUT
06105

OFFICE OF
THE ARCHBISHOP

October 19, 1982

Mr. and Mrs. Michael D'Angelo
22 Button Street
Meriden, CT 06450

Dear Louise and Mike:

I am thankful for the pleasant evening at your home, and also
for the gift of that unusual picture of St. Theresa, the Little
Flower.

I shall keep it on hand as a fitting rememberance of a beautiful
evening.

With kindest wishes in the Lord,

✝ John J. Whealon

Most Reverend John F. Whealon
Archbishop of Hartford

My husband greets Archbishop Whealon when he came to bless our new store and chapel at 9 Colony St., Meriden, Connecticut

On September 23, 1987, Archbishop Whealon came to bless our new store and chapel. I am with the Archbishop in our store.

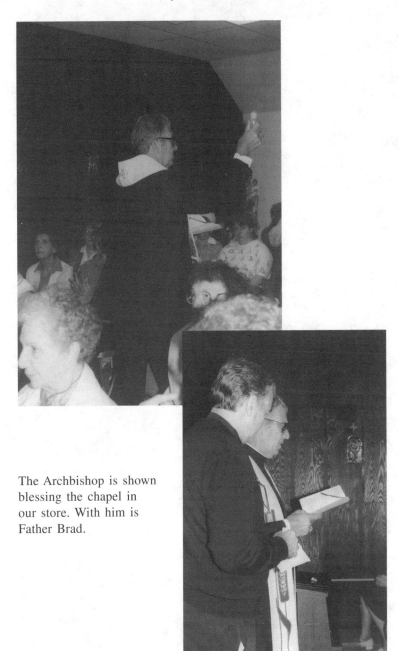

The Archbishop is shown
blessing the chapel in
our store. With him is
Father Brad.

Part 12

The Triumph of
The Immaculate Heart of Mary

— 1 —

WHAT MY LADY'S TRIUMPH MEANS

The first time my Lady stood on the rock in 1948 as The Golden Lady of Happiness, she said to me: "My Immaculate Heart has triumphed." In 1960, she said the same thing: "My Immaculate Heart has triumphed."

When she told me that, at that time, I did not even know how to pronounce the word triumph (let alone spell it). Invariably, I would say something like: "My Immaculate Heart has triumpheded . . ." not knowing how to say the word triumphed. When my first manuscripts about the visions were written, I left it up to my friend, who did the typing, to put in the correct spelling for the word triumphed. I always had a T somewhere in the word.

Although I knew next to nothing about Fatima, and I did not connect my Lady with Fatima until after I had seen my Golden Lady, I did know that Our Lady of Fatima had said: "In the end my Immaculate Heart will triumph." Even then, I never learned how to pronounce or spell the word triumph.

What is her triumph? It is actually an on-going condition. One cannot say that only one or two events constitute the triumph of the Immaculate Heart of Mary—and that is the end of her triumph. There will be no end as long as people have faith in Our Lady. Holy Mother Church has, from the beginning, encouraged devotion to and love for Our Lady. She worked her miracles and granted favors for about two thousand years. All such miracles and favors show Our Lady's triumph in one way or another: triumph over sickness, over plagues, over armies, etc.

When Our Lady spoke about her triumph to the children of Fatima and to me, she was not saying anything new. She was merely repeating what had been known about her since devotion to her started. She was the Lady who showed mankind that she was victorious in the past and will be in the future; as she said to me: (July 7, 1960) "My Immaculate Heart has triumphed. I will, now show the devil that I am the powerful one." The "powerful one" she always was. Now mankind will again see such power.

Because of this on-going triumph, it was reasonable for Mary to tell me, in 1948, that her Immaculate Heart has triumphed even when the world was still torn apart by the viciousness of World War II.

Most people could not see that triumph of Mary in world conditions starting in 1946. That was because most people see only the world they live in. They find it almost impossible to stretch that world backward into history or forward into the future. So it was easy for people in 1948 to look at the world they saw filled with the rubble of World War II and to ask: "What triumph?" Yet, Mary's triumph was there. Where was it? In love!

The triumph of Mary, whether in ages past or in ages to come always begins with love. One of the greatest and most powerful tools of the devil is to convince people that God does not love them when bad things happen and crosses are placed upon weary shoulders.

Yet, if people would only look within crosses, they would see love, God's love and also Mary's love. My Lady said to me, in 1960: "I come now to give love and to receive love." And this love has power: "I stand upon the world, upon the moon and upon the devil to show all men that my power is the greatest." That is triumph.

Yet, there are different ages of Mary's triumph. Ours is one of them; and my Lady appeared to me to show all that now is another age of her triumph: her golden triumph.

I will now explain Mary's triumph in our age and how clearly that triumph and her power can be seen.

— 2 —

VATICAN COUNCIL II AND
THE CATHOLIC LAITY

Vatican Council II! What was it like to be an average Catholic lay person during this era of Church history?

Many who lived through the first years following the Council entered a Catholic world totally unfamiliar to them. They became upset, confused and bewildered by what was happening to their beloved Church. A goodly number of these Catholics did not even try to find out what was happening. They found it easier to retreat into their own private world of I-give-up. The results: they left the Church.

The Council, itself, was not to blame for this sad state of affairs.

The Council produced many wonderful documents for the good of our Church and for the spiritual advancement of souls. If one were to study these documents and teachings, one would find within these pages words of wisdom inspired by the Holy Spirit.

However, the average Catholic lay person was not interested enough in these documents to study them. The fact is, most Catholics did not even know where to find the correct information concerning these documents so they could enlighten their minds. They left all that study to theologians who, we all thought, would explain what happened at Vatican Council II.

That was where the problems started.

The Council, as I said, brought about a great deal of good; however, it also lit fires which were created by the so-called extremists who tried to turn the Council's spirit of renewal into their own ideas of what this renewal should be. As a result, theologians who had secretly nursed pet ideas and theories which were contrary to the basic teachings and traditions of Holy Mother Church, felt that the time had come to let the world hear their voices. Without thinking about the effect that their words would have upon the unlearned lay person's spiritual life, these "experts" placed before the laity complicated, new and startling conclusions revolving around normal Catholic doctrines and moral teachings.

Most theologians *did not* stray from true Catholic teachings; however, they helped to create the lay people's problems because now there was the situation which resulted with theologians arguing with each other. That was unheard of before the Council. Lay people had always known that if one were to ask a question, ten or twenty learned men would give them the same answer.

The media (newspapers, magazines, even some Catholic publications), as expected, had a field-day with these controversies; reporting every remark made by theologians.

That caused tremendous confusion among the laity. Every statement, which could cause some kind of a clash between theologians was flashed across the world and ended up flooding the tranquil, undisturbed abode of the lay people. Many of these statements and remarks (perhaps some incorrectly reported) were accepted by most lay people as "Gospel-truth" even if these "new teachings" were contradictions of Catholic doctrine. After all, these people reasoned, these theologians should know what they were talking about.

On and on the doctrines and teachings of our beloved Catholic Church were abused and torn apart by those who should have known better; and the Catholics, who were comfortable with this "new" knowledge about their faith, repeated over and over what they heard and read in a parrot-like fashion which confused not only themselves but all they came in contact with.

And it was not only the noted theologians who caused so much confusion among the laity. This unauthorized "cause for change" was taken up by many priests and nuns as well.

I remember being present when a dear friend's grandson was being baptized. As the priest was pouring water over the infant's head, he said: "Now, I am baptizing this baby not because there is such a thing as Original Sin, but because this baptism is preparing the child to fight the temptations of life. He will now be protected from the world and sin."

I was shocked.

After the ceremony ended, I approached the priest and told him he had been wrong to say such a thing. I explained that the Church teaches that the Sacrament of Baptism cleanses us from Original Sin and it makes us holy with the gifts of the Holy Spirit.

He became angry and said: "Well, the book I read has the Imprimatur, you know! This is what the Council teaches!"

That factor, of priests telling lay people their own ideas about the doctrines and teachings of our Church caused more problems among the laity. What were we to think and who were we to believe?

I remember when I was a Sunday school teacher (or C.C.D. instructor as it was called) there was a huge banquet held for all the teachers in the diocese. Over three hundred men and women attended. I was one of them. The Archbishop was there with many priests and nuns. It was a festive event.

After everyone ate, the main speaker began his lecture. He was a young priest who had been present in Rome during the sessions of the Council.

Extremely brilliant, most knowledgeable and a proficient speaker, his mastery called all to attention. Silence filled the huge dining hall as his powerful voice took command of the situation. An excellent choice for the occasion; or was it?

He started his lecture by saying that he would speak about Vatican Council II. However, he would not explain the documents which had been accepted by the Council, but the ones which had been presented and then were rejected. He seemed to be angry because they were not accepted.

Then for almost two hours, he began to name names, mention these documents and explain precisely what was contained in each separate document; all of which meant nothing to most of the people who were present, including myself. We did not have the slightest idea what he was talking about. We did not

even know what documents had been accepted and he was trying to explain which ones were rejected. Before he finished,
half of the people in the room had gotten up and left.

The speaker did not care or else had no idea that he was
talking to lay people who had merely volunteered to teach
grade-school children and who had no training in theological
studies. The ones who arranged the affair surely made a mistake in the choice of the speaker and his subject to be presented.

Such mistakes were common following the Council and
deeply affected the average Catholic lay person.

The lay person who went dutifully to holy Mass, began to
hear or read in magazines and newspapers many unCatholic
ideas and teachings which were puzzling to say the least.

Many ordinary Catholic people, who were caught up in the
theological disputes of learned Church leaders through the
attempts of secular and religious newspapers and magazines
to present the "news" to their readers, began to confuse mere
speculation with truth in such a way that they readily accepted
any new ideas about doctrine if this idea appealed to them.

Papal infallibility often was cleverly turned into "personal
infallibility" wherein some Catholics felt that it was all right
to believe or to do anything they wanted to regardless of what
the Church and the Pope taught. The "I want to do this" and
the "I won't believe that anymore" became the role for any
Catholic who had looked for an excuse to justify the wrong
things which he did or planned to do or to believe.

Nothing was sacred to these extremists and their followers
as they went their own way tearing apart such doctrines and
teachings as: Hell, Purgatory, Heaven, Holy Communion, the
divinity of Christ, Adam and Eve and the role of the Blessed
Virgin Mary in the modern Church.

So, we, the lay people, quickly heard such "new teachings"
as: there is no more Hell or Purgatory and a Catholic does not
have to go to Mass if he or she chooses not to go. The sin of
deliberately missing Mass on Sundays and holy days "vanished" along with a host of other sins. According to these "new"

"truths" any Catholic could believe whatever he or she wanted to and to cast aside everything (in the name of religious freedom) that interfered with the person's life style.

As bad as that sounded, "the big one" was about confession. That seemed to appeal to a great many Catholics who did not want to go anyway. They, according to what they heard or read, no longer had to face the "dreaded" dark confessional.

In some parishes, the parishioners were told that all they had to do about their sins (mortal as well as venial) was to list these sins on a piece of paper which then would be burned along with the sins of others. Even if the people were told that only applied to venial sins (mortal sins still had to be confessed to a priest. Venial sins did not have to be confessed), many paid no attention and relished the idea of going to confession this "new way."

When I told Archbishop Whealon that a certain priest was teaching and using this method of confession, he replied: "Is he still using that hibachi thing? I will have to tell him again to stop."

All such conflicting ideas and teachings had a profound effect upon the average lay person and his or her faith.

I wonder if you can picture, in your mind, what the situation was like for the laity before and then after the Council.

One would have had to live through those years to personally experience the anguish and frustration of Catholics caused *not* by the Council, but by the priests and theologians who wanted to use the Council as an excuse for their wrong ideas about their Catholic faith.

Oh! I imagined that there were many Catholics who were delighted with the spiritual marvels which came forth from the Council. They were knowledgeable enough to understand the treasure which the Council was. But such Catholics were few and far between. I must confess that in talking to thousands of lay people as I travelled from city to city and state to state for over 25 years giving lectures and explaining to people the joys of their Catholic faith, I never met a person who actually knew what had happened at Vatican Council II. Instead, they would ask me question after question about something they had heard or read which greatly upset them.

After the Council, there were profound changes in the lives of Catholics. Before the Council, the average Catholic had experienced a marvelous sense of security found in their faith. A person felt that their faith was solid, unchangeable: the same yesterday, today and tomorrow.

The practicing Catholics never missed Mass on Sundays and holy days. Confession was usually once a week, before one received the Eucharist on Sunday. The lines, on Saturday evenings were long before the confessionals. A Catholic learned the answers to the questions of faith in a child's catechism. They believed in Heaven, Hell and Purgatory. Sin was sin: venial or mortal. No matter what a priest or theologian taught about doctrine or Church teachings, all said the same things.

There were the usual Monday evening novenas (always well attended), special devotions to saints, etc. No practicing Catholic ate meat on Fridays.

Suddenly overnight, things swiftly changed. No one could blame the Council for what happened nor the documents which the Council passed. Other factors entered the picture.

At that time when theologians began filling news print with their arguments and pet theories concerning the faith, numerous parish priests began to drastically change, not only the look of their churches, but also the way they thought Mass should be celebrated. Many such changes caused shock and anguish among the local parishioners. Added to these problems for the laity, there arose what became known as Christian Unity. There was an honest effort made by Church authorities to unite all Christian faiths, inviting dialogues with the leaders of Protestant denominations. There was nothing wrong with that. However, many lay people became very upset when they thought such actions meant that Catholics would have to compromise some of our most cherished beliefs such as love for and devotion to Mary.

Many Catholics did not know who or what to believe anymore.

For example, at one of my Crusaders' meeting, a woman came up to me and said: "My daughter came home from school—a Catholic school—and told me there was no more Hell."

I reacted: "What did they do with it?"

Others told me that Purgatory no longer existed. That everyone went to Heaven when they died.

Again: "What did they do with it?"

Another person came up to me and said: "Father told us we don't have to go to confession any more. We can tell our sins directly to God"

I replied: "And who will give you absolution?"

That was only the beginning. Like a virus spreading from one source of information to another, more startling events took place.

Some priests reasoned that the Council had given them permission (which it had not) to place individual tastes and preference above the traditional way Catholics had always viewed their faith and their churches. Rapidly making changes to suit their own ideas, fantasies and very large egos, they began to make changes which they never could have made before the Council.

Things became so bad that many Catholics no longer recognized their beloved Catholic churches.

Suddenly, people went to church for Sunday Mass and discovered there was no altar rail. It had been removed.

They were told that the reason why was that the rail acted like a fence keeping people away from Christ in the tabernacle; yet the majority loved to kneel at the altar rail to tell Christ they loved Him. They could no longer do that.

Catholics had been taught from childhood to show deep reverence for their Lord hidden in His golden tabernacle. They prayed in silence. Suddenly, they were told that the church is "God's home" and we are invited in to meet all our friends and relatives. Why not act as you would if they came to visit you at your home. As a result, the silent church began to be filled with loud activity as people who came to talk to the

Lord, preferred to talk to his or her neighbor, shattering the precious silence. If one dared to look back and tell the offenders to please be quiet "because you are in the presence of the Lord," the one requesting silence would be given a "dirty look" and told to "mind your own business." That happened to me several times.

Once, Archbishop Whealon told me, after a visit to a local church to say Mass, that he had never, in his life, heard such a racket when he was present in a church. The noisy congregation showed as little respect for their Archbishop as they did for their hidden Saviour.

With the silent respect for Christ in the tabernacle disappearing, other Catholic traditions began to fade out of sight. People no longer thought it necessary to genuflect before entering the pew. Gone were hats (I loved the Easter bonnets) worn by women, along with the "Sunday best" fashions. People, especially teenagers came to Mass, dressed as if they were going to a picnic in the country or a ball game or the beach.

Priests would say: "Come dressed anyway you want to. The important thing is that you come."

Some of the more "modern" priests would include in the Mass dancers, clowns, even some Pentecostal leaders running up and down the aisles shouting: "Praise the Lord," "Praise the Lord."

That happened in a church a friend of mine went to. He could not believe what was happening. He was extremely upset.

The long lines, which had always been there on Saturday evenings, as hundreds of Catholics went to confession, soon disappeared. These lines were replaced by long lines on Sunday morning when almost everyone in the church rose to receive their Lord.

That might have been commendable, except many, who received the Eucharist, believed that they no longer needed confession because they "never committed any sins." More than one person said to me: "I don't sin! I never murdered anyone!"

They had convinced themselves that there were only three

sins: murder, adultery and stealing, all of which they did not commit.

One woman, who was very ill in the hospital, and had not gone to confession since the Council, told a friend of mine who paid her a visit: "I want to see a priest to go to Communion. But you tell him not to hear my confession! I will not go to confession to any priest because I never did anything wrong like those who steal and commit adultery."

As a result, many once conscientious Catholics, lost their sense of sin completely overlooking their many faults and human weaknesses.

Added to all that, disobedience to proper Church authorities was rampant. Many Catholics would no longer obey the teachings of our Church: if such a teaching did not appeal to them.

When Pope John Paul II visited our country, the papers and magazines were filled with stories about Catholics who loved their Pope—however . . .! Then they would list all the things they did not agree with which the Pope had said.

It was sad to hear lay people make such statements. It was worse to hear a nun or a priest say the same things.

Then came the feminist movement which invaded the Church. Numerous disgruntled Catholic lay women and nuns began to make their voices heard. They demanded everything that the Church taught was wrong: abortion, women priests, active, sexual homosexual relationships, unmarried couples living together, remarriage of divorced men and women who had a valid marriage. Their greatest delight was to tell the world that they were Catholic.

As a result, little groups began to form which were called: "Catholics For Abortion," or "Catholics For Homosexual Activities," or "Catholics For Married Priests."

Of course they were wrong; however, they were also very powerful and gathered a large following of Catholics who agreed with their way of thinking. And they would not go away.

Even faithful Catholics began to be dragged into the feminist way of thinking.

One day a woman came up to me and said: "My daughter came home from school and told me that Sister said she could hardly wait to become a priest so that she can baptize all those little babies."

I could only shake my head in disbelief.

I remember when Pope John Paul II made one of his visits to our country. On a T.V. news broadcast, they showed a girl, at a Catholic school, about eleven or twelve years old. She was asked what she would tell the Pope if she could talk to him. She pulled out a sheet of paper and read: "I would ask the Pope why he will not allow women priests"—and this was *after* the Pope had issued a statement saying there would be no women priests.

Added to all that upset and confusion, extra church devotions—Monday night novenas, etc.—disappeared.

Starved for such necessary spiritual nourishment, many Catholics—some who had been my Crusaders—began to leave their faith and join groups of Bible students who loudly "praised the Lord" their own way. Several of my friends who thought they finally "found" the Lord in this manner, deeply hurt me by expressing hate for their Catholic faith and especially for the Holy Mother of God whom they had once dearly loved.

Things could only get worse—and they did! As the laity, along with numerous bishops all over the world, watched in dazed shock, thousands of nuns and priests gave up their vocations and walked away to "find something better." What a sensation that caused! Almost every news commentator interviewed at least one such former nun or priest.

I remember writing to a T.V. station asking why they did not interview the numerous priests and nuns who were faithful to the Church and to their vocations. The answer I received was that they "do not make news."

Added to all that confusion and unrest, the average lay person had to cope with official changes brought about by the magisterium which rocked their "unchangeable world."

Therein laid one of the reasons for the laity's state of perplexity.

Before the Council, the average lay person lived in a placid, calm, peaceful, nothing-ever-changes state of faith.

When they were faced with the official changes of the Church—all of them good—most Catholics were unprepared and shocked. They retreated to their personal safe world of: "But the Church never changes."

Yet, these changes came forth and had to be faced.

For example, the changes in the way Holy Mass was said.

Before the Council, the priest said Mass with his back to the people and spoke Latin. The laity sat in the pews, many of them not even knowing what was happening, praying to themselves or saying the Rosary. There were missals which could be read in English, but very few people used them.

Most people did not even know when it was time to receive the Eucharist, I was one of them. When I received, every Sunday, I would become very nervous waiting for the moment when I could leave my seat and go to the altar rail. I always welcomed the priest's beckoning nod of the head when he faced the congregation and made us aware that we could now come forward.

Suddenly, the whole procedure of the Mass changed. The altar was placed so that the priest could now face the people. English replaced Latin so the people could understand what was being said. Songs were suppose to be sung by everyone (no choir) but most people did not know how to sing them.

No one had to worry when it was time to receive Communion. They had only to follow everyone else to the front of the church where long lines would form. Not only that, but people would receive standing up, especially when the altar rails had been removed. (The priests never removed them in my parish church.)

Then a most unfamiliar sound reached the ears. At certain events or celebrations, the congregation would loudly applaud. Was this not disrespectful to Christ in the Eucharist? The first time I heard that noise, I wanted to cry. I felt so sorry for my Eucharistic Lord.

572 *Triumph of the Immaculate Heart of Mary*

Many people said to me as we entered the church: "Well, what new thing do we have to do today?"

Many priests, unofficially, added their own changes to our most Holy Mass.

We were told that the Eucharist was no longer the Body and Blood of Christ, but a "family meal." Pictures of a loaf of bread and a cup of wine began to be put on church hall walls and in private homes. There were words under these pictures such as: "Christ invites you to share a meal with Him," yet the Eucharist was not a "family meal," but Christ Himself.

The one thing which seemed to bother many people the most was the hand-shake or "kiss of peace."

I knew more than one person, who had been faithful church-goers, who stopped going when that was introduced. They simply did not want to shake hands with the person sitting next to them.

Confession, also, was not spared the changes.

The confessional was no longer that, but a Reconciliation Room where sinners could go to confess (horrors for some people) face-to-face with the priest!

Many people stopped going to confession, when they thought they had to face a priest in a well-lit room, until they learned that they had a choice. If they preferred the "old way" of not revealing who they were to the priest, they could still confess in that manner.

The main problem was that the laity were not well prepared for such changes. Later, when the confessional became the Reconciliation Room, Archbishop Whealon sent a letter, read at every Mass, explaining what was about to happen.

One day when I told the Archbishop how upset and confused most lay people had been about the liturgical revision of the Mass, he smiled and said: "We did not do too good with explaining that one." Then he paused and remarked: "We did better with confession, didn't we?"

We both laughed.

But the one change which caused the most anguish among the laity was not an official outcome of the Council. It was done by individual priests who seemed to have a problem with devotion to Mary and the saints.

I was shocked to learn how many priests did not love Mary nor did they pray to her. Suddenly, they began to reveal that fact.

A friend of mine told me that a priest told her that he doesn't "go" for "all that Mary stuff."

Another time when I was to give a lecture to a church group, I was told by the priest: "You better not give any lecture on Mary!"

I stood my ground and gave a lecture about Our Lady.

After the lecture, the priest came to me and said: "That was beautiful."

I was told that one priest stood up before the congregation and actually tore apart a Rosary telling everyone that we no longer needed Mary.

Many Catholics who truly loved Mary, came to me with tears in their eyes and asked me if they could still pray to Mary. Of course, I said yes.

Such priests, and others who followed their examples did not stop with words against Mary. They went a step further. They began to remove her statue (as well as the statues of Christ and the saints) from their churches.

Try to imagine, if you can, what it was like for Catholics to go to their parish churches and find that all the statues of Mary and the saints had been removed. They simply disappeared overnight. What a shock! What happened? Where did all the statues go? Why were they taken away?

The explanation: "We want to focus all attention on Christ in the Eucharist" did not heal the broken hearts of the faithful who had so loved the statues, who had prayed before them and had found comfort in the silent solitude of the church which told them that Mary, their Mother, was ever close to them in their hour of sadness.

The Council never told priests to remove all statues from their churches; but most lay people thought that the orders to do that came directly from the Council, and we could no longer honor our beloved Mother of God as we had in the past.

I was uncertain myself why the statues had been removed. I only knew that I missed them dreadfully. My own parish church kept the statues for which I was very thankful; but other churches in my city lost them.

I remember visiting a church where there had been a most beautiful statue of Mary. I was shocked to see only the empty pedestal. I stared at this with tears in my eyes, Mary was no longer there.

I went to another church and again: no statues. I looked around and I saw a small, narrow hallway next to the main altar. There, in that hallway were all the statues in one straight line as if they were waiting to be put on their pedestals. They were never replaced back into the place where they had been for decades. Then, they were gone.

Where did all these statues go? I was told by many of my friends that some of them were thrown into the land fills with the garbage. I knew where three statues went. I have them. Two were brought to my home by friends who rescued them from the land fills. One is a magnificent statue of Mary about 5-1/2 ft. tall. The other is an equally beautiful statue of Our Lord with outstretched arms about 4-1/2 ft. tall. Both statues were worth thousands of dollars.

A third statue of Saint Patrick, smaller than the other two, I found in a dusty antique shop where it had been brought by a priest who did not have the heart just to throw it away. I quickly bought it for a very low price.

Not only were statues removed, but also crucifixes and wall paintings.

I used to go to daily Mass at a church where there was a most magnificent, huge crucifix behind the altar. I would kneel in the front pew and look at the crucifix and love my Saviour.

One day, I went to Mass and the crucifix was gone. I was very upset. After Mass, I asked the priest what had happened to it. He said he had removed it.

I asked: "But why? I would look at that crucifix and love my Saviour."

He became angry and said, as he quickly walked away: "You can over decorate a church, you know!"

I found another church for my daily Mass.

Then there is this sad story to tell.

A young girl was very upset with the way her pastor had "modernized" her church by removing all the statues and the altar rail. She wanted to be married in a church which had kept its pre-Council look. She arranged to be married in the church I had been married in.

Meanwhile, before the wedding, the pastor of that church had called for funds to renovate the place. The funds were collected.

The day of the wedding arrived. You can imagine the bride's keen disappointment when she arrived for her day-of-days and saw what had happened in the time between making the arrangements and the wedding.

She hardly recognized the church. Not only were all the statues gone, and the altar rail, but all the magnificent, splendid, irreplaceable wall paintings behind the altar had been painted over and were no longer visible. I could share her disappointment when I, myself, paid a visit to that church and saw what the renovations had done. I considered it a disaster. Maybe the statues and altar rail could one day be replaced, but not the huge paintings which I had often admired.

There was no end to the changes the average lay person had to face. There were so many conflicting ideas, teachings and changes, some as I said from Church officials, others from individuals who had to get their ideas and ways into the picture, that many lay people did not know what to accept or whom to believe and follow.

However, as the years went by and Catholics got used to the changes made by the magisterium, calm became to settle over the laity and their faith.

There is no doubt that a great deal of damage had been done and many Catholics who left the Church never returned; however, the ones who would not leave began to see a different, more vibrant Church.

Many wonderful things happened not only to our Catholic Church, but also to the laity and their relationship to their Church as a result of Vatican II.

I wrote an article about Vatican II, which was published in "The Catholic Transcript" (Hartford, Connecticut) March 8, 1991. I called this article: "The Confusion, Fears and Joys Following Vatican II" I spoke, in that article, about many of the things I mentioned in this chapter but I ended it with a ray of hope and joy:

JOYS IN EXPANDED CHURCH

And there were joys in our expanded Church. The joys of understanding all the prayers being said during Mass, the joys of having laymen and women reading during the Mass, the joys of becoming more active members of each parish. The joys of giving one's time and energy to help others in all sorts of parish activities, the joys of sharing our faith with others. Those and many other joys came out of Vatican Council II.

But the greatest joy of all was to recognize and know Christ in the Eucharist as we had never known Him before.

Also, helping us laity through this most difficult time was a treasure given to our Church by God: Pope John Paul II.

Although some Catholics had developed a great dislike for the hierarchy and even for the Pope, most Catholics all over the world loved him dearly. He was a Pope for the people; but also a Pope who stood firmly against overwhelming odds proclaiming to all the true teachings and doctrines of our faith.

There is a saying which goes like this: Whenever there are serious problems within the Church, God will send a saint to straighten them out and give the correct answers.

Pope John Paul II was that saint for this most turbulent period of Church history.

In addition to the leadership of our beloved Pope, the bishops of our Church helped us sail over these rough waters into calmer seas through their guidance and concern. For those of us who wanted to listen to them and to obey, they produced many wonderful statements and documents.

One was the U.S. Bishop's letter on Mary called "Behold Your Mother."

When I organized a Marian Congress, approved by Archbishop Whealon in 1975, I presented an Audio Visual Film Strip based upon that document. When it was finished, the audience stood up and applauded. Mary was still, as she had always been and as the Council taught, a most important part of our Catholic faith.

— 3 —

THE SECOND VATICAN COUNCIL AND MY MADONNA MARIA'S TRIUMPH

One of the greatest triumphs of my Lady happened years before the downfall of the Russian Empire. Her triumph came after Vatican Council II.

As I wrote in Chapter Two, Our Lady's role as our beloved Mother had been threatened *not* by the Council but by what happened when many priests and theologians began to confuse the laity about devotion to and love for Mary. Article after article appeared, some in Catholic publications, stating that Mary had been deemphasized by the Council.

I clearly remember reading in the newspapers and secular weekly national magazines, during this time, headlines and news articles telling about how the Virgin Mary was being deemphasized in the Catholic Church and how her role was being downplayed by the Vatican Council Church fathers. I remember reading those news articles with sadness.

But then came the truth about devotion to and love for Mary as presented by the Council. At the closing of the third session on November 21, 1964, Pope Paul VI gave Mary a new title: Mother of The Church. This caused much joy among the laity as well as religious.

However, the damage which the extremists had done to Mary's place of honor and esteem had been unbelievably great. Instead of helping Our Lady as Pope Paul had intended, the decree became more fuel to be burnt in the fires of theological disagreement.

Famous theologians, well-known around the world, led the group who believed that Mary's role in the Church should be minimized. Their remarks together with ones such as emerged from another theologian's theory—that Fatima may have advanced many souls on their way to Heaven, but it put Mariology back 10 years—put the Holy Mother of God in a new light; one that was shaded with doubts about devotion to her. As a result this started a new trend to think of Mary more in the sense of liturgical veneration (her role in the Bible) instead of the one to whom hearts rise up with love during devotions to her. Many forms of this devotion such as saying the Rosary and Novenas to Our Lady were put aside by local pastors as being no longer needed or necessary. My beloved Monday night Novena to Our Lady of The Miraculous Medal was cancelled, along with Benediction and prayers to Our Lord in the Blessed Sacrament.

Before long, when Catholics went to church for Mass, they discovered in many churches that beloved statues of Mary had been removed. Some of these statues were merely thrown away. Some were hidden in a closet or in a dark corner of the church. I remember going to Mass at a local church and suddenly being startled. There had been a magnificent statue of Our Lady over a beautiful marble altar. In front of the altar were the words "Ave Maria." The altar and the words were still there, but the statue had vanished. All during Mass, I looked at the empty niche with tears in my eyes. In addition, Catholics who loved to say the Rosary during Mass were told that they now had to say prayers and sing songs. These changes in the Liturgy meant to focus all attention upon Christ and the Sacrifice of the Mass, were misunderstood by a vast majority of lay people; so instead of finding a new time to say the Rosary or favorite Novenas, many Catholics just forgot about these devotions.

This situation is the one which Our Lady foresaw when in 1945 she told the world through me: "Do not cast me aside."

As I mentioned before, in 1945, I could not imagine how Our Lady could ever be cast aside. As I write these words, years later, I can say that I lived through one of the most terrifying periods of Catholic history: the time when the Holy Mother of God was almost cast aside by the very ones who should have loved her the most.

I along, with thousands of lay people I talked to, became

sad and upset by the situation. Many asked me if it were a sin
to still pray to Mary.

Actually the Council never told priests to stop Novenas or
to take away beloved statues of Our Lady. Each priest decided
that for himself often with disastrous results. Lay people began
to look for other ways and means to satisfy spiritual hunger
which had been fed by loving devotions to Mary. Numerous
Catholics left their faith to join cults and fundamentalist Bible
groups thinking they had what the Church lacked.

It was into this type of a situation that I walked almost as
soon as I started my organization The Maryheart Crusaders. I
had formed the group in 1964 to teach people more about their
Catholic faith and to bring back into the Church fallen-away
Catholics. By the time I was holding meetings and giving lectures, I was on a battlefield being confronted by numerous
Catholics who no longer wanted to accept a teaching or doctrine of the Church, all saying: "We don't have to believe that
anymore because the Council said so." Their argument was:
"Well, Father said there is no more Hell" . . . or Purgatory . . .
or Confession . . . or "we don't have to go to Mass anymore.
It is no longer a sin."

All this became part of my Devil's Challenge and I was
going to fight for my Church, her teachings and doctrines. This
I did by my writings, meetings and lectures. The work was
exhausting and I still had a full-time job as a bookkeeper. I
also was very ill; however, I would not give up.

I was deeply upset and disturbed by all I had to encounter
on these battlefields; but what bothered me the most were the
remarks made about Our Lady; some of which are not fit to
print—and all coming from people who called themselves
Catholic. So most of my lectures were about Mary, her love
for us (none about my visions) and how we should honor and
love her. In a lecture I gave at Saint Sebastian Church in Mid-
dletown, Connecticut on December 5, 1971, I said: One of the
duties of The Maryheart Crusaders is to straighten out many
of the rumors and misunderstandings which have been making the rounds concerning our beliefs and teachings. Mary and

devotion to her have been included in these wild rumors. So many Catholics are being told that Mary is no longer needed, or no longer important.

I am sure that you have all heard how the Holy Mother of God has been downgraded by those who attempt to cast her aside.

You may wonder how is this possible! How could anyone presume that he or she has a right to speak against the great Mother of God!

The answer can only be that they see merely her human nature. They judge her as they judge other humans. They compare her to God and say: "He is God, she is but a created creature of God!" They add: "Do we need such a plain, human being to lead us to the Creator?" and they wrongly answer themselves with a loud: "No!"

Of course, Mary was only a human being, a creature of the Creator. Ah! but what type of a human being was she? What was there about her that was different? But more important: What did God think of Mary!

Ah! here is the secret of understanding Mary See her through the eyes of God.

How do we know how God saw Mary? How can we see her through the eyes of God? The answer is simple: Salvation History. What is Salvation History? It is the story of God's plan to redeem man after his fall from the heights of His grace. Where do we find Salvation History? The answer to that question is, the Bible.

Then I went on to explain Mary's role as the Mother of God as presented to us in Holy Scripture.

When I gave such lectures, many people would cry and feel such relief about devotion to and love for Mary. They would thank me for taking away their fears and doubts.

As can be seen by what happened after Vatican Council II, it was not the Church which caused the problem, but the devil's plan to cast Mary aside. It was what my Lady had foreseen when on January 26, 1945, I had been told: "Cast me not out of the world for such shall so anger your Creator's Heart that you shall pay with minds of fear and terror and an endless night of death."

However on May 7, 1946, God the Father told me that the message of January 26, 1945 will not come about because I so willingly accepted The Devil's Challenge: "Dear Child of Love, now I give to My children a promise. A promise that means great happiness for them. The message your Lady gave you on January 26, 1945, will not come about because you so willingly took upon yourself the task of fighting the devil and suffering.

"Wars will come and go throughout the centuries, but the world will not be destroyed for you will vanish much sin from the earth. But leave the message there for all to see what you stopped.

"If you had refused The Devil's Challenge then no other Child of Love could I have had. But you accepted so that the world will not suffer what Mary said it would. For you shall cause thousands to return to Mary's heart never to leave. And Mary's heart will be planted deep in the hearts of my children never to be blotted out by any force or power.

"The Mother of My Son will not be cast out of the world because you will bring her to the world in such a wondrous way that hearts and souls will turn to her with undying love and devotion."

Then on July 7, 1960 Our Lady said to me: "My Hour of Glory has arrived . . . my children shall flock around me in a most miraculous way . . . they will love me as I have never been loved before."

Now, as I write this chapter, I am seeing something which I never saw before mainly because the messages were in different note books filed only according to dates. Now, as I place in this chapter the messages according to subject matter, a most startling picture emerges.

In 1946 when I recorded the message from God the Father, I thought that my Devil's Challenge, as mentioned by Him stopped only the great punishment from Heaven. However, embedded in that message is a more profound prediction which

I never saw before writing this chapter. God the Father had also said to me: "The Mother of My Son will not be cast out of the world." Why? "Because you will bring her to the world in such a way that hearts and souls will turn to her with undying love and devotion."

In such words, there can be seen the union of my Devil's Challenge, my work for God, my Lady's shrine and how she was not cast aside when strong forces fought against her in order to do just that—to cast her aside.

The connecting elements between the events concerning Mary being cast aside are very plain to see. They are as follows: On January 26, 1945, Our Lady mentioned about the possibility of her being cast aside. On April 5, 1946 I was told about The Devil's Challenge, and I accepted it. On May 7, 1946, God the Father told me that Mary would not be cast aside because I accepted my Devil's Challenge, also because I would bring Mary to the world in such a wondrous way that hearts and souls will turn to her with undying love and devotion. On October 10, 1946, Our Lady told me about the shrine to her Immaculate Heart that she wanted in Meriden. On July 7, 1960, *before* the attempts were made to cast her aside, she said to me: "My Hour of Glory has arrived . . . My children shall say their Rosaries and they shall confess their sins, they will do penance for their sins, but most of all, they will love me as I have never been loved before."

By connecting all the facts, it is very obvious that the devil not only challenged God, which brought forth my Devil's Challenge, but he also challenged Our Lady. The devil, no doubt, said to Mary: "I will make your children cast you aside." On January 26, 1945, I was told about that challenge.

On April 5, 1946, I said yes to my challenge. On May 7, 1946, I was told that Mary would not be cast aside. Then I made known (as part of my job for God) my Lady's shrine And on July 7, 1960, my Lady gave her answer to the challenge made by the devil: "My Hour of Glory has arrived . . . My children will love me as I have never been loved before." And all this happened before there was the slightest hint that there would be attempts made to actually cast Mary aside. All the messages I have mentioned, thusly can be seen as predictions which did come true.

It was predicted that there would be attempts made to cast Mary aside. It was predicted that such would not happen. My Lady predicted that her children will love her as she had never been loved before. All of these predictions came true. And when my Lady stood upon the rock and said: "My Immaculate Heart has triumphed," this became part of her triumph. Our Lady was not cast aside and her children will love her as she had never been loved before. She knew that in 1948 and 1960.

This also becomes part of my triumph. I could have been caught up within the forces that wanted Mary to be cast aside. I could have refused The Devil's Challenge. I could have refused to make my Lady's shrine known. I could have refused to believe all I was told. But I did not refuse. I accepted and did God's holy will for me; so Mary's triumph is mine and my triumph is hers (as she told me on September 7, 1982): "But my dearest child, you are the one who accepted and won The Devil's Challenge. That becomes part of my triumph. Your triumph is mine and mine is yours. We are one."

— 4 —

FALSE VISIONS AND THEIR PREDICTIONS OF DEATH, DOOM AND DESTRUCTION MY LADY'S ANSWER HER TRIUMPH

Ever since I made my Lady known in 1960, there has arisen an untold number of "visions" vying with each other as to how and when our world will be destroyed. Whole books have been written concerning this subject and the writers have a "field day" explaining in gross details what Our Lady "said" here or there all pointing to the same conclusion: that this earth is condemned to a fate worse than the Biblical flood.

Such "visions" and "visionaries" greatly upset me not only because they threw numerous people into a state of panic and fear, but also because they pictured Our loving Mother Mary as one filled with vindictive anger ready to let fall upon poor, suffering humanity her wrath because of the sins within this humanity.

As the words of such visions spread far and near, they began to affect not only my Lady's messages, but my work for God, as well. While I was working day and night to straighten out rumors about Our lady brought about by the aftermaths of the turmoil following Vatican Council II, I also had to contend with the friends I knew who were caught up in these false visions. More than one of my Crusaders who knew about my Lady (most did not know) would leave me to go off to promote the death, doom and destruction focused upon by these "visions." I sadly watched several of my friends turn their backs on me and my Lady preferring to get involved in the false "visions" and these messages. One reason this happened was because I would not promote my visions and they wanted to become part of the excitement of spreading the visions which were being promoted by the false visionaries and their followers.

585

Not only did I have to see their involvement, but I often had to see a whole change in their personalities. They had been filled with joy when they heard about my Lady, but when they became consumed with the death-doom-destruction part of false visions, their joy would vanish as they agreed that Our Lady had to destroy the world because of all its evil, sin and corruption. All these friends, as I said many who left me, made sure that I heard the latest news from this vision or that one.

Sometimes even priests or nuns who knew about my Lady would scream and yell at me that "mystics" all over the world were talking about death, doom and destruction, why did I say that Our Lady spoke about peace, joy and happiness? One such nun yelled at me just before I gave my lecture at a church hall and so upset me that I could hardly talk.

At my Crusaders' meetings, I made it a point never to speak for or against any visions, my own included. Many people wanted me and my organization to become a promotion center for the "vision of the month," but I always refused. I said they could believe what they wanted to, but I had my own work to do for God and promoting visions (my own included) was not one of them.

Often after my lecture, when we were ready to leave, I would find all sorts of flyers on my book table put there by the promoters of false visions.

These flyers and booklets had been left so that the ones who came to the meeting would see them. I would gather them up and throw them away, never knowing who had placed them among my books and the booklets I gave out so that people could learn more about their Catholic faith.

Other times someone wanted me to get on a stage and speak about the false visions to hundreds of people. Of course, I refused to do that. I would not even do that to speak about my Lady.

All this confusion about visions was, without a doubt, part of my Devil's Challenge. It appeared to me that he created such a situation to not only hide my Lady but to make sure that her messages of peace, joy and happiness would never be accepted.

This whole situation became for me a trap to have me give up my Lady, her shrine and her messages. The pressure put upon me to not only promote such false visions, but to change my Lady's story *was enormous*. This pressure was always there throughout the years when I held meetings and gave lectures. Many of my dearest friends wanted me to agree with the "visions" of death, doom and destruction, but I would not. I knew what my Lady had told me and I was not going to change her story or her words. These friends would rush to see me, enter my home and immediately talk about their favorite "vision." They expected me to be just as excited about the Virgin's latest "message" as they were. They expected me to gleefully ask: "What else did she say?" But I was not excited nor did I ask such a question. Instead I would listen in silence, not willing to hurt their feelings, but crying because they did not care how much they hurt me. Sometimes at a meeting, everyone would be talking about the latest "message" from Our Lady before and even after my lecture. At times I wanted to give up, but I did not.

Other friends wanted me to join forces with the promotion centers which put out tons of literature, videos, magazines, etc. about visions of death, doom and destruction. I would answer: "They can do what they want. I must do my work for God which is not to promote visions but to teach adults more about their Catholic faith."

It can be well imagined what would have happened if I had fallen into this trap which the devil had set for me; and I knew that the trap was there. If the devil had won this battle and if I did join forces with the promoters of the visions of death, doom and destruction, if I did change my Lady's story, I would not be able to write this book about my Lady's triumph; because, if I had fallen into that trap the entire story of my Lady would have been changed. Her words would have been changed and her shrine would no longer be the shrine of love which she and God created.

The fact that I did not fall into this trap set by the devil is part of my Lady's triumph and mine. She and I worked together to bring forth messages of peace, joy and happiness, not messages of death, doom and destruction.

This battle between the devil and myself was a never-ending suffering for me. It was always there as new "visions" replaced the ones which faded away. Each new "vision" would attract the same followers many of whom became "vision chasers" running from one site of an "apparition" to another. I was amazed to find so many of the people I knew, who had very little income, suddenly find the funds to make a trip halfway around the world. It did not make sense to me; but as I was told once: "That is where Our Lady is alive." At a shrine, such as Fatima, they would say when I suggested they go there: "Our Lady is dead there. I am going where there is all that excitement." More than one person handed me a Rosary or a medal "blessed" by Our Lady at her new "home." I could not refuse the gift, but I would not believe Our Lady blessed it.

I did not blame the people who went running after and who promoted all these "visions" and "messages." They were searching for their own spiritual food and being at a place or talking about Mary in such a way seemed to satisfy some kind of a spiritual hunger in their hearts and souls. I would just be amazed when these people accepted any and everything which was said to be spoken by Our Lady. They seemed to have lost the ability to stop and think about the situation they were in. They didn't care if the bishop condemned the vision, all they cared about was that Our Lady said this or that.

There had to be a start to all this nonsense and there was. The outbreak started in the year 1960 almost as soon as my Lady told me to make her known. That was, no doubt, planned by the devil to contradict my Lady's messages of love, hope, peace and joy and to set the trap which I could have fallen into.

The year 1960 was anxiously awaited by Catholics all over the world. This was the year when the famous Fatima third secret would be revealed; and most everyone expected a message of *death, doom and destruction!* As the years went by, 1960 became known as "Doomsyear." I remember seeing a big poster on the door in my church in the hallway declaring that 1960 was "Doomsyear." I would look at that poster and say: "That can't be true. My Lady said the destruction would not take place."

This message (in spite of what has been written about this third secret) was never revealed. That not only disappointed millions of people, but it also lit a fire which even today is still burning.

Most of these millions of people expected the third secret to tell of just punishments for a sinful world filled with evil, corrupt people. To them, there was no other way for God or Our Lady to act. When the letter was not revealed, the next best thing happened. The people, who waited so long for the contents of the secret, found just what they had expected to find in the letter in the many false visions of death, doom and destruction.

The main problem with all the enthusiasts who embraced the messages of death, doom and destruction was they firmly believed that the only thing God or Our Lady can do about sinners is to destroy them and their world so that sin, evil and corruption will no longer exist. That method, of course, means that the world will no longer exist, but they don't think about such a thing. They only believe that when all evil, sin and corruption are destroyed, a new world will emerge filled with righteous, holy people.

Listen to these words from a book called "The Thunder of Justice" by Ted and Maureen Flynn (Published in 1993 page 299): "The cries of the prophets are unanimous in conveying the gravity of Our Lady's messages . . . The recent messages coming to us from all over the world say that the time of justice is at hand . . . The Blessed Mother . . . is preparing us and providing us with the information necessary to endure the chastisement ahead."

On pages 334-355, the authors list a variety of the messages of doom, death and destruction received since 1961.

Here are a few samples: (page 338) "Our Blessed Lady . . . warned the cup of Divine Justice was filling. . . ."

(page 339) "One visionary stated that the warning would be a thousand times worse than earthquakes . . ." "In order that the world might know His anger, the Heavenly Father is preparing to inflict a great chastisement on all mankind."

(page 340) "Our Blessed Mother . . . (said) that punishment is inevitable . . ." Our Blessed Mother said "There is so much sorrow in my heart, for many natural catastrophies and others created by man are coming."

(page 341) "Great catastrophies are coming upon humanity." This was said in 1988-1990. Also, "A chastisement worse than the flood is about to come upon this poor and perverted humanity." Also, "You are living the painful times of the chastisement. You are living the dark hour of the victory of my Adversary, who is the Prince of the Night."

This book goes on to mention "messages" after "messages" all filled with the threats of death, doom and destruction; such as (page 343) "Nothing will grow. The whole world will be hungry . . . San Francisco will be opened up and be swallowed."

(page 344) "That will be the end of San Francisco and New York." "The Antichrist is going to arise . . ."

Even the Church is not to be spared: (page 345) . . . the Church will start to crumble . . ."

(page 351) "The wicked will be crushed and eliminated . . ." ". . . the people given to evil will perish so that only one fourth of mankind will survive."

(page 353) "The sins of man are so black that they will poison everything upon the earth . . . The bodies of the wicked and of the righteous will cover the face of the earth . . . All plant-life will be destroyed as well as three-fourths of the human race."

By the time one gets through reading all these dire predictions from "Our Lady," one's stomach is "turning over" and fear shakes the whole body.

Of course, there are hints of hope among all these warnings

of what is to come; however, as the authors say on page 355, "Our Lady and Jesus have promised that those who do as the Blessed Virgin has asked have nothing to fear."

But what about the multitude who will not do what Our Lady asked, repent, be converted, pray? Or who do not even know what she asked?

Knowing human nature, we can be sure that a goodly number of "sinners" will never even believe these words of "Our Lady" let alone pray and repent.

Besides, we were told (page 353), "The bodies of the wicked and the righteous will cover the face of the earth."

So, the righteous, who do believe or are converted, are counted among the sinners and will be as destroyed as well as the wicked.

Let me analyze some of the above statements to find out just where these two authors are coming from.

First of all, I get a strong sense that they found great enjoyment in what they wrote. That being the case, I can only assume that they count themselves among the few who will, in some way, escape this great chastisement.

They remind me of a "saint" I was introduced to years ago. He had quite a following so I was asked to meet him and hear him speak.

As soon as he spoke, I knew he was a "Prophet of Doom." He described in great details about a terrible disaster just about ready to fall upon mankind, especially the United States. (That was in the early '60s.)

He said: ". . . and, I am telling you, there will be no work. People will starve . . . Everyone, all of you sitting here, will suffer beyond human imagination. Everyone will suffer— except me! I have been told that I will be spared. Isn't that wonderful?"

Well, I, for one, was not about ready to stand up and applaud; and I left not accepting the followers' claims that he was a living saint. I didn't mind thinking that I would suffer, but I thought that he should share our misery—at least a little of it.

To go back to the prophecies in "The Thunder of Justice":

one can see, in the few quotes I copied, several inconsisten-
cies or contradictions which obviously the authors cared little
about.

First of all, they said (page 353) "that three-fourths of the
human race would be destroyed," meaning that one-fourth
would survive.

At the same time, we are told that "all plant-life will be
destroyed." That does not make sense. Not even one-fourth of
the human race could survive if all plant-life is destroyed.

We are also told (page 353) "The sins of mankind will poison everything upon the earth . . ."

If "everything upon the earth" is poisoned, how could anyone survive?

Also, if "the wicked and the righteous are killed" (page 353),
and their bodies will "cover the face of the earth," what will
the one-fourth who survive do with all these billions of bodies: and if God is showing His wrath against sinners why would
He also destroy the righteous ones?

Also, when one reads about this "chastisement" which will
be "worse than the flood" (page 341), one wonders about the
promise made to Noah, after the flood: "(God said) . . . I will
establish My covenant with you . . . there shall not be another
flood to devastate the earth" (*Gen.* 9:11). What is it that is
"worse than the flood" which destroyed all of mankind except
Noah and his family?

However, the one thing which stands out very vividly, in
sharp contrast to our Church's teaching about Mary, is when
she is supposed to have said: (page 341.) "You are living the
dark hours of the victory of my Adversary, who is the Prince
of the Night."

When Adam and Eve were cast out of the Garden of Eden,
God said to the tempter: "I will put enmity between you and
the woman and between your offspring and hers" (*Gen.* 3:15).
The Church teaches that this passage can be understood as the
first promise of a Redeemer for fallen mankind. The woman's
offspring then is Jesus Christ.

When Mary is supposed to have said, on page 341, ". . .

the victory of my Adversary (Satan)," she is in reality admitting that the devil has more power than she or Christ; and he now is the victorious one pushing aside Mary and even Christ.

Would Mary appear to someone and declare that Satan has more power than she? Would she merely step aside and allow the devil to be the victor? The answer, of course, is no; and yet the authors of the book "The Thunder of Justice" are attempting to say that the devil is more powerful than Mary. That is nonsense.

As for the Church "crumbling" and falling apart (page 345)—an idea which the authors expand on the same page: ". . . for the Church is hurtling to nothing"—did not Christ say to Peter: ". . . you are Rock and on this Rock I will build My Church and the pains of death shall not prevail against it" (*Matt.* 16:18)?

The word prevail means triumph. The jaws of death, Satan and all his evil powers, shall not triumph.

Yet, for the authors to say, as they did on page 341, "the victory of my Adversary," they are trying to tell us that the Holy Mother of God proclaims that the Adversary, the devil has triumphed not only over all of humanity, but the Church as well.

The unfortunate thing about all these messages of doom, death and destruction is that they are so widespread and affect millions of people.

The book "The Thunder of Justice" was not the first one I read about these predictions of death, doom and destruction.

I have read all that was said in that book before; but I will admit that this book is able to frighten people as no other I had read. After reading the pages from 299-356, the reader's hair could either turn white from fright or "stand up straight."

It is very clear that is exactly what the authors intended. They surely showed no love for all of us "three-fourths of humanity" which is about to be destroyed or for the Church which is "hurtling to nothing."

It is also clear that the writers of such books (and numerous articles as well) have a very poor understanding of God and Our Lady.

They seem to relish the fact that they present a very cruel God and a heartless Madonna devoid of any love or compassion for poor suffering humanity or sinners.

Yes, the world perhaps deserved a great chastisement, but love becomes a bright light upon dark paths and love can save souls.

The whole world does not have to be destroyed because sinners walk the earth because each unrepentant sinner has his own eternal punishment to look forward to.

And just who are these sinners? They may be doing evil acts, but they are still God's beloved children whom His grace, if used, can turn the greatest sinner into a great saint.

Could Our Lady or the ones who write about these dire predictions judge sinners to the extent that three quarters of mankind has to be destroyed because such sinners wander the earth? If they do, they forget about these words from Our Lord: "If you want to avoid judgment, stop passing judgment. Your verdict on others will be the verdict passed on you. The measure with which you measure will be used to measure you. Why look at the speck in your brother's eyes when you miss the plank in your own" (*Matt.* 7:1-3).

If the whole world is to be destroyed because of sin and sinners, then each person has to accept the responsibility, for we all are sinners. We, ourselves, contributed to the fall of a fallen world; and there is no hand extended to help it rise if writers and "visionaries" and "mystics" constantly throw out threats of punishments, doom, destruction and chastisements. I, for one, believe that the love found in the Hearts of Jesus and Mary will raise a fallen world into the light of that love.

Everyone knows that sin and sinners exist, but the ones who like to condemn sinners and their world to destruction forget that Christ came to save sinners and their world, not to destroy them.

However, in spite of all the things that are wrong with such predictions, they do, in one way, serve a purpose.

If one were to fully comprehend the horror of sin (even little sins) and see sin as an insult to the love and goodness of

God, then one could say that sinners deserve all the punishment demanded by a just God.

What I find interesting about the visions of death, doom and destruction, is that even if some (most) are false they, in some way, explain what could have happened when God brings forth His rightful justice

However, one thing that is wrong with such thinking is that it is very one-sided. To see only the justice and anger of God is to see only one side of God or half of God.

When one explains who this God is, a person has to say He is a just God but they also have to say He is a God of mercy and love.

God could never be understood until one sees His love and mercy as well as His infinite justice.

Even though God, exploded with wrath and justice during the times of the Old Testament, His mercy and love for His children showed through.

The same God who told Abraham to slay his beloved son, Isaac, also sent a messenger to the grieving father who said: "Do not lay your hand on the boy . . . Do not do the least thing to him . . ." (*Gen.* 22:9-12).

Souls filled with the corruption of sin and evil, are deserving of God's anger and punishment; but still God does not forget that He sent His only Son to redeem such sinners because of His love and mercy.

Christ taught us to love our enemies, would He do less than that? He said, when accused of eating with tax collectors, "People who are in good health, do not need a doctor, sick people do. Go and learn the meaning of the words: "It is mercy I desire and not sacrifice: I have come to call, not the self-righteous, but sinners" (*Matt.* 9:11-13).

Would the holy Mother of God start appearing to people all over the world telling them that because there is evil and sin on earth, the whole world has to be destroyed?

I will add, is not this "poor and perverted humanity" worth saving? I think so, so do God and Our Lady who are both filled with love for poor, fallen humanity.

In one of these messages of death, doom and destruction Our Lady is quoted as saying: "Our Blessed Mother (said) . . . that punishment is inevitable . . ." Could this be the same, gentle, compassionate Mother who said to me on January 26, 1945: "My children of the world I stand before the throne of God to defend the children of the fallen world, and because of His great love for me, He will allow my heart to bring back the peace that is not in the world today."

She did mention that there could be a terrible destruction, but added: "I tell you this because my Father and your Father's love is so great that He will give you a way to prevent the destruction of the world *before* the Last Day" (January 26, 1945).

These are words of triumph, not defeat. Such words will rise loud and clear above the incident clamor of all the words from false visions about death, doom and destruction; and these words of love become another triumph of The Golden Lady of Happiness. If false visionaries declare that this great chastisement is on its way, then my beloved Lady stands in triumph and says it is not: "The world will not be destroyed before the Last Day by any force or power of man or by any force or power of God because now my heart will be planted deep within the hearts of my children. No force or power shall take my heart away from my children." (First promise)

Ever since my Lady said that to me in 1948, I have never stopped believing it. Also, I have never stopped believing that the world was mine and I would not let it fall to its own destruction, as these words show which I wrote on August 24, 1959: "Everyone says that 1960 is "doomsyear." Everyone—even my mother and my brother—are so filled with fear that the end is coming; but I have never had this fear because I firmly believe that our Golden Lady of Happiness will one day bring peace and happiness to the whole world. I believe that the world is only beginning to become a great, peaceful place and I also believe that our Catholic Religion is only beginning to become the religion of the whole world. So I firmly believe in all the peace and in all the goodness that will come to this earth—in spite of all the atomic weapons of destruction and in spite of people like the communists. Hitler tried to destroy the world and God. He did not succeed. Nor will anyone else because the world is mine and so I give it to God's Heart. I will not let it be destroyed. I will protect and give it great peace, joy and happiness.

In November of 1998, I began to study the words of the "visions" which appear to be false; which speak so much of death, doom and destruction. I found it very interesting to note that none of the visions I studied ever had Our Lady saying "My Immaculate Heart has triumphed."

As I was thinking of these facts, suddenly my Lady said to me: "The reason you have not seen or heard in false visions that my Immaculate Heart has triumphed, is that God would not allow the devil to utter such words. They were reserved for you alone. Only you, child of Love, have been given the grace to know the Triumph of The Immaculate Heart of Mary and to participate in my triumph."

THE GENTLE GOD OF LOVE AND MARY'S TRIUMPH

One of my favorite Biblical stories is told about an Old Testament prophet named Elijah (about 865 to 850 B.C.).

Elijah had a wonderful encounter with God one day outside his cave where he had found shelter. He was told: "Go outside and stand on the mountain and the Lord will be passing by." He went and waited.

First there came a strong and great wind crushing rocks—but the Lord was not in the wind. Then, after the wind there was an earthquake—but the Lord was not in the earthquake. After the earthquake, there was fire—but the Lord was not in the fire.

Then there was a tiny whispering sound. When he heard that, Elijah knew he had found the Lord (*I Kings* 19:11-13). The gentle voice was the voice of the Lord.

I have always thought of God as this "gentle voice." Even as a teenager, I did not like to hear anyone say that God is hard, cruel, uncaring and even heartless.

One of the first articles I ever wrote, I called: "God Can Laugh"; and I went on to explain how this God Whom "everyone" thought of as mean was in reality a God Who could laugh and become very kind and caring.

I remember going into a church and seeing a huge mosaic of a stern, almost angry Christ sitting in judgment. I looked at the picture and said: "Christ is not like that."

Yet, that is the way God and His gentle Mother are presented to their children by all the visionaries and promoters of the false visions of death, doom and destruction. I often wondered when I heard all these "messages" why the promoters are so angry.

Surely, they could only envision God as an angry tyrant

598

ready to unleash His powers of destruction because they, themselves, had some kind of a grudge against mankind. Why were all those self-proclaimed "righteous" people so eager to see the rest of humanity destroyed because of sin and corruption?

This "rest of humanity" usually did not include themselves. Even in sects and cults, their cruel, heartless "God" is ready—any moment now—to destroy all of mankind: except themselves (their Armageddon).

Such a God is not the one Christ told us about. When asked how to pray to God, Christ replied: "Our Father in heaven . . . give us today our daily bread" (*Matt.* 6:9:11).

Christ presents to us God as a loving Father caring for our daily needs: "What father among you would hand the son a snake when he asks for a fish?" (*Luke* 11:11).

After His resurrection, Christ said to Mary Magdalene: "I am going to My Father and your Father, to My God and your God" (*John* 20:17).

Seeing God as a gentle, loving Father is not what the Prophets of Doom want us to visualize.

Ah yes, there is sin and corruption in the world; and no doubt, the world does deserve the wrath of God. But hidden among all the evildoers, there are a multitude of human beings trying their best to carry on among the pitfalls of daily life filled with faith and goodness.

When Christ taught us to love our enemies, He said: "But I say to you, love your enemies . . . that you may be children of your heavenly Father for He makes His sun rise on the bad and the good, and causes rain to fall on the just and the unjust" (*Matt.* 5:43-45).

Who is there who has the right to tell God that he has to destroy the world because there are upon it sinners?

And who are the sinners? Could not the sinners of today become the saints of tomorrow if given a chance to repent?

If God allows the sinners to live and the corrupt world to exist is that the actions of a God seeking vengeance?

No. It is, instead, the gentle touch of a God filled with infinite love for His straying sheep; giving His children opportunity after opportunity for His saving grace to transform hearts and souls.

And it was this gentle God of Love who prepared the pathway upon which walked The Golden Lady or Happiness. Here is the Mother of that God of Love who comes forth as a brilliant ray of sunshine shining into a troubled, dark world.

If one can remember, at LaSalette (1846) Our Lady appeared to the two children and spoke about the harvest being spoiled and about the great famine which was to come. Yet, as she spoke her eyes were filled with tears. Her voice remained tender, gentle and sweet.

That is not the Madonna that the false visionaries speak about. They rather promote a Madonna who looks down from her heavenly throne with eyes and a heart filled with hate and vengeance waiting only to see all the evil-doers punished, even destroyed. They want the world to see the Mother of God who has lost the battle with the devil. He has won, they are saying, by filling the earth with so much sin and corruption that the only thing God can do is to destroy the world.

However, that is far from the truth. My Lady stands upon her rock in Meriden in pure triumph as she says: "My Immaculate Heart has triumphed. I will now show the devil that I am the powerful one. Tell my children that I say to them, my power is greater than the strongest armies and greater than the strongest hate. The world will know that there is hope—great hope—for peace, joy and happiness because I have come to bring peace, joy and happiness to mankind" (July 7, 1960).

She added: "The world has cried, now I will dry its tears because now I can show my power and my glory."

On July 12, 1960 she said to me: "Tell my children to hide behind my golden garments and there they shall find their protection. The devil can only advance so far. I have come now to force him to retreat. I have come as the loving Mother who protects her frightened children. Fear not, little ones, my hour of glory is at hand and when I win, my children will also win. I stand upon the world, upon the moon and upon the devil to show all men that my power is the greatest. Men shall see my power . . . I am the Mother who desires to protect her children . . . I have held my Son's hand and I have asked Him if I could protect my children. He has given me this power. As The Golden Lady of Happiness, I am the Queen of Love and Peace and I am the Mother who protects her beloved children."

Such words are words of triumph and they become another triumph of the Immaculate Heart of Mary.

— 6 —

MY LADY'S TRIUMPH: THE CONVERSION OF RUSSIA ENSLAVED PEOPLE WILL BECOME FREE

By the end of 1989, the world saw the most extraordinary event of the Twentieth Century; the downfall of Russia. Before one can fully appreciate this world-shaking occurrence, one would have to know a bit about the history of Russia before and then after World War II. During that period of time, Russia became a world power equal in strength to the United States with vast armies and weapons of war. With these armies and power, Russia was out to capture the world. She easily captured and enslaved millions of people in the countries surrounding her. Nation after nation fell into her clutches and nation after nation died agonizing, slow, painful deaths as Russian masters took control. Being an ally with countries which fought against Germany, Russia was given authority, as soon as Germany was defeated, to take control of half of that country. Soon, not only was there the horrendous Berlin Wall which divided the country, but nations surrounding Russia and Germany were also claimed by Russia as her own. The Red flag flew over half the world as the mighty Russia swallowed up countries which could not defend themselves. Fear ran through the hearts of the free nations as they were forced to watch the advancements of this Red Giant. Russia, being an atheist country destroyed in her own country and the ones she conquered not only freedom for the people, but religion as well.

What happened was predicted by Our Lady of Fatima when she said to the children on July 13, 1917: "If my requests are granted, Russia will be converted and there will be peace in the world. If they are not, Russia will spread its errors throughout the world, provoking wars and persecutions against the Church. Many good people will be martyred, the Holy Father

602

will have much to suffer; many nations will be annihilated." That is exactly what happened. But then came the words of hope (words which I have often repeated): "In the end my Immaculate Heart will triumph."

When my Lady first told me, in 1948, that her Immaculate Heart has triumphed, these words became a prediction of future events concerning Russia. She could see her triumph over Russia in 1917 when she said to the three children: "In the end my Immaculate Heart will triumph" and when she said to me in 1948: "My Immaculate Heart has triumphed."

When my Lady first spoke these words to me in 1948, Russia was becoming the most feared nation on earth.I remember reading articles in 1959 about this fear of Russia.

On July 20, 1959, I wrote: Yesterday I read a terrible article about the Reds and our country. The article said that a priest wrote it; but I can't be sure about that. The man who did write it claimed that within ten to fifteen years, our beloved, free country would be taken over by Russia without any Atomic War because there will be so many communists in the high offices of this country that they will just turn our country over to the Reds. The article said that the Reds would not even have to fight, they would just take the whole United States right from under our noses. The article said that our country is doomed and we are all asleep and so we will just let the whole United States slip into the hands of the Reds.

I began to worry so much about the facts which the article said were absolute truth, that I could not fall asleep. I love my free country and I want it to stay free. Each night I pray to the Sacred Heart of Jesus asking Jesus to place His divine mantle of love around our country and protect us from our enemies.

When my Lady told me in 1948 that her Immaculate Heart has triumphed, I knew nothing about what she had said to the three children in Fatima concerning Russia. I was to learn about Fatima only throughout the years. Yet, I myself, had been told about Russia even when I did not know what Our Lady had told the children at Fatima.

On August 15, 1946, even before my Lady appeared to me in 1948 saying her heart has triumphed, I was told by Mary: ". . . For your words and your examples and your love will become so implanted on the earth that you alone will save millions of souls from eternal damnation, and your influence will be felt throughout the world so greatly that nations will become peaceful and great powers will become meek and humble."

On July 7, 1960, I was told: ". . . Much remains to be done before true peace comes to this world, but I can now promise this peace. I also say that many, many hearts which *have been closed to God's love will repent and enslaved people will become free.*"

Without a doubt, my Lady's triumph, the triumph predicted by Our Lady of Fatima, came about by the freeing of enslaved people and nations. She predicted this years before the downfall of Russia began in 1989. This started her triumph over Russia when the Russian Empire began to fall apart.

My Lady's triumph concerning the downfall of the Russian Empire continued as more and more enslaved people became free.

In the "Fatima Family Messenger," dated October-December 1993, Father R. J. Fox wrote on page 2:

I had little idea what was ahead when the "news" which I was told was "dynamite"—was given to me in Fatima in July 1989. At the same time I was asked, "Would you share it through the Fatima Family Messenger as Sister Lucia now wants the word out to the world?"

Within months the world was changing dramatically and fundamentally. During those same months, as nations threw off communism peacefully, without any need for the atomic bombs the USA had stockpiled and word got out of what the Messenger had reported from Sr. Lucia, I was interviewed by Time magazine.

The Wall Street Journal, after talking to me, gave the interview front-page coverage concerning the Fatima prophecies and the words of Sister Lucia. All was reported.

By December 30, 1991 *Time* featured a picture of Mary on its cover together with a feature story for that issue telling of the role of Mary in a changing world. By February 24, 1992 Time carried extensive recognition of papal influence in the demise of communism, indicating a growing awareness of Papal-Marian roles in the breakup of the communist empire. I was interviewed early on by the senior religious editor of the Associated Press. (Cornell, AP religious editor, recently died.) I spoke to him in detail about the fulfillment of the promises of Our Lady happening. He wrote it up. Even with his seniority, the AP refused to carry his story, much to his unhappiness.

Anyone acquainted with the liturgical calendar of the Catholic Church who followed world events could not help but notice that Our Lady was not only keeping her promises made at Fatima but doing so on her feast days. By December 25, 1991, the Soviet red flag with the hammer and sickle of the Soviet Union was lowered for the last time over the Kremlin in Moscow. President Mikhail Gorbachev, successor to former dictators of the Soviet Union, announced his resignation and the end of the Soviet Union. One of his last acts was to send a letter to Pope John Paul II.

When the communist nations were freeing themselves from the tight grip of their leaders, the world watched and held its breath. Nothing like that, on so huge a scale had ever happened before in world history; especially since the war ended in 1944 and the "Cold War" began.

Everyone was stunned as they watched the daily events. I watched, filled with joy, knowing that all was my Lady's Triumph. I knew what was happening if none of the world leaders knew.

Russia watched also and as the events unfolded in 1989-1990, she began to walk the road to freedom herself from the communist grip. She began to set in motion tremendous changes and reforms of her own; as unsettling events started in her own country.

The daily headlines told the story concerning the triumph over the forces and power of communism:

> 10/8/89:   Thousands of Soviets March . . . against Communism.
> 11/17/89:   Freedom! Freedom! George Bush and Mikhail Gorbachev hold their first summit against a backdrop of upheaval in Europe.
> 10/27/89: Soviets to cut nuke forces in Baltic Sea.
> 10/30/89: Kremlin "frees" Hungary, East Germany.
> 1/4/90: Red's lock on power now at risk in USSR.
> 2/1/90: Soviet Communists Cave In!

And "Cave In" is exactly what happened. One by one nations which the communists had enslaved began to free themselves from Russia's grip.

Within Russia, herself, changes began to be made which were unthinkable only a year before.

On 2/8/90, the headlines read: "Soviet Reds Yield Power Monopoly. Party's dictatorship to end after 7 decades" (that is 70 years).

Then on April 3, 1965 (notes dated 4/8/65) when I still did not know all that Our Lady had told the children at Fatima about Russia, I was told: "There shall be, in Russia, a great spiritual awakening to destroy much of atheism. There will be a revolt, not against the government, but against atheism. The spiritual revolt will do much towards peace." (I told several of my friends this message and they signed statements saying that I did tell them at that time.)

This spiritual awakening came, but not until after 1989. That date began my Lady's triumph over Russia.

There was more wonderful news printed in large type in newspapers all over the world:

> 6/20/88: Giddy days for the Russian Church. Historic events signal growing respectability for long persecuted Christians. Moscow kitchen workers, soldiers and maids waited in long lines at hotels to snap up costly and usually unavailable religious books, medals and icon reproductions.

> 2/1/89: Gorbachev: We Need Religion.
> 2/1/89: As prayers are beard in the Soviet Union, Gorbachev meets John Paul II.
> 12/4/89: In the Ukraine, Catholics want their religion back.
> 12/2/89: Soviet Vows Religious Freedom.
> 12/24/89: Eastern Europe, Millions of Catholics are enjoying new religious freedom.

> 9/24/90: Kremlin Cathedral holds historic full service. . . the first full service allowed in more than 70 years in Russia's most important cathedral. Since 1918, it has been a Museum and closed to ordinary worship. 10/2/90: Soviet citizens guaranteed full freedom to worship . . . after 72 years of atheistic communism.
> 10/14/90: Crowd hears first church service since 1917 in Moscow's St. Basil Cathedral.
> 12/2/90: A Seminary opens. First fruits of the

Soviet Union's religious freedom. 12/15/90: Festive public Christmas returns to the Soviet Union.

9/4/91: Old-time Religion is back. The tables finally have turned. Churches are opening. It's the Communist Party whose property is being seized and padlocked. Millions of Bibles are rolling off presses that once churned out anti-religious tracts and other dogma. The re-emergence of religion as an open part of Soviet society started with . . . the demise of the Communist Party.

One of the best ways I can explain what happened is to quote the following article which was written in "Fatima Family Messenger" 1994.

ABOUT RELIGIOUS UPRISING IN RUSSIA

THIS IS PART OF
MY LADY'S TRIUMPH

"FATIMA FAMILY MESSENGER" 1994
We still get a considerable number of letters asking the above. *Some can see nothing happening, yet at the end of 1993 the secular television and print media carried headlines: "Religious Revival is Sweeping Russia."*

David Briggs, associated press writer wrote: A religious revival unparalleled in modern history is sweeping Russia."

Twenty-two percent of the nearly 3,000 respondents, including nearly a third of Russians under 25, said they once were atheists but now believe in God, according to the study released by the National Opinion Research Center at the University of Chicago.

After seven decades in an aetheist state, three quarters of Russians expressed absolute or a great deal of confidence in the church, a confidence rating nearly twice as high as Americans report.

"Since the mass conversions of the middle ages, has there ever been such a widespread and rapid change in religion?" asks the Rev. Andrew Greeley, a University of Chicago sociologist, in a report on the findings.

And as a true triumph for my Lady, this article appeared in the paper, September 27, 1990: "Soviets make religion legal."

Surely my Lady's triumph was not only a reality, but was seen by the whole world. Russia did enslave half the world, but Our Lady predicted her victory, and she won this great battle.

THE FEAR OF NUCLEAR WAR VANISHES: "THE WORLD WILL NOT BE DESTROYED BY ANY FORCE OR POWER OF MAN."

When the "Cold War" started after World War II ended, the first atomic bomb had exploded in Japan. That entered into history what became known as the "Atomic Age." Man had developed the means to destroy himself and his world.

A fear, which was never before known, descended upon humanity. From the end of World War II in 1944-45 until 1989, our country had, as its foreign policy, one item which was first on the list of situations to handle. That one item was to be prepared for a nuclear war started by Russia.

The threat from Russia, who was slowly devouring nation after nation through the use of her armed forces, was enormous and ever-present.

Russia became the enemy of the world, and especially of my country. There was such tremendous fear in the hearts of Americans that "everything" which happened in our country which brought any kind of trouble was said to be caused by Russia.

A good example was when, in 1965, all the whole Eastern states suddenly experienced a wide-spread power black-out, the first thought in everyone's mind was that the Russians had done "something" to "put out the lights."

I remember driving to the factory where my husband worked. I had the car radio on and as I drove along, the announcer was naming whole cities and whole states which suddenly lost all power. I said to myself: "What are the Russians doing?"

It was later explained that the power lines in Niagara Falls had malfunctioned and there was a chain reaction as each relay station became overworked and gave out.

The Russians were so proud of their success in capturing nation after nation that they would have a huge parade in Red Square each year displaying new and more powerful, frightening weapons of mass destruction; all of which helped to add to the fears of other nations not yet conquered by the "Red Giant." The worst and most feared weapons were nuclear ones. The Russians continued to build them; so we had to build our own arsenals filled with atomic bombs and weapons.

By the year 1989, there were enough weapons in stock to actually blow up the whole world. Also, across half the world there had been "constructed" what was called an Iron Curtain, free nations on one side, Russia and the communists on the other. Enemies we were.

To make matters worse, Russia developed the science and technology to send the first man into space. Fear was felt throughout the free world. Now it was said, Russia could rain down upon mankind all sorts of atomic bombs and hit any spot on earth.

However, my Lady had said to me in 1948 as one of her promises: "I promise that the world will not be destroyed . . . by any force or power of man . . ."

Then, suddenly, as a sure sign of my Lady's triumph, the fear of a nuclear war began to vanish. This was the direct result of the down-fall of communism and the dismantling of the Russian-communist empire.

The first hint of this triumph began in Poland in 1989. In an article in a newspaper, dated November 17, 1989, Lech Walesa said: "The Iron Curtain is no more . . . we have fought and we have won."

In another article dated, December 4, 1989, there were these words: "The currents of reform . . . have now swept away hard-line bosses in Poland, Hungary, East Germany and even Bulgaria. The breakthrough at the Berlin Wall was the most dramatic fall."

On December 18, 1989, "Newsweek" wrote (page 22): "Designing A New Era." also "Bush told the allies that (we) should promote human rights, democracy and reform within

Eastern Countries as the best means of encouraging reconciliation among the countries of Eastern and Western Europe."

U.S. News Magazine wrote (page 18) on December 4, 1989: "A Burial For The Cold War At Sea?" This happened: "Forty-four years after Europe was carved in two. . ."

The news continued:

> 10/27/89: Soviet to Cut Nuke Forces In Baltic Sea. U.S. willing to discuss its bases.
> 11/14/89: Democrats ask defense cuts as Cold War winds down.
> 11/23/89: Bush urges end at last to Cold War.
> 11/27/89: The Russians aren't coming. With peace breaking out, Nato's defense strategies are in for a shake-up.
> 1/4/90: Red's lock on power, now at risk in U S S R. Soviet Communists are lost in East bloc with power monopoly. President Mikhail S. Gorbachev will ask Communist Party leadership to break its seven-decade hammerlock on power . . .
> 1/24/90: "Red Menace" fading fast, CIA director tells Congress.
> 2/19/90: From nuclear arms to candy and beer. Converting Soviet defense factories to consumer-goods producers . . .
> 3/26/90: Attention, S A C: The War is Over! It's time for America to over haul its nuclear policy. The end of the Cold War should mean that the United States and the Soviet Union can begin to dismantle their nuclear arsenals.

And that is exactly what happened. Enemies, no more. My Lady's triumph!

There will, of course, be conflicts and even internal wars as countries try to come to grips with their own problems; however, the huge, world-wide threat of the Communists controlling every nation on earth ended when the Soviet "Red Menace" started to fall apart in the year 1989.

NOTE

This book is the beginning of The Story of Mary's Triumph. The story continues in Volume II, with added revelations not only about my Lady's triumph, but also about my Devil's Challenge and the battles I had to save my world. As I had written, such battles became part of my Lady's triumph. How? Because they show the power of love and grace. Our Lady did not need anyone to have a role in her triumph; but what she needed was an example or proof of the power of love and grace when used to fight the devil and temptation. Such an example can be seen in my story.

MY LOVE FOR TRUTH AS
EXPRESSED IN 1958: NOTES FOUND

Numerous times as I wrote this book, I have found or "been shown" notes or articles, which my Lady wanted in this book, in a way I can only describe as "miraculous": such as, picking up note books I had not intended to look in then a page found which I was not even looking for; finding a note book or book I had forgotten I had—just in time for the chapter I was writing—etc.

The following is a prime example of what I mean:

I had a book written about a psychological and religious study of visions and private revelations. I obtained this book in 1958. I read it then, but did not really enjoy it because it was filled with medical terms that I did not understand. But I did understand that the book spoke the truth about this subject and there had been problems in the past (as today) of false mystics and visionaries throughout the history of the Church. This book did an excellent job in explaining the false from the real.

As I read this book in 1958, I underlined many sentences which I agreed with; and I wrote a couple of notes. I reread the book in 1960 and again in 1972. But then I put it away in a closet where it remained until I suddenly discovered it a few days ago. When I did, I decided to reread it for I had completely forgotten what the author (Dr. Paul Siwek) had said. Again, I was not too interested in all the medical terms, so before I finished the book, I put it away again in a file case.

Yet, as I began to read another book, there was a very strong desire deep within me to finish reading the book. I could not get that idea out of my mind; so, I got the book and started to read from where I had left off to the end of the book.

When I got to the last page (page 222), I was amazed to find a note written in pencil dated August 1958. When I read the note, I was even more amazed. I called Father Brad and

617

read this note to him. He immediately told me to put this note in my book. He said it was absolutely astonishing that I had written such words *40 years ago* expressing my love for the truth. I also found a note I had written at the same time on page 123. And the "miracle" of it all is that I found these notes now just as my book "Triumph" is being printed.

The first note I wrote about my love for the truth (Page 123):

I so love the truth.
Correct all my mistakes
for I know I made them;
but find the truth: God's holy truth.

The second note I wrote (Page 222):

This is a wondrous book. It is filled with truth; and this truth is not hidden beneath marvels that have dazzled the eyes of so many so as to blind them to the truth. Look at my case and don't see marvels and such; for they might blind you. Look for and find the truth and God's love. If these are not there, then condemn me and my work for God. For without the truth and God's love, my work could harm souls.

Appendix

The following are some examples of photocopies of my original notes. Such notes go back as far as 1944. I have all the original notes mentioned in this book

May 17, 1946

Today I said to Jesus, "I don't want any of your messages to your children, lost. I don't care about my writings but I don't want your messages to them ever to be lost." (not about) And Jesus said, "Know, my little one, that for all time your writings will be read as you wrote them. No one single word will be lost by any force or power. Your writings and my messages will be spread over the whole world, yes, even as the Bible is spread over the whole world. For all time I will preserve all you have written so that all my children for all time) will know of my child of Love. They shall read not only the messages from Heaven, but the love you wrote, in your articles and writings

11/13/45

"the convent to prove to the world your love for me. You needn't ever make your love known to anyone because I, myself, will make your love and your name known to the world.

"But, my little one, write. Write long and hard. Write my love and my mother's love and give to the world that which I want them to have. Write as only my child of Love could write."

all this took place in the church of the Blessed Sacrament West 70th St. New York City

3/27/ 1944

To continue: Mary said that Jesus chose me to do a job of teaching His children things that He wants them to know.

She told me to write down all the things that Jesus tells me to write down because they are to be used after my death.

Mary said that I have made myself fit for the job of carrying her name to humans. She told me that she wants me to teach her name to all children because she is interested in all children and she is their mother and she wants them to know that.

She said that I am "to make a light shine on dark paths so that God's children can see the light and find peace and happiness." That is what she said and I repeated it over and over to make sure that I would remember it.

(Holy
Spirit)

Book I

march 27, 1944

③

would tremble over again. (I had
tried very hard to overcome all my
faults and to stay close to my Jesus.
Even then, I suffered great torment
from the devil and his evil ones,
when I was constantly tempted to
sin against all goodness and kindness.
These early battles with the devil
and temptation were as severe as
the ones I had years later.)
  But now she said that I was
completely over that line and
that I would always be safe.
  She told me that, in spite of
that fact, that the devil will still
be after me and I will still be
tempted. She said that the devil
hates me very much and that
he'll hate my work for God more
and that I must be always on the
lookout for him. (☞ This has proven to
be more than true ☜.) (sixty? words)
  But Mary said that if ever I
am tempted, I was to come running
and hide beneath the cloak of Jesus
and He will protect me.
  (She said that the Holy Ghost
will come to me and really inflame
my heart with the love for
Jesus and her and God. And that
He will give me the Gift of words
and all knowledge that I need
to do God's will perfectly — Gift S.H.)

This
have come
very true
true

Page 18

(note (at that time) I had no writings)

3/31/44

do not know us as we desire to be known

"Your job is to go forth into the dark wilds and gather up all of God's stray bewildered children and bring them home before they die from hunger.

"There are many things which you will not have the power to understand. But we use you to reach people who will understand them.

"Your writings will be left for the world so that others can understand and follow your examples.

"You are part of God's great army. You are on earth and you shall be sent where you are most needed.

God has chosen you to make known to the dark world many things which would otherwise not be known. You have a great, hard, important job to do! You will meet opposition and hate for the devil will be strong. But slowly and surely you will win because God wants His children back.

I have told mother this because
at that time, I was very I   Page 9 (4)
ambitious to convert the
whole world and I wanted to
convert all sinners right away   3/31/1944

"Do not expect to conquer the world.
Do not expect to convert millions. But
do start the landslide that will
make people stand up and take notice.
Cause an avalanche of love,
happiness and joy and show the world
how to find their own happiness, love
and joy.

"Teach a few and a great many
will seek you out to find what you
have taught others (after my
death)

" If you die and you have only
reached one person, that person
and your writings will be enough
to start a second crusade and
to end up with many walking the
right road to God."

OTHER BOOKS
By
Louise D'Angelo

The Catholic Answer to the Jehovah's Witnesses:
A Challenge Accepted (Spanish/Edition Available)
Louise D'Angelo/Paperback/Published 1981
Our Price: $12.00 + $2.50 Postage and Handling

Come Climb the Ladder and Rejoice Vol. 1
Louise D'Angelo/Paperback/Published 1996
Our Price: $12.95 + $2.50 Postage and Handling

Come Climb the Ladder and Rejoice Vol. 2:
The Prayer Life
Louise D'Angelo/Paperback/Published 1996
Our Price: $12.95 + $2.50 Postage and Handling

Come Home . . . the Door Is Open; an Invitation to
Reconciliation
Louise D'Angelo/Paperback/Published 1991
Our Price: $12.00 + $2.50 Postage and Handling

Too Busy for God? Think Again!
Louise D'Angelo/Paperback/Published 1981
Our Price: $5.00 + $2.50 Postage and Handling

Mary's Light of Grace: Marian Lectures
Louise D'Angelo/Paperback/Published 1973-1998
Our Price: $4.95 + $1.50 Postage and Handling

Send to:
The Maryheart Crusaders, Inc.
22 Button Street
Meriden, Conn. 06450

Bibliography

BIBLIOGRAPHY

By The Queen's Command
Lawrence P. Harvey
Publisher: John S. Burns & Sons
Glasgow

The Catholic Almanac
1994 Edition
Felician A. Foy OFM
Editor: Rose M. Avato

Our Sunday Visitor
Noll Plaza
Huntington, Indiana

A Catholic Dictionary
Donald Attwater
Third Edition
The Mac Millian Company
New York

Catechism Of The Catholic Church For The United States
    Of America (1994)
United States Catholic Conference, Inc.
Catholic Book Publishing Co.
257 West 17th St.
New York, N.Y. 10011

The Day That Time Stood Still – 1945
Article: Special Edition Of *Life* Magazine
Fall 1997
Time Inc.
Rockefeller Center
New York, N.Y. 10020

Exile Ends In Glory
The Life Of Trappistines Mother M. Berchmans, O.C.S.O.
Thomas Merton
The Bruce Publishing Company
Milwaukee

Fatima In Lucia's Own Words (Sister Lucia)
Postulation Centre
Fatima, Portugal

Fatima—Hope Of The World Magazine
Publishers: The Conventual Franciscan Friars At The
   Franciscan Marytown Press
Kenosha, Wis.

Fatima Today
Rev. Robert J. Fox
Christendom Publications
Crossroads Books
Route 3 Box 87
Front Royal, Virginia 22630

Fatima Secret
Emmett Culligan
Culligan Book Company
3435 Circle Road
San Bernardino, California 92405

Exploring Fatima
World Apostolate Of Fatima
AMI Press
Washington, New Jersey

Francis De Sales
Sage And Saint
Andre Ravler, S.J.
Ignatius Press
San Francisco, California

The Handbook Of Indulgences
Norms And Grants
Authorized English Edition
Catholic Book Publishing Co.
New York

*The Life Of Brother Andre—The Miracle Worker
    Of St. Joseph*
C. Bernard Ruffen
Our Sunday Visitor Pub. Division
Our Sunday Visitor, Inc.
Huntington, Indiana 46750

The Life And Revelations Of Saint Gertrude (The Great)
Christian Classics, Inc.
Post Office Box 30
Westminster, Maryland 21157

The Life Of St. Margaret Mary Alacoque
Most Rev. Emile Bougaud, D.D.
TAN Books And Publishers, Inc.
Rockford, Illinois 61105

Mary Vs. Lucifer
John Ireland Gallery
Publishers: The Bruce Publishing Co.
Milwaukee, Wis.

Miraculous Images Of Our Lady
Joan Carroll Cruz
TAN Books And Publishers Inc.
P.O. Box 424
Rockford, Illinois 61105

Marian Helpers Buttletins
Marian Brothers And Fathers
Stockbridge, Massachusetts 01262

Magazines Called: *Immaculate Heart Messages And Fatima*
Family Messenger
Published By: Fatima Family Apostolate
New Hope, KY 40052

The New Testament Of The New American Bible
St. Joseph Edition
Catholic Book Publishing Co.
New York

Our Lady Of Light
Chanoine C. Barthas and Pere G. Da Fonseca, S.J.
The Bruse Publishing Company
Milwaukee

Saint Gertrude The Great
The Herald Of Divine Love (1955)
Benedictine Convent Of Perpetual Adoration
Clyde, Missouri

Prophecies, The Chastisement, And Purification
By: Rev. Albert J. Hebert, S.M.
Books Obtainable From Author
P.O. Box 309
Paulina, LA 70763

Saint Catherine Of Siena—Doctor Of The Church
Igino Giordani
The Daughters Of St. Paul
50 St. Paul Ave.
Boston, Mass. 02130

Saint Alphonsus Liguori
Father D. F. Miller, C.S.S.R.
Father L. X. Aubin, C.S.S.R.
TAN Book And Publishers, Inc.
Rockford, Illinois 61105

*The Story And Relics Of The Most Holy Miracle
    Of Santarem*
Published By: St. Anne's Oratory
Apartado 1-33
2496 Fatima Cadex, Portugal

A Still, Small Voice
Fr. Benedict J. Groeschel, C.F.R.
Ignatius Press
San Francisco

The Sun Her Mantle
John Beevers
Publishers: The Newman Press
Westminster, Maryland

The Thunder Of Justice
Ted and Maureen Flynn
Max Kol Communications, Inc.
Signs Of The Times
6 Pidgeon Hill Drive S. #260
Sterling, VA 20165

A Woman Clothed With The Sun
John J. Delaney, Editor
Doubleday-Image
1340 Broadway
New York, N.y. 10036

The Woman Shall Conquer
Don Sharkey
Franciscan Marytown Press
1600 W. Park Ave.
Libertyville, IL 60048

Various Newspaper And Magazine
Articles (As Quoted)